$1

D1093503

BULWARK OF THE REPUBLIC

A BIOGRAPHY OF THE CONSTITUTION

JAMES MADISON

BULWARK OF THE REPUBLIC

REPUBLIC

A Biography of the Constitution

By

BURTON J. HENDRICK

Author of "The Lees of Virginia"

AN·ATLANTIC·MONTHLY·PRESS·BOOK

With Illustrations

Such is the World's great harmony, that springs
From Order, Union, full Consent of things.
— POPE's *Essay on Man:* III, 295–296

BOSTON
LITTLE, BROWN AND COMPANY
1937

THE ATLANTIC MONTHLY PRESS BOOKS
ARE PUBLISHED BY
LITTLE, BROWN AND COMPANY
IN ASSOCIATION WITH
THE ATLANTIC MONTHLY COMPANY

CONTENTS

ILLUSTRATIONS

INTRODUCTION

1937

IN 1831, something more than a century ago, a young French aristocrat came to the United States to investigate that new spectacle of popular rule, in which his faith, at that time, was not oversanguine. Four years afterward Alexis de Tocqueville, then thirty, published his *Democracy in America,* a work which has ever since remained a prime authority in the literature of government. Unlike most foreign visitors to the young, undeveloped country, De Tocqueville made a patient and deep study of the American system, to which he became a philosophic convert. The Constitution he regarded as the greatest ever framed; as for the Supreme Court, "a more imposing judicial power was never constituted by any people." The judicial prerogative of interpreting the basic law was, in his eyes, one of the greatest of human developments for the safeguarding of popular liberties. But the thing upon which this keen commentator laid especial emphasis was the absence, in America, of centralized administration. He came from a land in which the nation's capital extended its dominion to the remotest corners. In every detail of life the French citizen found himself in the closest contact with the national authority. His local taxes were collected by emissaries sent from Paris; his schools, his churches, the public roads, the bridges and ferries, the administration of petty courts, the police — all these were under the thumb of the royal government. No Frenchman could move from one section of France to another — from department to department, from town to town — without a passport issued by this omnipresent officialdom. The lack of an overweening Providence like this in the United States came to De Tocqueville as a refreshing breeze. It was, he insisted, the circumstance that made the United States such a radically different phenomenon from anything known in Europe. "Nothing is more striking to a European traveller in the United States than the absence of what we term the Government in the Administration. . . . The administrative power in the United States presents nothing either centralized or hierarchical

.

in its constitution; this accounts for its passing unperceived." No writer ever described more charmingly than De Tocqueville the town governments of New England; he contrasted them most favorably with the *communes* of France. The latter entities depended in practically all the details of administration on the bureaucrats of Paris, and were, in consequence, abandoned to "so incorrigible an apathy that they seem to vegetate rather than to live. . . . When, on the other hand, I observe the activity, the information and the spirit of enterprise in those American townships I see that society there is always at work."

Should De Tocqueville visit the United States to-day, he would find the situation considerably changed. That decentralization which he so admired in the first third of the nineteenth century is no longer the prevailing order of things. By decentralization the Frenchman did not mean what was understood in this country, then and afterward, as State rights; he was not thinking so much of government as of administration. Government in its large sense, he said, should always be centralized, but administration — the supervision of a thousand and one details of authority essentially parochial in extent and influence — should be entrusted to local hands. The danger to liberty came, the French prophet declared, when both government and administration were centralized. "It is evident that a centralized government acquires immense power when united to a centralized administration. Thus combined, it accustoms men to set their own will habitually and completely aside; to submit, not only for once, or upon one point, but in every respect and at all times. . . . A centralized administration is fit only to enervate the nations in which it exists, by incessantly diminishing their local spirit. . . . It may insure a victory in the hour of strife, but it gradually relaxes the sinews of strength. It may help admirably the transient greatness of a man, but not the durable prosperity of a nation."

So far as the conception of Nationalism is concerned, as distinguished from the system of local administration so precious to the Frenchman, recent developments in this country are not particularly new. The history of the Constitution, as outlined in the following pages, might be summed up in a single phrase: "From Nationalism to Nationalism." The proposal which the Virginia statesmen most forward in calling the convention presented to their associates was a plan for a national government. This is the beginning of the ensuing story. The fact that it closes with the recrudescence of the same note shows how deep a hold this aspiration has always had on the American people.   Phenomena, even in so progressive a nation as the United States, do not change.   One keenly alert for historic parallels could find many in the situation that confronted the statesmen of 1787 and that which faces their successors to-day.   It was then, as it is now, a time of social unrest. It was an age of strange economic doctrines, of currency inflations, of wild expansions of credit.   "Stay laws" to postpone the payment of debts were the rule everywhere, as moratoriums were in the recent depression — not then approved by courts and the public as they are now.   The relation between foreign debts and foreign trade seemed to be as little comprehended in the eighteenth century as in the twentieth.   Lawlessness as much appalled Washington as it does thoughtful Americans now.   Is it fantastic to see certain resemblances between Mr. John Llewellyn Lewis and Daniel Shays? Modern historians do not regard Shays as quite so odious a character as he appeared to the conservatives of his own time; possibly opinion a century hence will look upon Mr. Lewis with a more favoring eye than do many of his contemporaries; yet in defiance of law, in disregard of judicial pronouncements, the two figures, representatives of similar uprisings in two periods, have much in common. But perhaps the most suggestive similarity between the present age and that of a century and a half ago is the prominence of the perennial issue — commerce among the states.   That was the consideration directly prompting a "more perfect union"; that is the matter as uppermost in prevailing constitutional problems as it was in Washington's time.   It was not completely solved by the convention; it is not completely solved yet.   But the cries of contemporary reformers sound much like those in the discussions preceding Philadelphia.   "More power to Congress!" was the Hamiltonian demand for settling a confused fiscal situation, and "More power to Congress" is the slogan now on the lips of progressive thinkers.

Turn to those early sessions of Philadelphia, and particularly glance at the "plan" the Virginia statesmen brought to the convention.   These leaders had no desire to form a loose confederation.   Their Nationalistic outlook would startle even the most imaginative Americans of the present day.   They visioned a continental nation, exercising complete, unrestricted sovereignty, with the states reduced to the administrative districts which De Tocqueville afterward insisted was their proper function.   "Virginians, Pennsylvanians, New Englanders," might in future be useful words to describe geographic origin; as governmental designations they were to lose significance.   The "Fathers" foresaw the need of a new political being — the American citizen. State barriers they would have almost obliterated. Had James Madison won his battle in the convention, Virginia, Massachusetts, New York, and the proudest of the ancient commonwealths would have been reduced to "counties" in an integrated nation. No words were more deprecated in this continental viewpoint than "federation" and "federal." "National government" was the expression constantly on Virginian lips; "a government that operates not on states but on individuals." The scheme Virginia and Massachusetts fought for in 1787 would have satisfied the most extensive plans of the present administration. Had that constitution been adopted the most far-reaching recent legislation would not have been overruled. We should at present have a House of Representatives elected by the people, a Senate chosen by this House, and a President "appointed," not by an Electoral College, but by a "national legislature." Those who look with dismay upon a Supreme Court deciding the constitutionality of laws should keep in mind the even more extensive powers entrusted to the judiciary by the "Virginia plan." This established a so-called Council of Revision not unlike that exercised in Colonial times by the Privy Council of England. This Council of Revision, composed of the Executive and "a convenient number of the national Judiciary," was to examine all laws passed by the national legislature, as well as those of the several states. On all such measures it was to possess the veto power. But keep in mind an all-important fact: this veto was to be not a judicial, but a political prerogative; it was to be utilized for deciding not the constitutionality of laws, but their desirability as public policy. Thus the Supreme Court was to have two opportunities to set aside acts of Congress: first as part of the Council of Revision, and secondly in its capacity as a judicial body, passing on constitutional questions. This was the chief reason the Madisonian proposal was rejected. It made the courts a part of the legislative department. It thus upset that system of "checks and balances" which the framers regarded as indispensable to liberty. It was urged that the courts would have their power over legislation in due course, and a power that would be confined to their judicial capacity. "As to the constitutionality of laws," said Luther Martin of Maryland, "that point will come before the judges in their proper official character. In this character they have a negative in the laws. Join them with the Executive in the revision and they will have a double negative." Therefore the plan was dropped — fortunately for the future of the nation.

But probably, under the constitution proposed by Virginia, the constitutionality of acts of Congress would never have arisen. For the Congress under that system would have been a congress of virtually unlimited jurisdiction. Those problems of "strict construction" and "implied powers" that so plagued Jefferson and Calhoun would have cut no figure in history. The scope of Congress in legislation to-day would be almost as comprehensive as that of the British Parliament. For the Virginia plan gave the lawmaking department the right to "legislate in all cases in which the separate states are incompetent and in which the harmony of the United States may be interrupted by the exercise of individual legislation." That resounding, though rather indefinite phrase would have swept within its purview practically all the matters the suggested American parliament might choose to regard as its province. There would be to-day no Section 8 of Article I, with its list of topics to which the legislative right extends; there would be nothing in the present written instrument about "interstate commerce," "common defense," "general welfare," "army" and "navy"; nothing about laying taxes and imposts, and the other concerns to which the legislature, in the form finally decided, was to be restrained. The new American national sovereignty would reign supreme, subject only to such limitations as Congress should see fit to impose upon itself. In other words, it was planned that state lines should all but vanish and that the American people should be welded into that "consolidated union" so apprehended by Patrick Henry and George Mason. Under such an all-embracing authority in Congress the Rooseveltian regulations of industry, mining, trade, commerce, and agriculture, the price fixings and limitations of output, the regulations of labor, would have been "constitutional." Nothing that Congress should see fit to do would be "unconstitutional," for its dominion would be unbounded.

It is not likely that the advocates of an omnipotent Congress, in 1787, had in mind anything resembling recent developments. They would have centralized governmental power, but it is not likely that the same treatment would have been extended to the multitudinous details of local administration. The attempt of the existing régime to accomplish this administrative centralization and to do so under the protection of a Constitution erected on lines of definite limitations has produced one of the greatest "constitutional crises" in the annals of that document. This development appears, not only in those departures that loom largest in the public mind, — industrial codes, agricultural adjustments, regulation of bituminous coal, control of relations between employer and employed, — but in a multitude of other extensions of the central authority. The new American government now in process of formation is not only one which supervises interstate commerce under the widest definitions of that term, but one which engages in numerous activities intimately affecting the citizen in his everyday life. It gives financial relief to millions of unfortunates; it clears the slums in cities, assists the people in building homes, pays off the mortgages on the farm, constructs roads, parks, bridges, and transportation systems for localities, subsidizes Federal theatres, promotes literary and scientific research, furnishes amusement for the masses, and finances lighting plants and an infinite variety of public works. Plans are already under discussion that look ultimately to the assumption, by the national power, of primary education — a responsibility of government which, in the United States, though not in bureaucratic countries, has immemorially been regarded as the duty of small governmental units.

The newest Nationalism — or, as De Tocqueville would call it, centralization — represents a departure from the ideals of the earlier prophets, because it really amounts to an attempt to create a new American world. That is the significance of those four measures that have so astounded the conservative mind: the National Industrial Recovery Act, the Agricultural Adjustment Act, the Bituminous Coal Act, and the National Labor Relations Act. Some future Gibbon, uncovering the aspirations of the past from its superficially prosaic monuments, will be able to draw from these pieces of lawmaking the portrait of a new civilization. From them will appear a society of 130,000,000 Americans bearing little resemblance to the one in which they had been nurtured. Almost all the activities of life will be subject to the control of an outside power; the citizen, in his daily routine as well as in his avocations, will find a paternal government constantly at his elbow. For good or ill, the Rooseveltian measures substitute for the present body politic a new form of the American State. Through them all there runs the same general purpose. The regulation of industry, trade, business, agriculture, mining, and social and labor activities is to be only secondarily the responsibility of nation and state. It is to be transferred to a multitude of bodies, almost unofficial in character, operating under "codes" of their own manufacture. The United States is to be the scene of thousands of minute legislatures which, to all intents and purposes, are to exercise plenary lawmaking power. In the field of industry these authorities are to be the associations which, as informal groups, have grown up in connection with manufacture and trade. They are to have dispensation to legislate on all questions that arise in the complexities of business, to fix prices, regulate output, establish principles of competition, determine wages, — on the basis of collective bargaining with employers, — and decide such questions as hours and conditions of employment. They are to draw up "codes of fair competition" which are to have the force of law. The trade groups enforcing them can compel obedience, inflict fines upon refractory individuals, and have recourse to the United States courts to punish malefactors. The only power above them is the President himself. Under a benign and unenergetic Executive, the control of American industry could pass into the hands of thousands of trade associations. Under a President ambitious for power, this dominance could be concentrated in one man.

In the achievement of similar ends in the bituminous-coal industry a special commission is to be created in the Department of the Interior. Under this body are to be established twenty-three coal districts, each under the dominion of a district board. These boards will fix prices for coal and wages and establish working conditions of employees — again under a system of collective bargaining. Similarly the purpose of the Agricultural Adjustment Act is to give the Federal government complete control of agriculture, to regulate acreage and production and to control prices. Under the act the agriculturist is to have little independence as to the amount of soil he can plant, the kind of crops he can grow, or the prices at which he will sell them; practically his every activity is to become subject to the orders of representatives of the agricultural department.

Labor relations, in this reorganized society, are to be placed in the hands of a Federal Board, appointed by the President, and subsidiary boards placed in several parts of the country. These boards constitute a species of labor court, before which workers can bring their grievances, and which have the power to force employers to observe a new code of labor relations. In case of recalcitrancy the boards can call upon the United States courts to enforce their orders. The things these tribunals can compel employers to do are, mainly, to enter into collective bargaining for the establishment of wages and working conditions, a majority of the workers having the right to select representatives for this purpose, and to refrain from certain "unfair practices" such as forming unions of their own and discharging employees for belonging to workmen's associations and soliciting their fellows to do so. The right to strike is specifically recognized as legally inherent in the workingman.

These measures are intended to solve many of the distressing problems that have afflicted the people for a generation. Certainly the problems in question call for remedial treatment. American agriculture has passed through many crises in recent years. The attempts of successive administrations to remedy the evils, especially to bring the farmer adequate compensation for his products, seem only to have made a bad situation worse. In trade and industry devastating competition has reduced conditions to virtual anarchy. The best efforts to bring about a new order, under such agencies as trade commissions and antitrust laws, have accomplished little in the way of real reform. As for the coal fields, bankruptcy has followed bankruptcy, strike has succeeded strike, until the rich resources of the nation in a mineral that forms the basis of modern enterprise seem likely to develop into a curse rather than a blessing. The strife of labor and capital has demoralized American life for two generations. Point by point the employee has improved his status, but there is pretty general agreement that he has not yet attained his full share in the profits of his toil. A state of scarcely suspended war has prevailed for years between so-called "capital and labor" and there is a belief that the interposition of government, if it can establish a more equitable state of affairs, is justified.

Does the economic salvation of the American people lie in the old-fashioned system of uncontrolled private ownership and unrestricted competition or does a new régime, under Federal oversight, promise a more desirable solution? The Roosevelt administration believes that reconstruction of the social and economic structure is essential to any real improvement, and Congress, under its pressure, has passed the laws which revolutionize the entire agricultural, industrial, and social world.

It is one thing to decide that such a programme is desirable, and quite another, under the American system, to discover ways of putting it into effect. The difference between the American and most other governments is that the national legislature of America, in passing laws, must point to some definite section in the Constitution that grants the authority for the enactments in question. Such an *impasse* as has recently arisen in the United States, for example, would have been impossible in England. In recent years the British Parliament has introduced radical changes without ever raising the question of its right to do so. It has seriously curtailed the authority of the House of Lords, which meant a fundamental change in a governmental organization that had existed for nearly a thousand years, but no protest was made that it was trampling on the British Charter. Under the plan proposed by the Virginia leaders to the Convention in 1787, no constitutional difficulty would have confronted the new proposals. But the United States for a hundred and fifty years has been operating under a definitely written organ of government. Are there any grants definitely expressed or reasonably implied that make legal the new scheme? Are "codes of fair competition" warranted by the interstate-commerce clause? Is the proposed regulation of mining in accordance with a true understanding of the same provision? No assertion is made that this clause supports the wholesale regulation of agriculture. However, the Constitution does give Congress the privilege of levying taxes for "the general welfare" and the contention is therefore forthcoming that, under this indefinite permission, the levies made by the Agricultural Adjustment Act on processors for the benefit of food producers are in complete accordance with the American compact.

It is because the judicial department has outlawed certain of these innovations that the present crisis has arisen. There is no constitutional provision, it has decided, that justifies the national control of agriculture. The justices make no effort to explain the still unsolved riddle concerning the meaning of the "general welfare" clause, but insist that a tax laid on one part of the community for the benefit of another part is not a "tax" as that term is understood under the Constitution.

As for the National Recovery Act, the Court has discovered two clauses that make it illegal. That regulating "commerce among the several states" is not the one on which the strongest emphasis is laid. The slaughter of chickens in Brooklyn might be admitted to be interstate commerce, and the Recovery Act would still, according to the Court, be without Congressional power. Chief Justice Hughes and his eight concurring associates found an even more serious obstruction to this legislation than its declared repugnance to the commerce clause. This is that it involves an "unlawful delegation of power." The very first sentence of the Constitution is cited to prove the illegality of the thousands of little legislatures, composed of trade groups, which that act called upon to direct American industry. Consider Article I, Section 1: "All legislative powers herein granted shall be vested in a Congress of the United States, which shall consist of a Senate and House of Representatives." As long as this stipulation is observed, can convocations of steel manufacturers, or shoe men, or laundry owners, or kosher butchers, or dry cleaners, presume to wield that empire of legislation which the people have bestowed only upon their chosen lawmakers? For the Supreme Court insists that the authority with which the obnoxious act endows them is this power of legislation. The trade associations, under the Recovery Act, can establish rules of competition, determine prices, wages, and conditions of employment; such, the Court decrees, are legislative prerogatives that affect citizens in their most intimate concerns, which Congress itself must exercise and which it has no constitutional right to pass on to others. It is argued, however, that in certain instances Congress has done this very thing — that is, at times it has released its own right to legislate, and given it to extrinsic groups. The cases chiefly instanced are the Interstate Commerce Commission, which makes laws regulating transportation; the Federal Trade Commission, which exercises legislative privileges affecting industrial corporations; above all the Tariff Commission, which enjoys a delegated power to fix tariff rates. In these delegations, it is asked, has not Congress, with the complete approval of the Supreme Court, done precisely the thing which it is now said that body has no right to do — selected a group outside itself to legislate? But the present Court draws a sharp distinction between this Rooseveltian attempt to delegate power and the former ones. All the established commissions, it declares, are official bodies and are themselves created by law. Their members are appointed by the President and are responsible to him. Their lines of action are marked out in accordance with certain standards which Congress has set up. Thus they are really agents of Congress, carrying out principles which Congress has established. To create a few regular commissions is quite a different thing, the Court opines, from giving thousands of code makers roving commissions to invent standards of their own and apply them in practice. "If that conception shall prevail," says Justice Cardozo, "anything that Congress may do within the limits of the Commerce Clause for the betterment of business may be done by the President upon the recommendation of a trade association and calling it a code. This is delegation running riot. No such plenitude of power is susceptible of transfer. The statute, however, aims at nothing else, as one can learn both from its terms and from the administrative practice under it." As all the justices, even the most "liberal," were of a settled mind on this point, the Recovery Act may be regarded as one of those laws so palpably in violation of the Constitution that no reasonable doubt on the point exists, or ever will exist, whatever new Court may be appointed.

Irrespective of any new definitions of the commerce power, therefore, these plans for the regimentation of industry and agriculture, which in fact constitute the basis of the New Deal, are prohibited by the Constitution as it is interpreted by the present Court. Thus the *impasse* still exists and the President is still confronted by serious constitutional difficulties. Unless the Court decides that a new industrial America ruled by codes does not fly in the face of Section 1 of Article I, and unless it decrees that the national control of agriculture is warranted by the "general welfare" stipulation, — or some other so far uncited Congressional power, — it is difficult to see how this new transformation of American society is possible under the present organization.

But in one matter of transcendent importance constitutional interpretation has taken a progressive step. Under the recent cases the meaning of "commerce among the several states" has been redefined. Until the Court spoke on the recent labor-relations measure, its attitude on this question seemed to be fixed. The point had arisen in the clearest form in the legislation concerning the coal industry. In this the national lawmakers had set up commissions that were intended to exercise almost plenary domination. They were given a franchise to regulate working conditions at the mine, to fix wages and hours of employment, and similarly to determine output and fix prices at which the product could be sold. On what theory did Congress take to itself virtually dictatorial powers over an enterprise that had previously not been subject to its jurisdiction? Again the interstate-commerce clause! It was asserted that the mining of coal constituted "commerce among the several states." The Court dismissed the contention, set aside the legislation, and made a sweeping denial that this was the case. In doing so it gave what seemed a clear and permanent definition of the four words that have on many occasions taxed all its powers of fine discrimination.

The wraith of John Marshall was summoned for enlightenment. For a hundred years the Court, seeking solutions of contemporary problems, has turned to the writings of this most famous of its predecessors. "What is interstate commerce?" asked the Court in 1935, and Marshall, as always, was ready with a reply: "Commerce undoubtedly is traffic, but it is something more; it is intercourse. It describes the commercial intercourse between nations and parts of nations, in all its branches, and is regulated by prescribing rules for carrying on that intercourse." On this principle Chief Justice Hughes declared that the conduct of business within state lines, the manufacture of products carried on under local conditions, was not interstate commerce; that "intercourse" between state and state which Marshall believed necessary to fulfill constitutional requirements was lacking. On the reading put forth by the administration, said the present Chief Justice, Congress in its discretion could assume control of virtually all the activities of the people — in other words, perform the multitudinous acts of regulation and control which the Recovery Act had attempted. But were not these products intended, to a large degree, for interstate commerce, and did they not ultimately find their way into it? Yes, replied the Court. Then why, asked the government, were they not interstate commerce and therefore subject to be regulated by the commerce clause? Because there was no "intercourse" in the constitutional sense. While articles were in process of production or manufacture and while they lay inert in warehouses, they had not entered the commercial stream. In this immobile condition such materials were under the exclusive jurisdiction of the states in which they "rested." Did Congress ever have the right to take charge, prescribe conditions of labor and wages, even to regulate the prices at which they were to be sold? The opinion of the Court described the precise moment when this dominion of the general government arose. As soon as a manufactured article left the factory and started on its journey to another state, — as soon as a ton of coal began a similar journey, — then it established the "intercourse" which Marshall described as bringing it within the commerce clause. Chief Justice Hughes's opinion in the Bituminous Coal Law drew nicely this distinction. The process of mining was local, entirely within the states, and Congress, therefore, could not touch it with its laws. Above all it could not fix wages of miners or conditions of employment. But when the coal was once sent on its travels to different states or to foreign nations, then it assumed an interstate character. Congress could now step in and provide the machinery for fixing prices and regulating competition. Digging inert coal from the bowels of the earth was not commerce, but putting it on trains and starting it on its passage to other states was. On that definition of what constitutes "commerce among the states" and what does not, the Hughes Court seemed prepared to stand.

There are perhaps differences in the manufacture of steel and men's clothing from the production of coal that make the former interstate commerce and the latter a mere local enterprise, but the non-expert mind does not grasp them. A great steel mill, like that of Jones and Laughlin of Pittsburgh, draws its raw materials from fields lying outside Pennsylvania; it manufactures these into finished products and sends them into other states; these several transactions, now the Court declares, establish a "commercial stream" that makes it interstate commerce. A small clothing factory in Richmond, Virginia, imports materials from other states, transforms them into wearing apparel, and sells the result in all the forty-eight states. This again is "interstate commerce," subject to supervision under the historic phrase. It is not necessary to dissect the already cele-brated opinion further — to point out fine, metaphysical distinctions that make one commercial transaction a Congressional object of attention and leave the other out, and to reconcile the latest defini-tion with previous judicial attempts to explain a controverted sen-tence. What may fairly be said is that the five decisions rendered on April 12, 1937, create a new United States. The reign of Con-gress is now so sweeping that the Republic, in matters of industry, perhaps of agriculture, has become an integrated nation. Or pos-sibly it should be said that, if these pronouncements do not in them-selves create such a new society, others will presently do so, for the same processes of reasoning, and the same spirit of accommodation to events, that have extended the meaning of the Constitution to this point can easily push it into new fields. Thus the Nationalism which the framers had in mind, as will appear in subsequent pages, is brought nearer realization. That centralization in both adminis-tration and government about which Alexis de Tocqueville had so much to say may be the destiny, after all, of the transformed United States.

But all obstructions to the process have not yet been cleared. President and Court still face each other in combat. More than the interstate-commerce clause, as already indicated, divides these two departments of government. Two ways of resolving the *impasse* occupy the public mind. One is to follow the method the Constitu-tion itself provides and secure amendments that give the legislative branch unquestioned authority in all that relates to the American economy. Another hope lies in "judicial interpretation." It is asserted that the Supreme Court, when property is at stake, has found no trouble in uncovering constitutional justification for meas-ures protecting and solidifying its "welfare." The way in which the "due process" clause has been tortured to subserve such interests is cited as the most striking instance in point. Is it not possible that younger justices, more abreast of the times than several of the present incumbents, more in tune with the modern world, could devise interpretations that would inaugurate a new America? Amending the Constitution, it is urged, takes time; at best it is an uncertain process; whereas a new and invigorated Supreme Court could be installed quickly, and the desires of the people promptly written into law. After all, the personal equation enters in when reading the more obscure clauses of the Constitution; some doubt, in any event, enters into all Court decisions, especially those on which the judges are closely divided. Why not resolve this doubt in favor of the people as in many cases it has been resolved in favor of the "privileged"? The difficulty of framing amendments that would make sure the grants in question is advanced as another stumblingblock to realizing the desired changes in the accredited way.

Considerable misconception prevails as to the tediousness of the process of amendment. The succeeding pages shed some light upon this contention. In one hundred and fifty years twenty-one amendments have been added to the Constitution. For the most part these were changes on which public opinion had been definitely formed and, in consequence, they were adopted with little agitation or delay. As will appear, ten amendments — practically all of them regarded as precious guarantees of liberty and licensed order — were added in the first year of the general government. Of the remaining eleven, seven were proclaimed to be in effect within a year after Congress had proposed them to the states. It took ten months to secure ratification of one of the most momentous of them all, the Thirteenth, abolishing slavery. The Fifteenth, which extended the suffrage to negroes, went upon the books thirteen months after its presentation to the states. The Seventeenth, establishing the election of Senators by popular vote, required only a year. The Eighteenth, introducing prohibition, took thirteen months. The Nineteenth, introducing so radical a change as woman's suffrage, received the necessary state approval in fourteen months. Prohibition was repealed in less than a year. The next to last amendment to be adopted, the Twentieth, providing, among other things, for the meeting of Congress on January 3 and the inauguration of the President on January 20, went into effect eleven months after receiving the approval of Congress. The four amendments that took a longer time were the Eleventh, making it impossible for a citizen to sue a state — which was not a matter on which quick action was important; the lamentable Fourteenth, supposedly giving civil rights to negroes, on which public opinion was passionately divided; and the Sixteenth, making constitutional an income tax. The prevailing idea that amendment is a slow and disheartening method is thus shown, by actual experience, to be a myth. If a strong public sentiment exists at the present time for completely changing the relations of nation and state and giving Congress unquestioned jurisdiction over agriculture and all phases of industry, the necessary amendments can be attained in a very short time — even shorter than the examination made above discloses.

The search for historic parallels is always an engaging occupation, and for the struggle now taking place between the Executive and the legislature, engaged in one camp, and the judiciary in another, there are many precedents. The ensuing pages will describe several encounters of the kind. Such contests began with the founding of the government itself. The first, on a large scale, came in 1798, with the Virginia and Kentucky Resolutions. This was a "reform" more annihilating than anything propounded in recent times, for it contemplated the split-up of the nation into an assortment of independent commonwealths, each having an absolute veto over acts of Congress. Though advocated by Virginians, it amounted to a complete reversal of the original Virginia plan, for this gave the general power the right to veto the acts of state legislatures, whereas the innovation of 1798 would have given states the right to set aside the acts of Congress, so far as constitutionality was involved. Under it the Federal courts would have been completely shorn of the prerogative of judicial review. This represented Jefferson's first attempt to dissolve the "Consolidated Union," and the Supreme Court as its cementing force; his administration as President was a continuous battle with the judiciary, a warfare unremittingly pursued during his long retirement. His hostility was more than a matter of words; it found expression in action. Jefferson's abolition of the Adams circuit courts, his law limiting the Supreme Court to one session a year, his attempts to get rid of disliked judges by impeachment — such was his programme for depriving the judiciary of power over the Constitution. Nullificationists from 1829 to 1833, again adopting this proposal, sought to substitute for courts, on constitutional questions, state legislatures or state conventions. Buchanan interfered with the Court in the Dred Scott case; the radical Reconstructionists in 1868 muzzled Justice Chase and his associates; Grant appointed two judges in 1870 upon whom he relied to upset the legal-tender decision.

Here are "constitutional crises" in which the independence of the judicial department was the issue in question. The tribulations of Chief Justice Hughes and his brethren are therefore nothing new. Marshall's efforts to maintain the influence of his Court is the comparison that looms most prominently. Those who assembled on January 20, 1937, to witness the administration of the oath by the Chief Justice to Franklin Roosevelt could profitably have reverted to a similar scene that took place one hundred and thirty-six years before, when Chief Justice Marshall performed the same rite for Thomas Jefferson. On both occasions the outward scene was all harmony and good feeling, but, on both, two strong men faced each other with widely different opinions of the rôle that the judicial department should play in the American system. That solemn moment in 1801 started one of the fiercest contests that American history has known, and similarly the peaceful meeting in January 1937 has proved to be the prelude to a struggle that promises to be historic. Just as Jefferson found himself confronted by a Court entirely selected by his political antagonists, with "predilections" different from his own, so Franklin Roosevelt has inherited a judiciary largely formed by Presidents standing far apart from him in conception of governmental power. The conflict in both instances was probably inevitable.

Not impossibly the historian who, a half century hence, reviews the "constitutional crisis" of 1937 will find it chiefly interesting for its revelation of one great weakness in the fundamental instrument. Perhaps by that time this lapse will have been rectified by amendment. That is Article III, which deals with what the Constitution itself calls "the judicial power." This power, which, in many ways, has developed into the greatest of all, was left by the framers in indefinite shape. So far as the "one Supreme Court" for which it provides is concerned, they merely prescribed that the judges serve during "good behavior" and that they receive a fixed compensation, not to be decreased during their term of office. No other courts were imperatively established, their creation being left to the discretion of Congress. No number of judges of the Supreme Bench or on the "inferior courts" was set forth. That too was left for Congress to determine. The appointment of all judges, Supreme and "inferior," was placed in the hands of the President. The result is that the President and Congress, working in harmony, have this third department of government, which many look upon as superior in authority to both, at their mercy. Congress can eliminate all the district and circuit courts from the national system; it can reduce or increase the membership of the highest Court at pleasure; and thus the President and the Senate, in their choice of incumbents, can "dominate" the whole extensive régime of constitutional law. And the Constitution gives them an even greater power. The second section of Article III concerns itself with jurisdiction. On the surface it seems wide-sweeping enough to satisfy the most Nationalistic mind; it extends to all cases "in law and equity arising under this Constitution" and "the laws of the United States."

That evidently gives the judiciary the right to enforce and interpret the measures of the national legislature. But a careful reading shows that it is only by the sufferance of Congress itself that this great authority can be wielded. Original jurisdiction in all these cases is the province of the "inferior courts," not of that loftier body which is now so conspicuous in the public eye. The Supreme Court has original jurisdiction only in "all cases affecting ambassadors, other public ministers, and consuls, and those in which a State shall be party." In other concerns, including "the laws of the United States," — all the legislation passed by Congress, such as the laws that now occupy the centre of the stage, — its jurisdiction is appellate. It passes on them only as they come up on appeal from the "inferior courts." But there is a final clause that, in the event of a hostile and revolutionary Congress, can reduce Chief Justice Hughes and his companions to helplessness. They are to exercise their appellate power "with such exceptions and under such regulations as the Congress shall make." An act passed by the House and Senate, therefore, can limit the Supreme Court to considering only cases affecting ambassadors, consuls, and those in which a State shall be a party, for those are the only matters in which the Constitution gives it express original jurisdiction. Such departures as National Recovery Acts, Agricultural Adjustments, Bituminous Coal, Hot Oil, Tennessee Valley Authority, Minimum Wage, and Child Labor can be snatched from its consideration. How this power was used in Reconstruction times will appear in an ensuing chapter. One of the greatest prerogatives possessed by Congress is that it can instantaneously destroy the great Court and the entire judicial hierarchy that has so frequently placed itself athwart its path.

This weakness in the American system has not escaped foreign observers. No shrewder mind ever analyzed the Constitution than James Bryce, who, after writing *The American Commonwealth*, served for many years as British Ambassador at Washington. No sincerer friend of the United States ever lived. In the whole American plan of government nothing so impressed this student as the Supreme Court. Like most British publicists, and like his French predecessor De Tocqueville, he regarded the judiciary as America's greatest and most original contribution to the science of government. But in the failure of the Constitution to guarantee the existence of that Court, especially in its failure to fix the number of judges, he detected a great peril of the future. The following passage, written fifty years ago, must be regarded as one of the most inspired prophecies in all political literature. Commenting on the legal-tender decisions of 1870–1871, Lord Bryce says: —

"This method [that is, this method of appointing judges to obtain the reversal of a judicial decision] is susceptible of further and possibly dangerous application. Suppose a Congress and President bent on doing something which the Supreme Court deems contrary to the Constitution. A case arises under it. The Court on the hearing of the case unanimously declares the statute to be null, as being beyond the powers of Congress. Congress forthwith passes and the President signs another statute more than doubling the number of justices. The President appoints to the new justiceships men who are pledged to hold the former statute constitutional. The Senate confirms the appointments. Another case raising the validity of the disputed statute is brought up to the Court. The new justices outvote the old ones; the statute is held valid; the security provided for the protection of the Constitution is gone like a morning mist."

But the future of the United States is not so desperate as that, despite the present struggle between the Executive and the judiciary. This nation has weathered "crisis" after "crisis" in the course of a hundred and fifty years, and popular liberties will survive, whatever the outcome of the present contention. The wings of the Supreme Court have been "clipped" before and they may undergo this mutilation again. Its story has been an alternating one of power and weakness; even though it suffer another curtailment in the present generation, it will undoubtedly rise into strength in the future. It has survived even more violent "onslaughts" than that of 1937. So far it has experienced no such humiliation as Congress visited upon its head in 1868 when, so far as any review of the Reconstruction Acts was concerned, the Court was virtually wiped out of existence. And time and public opinion affect the Court as they affect all things human. Never has the "flexibility" of this august tribunal, even its resiliency to public opinion, been so manifest as now. The process of "packing" has not been necessary, in 1937, to bring about complete reversals in its most exalted judgments. Such changes have been announced in the domain both of national and of state affairs. Little more than a year after its decree that production and manufacture are not interstate commerce, the Court has turned its back flatly upon its own definition and boldly proclaimed that they are. Such self-repudiation is as complete as the position, in 1870, that Congress could not make its national currency

legal tender and, in 1871, its declaration that it could. The appointment of sympathetic justices was the preliminary to the reconsideration of the eighteen-seventies, but the latest "repeal of judicial decision" was obtained without any change in personnel.

The present Court has taken a stand even beyond any of its
predecessors; it has not only annulled one of its own opinions, but
has informed the nation that it was doing so. One change in the
Federal structure, the importance of which has been almost lost
sight of in the alarum of the greater battle, is taking place. The
practice of setting aside state laws passed in the interest of "social
justice" is falling into the discard. The use of the "due process"
clause for defeating humanitarian legislation, which so irritated
Oliver Wendell Holmes, will soon be a thing of the past. Minimum
wages for women, — probably also for men, — maximum hours of
labor, are no longer beyond the province of the states. The prevailing views of Justice Peckham and Justice Sutherland on these
points the Court has overruled. It is no longer an "impairment of
contract" and therefore a deprivation of liberty without "due process" for a state to prohibit working hours of more than ten a day,
or the payment of wages that doom the recipient to a life of squalor,
if not degradation. This epochal change in law and attitude came
on March 29, 1937 — a date that promises to be a great one in the
annals of America's highest tribunal. In a majority opinion, written
by Chief Justice Hughes, the constitutionality of a law of the State
of Washington providing minimum wages for women was upheld.
This judgment involved no inconsistency on the part of the Chief
Justice, for he had steadily maintained the validity of such legislation, but it did involve a change in the attitude of the Court as a
body, for it had previously set aside such laws, notably that of the
District of Columbia in the case of *Adkins* vs. *Children's Hospital*.
One phrase of Chief Justice Hughes's discourse lifts it to a high
plane of moral courage. In casting aside precedents, in "reversing
itself" if you will, the judicial mind customarily proceeds in wary
ways of its own. It ingeniously discovers fine points on which the
case under consideration differs from the one in which the precedent
was established. Its usual method of taking positions inconsistent
with its past has been, in the words of Chief Justice Taft, *sub silentio*.
But there was no indirection in this instance. The Chief Justice
brushed aside, almost impatiently, subterfuges of the sort. He boldly
proclaimed: "The case of *Adkins* vs. *Children's Hospital* should be,
and is, overruled." That is, the Court had seen a new light and made
no effort to conceal the fact that it had changed its mind. In open

meeting it proclaimed its conversion.   In the matter of social legislation, and the supposed impediment presented by the outworn "due
process" business, the Court has simply turned its face in a new
direction and has taken a stand in harmony with the best purposes
of the modern world.   These are brave and reassuring words, and
in themselves indicate that, whatever the outcome of temporary controversies may be, the part of the judiciary in the American scheme
of things is by no means at an end.

PROLOGUE

PROLOGUE

THIS volume makes its appearance in June 1937, one hundred and fifty years after the framing of the Constitution by the Philadelphia Convention. The period covered by this century and a half is usually regarded as one of the most revolutionary in history. If we were asked what was its predominant characteristic, the reply would almost certainly be the tendency to change. The era stretching from the creation of the American Constitution in 1787 to its sesquicentennial in 1937 is the least static in history. Scarcely anything that the human race looks upon as sacred has escaped mutation. Science, religion, literature, social and industrial life, education, the mechanics and economics of existence — instability has been the law of life in all these departments. In political organization, in the art of government, this spirit of eternal restlessness has been especially marked. Few peoples at the present moment are living under the systems which their ancestors upheld a century and a half ago. Since 1787 civilization has been a world of tumbling thrones, prostrated dynasties, overturned constitutions — of new empires, new republics, new and constantly varying conceptions of the state. Yet in this epoch of upheaval one political entity has remained intact. The Constitution of the United States of America is essentially the same instrument to-day that it was in 1787. Almost alone of all the civic organizations that existed one hundred and fifty years ago it has withstood the storms that have overwhelmed mankind since the day of its adoption. At the outset of our study, therefore, we are confronted by one arresting paradox: the youngest of the great nations is at the same time the oldest government.

Nothing enforces this lesson so graphically as a glance at the map of the American and European world, as it was familiar to the statesmen of the Philadelphia Convention. It is worth surveying in some detail. Little shall we discern in its aspect to-day that met the eye in 1787. The physical globe — the continents, oceans, rivers, islands, and the like — has undergone only slight transformations. But those artificial creations of man known as nations and governments, indicated by imposed boundary lines, show scant resemblance to the phenomena of the present day. Even our own Western Hemisphere, still called the New World, has experienced startling alterations. On the map of 1787 all of South America was under the domination of the Spanish and Portuguese monarchies. Central America and nearly all of North America extending from the Mississippi River to the Pacific Ocean was ruled by Spain. This land is to-day the home of independent, self-governing republics. Canada was then subservient to the British Parliament; it now governs itself under what is essentially a constitution, the British North America Act of 1867. In Europe almost the only governmental form approximating that of 1787 is the Kingdom of Great Britain. Yet here the likeness is only external, for the democracy at present masquerading under the shape of monarchy hardly suggests the personal rule of George III. On the Continent metamorphoses have everywhere taken place, not only in substance, but in form. In a century and a half France has lived under three monarchical régimes, two empires, three republics, a Directory, a Consulate, and a bewildering succession of constitutions. Spain has known an alternation of despotisms, republics, foreign interventions, dynastic wars, constitutions made only to be trampled under foot, and has finally attained an appropriate climax in contemporary anarchy. Italy, in 1787, was only a name; the land was split into a group of kingdoms, duchies, papal states and republics, most of them under foreign domination; its present unity dates only from 1870, and even the monarchy then established has in recent years changed to a dictatorship. In 1787 Germany was also a congeries of large and small kingdoms, principalities, and dukedoms; in the last sixty years it has been empire, republic, and Fascist state. Russia, a mediæval autocracy in 1787, has become a Communistic society. Poland, though it had undergone one partition, then filled a large space on the map of Europe. Switzerland was a republic in 1787, as it is to-day, but its present constitution dates from 1874. The Holy Roman Empire, still extant when the Constitutional Convention was sitting, gave way to the Austro-Hungarian imperium of the Hapsburgs, and that in turn to the multitude of small nations that came to life after the World War. The Ottoman Empire, a century and a half ago, comprised all the Balkans, part of northern Africa and Egypt, Asia Minor, Syria, Palestine, and a vast extent of territory reaching as far as the Persian Gulf. This structure has crumbled, and a variety of new nations, mere geographical names in 1787, have risen on the ruins. Even the supposedly unchanging East has shown no permanence. India, in 1787, was for the larger part still under the domain of its native princes, British encroachment having only just begun; in China the now vanished Manchu Empire was intact; Japan, ruled by an absolute Emperor in 1787, now — ostensibly at least — is governed by a cabinet responsible to Parliament.

Wherever we look, therefore, changing governments, discarded constitutions, revolutions, and usurping dynasties have been the rule. Only the charter drawn up by the fathers of 1787 has suffered little change. The political form which European statesmen of the eighteenth century — that based "on the consent of the governed" — regarded as the most volatile and transitory has proved, in the vital test of circumstance, to be the most lasting. It has endured even the supreme trial to which European governments have been unequal — that of civil war. When the clash came in 1861, European philosophers heralded it as the collapse of the American experiment. One of the literary curiosities of all time is a book by Edward Augustus Freeman published in 1863, entitled, *History of Federal Government from the Foundation of the Achaian League to the Disruption of the United States* — a work which the great historian subsequently published as *The History of Federal Government in Greece and Italy.* When one thinks of the United States, maintaining its vitality in the tumultuous age extending from 1787 to 1937, we are reminded of the Abbé Sieyès, whose active life spanned the miscellaneous excitements that ravaged France from 1748 to 1836. When asked what had been his chief accomplishment in this period, the Abbé, once fellow Consul with Bonaparte, replied: "I have survived." So has the American Constitution, and in so doing has met successfully the most searching of tests.

What is the explanation? Other circumstances than the frame of government must be considered. The influence of climate, soil, natural resources, abundance of land, racial inheritance, national character, and habits of life cannot be disregarded. The slightest acquaintance with American history, however, will show that the main reason for the vitality of that organism which we call the United States of America is found in the Constitution itself. Walter Bagehot said that the men of Massachusetts Bay — by which he signified the American people — could have made any constitution work. The compliment is not quite deserved. These same men were making a sorry mess of the constitution — the Articles of Confederation — which this new instrument supplanted. It was precisely because they could not make that earlier form of union succeed that they brought forth another which has proved more practical. A mere piece of parchment presides over what still is, despite certain ominous manifestations, one of the two stable governments of the world.

Anyone who embarks on a survey of one hundred and fifty years finds an abundance of material. The American Constitution has produced a great literature of its own. Walter H. Page believed that, though American literature in its imaginative aspects left much to be desired, in political writing at least this country stood preeminent. Many of the works dealing with the formation and history of the Constitution belong to this class. The *Federalist,* the letters and speeches of Madison and Hamilton, the works of Daniel Webster, John C. Calhoun, and Abraham Lincoln, the Commentaries of Joseph Story, Chancellor Kent, and Thomas M. Cooley, the *Reports* of the United States Supreme Court, are legal classics everywhere. Certain histories, such as Bancroft's *Formation of the Constitution* and George Ticknor Curtis's *Constitutional History of the United States,* are indispensable to the student of free institutions. Several of the greatest works on the subject — De Tocqueville's *Democracy in America,* Bryce's *American Commonwealth* — are by foreigners; another, the exhausive *Constitutional and Political History of the United States,* is the tribute of a German scholar, Hermann von Holst, who lived and wrote in Germany, but subsequently settled in the United States and became professor at the University of Chicago. In more recent times such books as Charles Warren's *Supreme Court in United States History* and *The Making of the Constitution* maintain this high tradition. But the story of the Constitution is more than a succession of court decisions. That chronicle is a living thing, involving men and events. It is not only judicial interpretation; it is biography and history. It has set the stage for many of the most stirring American crises and personal conflicts. It might be argued that these human struggles, and not court proceedings, have been the really vital influences in its survival. No President knew less constitutional law than Andrew Jackson. Yet it is doubtful whether many judicial edicts accomplished as much in establishing the Constitution as did his handling of the nullification crisis. Webster's reply to Hayne did more to make that Charter the realized possession of the American people and to cement disharmonious states into a nation even than the decisions of John Marshall. One of the most eminent of modern constitutional authorities, Andrew C. McLaughlin, says that the greatest of constitutional decisions was rendered, not by the Supreme Court, but by Grant when he forced the surrender of Lee. This proved to be a decision — beyond the power of any court to pronounce — that settled a seventy years' argument on the nature of the Union and the legality of secession. Similarly the failure of the impeachment of Johnson did what court proceedings could never do in making inviolate the Presidential office. These developments of the Constitution are its flesh and blood and nervous system, giving vitality to what had previously been little more than a skeleton of government. They explain an anomaly that has astonished foreign observers — that of a people concentrating on a written document the intense loyalty and devotion which other peoples have bestowed on dynasties. An English observer once remarked that the American Constitution, as a symbol of union and national coöperation, performed the same service in the United States that the Royal Family did in England.

The succeeding pages, therefore, treat the Constitution in terms of biography, and biography in two senses. It is the story of the instrument itself, its formation, the causes that brought it to life, its struggles for survival, its triumphs and failures. It is again a survey of the men most identified with its progress. Who were chiefly responsible for its creation? Who in subsequent years were its enemies, who its friends? Consider the greatest of American statesmen — what did they think of this document? What did they do to uphold or destroy it? The Constitution, like everything else, is first of all biography. It was made by men; it was made for men; it has succeeded and failed to the extent that it has fulfilled human aspirations. This is the reason that the present writer, leaving questions of jurisprudence to more experienced and competent hands, deals with our great charter in its biographical aspects.

BOOK I

THE UNITED STATES BECOMES A NATION

I

In the latter days of March, 1785, two commissions, one representing Virginia and the other Maryland, met at Mount Vernon, under the vigilant supervision of Washington. The gathering attracted little attention at the time, and has not figured extensively in history since. Yet its outcome, two years afterward, was the Constitution of the United States. The delegations foresaw no such transcendent result. Their purpose in meeting at Mount Vernon was merely to compose differences between the two states on commercial matters. The deliberations were friendly and informal, and ended in creating a federation, or something that resembled a federation, uniting Virginia and Maryland. Between the "ancient dominion" and Lord Baltimore's proprietary flowed the Potomac, a river that performed the double purpose of joining and separating these noble commonwealths. For two hundred years the navigation of this stream had caused constant bickerings, and it was to settle these quarrels that the distinguished Virginians and Marylanders had met in amiable argument. The constitutional question involved was thus that "interstate commerce" which was an active difficulty in the eighteenth century, as it is to-day. A year afterward came Virginia's call for an assemblage of all the states at Annapolis, a proceeding that, in its turn, led to the great Convention in Philadelphia in 1787. This Annapolis "scheme," as Madison called it, was the immediate consequence of the Mount Vernon treaty. "It seems naturally to grow," Madison wrote Washington, December 9, 1785, "out of the proposed appointment of commissioners for Virginia and Maryland concerted at Mount Vernon, for keeping up harmony in the commercial relations of the two states." The cradle of the American Constitution was thus the home of Washington, and the chief impelling purpose that led to this new form of government was the necessity of regulating commerce. The thousands of visitors who to-day flock to Mount Vernon not only are treading the soil that formed the birthplace of their National Charter, but have before their eyes, in the leisurely flowing Potomac River, the great geographical fact that made inevitable a "more perfect Union."

Nothing could be more appropriate than that the rooftree of Washington should have been the scene of the first step in creating one nation out of thirteen discordant commonwealths. No spot could more truthfully have symbolized the instinct towards strong and permanent union that found expression in the Constitution. No one man had done so much to bring America to this final act of coöperation as the quiet but forceful gentleman who, two years previously, had retired to his Potomac home, seeking, as his only reward for his public services, a peaceful old age. "At length, my dear Marquis," Washington wrote Lafayette,[1] indulging in one of his rare sentimental outbursts, "I am become a private citizen on the banks of the Potomac, and under the shadow of my own vine and my own fig tree, free from the bustle of the camp, and the busy scenes of public life, I am solacing myself with those tranquil enjoyments of which the soldier, who is ever in pursuit of fame, the statesman, whose watchful days and sleepless nights are spent in devising schemes to promote the welfare of his own, perhaps the ruin of other countries, as if this globe was insufficient for us all, and the courtier, who is always watching the countenance of his prince, in hopes of catching a gracious smile, can have very little conception. I have not only retired from all public employments, but I am retiring within myself, and shall be able to view the solitary walk, and tread the paths of private life, with heartfelt satisfaction. Envious of none, I am determined to be pleased with all; and this, my dear friend, being the order for my march, I will move gently down the stream of life, until I sleep with my fathers."

The Revolutionary veteran who wrote these lines little understood that the most difficult years of his life lay ahead, and that an even greater task than war — the nationalization of his disordered country under a constitution, the launching of the new Union on lines which, in the main, still endure — would call him from the gentle existence he forecast. Had the United States resembled the peace and quiet of that Mount Vernon which he so charmingly portrays, Washington might have achieved his dream. But that placid retreat was not representative of America as a whole. Outside its confines, when Washington retired at Christmas, 1783, everything was turbulence and distraction. And no one knew so well as the lord of Mount Vernon the nature of the country that he was leaving behind. No one had had his opportunities for ob-

[1] February 1, 1784.

servation or had drawn from them more accurate conclusions. The greatest test of government is probably war — especially a war waged for independence, for such a crisis demands universal sacrifice, unselfishness, and coöperation, the power of massing all national forces, spiritual and material, to one great end. These virtues America had displayed only to a moderate extent in the first contest with Great Britain. It was because Washington had experienced this failure, because he had fought an eight-year war without a government at his back, that he, practically above all other men, felt the need of a strong central power. Perhaps, after all, we should not go to the Mount Vernon compact of 1785 for the beginnings of the Constitution, but to Valley Forge in 1778. For in that trying season the ineptitude of a feeble Congress and the need of an energetic civic organization had appeared most glaringly. The four men chiefly responsible for establishing the Constitution as the all-powerful force in America were Washington, Madison, Hamilton, and Marshall. Is it not significant that three of these spent that winter at Valley Forge, and learned at first hand the impossibility of conducting large concerns without the support of a united and vigorous people?

It would be a simple matter to trace Washington's career and demonstrate that his whole life had been a preparation for his culminating work in the establishment of the Constitution. Certainly by character and experience no man could have been more adapted to this task. Perhaps Washington's most striking quality was his sense of order. Disorganization, whether in his Mount Vernon estate, the deliberations of Congress, or the management of the army, was obnoxious to his soul. The man was as methodical as the solar system. His recently published diaries have disappointed many admirers; there was nothing Pepysian about this conscientious recorder of plantings, the behavior of his animals, the steady progress of his crops, the visits of friends, the state of the weather, the prices of tobacco and wheat; nothing of those political details and struggles of party politics so dear to John Quincy Adams. Even in the great period of the Philadelphia meetings all that appears in Washington's diary, day after day, is "Attended convention," with an occasional reference to tea drinkings and visits to the playhouse. This seems to indicate a matter-of-fact range of interests; at least it shows a disposition precise, observant, concerned above all with the proper arrangement of time and circumstance. And such had been Washington's manner from childhood. Significantly his first interest as a schoolboy was mathematics, his first occupation that of a surveyor.   One cannot spend his early years running boundaries and measuring angles without developing a sense of system and exactitude, and these qualities the youthful Washington presently carried into his civic and military life.   Not many letters of Washington's early period have survived, but his account books are intact and are as definite as one could ask for the practical details of his life — the receipts of his surveying, purchases of land, and the like.   In his letter to Governor Dinwiddie, in 1754, when engaged in the Ohio campaign, Washington shows the same concern over the neglect of his men — the failure to pay them regularly, and to supply clothing and shoes — that he afterward evinced for the soldiers of the Continental Army.   Washington's interest in the practical and precise has led many, mistakenly, to deny him imagination; but that his mind was, first of all, neat and practical, given to logical thinking, proved an asset of immense value to his nation in the constitutional crisis.

Certainly the Continental Army, at the time Washington assumed command, offered opportunities in plenty for talents of this kind. The General's first emotion, on assuming this responsibility, was amazement at the aspect of disorder it presented.   The real explanation, as he quickly discovered, was not the men, but the absence of anything resembling an American government.   It has become fashionable to-day to write disparagingly of the Revolutionary soldier — of his rags, his unmilitary bearing, his lack of discipline, sometimes even his lack of courage and skill.   This was not the attitude of Washington, who paid high tribute, many times, to the soldier's bravery, his willingness to endure hardship, his patriotism and spirit of sacrifice.   The trouble was not with the man in the ranks, but with Congress, which neglected him in the field, left his family destitute, and provided neither the food nor the arms with which he could make a creditable showing.   Absence of centralized government — that was the thing which made Washington's days so difficult and prolonged the war.   Fighting the most powerful nation in the world with no government worthy of the name in his support — this is what explains the early disasters of the Revolution.   And the enemy confronting Washington at every crisis was the lack of a national sense — the habit of viewing everything from the standpoint of local interest.   Washington from the first comprehended his problem as a whole, and demanded a continental army, while the states, despite the bad demonstration made by the militia, placed their main reliance on undisciplined levies. The thirteen commonwealths had drawn up a Declaration of Inde-

GEORGE WASHINGTON

MOUNT VERNON

ALEXANDER HAMILTON

JOHN JAY

pendence in which they pronounced themselves "the United States of America," but Washington, little given to sarcastic outbursts, described them as the "Disunited States." The difference in conception of the American State that formed the main political issue for the first seventy years of the Republic, and finally led to civil war, appeared in Washington's earliest campaigns. Though born in Virginia, in the section especially conspicuous for local pride, the General immediately took his stand for a broader doctrine.

From his first days Washington was a Continentalist — a man to whom state lines were not so important as a strong national system. "I have learned," he wrote, December 20, 1776, to the president of Congress, "ever since I have been in the service, to discourage all kinds of local attachments and distinctions of country, denominating the whole by the greater name of American, but I have found it impossible to overcome prejudices." He had recommended a national army, but Congress responded with eighty-eight battalions — a force that embodied all the evils with which the General was contending. For this new army was built on principles of particularism. The levies were to be raised not by Congress, but by the states, a quota being assigned each one. They were to be armed and clothed by the states, and the officers were to be selected by their localities, not by the central government. What the scheme really signified is that the American people did not regard Congress as the ruler of the war, that they did not realize the existence of a national government, that the only "countries" that controlled their consciousness were the states. In the retreat through the Jerseys there were many painful demonstrations of this attitude. The region south of the Potomac — and the future was to show this clearly — was not the only section where devotion to the native soil was the only conspicuous form of patriotism. Washington attempted to persuade New Jerseyites to swear allegiance to the United States. "What," they answered in amazement, "is the United States?" The only country they knew was New Jersey. A member of Congress from that state arose and denounced Washington's action as most improper! Thus at every point and in every crisis Washington, the Continentalist, the upholder of national authority, the enemy of sectionalism, was met by this general indifference to centralized power, this insistence on local allegiance, and this hostility to union. It was the antagonism chiefly responsible for prolonging the war for seven agonizing years.

A thousand other incidents of the Revolution indicate how slow a growth was Nationalism in the one-time British colonies;

everywhere there were Virginians and Pennsylvanians and Massachusetts men, but very few Americans. Washington, however, was one of this small company. Perhaps, amid all its discouragements, the greatest service rendered by this war was the education of the Commander in Chief on national lines. Certainly the need of a strong central government, superseding the states in certain well-defined functions, but not obliterating them, was the lesson Washington drew from the conflict. This need runs through all his letters of the time. Whether writing from the Heights of Harlem at one of the most disheartening moments of the war, or from his camp at Morristown or Valley Forge, the glaring defect of the continental organization — the lack of union — is ever present. Washington was no constitutional lawyer, no student of Blackstone or eighteenth-century philosophers, no man skilled to draw a frame of government, but seven years in the open camp had taught him practical lessons beyond the purview of the closet scholar. In a letter to William Gordon, written soon after the establishment of peace, he set forth the convictions that had been drawn from the battlefield. "Certain I am that unless adequate powers are given to Congress for the general purposes of the Federal Union that we shall soon moulder into dust and become contemptible in the eyes of Europe, if we are not made the sport of her politics. . . . To suppose that the general concerns of this country can be directed by thirteen heads, or one head without competent powers, is a solecism, the bad effects of which every man who has had the practical knowledge to judge from that I have, is fully convinced of; though none perhaps has felt them in so forcible a degree. The People at large, and at a distance from the theatre of action, who only know that the machine was kept in motion and that they are at last arrived at the first object of their wishes, are satisfied with the event, without investigating the slow progress to it or the expenses which have been incurred, and which they have been unwilling to pay — great part of which has arisen from that want of energy in the Federal Constitution, which I am complaining of, and which I wish to see given to it by a Convention of the People."

When Washington, in this and other writings of the time, refers to the "Constitution" and the "Union," he means the Articles of Confederation, adopted, after much hesitation and wrangling, in 1781, and to the loose and weak federal organization founded upon them. That this futile scheme of central government should be discarded and a genuine plan of Nationalism erected on its ruins was the conviction with which he emerged from the war. The Congress of the Confederation had impressed him no more favorably in peace time than in the midst of hostilities. Ineffective as it had proved at the height of the conflict, it lapsed into a more contemptible state after the British forces departed for England. Its treatment of the army once more exemplified its irresponsibility and lack of public spirit. In these men who had obtained independence Congress apparently felt little interest. It still regarded the men as armies of the states, not of a federal government. It recognized no responsibility for their present or future. The soldiers' wages had not been paid in war time — why should these arrears be compensated now? Let the men be turned adrift, finding their way home as best they could — transformed, that is, virtually into bands of tramps, begging food and shelter on the highway and foraging on the civilian population. The Commander did not approve the excesses of the neglected Continentals, — their threats of rebellion, their plots to establish a monarchy with himself as king, — but he respected the distracted soldiers and officers more than the complacent statesmen responsible for their plight. The lesson that he drew from this demoralization, as from other evidences of Congressional weakness, was the need of a strong central power that could perform the duties and fulfill the obligations of responsible government. The one aspiration he entertained for the United States appears frequently in his correspondence: he wished it to become "a great, a respectable and a happy people." And this conception of "people," not of "states," was one that constantly ruled his mind. No man wrote more scathingly than he of those Virginia planters who were chiefly concerned in subordinating the welfare of the American people to local interests. Why, he indignantly asked Benjamin Harrison, had Virginia refused to give Congress power to lay an impost, so that money could be obtained to pay interest on its debt and meet the ordinary expenses of government? Why treat the "Union" with such contempt and make it so impotent? Who are Congress, he asked, but "the people"? Is it not "selfish and futile" to ring "an alarm bell" against entrusting them with the "monies" necessary to repay the money they have borrowed? "I am decidedly of the opinion that if the powers of Congress are not enlarged, and made competent to all *general purposes*,[1] that the blood that has been spilt, the expenses which have been incurred and the distresses which we have undergone will avail us nothing, and that the band which at present holds

[1] Italics in original.

us together, by a very feeble thread, will soon be broken, when anarchy and confusion must ensue."

Indeed those months of uncertainty and turbulence, between the signing of the treaty of peace in September 1783 and Washington's retirement, on Christmas Eve, to Mount Vernon, are among the most distressing in his life. The apparent failure of the nation to grasp the meaning of independence was the worry that constantly preyed upon his spirit. It was the theme of his discussions with public men and the subject of his letters to influential generals and statesmen. Washington is commonly regarded as untalkative, especially as one not likely to force his private views on public notice, but on this subject he was never lacking in eloquence and self-assertion. Even when the "celebrated Mrs. Macaulay" paid her visit to Mount Vernon, the topic on which her host had most to say was the need of union among the states. Several of the most stirring episodes in Washington's life took place at this time — his circular letter on laying down his command, the address at Princeton in August, and finally, on December twenty-three, his speech to Congress surrendering his commission as Commanding General. In these the question nearest his mind — the need of a strong Union in place of the existing weak Confederation — comes always to the front. "The establishment of the national security" was a theme of which he never tired.

One of the two or three of Washington's greatest papers is the letter addressed to the governors of the states, in June 1783, on disbanding the army. Its subject is the need of forming a national government, of solidifying the American success and guaranteeing its future. So powerfully is the subject urged that it gave umbrage to certain advocates of particularism, especially in Washington's own state, Virginia. Edmund Randolph seemed to regard it almost as an impertinence. "The murmur is free and general," he wrote to Madison, "against what is called the unsolicited obtrusion of his advice." Washington really intended this letter as his final testament to the American people, never dreaming that, nearly fifteen years afterward, he would deliver another farewell address, reëchoing many of the sentiments of this earlier admonition. The two documents — the letter to the governors, of 1783, and the farewell address of 1796 — should be taken together, as the expression of Washington's views on the destiny of the American people and the way of making it certain. To him, in the governors' address, America was no congeries of inharmonious states. "The citizens of America" are the "sole lords and proprietors of a vast tract of continent, comprehending all the various soils and climates of the world, and abounding in all the necessaries and conveniences of life." "Heaven has crowned all other blessings, by giving a fairer opportunity for political happiness, than any other nation has been favored with." The American State had come into being at an auspicious age — the age of new philosophies in free government, the spread of science and invention. In this new world will America "be respectable and prosperous, or contemptible and miserable, as a nation"? It all rests with Americans themselves. "This is the time of their political probation; this is the moment when the eyes of the whole world are turned upon them; this is the moment to establish or ruin their national character forever; this is the favorable moment to give such a tone to our federal government as will enable it to answer the ends of its institutions; or this may be the ill-fated moment for relaxing the powers of the Union, annihilating the cement of the Confederation and exposing us to become the sport of European politics, which may play one state against another, to prevent their growing importance and to serve their own interested purposes. For, according to the system of policy the states shall adopt at this moment, they will stand or fall; and by their confirmation or lapse it is yet to be decided whether the Revolution must ultimately be considered as a blessing or a curse — a blessing or a curse, not to the present age alone, for with our fate will the destiny of unborn millions be involved."

Certainly here is manifest imagination of a lofty order. These sentences show that Washington had what few men of his generation possessed — a clear view of the future of America, its possible significance in history, the lines along which lay its natural development. When one compares these views with the narrow conceptions of the governors to whom his letter was addressed (a Benjamin Harrison, clinging to a Virginia plantation as the most desirable unit in the future America; a George Clinton of New York, foe to union because union would deprive him of the political ascendancy obtained from the existing régime), the distance between a farseeing statesman and a parochial mind stands out in broad relief. The denunciation of Charles Lee at the battle of Monmouth is usually cited by those who wish to prove that Washington possessed human emotions; but his capacity for resentment was strong and unsleeping when directed against men and communities that interfered with his plans for federal union. His personal animosity was directed against those Virginians, Mason, Patrick Henry, and Richard Henry and Arthur Lee, who were most pertinacious enemies of constitutional union. In his view they were "desperate men" and "designing characters"; their opinions were those of "chagrined and disappointed men." Their behavior was "insidious," "intended to alarm the fears and inflame the passions of the multitude."

And in what way could the American people assure themselves of their splendid inheritance? Here again Washington, as always, was precise. "There are four things which, I humbly conceive, are essential to the well being, I might even venture to say, to the existence of the United States, as an independent power. First. An indissoluble union of the states under one federal head. Secondly. A sacred regard to public justice [that is, the payment of debts]. Thirdly. The adoption of a proper peace establishment [that is, an army and navy]. Fourthly. The prevalence of that pacific and friendly disposition among the people of the Union, which will influence them to forget their local prejudices and policies; to make those mutual concessions, which are requisite to the general prosperity; and, in some instances, to sacrifice their individual advantages to the interest of the community. These are the pillars on which the glorious future of our independency and national character must be supported."

II

But it did not need a Revolution and the period of distraction that ensued to implant in Washington's mind this ideal of Nationalism. It had been his possession from boyhood days. Even in the colonial time, the interest of this young pioneer had extended beyond the Virginia that absorbed the allegiance of most of his companions; his thoughts kept roving into the Allegheny country, his political imagination was concerned with the fusion of all Americans into one people. The earliest Washington fame was derived not in exploits as a Virginian, but as the leader in expeditions whose purpose was to add the Western country to the American domain. The early trips to the Ohio, the Braddock campaign, the conquests of the French and Indian, constituted an apprenticeship not only in war, but in statesmanship. It is not a poetic fancy that sees all Washington's days, from his youthful surveying expeditions on the Fairfax estate to the surrender at Yorktown, as progressive steps to this culmination. For always this frontiersman was leaving his Potomac home and extending his course to the west. Only once did Washington set foot outside the United States, but, so far as the American continent was concerned, he was the most traveled American of his time. No American had ever traversed so much of the Western country, and in no man's inner vision did it gain such ascendancy. He made six trips to this wilderness, the first in his eighteenth year, the last in his fifty-second; besides this he explored the Mohawk region of New York, while his campaigns made all the older sections, New England, New York and Pennsylvania, as familiar as his native soil. Nor did this passion for the West cease with his retirement, to Mount Vernon, on Christmas 1783. Eight months after settling down to the rest he describes to Lafayette, Washington started on his last excursion to unknown America. Traveling on pack horses, fording streams, sleeping in the open, sometimes in the rain — here we have the genuine pioneer. And in this open country we exchange the taciturn Washington for the conversational, almost garrulous one; at least the occasional

Indians encountered, the stray white men assembled for the night at an inn, found the military leader of whom they had heard so much not especially silent. The man kept plying them with questions — and questions that disclosed one absorbing interest. Navigable streams, suitable for transportation, seem to have been his main concern. Was there water enough in a particular river to float rafts and bateaux? What was the shortest land route between the north branch of the Potomac and those rivers emptying into the Monongahela? Washington for years had been turning over in his mind the most practical route to the Western country. The days of canals, railroads, motor travel and airplanes, was far in the future. The only way to bring the peltries and produce of the Northwest to the Atlantic and to start immigration into the Ohio country was to load them on flatboats and make slow progress on the rivers.

Thus long before definite plans had taken shape for linking the continent into one political Union, Washington was busy with personal investigations that had as their end the amalgamation of East and West by physical means. That the task was a difficult one his tentative proposals show. Probably no more tortuous scheme of navigation was ever devised than the route which Washington planned as the most practical for giving settled America access to its Western wilderness. Almost every river in the East and the tramontane country — the Potomac, the North Branch, the Great and Little Kanawha, the Greenbrier, the Cheat, the Youghiogeny, the Monongahela, and the Ohio — was to be part of the undertaking, while portages connecting the arteries, and canals around the cataracts, were to be built without end. Indeed, as we look to-day at this complicated programme of Western transportation, it seems more to testify to the determination of its projector than ever to have held the prospect of success. But the investigation was useful to Washington in other ways than the difficult engineering. The whole proved to be a lesson in constitutional law. His studies gave the first intimation of the meaning of "interstate commerce," and perhaps no single discovery reënforced so concretely his conviction that a strong central government was needed. The fact that made him pause was a geographical one, as are most facts that determine national destiny. In order to make the East brother to the West one would be obliged to drift down, in his flat-bottomed boat, to the point where the Cheat River entered the Monongahela. A reference to the ordinary map shows where this point lies. It is just two miles north of the boundary that separates Virginia[1] and Penn-

[1] Now West Virginia.

sylvania.   That is, the point indispensable to Washington's dream was in Pennsylvania — only two miles in, but quite far enough to raise difficulties.   "Which gives command thereof to Pennsylvania," is Washington's notation in his diary.   The problem could not be solved, that is, except in agreement with a state not famous for a compromising spirit.   That Pennsylvania would impose a veto, Washington well understood, for the provident Quakers were not inclined to facilitate the shifting of Western traffic from Philadelphia to Alexandria on the Potomac.   Only some central authority, possessing control over commerce between the states, could establish such an interstate traffic route.   Maryland was another obstacle, for its control over the Potomac was more comprehensive than Virginia's, and it was as ambitious for its own port of Baltimore as were Virginians for their darling harbor.   Thus Washington returned from his six weeks' hardship with two convictions, the result of personal observation : that only by such a zigzag line of land and water transportation could his "Western empire" be made a part of the United States, and that only by a union of the states themselves could the plan be effected.   His inland voyage, undertaken as an inspection tour of his "lands and tenaments" in the West, became an incentive to Constitution making.

This trip reënforced Washington's lifelong conviction in other ways.   The hoped-for Union was more than a mere means of establishing trade and transportation among the states.   Only such a Union, Washington believed, could make secure the results of the Revolution and protect the new nation from falling again into the clutches of Europe.   This idea runs all through his correspondence of the period.   No American of the time seemed to have such a grasp of this impending danger.   Here was imagination again! The forces working against the safety of the United States he had observed with his own eyes.   The United States, as fixed by the Treaty of Paris, consisted of two well-defined and sharply separated units.   Its territory extended from the Atlantic Ocean to the Mississippi River, but it was bisected by the Allegheny Mountains — an almost impassable barrier, or rather a barrier that could be crossed only by a few passes, the most available the Mohawk Valley in the north and the Potomac Valley in the south.   If America had developed in accordance with European precedent, this mountainous wall of the Alleghenies would have split the continent into at least two separate nations, would have done for the Western Hemisphere what the Pyrenees had done for Spain and France.   Though the tramontane region was rapidly filling with settlers, Washington well understood that this new population, even though the larger part came from the Atlantic states, — there was also a considerable contingent of immigrants from Europe, — would not necessarily keep allegiance to their native country. The consideration that mainly directs human conduct, this realistic statesman never tired of iterating, was self-interest, and unless the new nation made it worth while for these pioneers to maintain their allegiance, they would drift under the influence of more complaisant neighbors. Their chief occupations were agriculture and trapping; unless they could sell their wheat and furs they would fall into distress; their most available entrepôt, but not the inescapable one, was the Atlantic seaboard. No market could be obtained without transportation routes, and in that period even passable oxcart roads were unknown.

If Virginia and the other states should let their compatriots pursue an independent life west of the Alleghenies, neglecting them and providing no facilities for crossing the mountain ranges, there were other nations that might show a more friendly interest. On the western side of the Mississippi, for example, was Spain, upholding definite claims to most of trans-Allegheny America and maintaining very definite sway over the mouth of the Mississippi at New Orleans. Spain, Washington declared, was behaving in a stupid fashion in excluding Americans from the use of the Mississippi, — that is, if she was thinking of her own future, — for if the trans-Allegheny settlers were permitted to float their products down the great river, this new country would have good reason to attach itself to the Spanish empire. Perhaps, Washington said, more enlightened Spanish statesmen would see this opportunity, and then secession movements might start in the Northwest country. More likely dangers of the same kind would be created by England. That England had abandoned hopes of reincorporating America, or at least part of it, in the British Empire, Washington did not believe. Franklin, at the peace conference, had outwitted the British negotiators and established the Western boundary at the Mississippi River; England was still smarting from this defeat, and still retained such posts as Niagara, Detroit, and Vincennes, finding pretexts in plenty for refusing to fulfill her treaty obligations and surrender them; these, especially Detroit, might easily become focal points for the Western American trade. The result would be the binding, by "self-interest," of the American Northwest to Britain, and its ultimate loss to the new Republic.

Those who picture Washington as chiefly concerned with enhancing the value of his Western lands are thus mistaken; that was a subordinate matter; his inspiration in planning his complicated Potomac route to the West was statesmanlike, intended to thwart the schemes of Britain and link the Northwest to the East by the firmest of chains. The peopling of that country he foresaw; moreover, he declared, this growth would take place rapidly — far more rapidly than the settlement of the Atlantic Coast. At Princeton, before the disbandment of the army, he wrote to Chastellux, October 12, 1783, revealing the emotions aroused by his recent trip to the Mohawk Valley — the route to the West that proved to have greater advantages than the one he had planned by way of the Potomac: "Prompted by these actual observations I could not help taking a more contemplative and extensive view of the vast inland navigation of these United States from maps and the information of others; and could not but be struck with the immense diffusion and importance of it, and with the goodness of that Providence, which has dealt her favors to us with so profuse a hand. Would to God we may have wisdom enough to improve them. I shall not rest contented until I have explored the western country and traversed those lines, or a great part of them, which have given bounds to a new empire." The fear of British encroachment was an ever-present one, as appears from a letter to Benjamin Harrison, then governor of Virginia, immediately after his return to Mount Vernon. "The disinclination of the individual states to yield competent powers to Congress for the federal government, their unreasonable jealousy of that body and of one another, and the disposition which seems to pervade each, of being all-wise and all-powerful within itself, will, if there is not a change in the system, be our down-fall as a nation. The powers of Europe begin to see this, and our newly acquired friends, the British, are already and professedly acting on this ground, and wisely too, if we are determined to persevere in our folly. They know that individual opposition to their measures is futile and boast that we are not sufficiently united as a nation to give a general one. Is not the indignity alone of this declaration sufficient to stimulate us to vest more extensive and adequate powers in the sovereign of these United States? For my part, although I am returned to, and am now mingled with, the class of private citizens, and like them must suffer all the evils of a tyranny, or of too great an extension of federal powers, I have no fears arising from this source; but I have many, and powerful ones indeed, which predict the worse consequences, from a half-starved, limping government, that appears to be always moving upon crutches and tottering at every step."

And his greatest fear — it should be repeated — was the absorption of the United States, or a considerable part of it, by a European power — above all, by Britain. Another letter to Harrison, urging the adoption of the Potomac route, sets forth this apprehension. "I need not remark to you, Sir," — the date was October 10, 1784, almost immediately after Washington's return from his trans-Allegheny trip, — "that the flanks and rear of the United States are possessed by other powers, and formidable ones, too; nor how necessary it is to apply the cement of interest to bind all parts of the Union together by indissoluble bonds, especially that part of it, which lies immediately west of it, with the middle states. For what ties, let me ask, should we have upon those people? How entirely unconnected with them shall we be, and what troubles may we not apprehend, if the Spaniards on their right, and Great Britain on their left, instead of throwing stumbling blocks in their way, as they do now, should hold out lures for their trade and allegiance? What, when they get strength, which will be sooner than most people conceive . . . will be the consequence of their having formed close connexions with both or either of those powers in a commercial way? It needs not, in my opinion, the gift of prophecy to foretell. The western settlers (I speak now from my own observation) stand as it were upon a pivot. The touch of a feather would turn them any way. . . . It only wants a beginning. The western inhabitants would do their part. Weak as they are they would meet us at least half way, rather than be driven into the arms or be made dependent on foreigners; which would eventually either bring on a separation of them from us, or a war between the United States and one or the other of those powers."

These words are certainly those of a statesman, and of an imaginative statesman, who deprecated petty jealousies and ambitions, who was thinking of the prosperity and happiness, not of localities, but of the whole. There was little of the Jeffersonian about Washington. He did not think the future of the United States lay in a one-sided development, but in the nurture of all the advantages with which heaven had endowed the country. An agricultural democracy was not his exclusive purpose, though he did not disregard that ideal; he believed also in commerce, in industry, in the exploitation of all resources. And, above everything else, he believed in union. The favorite words upon his pen and lips at this time seemed to be "Union" and "National"! Everywhere Washington turned, the inevitability of a powerful central authority was enforced on his mind. The transportation route across the Alleghenies, which meant the growth of the West and its "cementing" to the old America, could not be accomplished, as he well understood, by one state, or two or three; only by enlarging the powers of Congress could this, and many other ends, be made reality. Thus, in the list of those men chiefly responsible for the Federal Constitution must be placed the name of Washington. "It would seem," writes Herbert B. Adams, "as though all lines of our public safety lead back to Washington, as all roads lead to Rome." Fifty years before Daniel Webster exclaimed, "There are no Alleghenies in my politics," Washington had framed the same idea as the guiding principle of his political action.

III

What basis was there for this Washingtonian belief that, without union, the United States would disintegrate and not improbably fall within the influence, perhaps the sovereignty, of a European nation? Reasons existed on all sides for this apprehension. Even in his own state of Virginia adverse forces were at work. The group of aristocrats that had opposed separation from Great Britain, and had fought the Declaration of Independence, were still more amiably disposed towards Great Britain than towards the shipbuilders and codfishers of New England. This attitude, confined to a few, — such as Meriwether Smith and Carter Braxton, — represented the extreme of particularism, but the general disorganization of the United States immediately after separation from Great Britain gave encouragement enough to those forces in England who regarded reunion as not impossible. The fact is that in 1783 America, for the first time in its history, had been released from leading strings. From the settlement of Jamestown in 1607 to the Declaration of Independence in 1776, the British Crown had acted as supervising authority, a powerful force that, despite temporary divagations, kept the colonies on an even keel. From 1776 to 1783, the war with England and the consciousness that only by staying together could the enterprise succeed maintained a fairly stable equilibrium. But, peace once signed, both these centripetal influences disappeared. The states were now free and independent, unloosed for the first time from parental control, and immediately began to behave like the unruly children that, in many respects, they were. They really had only one thing in common: they were, despite the influx of other peoples, for the most part of the same English race; they spoke the same tongue; they were overwhelmingly Protestant in religion and had an identical political and institutional background. This was indeed a powerful common inheritance; but there were differences and jealousies that exercised a strong separative influence. The South was wholly agricultural; the North was largely commercial and urban; Virginia was Anglican in religion; Maryland, to a great extent, was Catholic; Pennsylvania and Delaware were Quaker; New England was Congregational, while Presbyterianism flourished in other sections. Absence of communication had caused little social intercourse; dislikes and antagonisms had developed; the citizen of each state usually referred to his state as "my country." Not only were states hostile to one another, but most states themselves were split into sections and classes, with mutual dislikes. This disintegration of sympathy and interest naturally inspired hopes in the old mother country that the Rebellion was not yet ended, that America was incapable of organizing into a nation, and that it could still be kept in subordination — if not political, at least economic and commercial.

The best light upon this prospect is obtained from the official correspondence of such foreign representatives as were attached to the new government. Most foreign countries declined, during this period, to send regular ministers. How was it possible, they asked. There was really no central government to which emissaries could be accredited. They could not dispatch thirteen ambassadors to thirteen states, nor could the so-called United States be expected to send thirteen diplomats to each of the courts of Europe. France was the only great country which maintained anything resembling an embassy at Philadelphia. From 1779 to 1792, it was represented by two clever diplomats, the Count de la Lucerne and, when he returned home, Louis Guillaume Otto, as chargé d'affaires. Their official communications describe the new nation as a distracted place. The same information was conveyed to London by British correspondents in America. England, it is true, had no minister to the United States, but it did have a secret agent. And this emissary was none other than the renegade American, Edward Bancroft. This man, for eight years, had served as secretary to the American headquarters in Paris, drawing pay from Congress; and all this time had been receiving a salary from the British Foreign Office as compensation for betraying American secrets. Bancroft's usefulness as spy did not cease with the conclusion of peace. Armed with letters of introduction from the unwary Franklin, and still on the British payroll, he spent several months at Philadelphia, from 1783 to 1784. The nature of his mission is fairly evident from his letters to British officials. The purpose was to discover the most efficacious means of forcing the American states back into the British Empire. At least Bancroft's communications give copious advice on that point.

Washington knew nothing of Bancroft or his reports; if he had read them, however, his suspicions of British ambitions would have been strengthened. British encroachment in the trans-Allegheny region was the danger especially feared by the Commander in Chief, but Great Britain was able to threaten the new republic also from the east. The part that the West Indies and American shipping generally had played in colonial development is a familiar story. To-day, with the vast ramifications of American foreign trade and the tremendous development of American industry, it is difficult to realize the importance of the Leeward Islands in this early day. For certain sections of the nation, however, especially New England, they were a matter of life or death. An overmastering part in the economy of New England was played by so humble an article as molasses, the great West Indian product. So busy growing sugar and transforming it into molasses were the plantations of English, French, and Spanish islands in the Caribbean that they had no time for producing the food, as well as the lumber, barrel staves, and other articles, essential to the industry. The exchange of New England products for this sugar and molasses — the latter, distilled into rum, was used as a medium of exchange in the great fur trade with the Western Indians — was the basis of ante-Revolutionary prosperity. Most of the carrying trade between West Indian and American ports and Great Britain was likewise in the hands of New England and the Middle states. New England was a great shipbuilding centre, annually providing the British Isles with hundreds of new vessels. Practically the entire product of the "staple" states — the tobacco of Virginia, the indigo and rice of South Carolina, and the like — similarly found an exclusive market in British ports.

Since 1651 the entire economic life of the colonies had been only one aspect of that of Great Britain. The Navigation Act passed that year, confining all American trade to England and British possessions and to British ships, had had the effect of welding the colonies and motherland into one economic nation, trading exclusively — except when the laws were evaded — within itself. The closing of American ports to British ships at the beginning of the Revolution naturally produced a sudden and violent change; the disorganization would have been even more profound had not France, Spain, and other European countries given great trade advantages to their new allies and friends and, in a measure, taken the place of Britain. But the establishment of peace, in September 1783, presented a disheartening prospect. American goods and ships found the ports of Spain, France, and Holland, both in Europe and in the West Indies, closed to them.[1] Trade from America to England, on which the colonies had become rich in colonial days, came to an end. The Navigation Act, under which this commerce had developed, applied only to members of the British Empire; and the United States had now become, so far as Britain was concerned, a foreign country, and could therefore no longer shelter within its encompassing range. As a result the United States, in an economic sense, was a waif among the nations. Its West Indian trade — except for such smuggling as naturally took place — was at an end; New England had no purchasers for her food, her fish, her lumber; Virginia tobacco could enter England, its one great market, only surreptitiously, and all the rest of the native American products were similarly left without a port. American shipping, including both the shipbuilding trade and the use of American bottoms as carriers, fell at a blow, for under the Navigation Act only British ships could be used in British trade. Thus as far as material prosperity was concerned the American states were in a far worse position after gaining their independence than in the days of subjection. Americans were free men politically, but in all that affects economic welfare they were still under the thumb of Britain, which showed few signs of mercy.

This new dependence is most important in the present connection, for it was one of the most potent influences in the formation of the Constitution. Certain enlightened men saw in the crisis a great opportunity for statesmen. There were imaginative philosophers who, even at that time, after all the bitterness of the Revolution, believed that the welfare of the two nations, and of the world, depended on friendly coöperation between the Anglo-Saxon nations. That the two peoples would forever remain politically separate was evident, but the belief prevailed in certain quarters on both sides of the ocean that they could be reunited in an economic sense, and that such a reunion would promote their own happiness and comfort and also contribute to the peaceful progress of the world. Concretely this attitude took the form of a proposal that

---

[1] The explanation is a little complicated. While they were in the British Empire, the American colonies could trade only with Great Britain and its possessions. This arrangement came to an end with the Declaration of Independence. France, Holland, and Spain, American allies, at once stepped into the position occupied for more than a century by England. The peace with Great Britain, in 1783, created the new situation described in the text — British trade was admitted to American ports, but America was shut out of Britain. Then France, Holland, and Spain no longer had the market in America they had enjoyed in war time. American trade again reverted to England. Having lost their *quid pro quo*, the European nations returned to the old discrimination against the United States.

the trade relations preceding the Revolution be restored and the Navigation Act be extended so as to bring again within its protection the old-time colonies. The effect of such a family relationship on history would have been almost incalculable. English statesmen who favored this restoration were mainly those who, in Stamp-Tax days, had championed the American side — Burke and Shelburne, supported by the brilliant son of Lord Chatham, that William Pitt who, although only twenty-four, was already a great Parliamentary figure, Chancellor of the Exchequer in the Shelburne Cabinet and destined soon to be one of the most eminent of English Prime Ministers and leader of the British Empire at one of its greatest crises. Soon after the conclusion of the treaty of peace, Pitt introduced a bill which would have established the trade relations between the United States and Great Britain that had prevailed before 1776. But public opinion in England did not sustain this enlightened view. The King, unreconciled to the separation and especially bitter at the favorable terms Franklin had exacted at the peace, was outspoken in hostility. To George III all Americans were "knaves"; their departure from his rule he affected to regard as "good riddance." "The American cannot expect," he said, "nor ever will receive any favor with me."

Other Britishers saw in this trade situation a means of forcing the rebels back into the British Empire. A slow process of economic strangulation might accomplish that which the troops of Cornwallis had been unable to effect. This was the attitude that Edward Bancroft, the American spy in British employ, now reflected. His letters and "informations" from Philadelphia, in 1784, advocated this policy. "If the views of His Majesty's ministers," wrote Bancroft on August twenty-six, "extend towards the recovery of the sovereignty of the new United States, or towards a dissolution of their Confederation, or of their present connection with France, these ends will be best promoted by an adherence to the system of excluding American vessels from the British plantations [1] and American shipping from the advantages of being sold and employed in this Kingdom. Because, in fact, such exclusion will render the situation of many of the states, and particularly those of New England, in respect of commerce, much worse than it was when they were subject to the British crown and to the British navigation laws. Of this truth many persons in those states are already convinced; and it seems to me highly probable that, if such exclusions be continued, and a fixed determination be manifested them by this government, the

[1] That is, the British West Indies.

people of New England, North Carolina and, perhaps, some other states, will, in less than twelve months, loudly clamor against the Confederation, and openly concert measures for entering into something like their former connections with Great Britain."

Franklin, in a letter to the President of Congress, warned his countrymen against this danger. Already a plot was afoot, he said, to make one of the "numerous progeny" king of the old-time transatlantic possessions. "With respect to the British court we should, I think, be constantly on our guard, and impress strongly upon our minds that, although it has made peace with us, it is not in truth reconciled, either to us or to the loss of us, but still flatters itself with hopes that some change in the affairs of Europe, or some disunion among ourselves, may afford them an opportunity of recovering their dominion, punishing those who have most offended and securing our future dependence." The views outlined by Bancroft presently solidified into fixed British policy. America was to be treated as an "alien" country, totally shut out from that commerce which had been the cause of all its prosperity and on which its very existence seemed to depend. If this programme had been adopted partly in the hope of forcing the erstwhile colonies back into the British Empire, it most grievously failed. Instead it had the result of welding thirteen quarreling states into a strong Federal Union. The British statesmen who framed this trade policy must be enrolled among the makers of the American Constitution.

IV

There were thus two forces, from 1783 to 1787, threatening American union in favor of Britain: the Appalachian barrier separating the thirteen states from their new territory in the West, in which England, despite the treaty of peace, still held the dominating posts and to which the old America had virtually no trade routes; and the policy of death Britain was so successfully applying to American commerce. When one state prohibits the products of another from entering its ports the remedy seems fairly obvious. The state discriminated against usually retaliates and closes its ports to the trade of its inhospitable rival. This has always been the procedure, from ancient to modern times; tariff wars, foolish as they may be, are among the commonplaces of history. If Britain shut American products from her ports, — or, what was the same thing, levied destructive duties on them, — obviously America should exclude English manufactures. But that was something beyond the powers of Congress. The United States, despite its name, was not a union; it was the loosest kind of federation. Congress possessed only such shadowy powers as were given to it by the Articles of Confederation. The right to tax, and to levy duties on imports, it did not possess. In all the thirteen states there was not a single federal customhouse or customs officer. Massachusetts and Virginia had their customhouses, as did many of the other states, and the right to collect duties, from the earliest days, had been a colonial function. In order to fight Great Britain with her own weapons, therefore, it would have been necessary for thirteen states to levy simultaneously identical duties on British products. Such unanimity could not be obtained. State interests and jealousies stood in the way. Massachusetts did pass an exclusive law against Great Britain; the only result was that other states "got the business." Certain communities, such as Rhode Island and New York, found the traffic very profitable, for it enabled them to levy tribute on neighbors, such as Connecticut and New Jersey, which, having no foreign commerce of their own, were obliged to obtain their foreign necessities from these avaricious compatriots. Connecticut, placed between Rhode Island and New York, was compared to a "cask tapped at both sides," and North Carolina, between Virginia and South Carolina, to a "stump bleeding at both ends." And so long as the Articles of Confederation remained the American "constitution," this situation was irremediable.

The domestic politics of America, from 1783 to 1787, revolved largely around one question. Readers of the newspapers and memorials of that period are constantly meeting the word "impost." This was a plan to give Congress power to assess a 5 per cent duty on foreign products. As Congress had no such authority, this proposal amounted to an amendment of the Articles of Confederation. But here another difficulty arose. For the Articles could be amended only by unanimous consent. Imagine that, at the present day, the consent of every one of the forty-eight states should be necessary to pass a tariff bill! That was the situation our ancestors were confronted with a century and a half ago. And the result was the same then as it would be to-day. The impost was kicked around from legislature to legislature; some states gave consent, others consented with qualifications that again illustrate how widely the local spirit prevailed: the duties must be collected by state officers and paid into state treasuries; the power should be granted for a stipulated period, fifteen or twenty-five years. Certain states at one session granted the impost only to withdraw it at the next, while others — the most conspicuous offender was Rhode Island — never granted it on any terms. The fact that the smallest of the states, by refusing its consent, could prevent Congress from exercising the main prerogative of government — taxation — and do so from purely selfish motives was a sufficient demonstration of the contemptible weakness of the new republic.

And Great Britain fattened on the situation. So far as America was concerned, she reveled in a system of unilateral free trade. She excluded American goods and ships from her ports by heavy duties, but entered her own products in all ports of America duty free. More than that, her merchants and factors began to overrun the United States. They opened shops in Boston, Philadelphia, and other towns, underselling Americans and driving them out of business; they sailed up the rivers of Virginia, disposing of their goods directly to the plantations, extending long-time credits that local tradesmen could not offer. Of course this British policy was a foolish one. The principles of trade, despite the appearance of a new luminary, Adam Smith, were not then understood. The fiscal situation, in the post-Revolutionary period, resembled that which has prevailed between America and Europe since the end of the World War, with positions reversed. Then Americans owed England large sums of money, the payment of which was angrily demanded, just as England and the Continent owe vast debts to the United States to-day. But America could then pay England only in goods, which Britons refused to admit. This situation could continue only so long as America had specie to ship, and for the two or three years following the Revolution every vessel leaving American ports carried gold and silver to settle trade balances, until the country was completely stripped of the precious metals. Almost the only man who grasped this fallacy was that same Edward Bancroft who had advised this sort of pressure as a means of forcing America back into the British Empire. If this aim should be abandoned, he wrote in one of his "informations," it might be well to restore "the former intercourse" of the United States "with the West Indies, and the sale of their shipping to Great Britain," to enable "them to buy and pay for greater quantities of British manufactures than they can otherwise do."

This enlightened idea made no impression on British statesmen. Why should they grant reciprocal trade advantages to Americans, since they had all the American trade without extending such favor? Even Pitt, who had proposed a more generous policy, had, by 1786, become reconciled to this situation. One of the piquant episodes of the time is the meeting that took place in October between the youthful Chancellor of the Exchequer — he was now twenty-six — and John Adams, the first American diplomatic agent to Great Britain. That Adams appeared as American Minister was in itself a humiliation, for England had sent no minister to the United States and refused to do so; King George had said that a British Minister in America "can never be agreeable to me, that revolted state certainly for years cannot establish a stable government." Adams had to meet jibes and insults at every turn. What did he represent — one, or thirteen, nations? What was the use of making an agreement with Congress, when each state could repudiate it? American attempts to borrow money were jeered at. Congress, the bankers pointed out, had complete power to contract loans, but no power to pay them. Attention was constantly called to the large outstanding loans America had floated in France and Holland, for which the interest had long been in arrears.

Adams stood this ridicule as well as his irascible temperament permitted. He could hardly do otherwise. He knew that the criticisms, unpleasantly as they were sometimes worded, had justification in fact; besides he had been sent to England to negotiate a treaty of commerce and remove British restrictions against American products and shipping, and patience was a virtue the crisis sorely needed. And now he, a man of fifty, found himself closeted with this statesman of twenty-six. His reception was most courteous, and the ensuing talk, though lively on both sides, was conducted with the utmost good nature. The discussion covered all points at issue between America and Britain: the evacuation of the Western posts; the large number of negroes Sir Guy Carleton had carried from America; above all, the proposed treaty of commerce and the abandonment of British restrictions on American trade. On all matters, except the last, Pitt displayed a conciliatory attitude. Adams again protested against a one-sided system — the prevalence of free trade for British products and British ships in American ports, while American products and American ships were virtually excluded from British possessions. He tartly called attention to the navigation act that had recently been adopted by Massachusetts, closing Boston and other Massachusetts harbors to Englishmen. Unless Britain relented, Adams declared, such would soon become the policy of all the states. But Adams knew that this was an empty threat, and so, apparently, did Pitt. To the older statesman's assertion that America had the right of regulating her own commerce, and that England and other parts of Europe had need of many American products, the Minister yielded a polite assent, but "Englishmen," he added, "are much attached to their navigation." "And Americans to theirs," answered Adams.

"But the United States has now become a foreign nation," said Pitt.

Adams replied that Britain's present commercial policy was sure to drive American trade into the hands of France and other European countries.

"That," replied Pitt, "I do not deny. But you will admit that we have a right."

"Certainly I do," said Adams, "and you, sir, will allow that we have a right too."

"Yes, I do, but you cannot blame Englishmen for being attached to their ships and seamen which are so essential to them."

"Indeed I do not, sir," replied Adams, "nor can you blame Americans for being attached to theirs, which are so much fewer and so much more essential to them."

"No, I do not blame them," said Pitt; and then Adams proceeded to push his argument. Was not the real point at issue Great Britain's determination to prevent the growth of an American merchant marine and an American navy? This contention, of course, the British statesman deprecated, but Adams stuck to it. But this and conversations with other Cabinet members, in particular Lord Carmarthen, Foreign Secretary, accomplished nothing to the immediate purpose; their chief bearing was on the constitutional side. Congress had really conferred no power on Adams to negotiate, because it possessed no power itself. Pitt and his confreres smiled and insisted on British rights. Adams fumed and protested the injustice and unwisdom of British policy, but there his ability to act ended. He knew that, could he present Britain with an ultimatum closing all American ports to English shippers, just as British ports were closed to American, he could immediately reach an agreement. But the rulers of the old mother country knew, just as well as did Adams, that Congress had no power to take such action. Only a real constitution could confer such authority, and the possibility of a constitution was remote. Over and over again Adams made this point in letters to John Jay, Secretary for Foreign Affairs. "America at present has no party in her favor. . . . Patience, under all the unequal burthens they impose upon our commerce, will do us no good, it will contribute in no degree to preserve the peace with this country. On the contrary, nothing but retaliation, reciprocal prohibitions and imposts, and putting ourselves in a posture of defence, will have any effect. . . . Confining our exports to our own ships, and laying on heavy duties on all foreign luxuries and encouraging our own manufactures, appear to me to be our only resource. . . . Nothing but our strength and their weakness will, in my opinion, protect us from such a calamity. They will never again pour large armies into the United States, but they think they can distress us more, by cutting off all our trade by their shipping, and they mean that we shall have no ships nor sailors to annoy their trade."

Thus Washington at Mount Vernon, casting his thoughts beyond the Alleghenies and contemplating the opportunities and dangers presented by that region, and John Adams, in lonelier seclusion in Grosvenor Square, observing the commercial helplessness of his own country and the likelihood that the crushing process of British statesmen might reduce it to annihilation, drew from their respective outlooks the same lesson. The American states must federate into a strong union or be destroyed.

V

Meanwhile two powerful allies had joined forces with these venerable statesmen; the two most remarkable young men in the constitutional story were as active in Congress, at Philadelphia, as were their seniors in other fields. After the establishment of peace these precocious advocates of union, James Madison, of Virginia, aged thirty-two, and Alexander Hamilton, of New York, aged twenty-six, had been sent to the Federal legislature. Madison, like Washington, was an inheritor of the Virginia tradition; the son of a large tobacco proprietor and county lieutenant for Orange, he had spent a studious boyhood, had given most of his time to books, and at Princeton, under the inspiring Witherspoon, had become so engrossed in history, the classics, the pursuit of philosophers, especially the philosophers of government, — devoting, according to his own statement, only three hours out of twenty-four to sleep, — that he had returned to Virginia, on graduation, weak, pallid, and permanently broken in health. Yet his slight and diminutive figure, for the next thirty years, assumes, if not a dominating, at least an influential significance in all the crises of his country. For it was by pure intellect, not by personal grace or magnetic force, that Madison became one of the great men of his day. His exterior, indeed, was far from impressive; neither did he possess the overmastering will — as did Hamilton — that compelled contemporaries to follow his lead. "The great little Madison" — such was the phrase bestowed upon him at first meeting by that lively widow, Dolly Payne Todd, who presently became his wife; and the expression has fixed that fragile figure ever since in the American portrait gallery. Small of stature, slight of frame, light-haired, hazel-eyed, with a high forehead, a long oval face, clad as soberly as a Presbyterian parson, shrinking in manner, hesitant in his approach to others, never prone to advance himself or his views, possessing a modesty that at times seemed mere shyness — Madison was a man destined rather to be the brains of a reform than its heroic champion. From childhood he had embodied these quiet virtues. His birth gave him high position; as the oldest son he was heir of Montpelier; all his antecedents were of ancient Virginia; yet Madison, the child and young man, was, in many ways, far removed from the Virginia type. Those outdoor sports — horses, hunting and cockfighting, drinking and gambling — that were regarded as essential qualities of the Virginia gentleman were not his favorite course of life. Books, not saddlebags and foxhounds, were his constant enjoyments, even as a boy. The study of the ancient democracies, not the love-making so popular in Virginia, was the liveliest pursuit of his adolescent years. He was not a dancer, like Washington, nor given to scraping the "fiddle," like Jefferson.

At the age of twenty-one Madison in most paternal fashion writes his friend Bradford, three years his junior, then residing at "The Coffee House" in that dangerous Quaker city, Philadelphia. There are injunctions against "the follies of mankind" and the necessity of "framing our economy according to the precepts of wisdom and religion." "A watchful eye must be kept on ourselves, lest, while we are building ideal monuments of renown and bliss here, we neglect to have our names enrolled in the annals of heaven." As for himself, Madison affirmed that he was safe from undue temptations, for he was sickly and did not look forward to a long life. He had, indeed, "exchanged time for eternity," but one so young as Bradford, so vigorous, so full of "health, youth and fire . . . must tread warily." He recommends for his friend's reading "History and the science of morals . . . seasoned with a little divinity now and then." Bradford must not "suffer those impertinent fops that abound in every city to divert you from your business and philosophical amusements." Instead he should show his "indignation at their follies" and keep "them at a becoming distance."

"I am luckily out of the way of such troubles." Indeed at this moment Madison was spending his time "instructing my brothers and sisters in some of the rudiments of literature," writing notes, still preserved, on the Gospels and Acts of the Apostles, and "studying the whole field of theological literature." In his early existence there seemed to have been no Belinda such as eased the scholarly activities of the youthful Jefferson, and no Sally Fairfax such as distracted the military exercises of Washington. The one love story of Madison, preceding his ideal marriage with Dolly, was quite in keeping with the details sketched in these early letters. That Madison should wait until he was thirty-two before falling in love is significant of an unimpassioned nature. His choice was Miss Catherine Floyd of New York, only sixteen years old, and full of the vivacity in which her mature lover was so lacking. Yet the two became engaged — largely, it is said, through the agency of the young lady's father, who admired the Virginian and saw in him a coming man. Madison's calls upon his fiancée too often took the form of conversations with the father on the misbehavior of Congress and the need of the impost — subjects that did not, at the moment, interest the lady, especially as there was a young clergyman, not far distant, only too eager to introduce other themes. This wooer also possessed another attraction unknown to Madison; in the words of Miss Floyd's aged and reminiscent aunt, he was given to "hanging around her at the harpsichord." Presently Madison received a letter from his fiancée informing him that he was dismissed; his feelings were not assuaged by the fact that this missive was sealed with "a bit of rye-dough." Jefferson wrote in most comforting style, informing him that "firmness of mind and unremitting occupation will not long leave you in pain."

If the youthful Madison presents certain priggish qualities, it was a priggishness that did excellent service for his country and the Union. For the absence of what many would regard as more vigorous qualities left the young man free to pursue his studies in the art of government. Heir to a beautiful estate, seemingly assured of a comfortable income, his lot was to be the approved Virginia one of "statesmanship." That he was set apart, not to engage in frivolity or even humane enjoyment, but to become one of the chief artificers of the Constitution seemed almost, with Madison, a premonition. At any rate, consciously or unconsciously, he shaped his course, from early boyhood, to this end. He early tried his hand at writing, developing on the model of the *Spectator* the style which subsequently adorned the *Federalist*. Afterward he liked to quote the Addisonian injunction that "fine writing consists of sentiments that are natural, without being obvious," and Swift's dictum that a good style consists of "proper words in their proper places." Probably the times had something to do with the subject on which the youthful Madison chose to exercise his literary genius. In his early period the one subject of discussion was the British Constitution. He was fourteen when the Stamp Act was passed, and became a juvenile reader of the unending pamphlets, resolutions, newspaper letters, reports, and debates that followed that legislation. The year he entered Princeton, 1769, Charles Townshend's legislation taxing the colonies was the theme of continuous debate in the faculty and student body. The most outspoken critic of the British policy was the president, John Witherspoon, recently imported from Scotland to direct the intellectual processes of young America. Madison himself was one of the organizers of the American Whig Society, in which denunciations of the duty bill were everlasting gospel. His friends and associates formed perhaps the most celebrated group of young men then extant in America, and that he became the intimate of such a fraternity shows that he was more than a bookworm and "dig." Brockholst Livingston, afterward Justice of the United States Supreme Court; William Bradford, son of the "patriot printer of 1776" and Attorney General in Washington's Cabinet; Hugh Henry Brackenridge, destined to a miscellaneous career as poet, novelist, judge, and leader in the "Whiskey Rebellion" of 1794; Aaron Burr, political adventurer and Vice President of the United States; Morgan Lewis, Governor of New York; Henry Lee, "Light Horse Harry" of Washington's army and Governor of Virginia; Aaron Ogden, Governor of New Jersey; Philip Freneau, vituperative poet and satirist of the Washington administration; and the Reverend Samuel S. Smith, Presbyterian divine and later President of Princeton — such was the coterie of young men in whom Madison found instructive companionship. Nassau Hall, then Princeton's one building, resounded with discussions on British policy and British constitutional law; judging from one of Madison's freshman letters, the tribulations of John Wilkes also occupied the undergraduate mind. The year 1769 also marked the rise of Junius, who similarly became a hero to this Madison and Livingston contingent. One surviving letter of Madison's shows him in more animated light, when he formed one of a party of students who, in black gowns and hoods, amid the death toll of bells, turned out at midnight to register their disapproval of the Tory state of New York, which had declined to accept the Nonimportation Agreement and had written the merchants of Philadelphia asking them to take the same course; the purpose of this midnight assemblage was to burn a copy of this unpatriotic missive.

For the ten years following Princeton, from 1771 to 1781, Madison fulfilled his rôle as a member of the leisure, public-serving, Virginia upper class. He did not enter the Revolutionary army — his health disbarred him, and thinking, discussing, and writing were his more suitable contribution to the cause. The years 1771–1776 are especially fruitful in their bearing on Madison's part in the

American triumph, for this period was given largely to the study of republics, ancient, mediæval, and modern.   There was hardly a Greek city that had experimented with this dangerous form of rule whose successes and failures Madison did not master in detail. "My customary employments," he wrote Bradford, "are solitude and contemplation."   Virginia in those days took meditative young men seriously, especially when they were the sons of established families, and pressed them into public use.   Appropriately, therefore, Madison, in 1776, emerged from scholastic retirement, and for the next seven years applied in constitutional and legislative chambers the precepts so sedulously acquired in study.   In 1776, aged twenty-five, he represented Orange County in the Virginia Constitutional Convention; from 1777 to 1779 he was a member of the Virginia House of Delegates and the Council of State, while from 1779 to 1783 he was one of the Virginia delegates in the Continental Congress.   In all this public work there was a consistency in service and method.   Always the young Virginian is the constitutionalist; always his name signifies certain ideas; always he is the writer, the "penman," the person selected to draw up resolutions and memorials; seldom is he the debater.   He was apt at making motions, but not given to making speeches about them; he was indefatigable in committees; his favorite methods, that is, were colloquial, not forensic.   Perhaps Madison's ideal contribution at this time was as a member of the Virginia Council, a group of eight men elected by the House of Delegates who had revisionary power over acts of the popular chamber.   It was the republican successor of the Royal Council that had ruled the colony in the days of the Virginia "Barons," and was composed of the most venerable dignitaries of the state, several of whom had served the King in the same capacity.   The manner in which this young man so quickly attained this high position is significant.   Madison was a candidate for the House of Delegates in 1777, but his rigid principles caused his defeat.   He regarded the universal practice of "treating" — of providing the electorate with liberal potions of rum on election day — as demoralizing to public virtue, and refused to propitiate Demos in the good old-fashioned way.   An opponent less scrupulous, but, on the side of statesmanship, utterly obscure, "treated" in wholesale fashion and won the coveted seat.   But the sequel disclosed the hold Madison had gained in the respect of the legislature, for it at once elected him member of the Council.   Evidently this slight boyish figure, seated amid the bigwigs of Virginia, made a favorable impression, for after a year of the Council Madison was sent to the Philadelphia assembly, a body that sorely needed men of talent, for in 1779 it had sunk to a new level of ineffectiveness.

Meanwhile Madison had made that friendship which was to last for fifty years and exert so profound an impression on American politics. That he and Thomas Jefferson should become fellow spirits is not surprising, for the two men had everything in common. Both were thinkers rather than doers; both, as students, were interested in the same things — philosophy, government, history, science; both were writers, and both figured in the Revolution, not as soldiers, but as legislators and statesmen. It was these sedentary aspects of Madison that Jefferson chiefly recalled, in his old-age reminiscences of his friend. The phrases Jefferson applied to the Madison of this youthful period confirm the portrait derived from other sources: he mentioned his "consummate powers," his "pure and spotless virtue," his "extreme modesty," the "habit of self-possession which placed at ready command the sources of his luminous and discriminating mind and his extensive information . . . never wandering from his subject into false declamation . . . soothing always the feelings of his adversaries by civilities and softness of expression." Probably few remarkable men have been so influenced by another as was Madison by Jefferson, and naturally the qualities especially evident in Jefferson's recollection were the compliant ones; yet in one conspicuous episode, at the convention of 1776, Madison had displayed aggressive qualities. That was the assemblage of Virginia worthies which, besides approving its Resolution of Independence and the Virginia Constitution, also adopted George Mason's much celebrated Bill of Rights. Religious freedom had for several years been Madison's chief preoccupation; though a Christian, he regarded unfavorably a state religion, going so far as to say that New England was ahead of the other colonies in asserting popular rights for the reason that that region had no established church. "Religious bondage shackles and debilitates the mind," he said, "and unfits it for every noble enterprise." George Mason, whose reputation had suffered somewhat because of his opposition to the Federal Constitution, was then one of Virginia's imposing men; he was fifty-one, in the full maturity of his powers and influence, and for a youngster to fight his first legislative battle against this veteran indicates that there was more in Madison than the deprecating manner which his contemporaries enlarge upon. For Mason's article on religious freedom, in his Bill of Rights, said that "all men should enjoy the fullest tolerance in the exercise of religion." Madison objected to the word "tolerance" and combated it in committee of the whole. It seemed to assume the existence of an established church and implied that dissentients were not to be punished for not accepting it. Such a conception was not in accordance with Madison's ideas; in his quiet, unassuming, respectful, but still positive manner, he argued that there should be no established church; that none should be recognized by the state, and that all should be protected. But this, a commonplace of America to-day, was not generally agreed to then, especially in Virginia, where so vociferous a democrat as Patrick Henry was advocating state appropriations for the support of clergymen. In committee of the whole Madison did not carry his point, but he was still persistent and took his argument to the convention. And here he won, the result being that one of the most decisive paragraphs in Mason's Bill of Rights — "that all men are entitled to the free exercise of it [religion] according to the dictates of conscience" — was the work, not of himself, but of this twenty-five-year-old boy. It is a clause that has directed American history in an important regard, and Madison's tenacity in this matter of profound conviction discloses that he possessed sincerity and determination. It was his first triumph in constitution making.

These were qualities much needed in the new field to which Madison was called in 1780. Congress then illustrated the American political character in its most disastrous phases. Washington had learned the need of a strong central government in the army: Madison now drew the same lesson from his service in Congress. Both experiences emphasized an identical trait: only by a strong central government could the American cause be saved. The fact is that Madison's so-called elevation, from the Council of State in Virginia to the national Senate in Philadelphia, was no promotion. Washington had complained, in his letter to Harrison, that Virginia leaders looked upon service in their state legislature as more honorable than that in Philadelphia, and Madison, as he first surveyed his new brethren, could easily have verified the criticism. The great Virginians who had participated in the early Continental Congress had all departed. Where were Thomas Jefferson, Patrick Henry, George Wythe, Richard Henry Lee, Thomas Nelson, Edmund Pendleton, and others who had early piloted the new nation in the path of revolution? All had left the Congress, and most of them were in the legislative service of their native state. Their absence had more than a personal meaning. It illustrated the American point of view — not confined to Virginia, but almost as rampant in New England — which was destined to confound American politics for a century. The early enthusiasm for the United States had diminished; the entity important in the national mind was not the Union but the State. The war was not yet finished; indeed it had then reached its most discouraging *impasse;* it still called for united effort, but the spirit of coöperation had almost disappeared.

Madison soon found that the body to which he had been called was hardly a legislature; it was a kind of mediæval diet, in which states and not persons were represented. There was no such thing as an American citizen; there was no such character in Congress as "the gentleman from Virginia," the "gentleman from Massachusetts," and those other regional statesmen with whom Americans have become so familiar. When the roll was called, the question was not whether Mr. Jay was present, or Mr. Roger Sherman; the point was whether New York or Connecticut was at hand. When the vote was taken no one asked how Mr. Wilson or Mr. Pinckney had cast his ballot, but how had Pennsylvania or South Carolina voted. No member ever proposed that an excise tax or duties for raising the revenue necessary to pay the expenses of the war should be levied, but that a "requisition" should be made on their respective states — most of which neglected to comply with it. Madison found that his modest stipend as Congressman was not paid by the central government but by the State of Virginia — that is, when it was paid at all. The salary was usually so much in arrears that he was slow in liquidating his boarding-house bill and lived sometimes by borrowing money of a patriotic Jew, Haym Salomon, who generously made advances to needy Congressmen without interest. Jefferson, in one of his letters, records that the "horses of members of Congress were sometimes turned out in the street, because the livery stable keeper was unpaid." Things like these would have been endurable had they only signalized that the country was poor and struggling under great burdens; unfortunately they merely pictured the indifference of the American people towards their legislature. The fact that in the period of Madison's service it became what the French statesman Vergennes called an "ambulatory body" showed the state to which it had been reduced. Congress, in the year of triumph 1783, — when Great Britain acknowledged American independence, — had no home, but wandered from place to place. A mob of soldiers, furious at not receiving any wages for six years, assailed the lawmakers in Philadelphia, threatening to imprison them until their arrears were paid. When Pennsylvania refused its protection, the statesmen mounted their jaded horses and adjourned to Princeton, where Madison found himself on familiar ground in old Nassau. This not proving a satisfactory headquarters, Congress took up a temporary station in Annapolis; then it went to Trenton, and finally to New York. But the place of meeting was not so important, for at times there was no Congress to meet. Members were most lax in attending to their duties; a law practice at home, or the harvesting season, had prior claims. One of Richard Henry Lee's letters pictures him, a desolate figure, in cold lodgings, the snow piled high outside, half dead with the gout, wearily waiting in Trenton for Congressmen to appear in sufficient force to provide a quorum.

Thus the interest everywhere was the state — the state; the central government was disregarded. Madison witnessed several Congressional episodes that evidenced this absorption in local concerns. The most significant came in the early part of 1783. It was not until this crisis arose that Madison realized how far apart he was from many of the great men of his own section. With Washington, — a mighty ally, it must be confessed, — he found himself aligned against Patrick Henry, the Lees, — Richard Henry and Arthur, — Harrison, and others. The hostility of this faction reached its most provocative pitch in the last days of December, 1782. At that time there were two pressing financial questions before the country. Congress needed $3,000,000 for the expenses of 1783; this would enable that body to pay clamoring soldiers, to meet interest on the national debt, domestic and foreign, also long overdue, and to pay the ordinary expenses of government. According to the Articles of Confederation Congress could raise this money only in one way, by "requisition" on the states, assigning to each its "quota." The amount due from Virginia on this basis was $400,000. The other question at issue was the adoption of a permanent method of raising a national revenue — for experience had shown the futility of depending on this "requisition." The method most generally favored, as already explained, was a 5 per cent duty laid on imports. To this impost Virginia had given its consent. But in these last days of December, on the eve of adjournment, the Virginia House of Delegates passed a resolution, not only withdrawing its approval of the impost, but notifying Congress that only $50,000 out of the $400,000 due on its "requisition" would be paid. That is, it not only refused to contribute — in any adequate fashion — to the budget of 1783, but declined to enter into any agreement for a permanent revenue system. The Virginia leaders who were fighting all movements for a constitution, or any effective federal union, were responsible for this backward step. Richard Henry Lee had been declaiming against Congressional "lust for power"; Arthur Lee — at this time a member of Congress — had had much to say of the danger of giving "control of the purse and sword" to the same hands; and Patrick Henry was already descanting on his favorite plan of an independent Virginia nation, to include the Northwest Territory, which was to be cut up into several republics, all to be dependencies of Virginia. Benjamin Harrison, in a letter to the indignant Washington, said that the revocation of the impost and, in large part, of the requisition was the work of the Lees, who had taken advantage of a "slim house" and their own parliamentary skill to engineer the resolution through. It was the greatest blow struck up to that time at the proposed union.

The episode shows Madison in his bravest mood; the scene that subsequently took place in Congress brings forth an entirely different character from the shrinking boy of a few years before. For Madison now arose in Congress and vehemently denounced his own state. The question before the house was the still unsettled matter of the impost. On this subject Madison had already expressed himself with angry emphasis. His proposal now was an amendment to the Articles of Confederation which would enable Congress, at sword's point, to collect requisitions due from delinquent states. "The situation is such," he wrote Jefferson, "that two or three vessels of force, employed against their trade, will make it their interest to yield prompt obedience to all just requisitions upon them." Madison's solution of the difficulty, that is, was in the nature of civil war. His emotions may be conceived, therefore, when Theodorick Bland, one of his Congressional colleagues from Virginia, arose, on January 27, 1783, to explain the position of the ancient Dominion. He had received "sundry papers" from the executive of Virginia, which should be presented to Congress. The first was the one limiting Virginia's requisition to $50,000; the second was that withdrawing its consent to the impost. The debate that ensued lasted several days, the chief speakers being Madison, Alexander Hamilton, and Arthur Lee. At times it was animated and bitter, and both Madison and Hamilton turned ferociously on Lee, upholder of Virginia's defalcation. Madison rejected the "idea of erecting our national independence on the ruins of public faith and national honor." He admitted his embarrassment in pressing his contention in view of the instructions of his own state; still, a member of Congress must think, first of all, of the national welfare, not of local concerns; he was also persuaded that, had the legislature of Virginia completely understood the situation, "it would not have repealed the law in favor of the impost, and would even now rescind the repeal."

Hamilton directed his remarks at Arthur Lee in his usual sledge-hammer fashion. Why beat around the bush? Everybody knew why Virginia and Rhode Island were hostile to the impost. The present system enabled Rhode Island to levy exorbitant taxes on all foreign goods imported into Connecticut, and she was not disposed to relinquish that profit. Nor was Virginia's motive more commendable. The money raised from these duties was to be used, in part, to meet the interest on the Federal debt. Most of that debt was held by Massachusetts and Pennsylvania, which was only another way of saying that these commonwealths had borne the financial burden of the war. Pennsylvania had bought $4,000,000 worth of the war certificates — what would to-day be called the "bonds" — of the Revolutionary government; Massachusetts $2,360,000; while Virginia, though the largest state, had invested only $400,000. "The true objection on the part of Virginia," Hamilton declared, "was her having little share in the debts due from the United States, to which the impost would be applied." There were further remarks from Mr. Lee; certain gentlemen had said that, without the taxing power, the existing Confederation was a "rope of sand"; he would prefer that to a "rope of iron."

VI

The chief result of these debates was thus to widen the breach between the advocates of a loose confederation, such as already existed, and those of a powerful centralized national organization. But economic and commercial forces, as ever, were proving more effectual than parliamentary discussions. Events in the Potomac region began playing into Madison's hands, and he was quick in using them to make real his cherished plan of "federation" (or, as he spelled it in those early times, "foederation"). If a map of the Potomac region is examined, one surprising fact at once becomes apparent. The boundary line separating Virginia and Maryland does not run in the middle of the stream, as is usual in such situations, but is formed by the southern bank of the Potomac. That is, this famous river is not, as is popularly supposed, a Virginia watercourse; the river as a whole is part of Maryland. This had been the case since this northern part of Virginia, in 1632, was separated from its parent colony and transformed into a proprietary for Lord Baltimore; those responsible for making this boundary, three centuries ago, little realized that their friendly disposition to Maryland was to assist in the formation of a constitution of which they did not have the slightest intimation. For the accident that the sovereignty of Maryland extended to the southern bank of the Potomac gave Washington and Madison the excuse for the first step that led to the Philadelphia Convention. In the Virginia Constitution, adopted in 1776, this boundary was accepted, though in the same clause Virginia insisted that its free navigation of the Potomac should never be interfered with. It was one thing to set forth this claim and another to make it the fact; Maryland, having jurisdiction over the whole width of the Potomac, could prevent vessels destined to Virginia ports from entering the river, and could impose other restrictions destructive to Virginia commerce. In a visit to the Northern Neck, in 1784, Madison heard that Maryland was preparing to enforce measures against its neighbor state. Yet Virginia similarly possessed exclusive and counterbalancing advantages. The entrance to the Chesapeake, for example, was entirely in her possession; both the capes, Henry and Charles, were Virginia ports; she could therefore exclude all Maryland ships from entering the great Bay and, by the same token, from gaining access to the Potomac itself. Virginia had long maintained lighthouses, buoys, and other aids to navigation in the Chesapeake and the Potomac; these were just as necessary to Maryland as to herself; was it not unjust that she should have to bear the whole expense?

Here was opportunity for trouble; here were precisely the circumstances that, in ancient countries, had produced war. Maryland closes the Potomac to Virginia: Virginia retaliates by closing the Chesapeake to Maryland; much less serious disagreements have caused nations to fly at one another's throats. In 1783 Madison withdrew from Congress, having served the three years which was then the statutory limit, and retired to his library at Montpelier. Here he diversified his studies; zoölogy, especially the zoölogy of the American continent, became an absorption; Jefferson, when later in Paris, had a standing instruction to purchase for him "such books as may be either old and curious or new and useful." But his mind was faithful to the main subject, for Jefferson was also enjoined to send him "treaties on the ancient or modern Federal Republics, on the laws of nations, and the history, national and political, of the new world: to which I will add such Greek and Roman authors (where they can be got very cheap) as are worth having and are not in the common list of school classics." Such was the type of mind that drew up the American Constitution! But Madison — he was now thirty-two — was not to be left solely to theoretical contemplation of political problems. Virginia's great men at that time commonly vacillated between Congress and the House of Delegates, and now Madison was called upon again to resume his legislative work in Richmond. The most pressing question was the navigation of the Potomac. What was the best procedure, Madison asked in a letter to Jefferson, — it was a year before the latter's departure for France and he was then a member of Congress in Annapolis, — to take aggressive action, extend Virginia laws on the Potomac, or for the two states to appoint commissions and arrive at a peaceful settlement? The latter, by all means, replied Jefferson; he talked the matter over with prominent Marylanders, who at once approved the plan. Commissioners were consequently appointed — for Virginia, James Madison, George Mason, Edmund Randolph, and Alexander Henderson, the first three important members of the subsequent Constitutional Convention; and for Maryland, Samuel Chase, Thomas Stone, Daniel of St. Thomas Jenifer, and Thomas Johnson. Before these gentlemen could come together another historic event had taken place, for Washington had made his trip to the Western country and laid out his transportation route from Virginia to the Ohio. In this connection, it will be recalled, he had discovered that his plan, because his river system entered Pennsylvania, was an interstate matter. It seemed indispensable that Pennsylvania be invited to coöperate, and, in fact, an invitation for such coöperation had been sent and accepted. Thus, both east and west, the idea of interstate commerce was becoming a reality.

Washington was naturally interested in Madison's Potomac plan, and informally dropped in on the delegates when they met in Alexandria, in March 1785. He found them in somewhat doubtful mood. Facilities for transit were slight in those days, and, the notification not having reached them, Madison and Randolph had not appeared, although their associates had been waiting four days. Washington's concern is evident from his diary. On March ten he paid a visit of a day and a night to George Mason; he was busy dining with other members of the delegation, and was sending his carriage back and forth to conduct the negotiators to the meeting place. Finding the commissioners undecided what to do in the absence of Madison and Randolph, he strongly advised them to proceed, and suggested, since the quarters selected at Alexandria seemed unsatisfactory, that the session be adjourned to Mount Vernon. Thus Washington, though not a member of the Virginia contingent, dominated the convention; the confabulations under his roof lasted for four days; and the document drawn up — really a treaty between Virginia and Maryland — was promptly named "the Mount Vernon" compact.

This Mount Vernon compact, next to the Constitution itself, is the most historic paper in our constitutional history. Emphasis is usually laid on the Annapolis Convention of 1786 as the first step in the process that culminated in Union; but so far as the initiation of ideas was concerned, the several agreements drawn up in early March, 1785, at Mount Vernon, were more important. For this Mount Vernon compact contains many of the principles that ultimately formed the basis of the Constitution. That only two states formed the understanding is true, but two states were sufficient to establish the principle of interstate organization which is the nucleus of that instrument. Maryland consented to admit Virginia freely to the navigation of the Potomac; that is, she withdrew the threat, always present, of "occluding" — a popular word of the time — the entrance of that river to the sister state and framing restrictive measures after Virginia's vessels had gained access. Virginia, on her part, contracted to let Maryland vessels pass without hindrance — that is, without the payment of duties — the capes of the Chesapeake and to enjoy all the navigation rights of those waters. A great page in constitutional history unfolds as one reads this interstate agreement of 1785. We foresee New York, several years after the Constitution was adopted, attempting to close its rivers and sounds to the steamboats of its neighbors; we glimpse the coming Daniel Webster proclaiming before the Supreme Court, presided over by John Marshall, the rights under the "commerce clause" of all states to have free entry into the waters of its associates, and Marshall's decision, *Gibbons* vs. *Ogden,* which sustained that right. It was a decision, says Beveridge, that "has done more to knit the American people into an indivisible nation than any one force in history except only war"; and this principle, expressed so indefinitely in the Constitution that a great legal battle was required forty years after its adoption to reduce it to permanent form, was set forth explicitly in this Mount Vernon compact of 1785.

Another conception which has done more perhaps than any one influence to establish peace and lay the foundations of industrial and agricultural greatness appears in this same parchment. Virginia and Maryland agreed that there should be no trade barriers between them; the products of each were to enter, without the payment of duties, the ports of the other. Here is that principle of interstate free trade which now exists among forty-eight commonwealths — a system which has made the United States the greatest free-trade nation in the world. Again the Mount Vernon compact provides that these two states should levy identical import duties against other nations — thus establishing, as a rule for themselves, the idea which Washington, Madison, and others were urging as a necessary safeguard for the thirteen states, and which, two years afterward, was inserted in the Constitution. Here were two great principles of interstate coöperation, but the framers of the compact had in view other proposals — proposals afterward embodied in the Constitution. They suggested that, at a future meeting, Maryland and Virginia should adopt measures for a common monetary system. In fact these two neighboring commonwealths were sensibly drawing together into union — union none the less because membership was so limited.

But reasons for its extension soon appeared. Maryland and

Virginia presently discovered that other states were concerned in the navigation of the Potomac and the Chesapeake. The Susquehanna River, for example, then a more important element in transportation than now, empties into the Chesapeake. Did the two communities directly bordering that body imagine that they could exclude Pennsylvania from utilizing its waters? In that case, Pennsylvania could easily retaliate: what, for example, would become of Washington's river route to the West, a part of which would need the consent of the none too friendly Quakers? A plan was afoot for connecting, by canal and otherwise, the Susquehanna and Delaware rivers; and so it appeared that Delaware must be added to the commercial alliance. Thus, step by step, the field of union was broadening. Evidently a new conference would be necessary to round out the scheme; accordingly Maryland, on November 22, 1785, issued an invitation to Virginia, Pennsylvania, and Delaware to meet representatives of her own, to frame an enlarged Mount Vernon compact — one this time to comprise four states. The Union was extending — but extending in a way which Madison disapproved. The association of these four "countries" looked too much like the growth of one of those separate groupings which at this time threatened the amalgamation of thirteen states. Should this four-power commonwealth be formed, undoubtedly the states south of Virginia would establish a federation of their own, and those north of Pennsylvania would organize a nation in the North. The one man responsible, above all, for checking this development was James Madison. His reputation as one of the builders of the Constitution rests largely upon his action in face of so great a danger. Events were moving rapidly. By the end of the year Pennsylvania and Delaware had accepted Maryland's invitation; and now Madison acted decisively. Why confine the proposed commercial covenant, he said, to four states and thus form a confederation within a confederation? Why not invite all the states, and establish a general unison on this subject at least — the control of navigation and commerce? There were forces within Virginia, Madison well knew, intensely hostile to such coöperation. Certain leaders, as noted above, were advocating trade agreements with England rather than with their Northern brethren. That the Lees had resorted to clever parliamentary methods in withdrawing Virginia's consent to the impost has already been described; and now Madison did not hesitate to indulge in a little deception of his own. At the time he was a man suspect; his advocacy of national measures was well known, so much so that his suggestion of any conciliatory motion would immediately arouse the opposition of the powerful anti-national men.

But there was one man in the Virginia legislature who was trusted by both sides. This was John Tyler, for several years Speaker of the House, subsequently to be Governor of Virginia, member of the United States District Court, and father of an American President. As the session of the House of Delegates for 1785–1786 was drawing to a close, Madison took Tyler aside and placed in his hands one of the most fateful documents in American history. This was a resolution accepting Maryland's invitation to a four-state convention, but enlarging it so as to include all the thirteen. The place appointed for the meeting was Annapolis — selected, Madison afterward said, because it was so far removed from the North and the "marts of trade." The proposed meeting was to be strictly limited in scope — it was not to frame general articles of government, but to take in consideration the trade of the United States "and to consider how far a uniform system in their regulations may be necessary to their common interests and permanent harmony." Thus it was not to be a constitutional convention, but a kind of river and harbor congress. That Madison entertained larger hopes his correspondence shows. For years the conception of national union had filled his thoughts. His mind, like Washington's and Hamilton's, was in a state of unsleeping vigilance. Yet he knew the need of approaching the grand consummation by degrees. Annapolis, he hoped, would bind the states into a commercial union.

Madison's ruse succeeded; on the last day of the session the resolution was called from the table and rushed through the house. The fact that the modest member from Orange was the person who had outwitted the foe remained a secret for several years — until the object at which Madison had been really aiming, the Constitution of the United States, had become an actuality.

VII

Yet in this Annapolis Convention, which came together in May 1786, Madison was not the most powerful influence. Leadership in the assembly for which the Virginian was responsible passed to another man — one quite unlike the Montpelier philosopher, but one who, like himself, had been unceasingly working for Nationalism. Perhaps the great advantage of Alexander Hamilton at this time was that his background had been so different from that of his co-workers. For Hamilton, by birth, was not an American; he came from the tiny West Indian island of Nevis, in the Caribbean. Hamilton never saw the country whose destinies he was to have so potent a hand in shaping until his fifteenth year; because of this he was a man without local allegiances. He was not a Virginian, a New Yorker, or a New Englander; the prejudices and loyalties the sons of section had absorbed in childhood formed no part of his mentality; he was, in no mere rhetorical sense of the word, an American, and had no outlook except a continental one. Thus as the several problems engendered by independence arose after 1776, Hamilton saw in them not a means of fulfilling the destiny and reaping the advantages of a Virginian; he surveyed them from the standpoint of the country as a whole. Alone among the great men concerned in forming the American State, Hamilton needed no conversion to the Union. From the day the almost friendless boy disembarked at Boston, America signified nothing to him but a great national expanse, under one form of government. The accusation, afterward so freely made, that Hamilton cared nothing for the states and would willingly have erased state lines was virtually true, and in this conviction, so far as his work as an agitator for the national government was concerned, lay his strength.

It is an interesting circumstance that the West Indies should have given the new American and French republics of the late eighteenth century, at almost the same time, two of their most romantic characters: in 1772 Nevis sent to the United States its future constitution maker, while in 1778 Martinique sent to Paris that Josephine Tascher de la Pagerie who was to become, first, wife of a leader of the French Revolution, and afterwards Empress of the French.   Little as they had in common from the standpoint of intellect or character or temperament, both owed much to the circumstances of their early life.   It should not be forgotten that Hamilton was half French, his mother being Rachel Faucette, of Huguenot origin, who transmitted those traits of fire and impatience that so startled the matter-of-fact Americans of his day; while his father was that James Hamilton, son of the Laird of Grange in Scotland, who may have been responsible for the hard-headed qualities his son introduced into the American system.   Though these characteristics — on one hand impulsiveness, fierce determination, passion, romance, and on the other a stern sense of reality, a cold-blooded allegiance to facts — went along hand in hand throughout Hamilton's career, probably the exterior man suggested the maternal rather than the paternal stock.   This inheritance was excitable, headstrong, even turbulent.   Both Hamilton's mother and grandmother, in their domestic relations, had defied the conventions.   His grandmother, Mary Faucette, famed for beauty and intellect, for fearlessness and unchecked will, had scandalized even the easy-going society of the Caribbees by separating from her husband and taking up an independent abode on St. Kitts; Hamilton's mother, daughter of this self-assertive lady, and, like her, a beauty and a wit, had found herself, at the age of sixteen, forced into marriage with a Danish Jew whom she abhorred, and who, from all accounts, treated her cruelly.   From him she fled to her childhood home and entered into an irregular union with the Scotsman, James Hamilton, of which the fruit was the future American statesman.   John Adams's coarse description of his political rival as "the bastard brat of a Scotch peddler" was true to the extent that Hamilton's birth was illegitimate, but inaccurate as an intimation of his ancestry and mental inheritance.   For Hamilton's father was a member of Scotland's foremost ducal house, while his mother's family had been for a century a political and social leader in the British West Indies.

And the romantic and intrepid qualities Hamilton derived from his French mother are hardly suggested by Adams's description. The family, if erratic and high-spirited, was devoted to things of the mind.   Hamilton's mother, in a day and in a place where women were restricted to domestic employments, had a mastery of English, French, and Spanish, was educated in music as well as embroidery, and had been trained in riding and out-of-door sport.   But the Faucette blood was, above all, imperious, insistent on command, not overpatient with opposition. It is therefore no mystery where Hamilton acquired his energy, his contempt for spirits less audacious than himself, the fierceness with which he rushed at the goal, and the tactlessness and outspokenness which, while they did not block the masterwork of his life, prevented him from ever becoming a great political leader. As a child, we are told, he was puny, but also passionate, difficult of control, and given to spells of fury. The most famous episode of his early days fits in well with his mature character. When he was ten, the worst hurricane in a century descended on his island. While the other inhabitants were rushing to the safety of their stone houses, Alexander, remembering that his aged aunt lived on the outskirts and might not have the strength to save herself, beat his way in the open against rain and destructive winds, reached her home, barricaded the windows, and fixed in their place all the protective devices this storm-swept island had prepared against such dangers. It was an early test of Hamilton's gift of working most successfully when the difficulties were greatest, an eloquent prelude to the supreme moment of his life when he entered the Poughkeepsie Convention with all the big party leaders, four fifths of the members, and the overwhelming majority of the electorate against him, and by sheer will forced that body to ratify the Constitution.

From this maternal inheritance Hamilton derived not only his determined impulsive nature, but his looks. Probably few men, by mere presence, have exercised such influence on their age. Brilliant as were Hamilton's writings, persuasive as were his orations, it was chiefly by personal discussion that he bent men to his purpose. He went much into society, and it was his talk across the dinner table, or his more intimate corner conversations, that exercised the most powerful effect upon events. Just where Hamilton obtained his extensive knowledge of history and human institutions was a mystery to his friends, but this made him a formidable opponent, on the platform, in the press, and in private talk; to listen to him for half an hour was an education in the topics that were exciting the public. Charm and magnetism, of course, explain a good deal; and these were qualities not drawn from his Scottish father, but from his mother and grandmother. We feel to-day this compelling personality in the Trumbull portrait. The tilt of the head, the fire and vivacity of the eyes, the firmness of the mouth and chin, the sharp, clear-cut features — here is sufficient explanation of the eager soul who held captive such diverse characters as Washington and Madison, and proved so convincing in the legislature and at the bar.

It is said that in his tensest moments Hamilton's blue eyes would turn black, the friendly, even humorous, lines of his mouth become tight-set, and his slight and diminutive figure seem to take on added stature. The man's fondness for fine clothes also reflected his neatness and precision of thought. Jefferson's slovenliness in attire was only another reason, in Hamilton's view, for mistrusting the man's political garments. His rival's lack of ceremony was also offensive; no one could imagine Hamilton, at a Presidential inauguration, walking, unattended, to the scene. His own chestnut hair was always carefully brushed and queued; his coats were tailored in the latest mode; his laces and ruffles were always spotlessly white; his silver buckles were invariably shining. One of the charms of Hamilton is that he is always young; he died at forty-seven, before the slightest signs of decay had appeared, and thus we have no image of him other than that of the well-kempt, slender figure, dignified, aggressive, the most romantic statesman in American annals, if not the most heroic.

Despite the man's attraction, there was a certain quality of steel that, to his contemporaries as well as succeeding generations, has made him a character rather admired than loved. Hamilton never sought the affections of the people, and not infrequently expressed his low opinion of his fellows. To-day his name means to the average American the man who called the populace a "beast"; who, in framing the Constitution, was more interested in maintaining the rights of property than the "rights of man"; who called the British House of Lords "a noble institution"; who even looked tolerantly upon a King; who, in default of a monarch for the American nation, wished a President and Senate for life, and was so strongly in favor of a powerful national government that he would almost have obliterated state lines and cemented the whole country into a centralized power. These things can be easily exaggerated to Hamilton's disadvantage — and the present tendency is to exaggerate them. The fact is that Hamilton was no more a Nationalist, and no more in favor of reducing the states to administrative districts, than was James Madison, or Rufus King, or Charles Cotesworth Pinckney, or John Rutledge, or Edmund Randolph, or many of the other founders of the Constitution, including probably Washington himself, and certainly was no more hostile to democracy than Gouverneur Morris or Roger Sherman, or Elbridge Gerry, or John Dickinson, or nearly all his contemporary statesmen.

The constant harping on these Hamiltonian beliefs has obscured

the fact that Hamilton, in Revolutionary days, was a patriot of
Samuel Adams fervor; that he wrote articles approving casting the
tea into Boston Harbor; that his early fame was derived from
appearances on the stump, defying King George in best Son-of-
Liberty strain, and from his articles in Holt's Whig newspaper
holding up to scorn that arch-Tory, Samuel Seabury, afterward
first Episcopal Bishop of New York. When a student at King's
College, his demonstrations brought disapproval from its Tory
president, Dr. Cooper. On the great question of American submission to British pretensions, Hamilton was distinctly a revolutionary. The early Continental Congress had no greater admirer;
his articles on the Reverend Mr. Seabury were a "Vindication" of
the Philadelphia statesmen, in all their acts. Hamilton was only
seventeen years old at the time, but the pamphlet was generally
attributed to John Jay. Yet when it came to reorganizing the country wrested from the British Crown, his position was conservative.
It is a simple matter to explain this by his early environment.
Despite the equivocal nature of his birth, Hamilton's ancestors on
both sides were aristocrats. The West Indian society into which he
was born, with its sugar grandees, its slaves, its absence of a middle
class, represented a more exclusive social and political organization
than did the planter oligarchy of Virginia; naturally therefore, it is
assumed, Hamilton would cling to property and privilege. But
there was doubtless something more fundamental than this. Hamilton's all-mastering quality was a sense of order. Turbulence in the
body politic he regarded as a greater evil than temporary injustice.
His literary style, brief, pointed, staccato, was precisely like the
man; he was a devotee of seemly public behavior, of law, and of
honesty in meeting obligations. The absence of these essentials in
the America of his day affected Hamilton's primary instincts. In
this the young lieutenant colonel was much like Washington. Government, he believed, was impossible without energy, and energy was
the last quality of the Continental Congress in its latter years.
Financial integrity, in Hamilton's view, was the bedrock of constitutional order. In 1786 every state was flooded with paper
money; Congress had recently "stabilized" its currency at the rate
of forty dollars to one Spanish gold dollar; debtors were in open
rebellion against the creditor class, and mobs were attacking the
courts; the air was full of the wildest schemes of repudiation and
spoliation. Thus Hamilton needed nothing but the prospect before
him as argument for a powerful, honest, debt-paying American
government. Not admiration for tradition and aristocracy, not

the study of unstable Greek democracies, had made him a Nationalist; the question, as he saw it, was the disappearance, or the survival,
of America as an independent empire.   The problem was a practical
one, arising from the circumstances immediately at hand.

And so it happened that, from his first glimpse of the central
so-called government, Hamilton became the leading advocate of
change.   From 1780 until 1787 his mind seemed riveted on one
subject — a convention for the creation of a strong and stable constitution.   One of the most important documents in American
political literature is the letter Hamilton addressed to James Duane,
September 30, 1780.   At that time the United States was still a
revolutionary government; the Articles of Confederation had not
been adopted; the war was still in progress.   Hamilton was only
twenty-three years old; that he should have written these mature
views is not more surprising than that one of America's leaders at
the bar and one of the conspicuous men in Congress, James Duane,
should have solicited his advice.   What, in your opinion, — such
was the query Duane had proposed to Washington's young aide-de-
camp, — is the trouble with the American system and what changes
would best fit the situation?   Hamilton replied immediately and
succinctly: "The fundamental defect is a want of power in Congress."
How could that be remedied?   A convention of all the states should
be called, to meet the following November, and formulate a genuine
National Union.   The plan which Hamilton now exhibited to
Duane has been frequently described as the embryo of the Constitution adopted several years afterward.   This is an exaggeration,
for the scheme which Hamilton outlined provided for no executive and still confided legislative ability to a single house of
Congress.   But in the enumeration of the powers to be granted his
single chamber, Hamilton's proposals were almost a forecast of the
Constitution of 1787.   The body would possess the complete attributes of sovereignty — authority to levy taxes, external and internal, to make appropriations, to regulate commerce, both foreign
and interstate, to control foreign affairs, make war and peace,
negotiate treaties, raise and equip armies and fleets, establish courts,
coin money, and charter banks.   All the territory the states possessed
or claimed to the west was to be ceded to this central government;
thus the Hamiltonian outline foresaw the policy afterward pursued
in the several cessions and the Northwest Ordinance of succeeding
years.   But the principle that underlay this precocious visioning of
the future United States is its most illuminating point.   That principle was the idea of genuine union, with its essential corollary of

a diminution of state authority. It was this emphasis that made Hamilton's proposed constitution, at that moment, seem immature, and rendered it impossible of acceptance. Yet it was the conception which the young political philosopher kept ever before the American public from this time forward. He caused resolutions in the New York legislature to be introduced favoring a Constitutional Convention. His brief service of eight months in Congress, in 1783, was largely occupied, in debate and in private conversation, with popularizing his idea of union, and of a Constitutional Convention to achieve it. His pen was busy on the same theme in the public press. The very title to a series of articles written in 1781 epitomizes Hamilton's work for his adopted country: this was "The Continentalist," and the word describes the farseeing statesman even better than the "Federalist."

The Annapolis conference called through the influence of Madison to discuss trade relations among the states accomplished nothing in that direction; it was chiefly useful in demonstrating the need of that coöperation on which Hamilton had been insisting for so many years. It proved to be a conference not of union, but of disunion. Madison's effort to draw all the states together for sympathetic arrangements in trade was a failure. The most conspicuous disappointment was the absence of New England, for not a single one of the Eastern states regarded the matter with favor enough to send delegates. New York was almost as neglectful, but one of its two delegates was Hamilton — the equivalent of a cohort of less imaginative statesmen. Four other states appointed representatives, none of whom took the trouble to make the journey to Annapolis; thus that celebrated convention, in which many pretend to detect the germs of the Federal Constitution, embraced the ambassadors of only five states — New York, New Jersey, Pennsylvania, Delaware, and Virginia. Evidently the desire for coöperation in trade matters was not extensive. Instead, at this particular moment, North and South were engaged in a violent dispute over the navigation of the Mississippi; that stream was still under the jurisdiction of Spain, which excluded Americans from its traffic; Virginia insisted that the settlers in her "backlands" have access to its waters, threatening to join her fortunes to the mother country unless New England coöperated with her in obtaining the privilege; New England, far more interested in the fisheries on the Grand Bank, cared nothing for Virginian aspirations or threats. Thus, at the moment when the half-reluctant delegates gathered in that Annapolis statehouse where, three years before, Washington had handed back to Congress his commission as commander of the victorious forces, the spectacle that confronted them was not the one which they had assembled to contemplate, good feeling and coöperative effort, but hostility and disunion.

From this sorry pass the Annapolis Convention was lifted by the genius of one man — that Alexander Hamilton who had now attained the age of twenty-nine. The convention had been called to discuss such practical, possibly sordid matters as the regulation of interstate trade and the use of interstate watercourses; but the swift delegate from New York seized the occasion to concentrate the country's attention on loftier purposes. All bodies, official and unofficial, with which Hamilton had been concerned up to that time had been used to further the cause nearest his affections — that of National Union; it was in keeping with this fixed idea, therefore, that he should see a new opportunity in this assemblage of unenthusiastic delegates. In fact the convention soon demonstrated that it could not agree on anything, and would soon have broken up in sullenness had not the New Yorker suddenly assumed command. He showed his parliamentary skill by picking out a phrase which New Jersey had included in its instructions to delegates. Never has a parenthesis in a state paper served a grander historic end. For New Jersey, not regarded previously as a leader in the creation of an American union, in specifying the usual commercial subjects on which her delegates had been instructed to negotiate, had added these four words: "and other important matters." The phrase now formed the theme of Hamilton's discourse. No precise record of that Annapolis Convention is extant; probably there was not much speech making, Hamilton, as always, relying upon private talk to bring forth his argument. Only one surviving paper gives an insight into the deliberations, formal and informal, and this is Hamilton's composition. It is said that the first draft contained more daring statements than certain Virginians, notably Edmund Randolph, were willing to subscribe to, and that Hamilton toned the argument down in the interest of harmony. But the final document was sufficient for all purposes. It declared, quoting New Jersey's extension of powers, that there were other things than trade to be considered in calming the existing unrest. New Jersey's suggestion of "extending the powers of their deputies to other subjects than those of commerce" was an "improvement on the original plan." It was impossible to settle trade matters without considering other concerns of even greater importance. What these were was so well known that they need not be "particularized." The Annapolis Convention therefore unanimously recommended — and this was its great accomplishment — that a convention of all the states be held at Philadelphia "on the second Monday of May next, to take in consideration the situation in the United States, to devise such further provisions as shall appear to them necessary to render the Constitution of the Federal government *adequate to the exigencies* of the Union, and to report such an act for that purpose to the United States in Congress assembled as, when agreed to by them and afterwards confirmed by the legislature of every state, will effectually provide for the same."

Congress and the several states — except Rhode Island — subsequently agreed to this proposal, and thus the Constitutional Convention, for which Washington, Hamilton, and Madison had been struggling for ten years, became a reality. Naturally all three men became delegates.

VIII

Although Washington presided over the Constitutional Convention, its work was mainly the achievement of the younger generation — the generation that had come into effective influence after the Revolution. The extent to which Washington swayed the deliberations is not known. As many of the most important decisions were taken out of doors, in those caucuses or groups that settled programmes, and as the Virginia delegation was given to such discussions, the likelihood is that his authority was constantly felt. Washington was no debater, but he had his way, by nods of approval or deprecating shrugs, of expressing his opinion — signs that would have infinitely greater weight upon the body than a thousand fiery orations.

Certain other dignitaries present recalled the days of the early Continental Congress, but few of these veterans were particularly active. Benjamin Franklin was now eighty-one, so feeble that his speeches were read by his colleague, James Wilson; his ideas made no impression, although he was heard with the respect due his years and fame. His interventions were mainly of a conciliatory nature, intended to calm an excited atmosphere, but his proposals for the most part were futile and even, at times, absurd. John Dickinson cut no glorious figure; his constant insistence on the "rights of property," his desire to make the Senate a duplicate of the British House of Lords, in which leading "families" should have representation, fell upon unappreciative ears. George Wythe, preceptor in law and government to most of the public men of Virginia, and Robert Morris of Pennsylvania, "financier of the Revolution," both sat in the convention, but silently, for Madison's *Debates* do not record a solitary contribution from these experienced statesmen. Even more noticeable were several important absentees. Patrick Henry and Richard Henry Lee had been elected delegates, and both, having no sympathy with the purposes at hand, refused to attend. Samuel Adams remained in democratic seclusion in Boston; John Adams, in London, was still attempting vainly to wring trading concessions from hostile British statesmen.   Thomas Jefferson was serving as American Minister in Paris and observing the growth of a revolutionary explosion even more destructive than the one he had fomented eleven years before.   John Hancock was in Boston, governor for the second time, his life still made miserable by gout and by the insurrectionary behavior of the Massachusetts peasantry under Daniel Shays.   Practically the only leaders of the Continental Congress who played great rôles in 1787 were James Wilson of Pennsylvania, now forty-five years old, and Oliver Ellsworth and Roger Sherman of Connecticut, a worthy pair whose interposition at the most critical moment proved decisive.   Thus the American Constitution was the work of young men.   The habit of regarding the present as the era of youth receives a shock when we consider the statesmen who created the system under which we live.   Hamilton was thirty; Madison thirty-six; Edmund Randolph, whose resolutions formed the basis of the early debates, was thirty-four; Paterson, author of the so-called New Jersey plan, was forty-two; Gouverneur Morris, who reduced the Constitution to its present literary form, was thirty-five; and Oliver Ellsworth was forty-two. On the whole the Constitutional Convention was a conservative body, insistent on preserving property rights and not overtrustful of the populace, but it was not an organization of weary, disillusioned old men, impervious to new ideas.

Next to Washington the most conspicuous figure was Madison. The General sat on a dais, as became his office as chairman, and directly before him, in the middle of the front row, with associate delegates ranged on both sides, Madison had selected his vantage ground.   This position was not preëmpted from vanity or ambition, but as a matter of convenience.   Madison entertained a loftier vision of this assemblage than did most of the members, and had assigned to himself the duty of immortalizing the proceedings. The Virginian, in addition to his other claims to fame, proved to be the greatest reporter in our history.   American journalism has no feat to compare with his record of the Constitutional Convention. Many works have been written describing that event, but Madison's *Debates* still remain the source to which all interested in our national beginning must go.   For they not only constitute the most authentic report available of the speeches and votes, but are full of emotion and human nature.   Unconsciously the leaders draw their own characters; their views give a perfect picture of the prevailing attitudes of the time on life and government.   Drama is not lacking, for at crises the rivalries, aspirations, the personal and sectional dislikes, can be felt. In these pages New England and Virginia frequently glare at each other; Connecticut and South Carolina indulge in unexpected caresses; a pygmy state like Delaware hurls defiance at its great neighbor Pennsylvania; and Massachusetts, with a self-confidence which was afterward to become a high light in American politics, reads lessons in the art of government to its less enlightened associates. The essential element in drama, suspense, is always present; whether the Convention is to result in a form of government or is to break up in disorder is always in doubt. Cabals, "deals," the mutual give and take without which association in government is impossible, constantly appear in this sober chronicle.

Yet there was little suggesting conflict in Madison's appearance as he made this record. His slight boyish figure, clad in black, constantly bending over the desk, pen busily inscribing the tumultuous relation, frequently rising to make contributions of his own to the narrative, is forever fixed in the American story. The reason for this voluntary industry Madison has explained. He had read much in "the history of the most distinguished confederacies, particularly those of antiquity, more especially in what related to the processes, the principles, the reasons and the anticipations which prevailed in the formation of them," but had been impeded by the absence of authentic records. He determined that the future should not be left in the dark concerning the beginnings of what, he felt sure, was destined to be the most impressive of attempts at self-government. Therefore he had selected this commanding seat "in front of the presiding member," not, however, facing Washington, but his colleagues. "In this favorable position for hearing all that passed, I noted, in terms legible, and in abbreviations and marks intelligible to myself, what was read from the chair or spoken by the members; and, losing not a moment unnecessarily between the adjournment and reassembling of the Convention, I was enabled to write out my daily notes during the session or within a few finishing days after its close, in the extent and form preserved, in my own hand. . . . I was not absent a single day, nor more than a casual fraction of an hour in any day, so that I cannot have lost a single speech, unless a very short one." As the Convention remained in session four months, with only occasional intermissions, Madison's performance, even as a feat of endurance, was a creditable one.

Thus the deficiency which Madison had so sorely felt in studying the Amphictyonic League, the Lycian League, or the Italian republics of the Middle Ages, does not affect his successors to-day who seek to penetrate the springs of the American Constitution. Some may desire even completer details than his compendium, but they are quite sufficient for most purposes. They are a far better guide to the convention than most of the confused narratives which modern writers have based upon Madison's report. On most of the questions that had stirred America for the preceding ten years there was little disagreement. On that subject of "more power to Congress" which Hamilton had been demanding since his teens the delegates were little disposed to argue. Certain happenings in Massachusetts and Pennsylvania in the few months preceding the convention had dispelled all doubts as to the need of a government with "power." Massachusetts, in particular, had been definitely converted by the spectacle of large sections of her own people engaged in property destroying, riot, and rebellion. Probably Mr. Daniel Shays, with his army of debtors burning courthouses, attacking judges and lawyers and all forces that had been sent to disperse his malcontents, until a large part of western Massachusetts had been reduced to anarchy, furnished quite as persuasive an inducement for well-conducted government as the pleas of statesmen. Modern writers have found some justification for the Shays insurrection, and uprisings of recent times — farmer disturbances in Iowa and other states, for example, aimed against courts and judges engaged in foreclosing mortgages — have had certain features in common with it, but the conservative defenders of social order that prevailed in the Constitutional Convention saw in it not a vindication of agrarian rights, but mob rule and a riotous attack on "property." Even Washington's horror appears in his letters. This prevailing chaos in one state, and the knowledge that similar tinder boxes were smouldering in others, ready, on the slightest incitement, to burst into flame, proved a strong argument in the hands of the statesmen who could see in a powerful national government the only means of maintaining the public peace. The large attention devoted to the militia in the debate seems disproportionate to an age that does not esteem highly this amateur method of defense, but if one seeks the explanation of that clause in the Constitution that gives Congress power to "provide for organizing, arming, and disciplining" this civilian army, and to call it forth to "suppress insurrections," it will be found in the Shays rebellion already experienced and the numerous explosions that threatened other parts of the country.

Thus on the need of a new government, continental in scope,

there prevailed, at the moment when Washington's gavel called the assemblage to order, practically no disagreement. On certain of its features — decisions that assumed subsequently a greater importance than they did in the summer of 1787 — there ensued little argument. That there should be a Congress and that it should consist of two houses was the majority opinion. That there should be an executive — something unknown under the Articles of Confederation — was an idea that aroused little opposition. Certain questions involving this executive caused a good deal of discussion, — whether he should be one person, or two, or three, whether he should work in coöperation, especially in exercising the veto, with some body resembling a privy council, the method by which the executive should be chosen, whether by popular vote, or by Congress, or by the Electoral College finally adopted, — but this discussion never reached the acrimonious stage. That Congress should have the power for which so many leaders had long pleaded in vain — to levy taxes, duties, imposts, and excises — was accepted with the most perfunctory debate, nor did any delegate now rise to insist, as so many had been insisting in state legislatures, that this — the one supreme function of government — should be given only for fifteen years, and that the taxes should be collected by the states and paid into the state treasury. All such absurdities had long vanished into the discard. Nor did hostility show itself to the vital matter that in itself was responsible for the Philadelphia gathering — that Congress should regulate commerce with foreign nations, and among the several states. Everyone now agreed that no state should be permitted to levy import duties on the products of another, and thus, at one blow, fell that practice which, in the *likin* of China and the *octroi* of European nations, had made the localities of the same countries almost foreign nations to one another.

The terse action on this and other points on which constitutional history has since turned — and which are still questions of fierce controversy — almost shocks one. The explanation, of course, is that these subjects had been matters of endless harangue for fifteen years, in legislatures, pamphlets, and in Congress. The phrase that frequently appears, "agreed to, *nem. con.*," tells this story of acquiescence. *Nem. con.* abbreviates the familiar Latin expression *nemine contradicente* — with no opposing voice; in other words, the decision is unanimous. Thus the clause for regulating commerce with foreign nations, and such, was agreed to *nem. con.* That exclusive right of Congress to "coin money," of which so much has been heard in recent years, similarly passed *nem. con.*   Perhaps no article caused so much excitement in the first half of the nineteenth century as that requiring the surrender of fugitive slaves.   It aroused no discussion in the Constitutional Convention; there it was adopted *nem. con.*   No sentence has so puzzled lawyers, and so perplexes amateur jurisconsults to-day, as that authorizing Congress to levy taxes "for the general welfare."   Some contemporary writers see in these words justification for any legislation Congress deems desirable for the good of the people — see in this innocent clause, that is, a means of destroying the Constitution itself.   But the wise men of 1787 shed no light on the problem.   The phrase was a familiar one — it appears in the Articles of Confederation, where it certainly conveyed no such universal power as is now sometimes claimed for it; it also appears in the preamble to the present Constitution, amid the pious listing of the reasons why that instrument was framed.   If the gentlemen at Philadelphia intended to give Congress power to negative the Constitution as a whole, they did so with a cheerful casualness.   On the "general welfare" clause there was no debate; it "was agreed to, *nem. con.*"   Another *nem. con.* provision was the one on which John Marshall founded the doctrine of "implied powers" — the one that gave Congress the right to pass such laws as were "necessary and proper" to carry the enumerated powers into effect.   Such ordinary attributes of sovereignty as the declaration of war and peace, the establishment of an army and navy, the control of relations with foreign nations, of immigration and naturalization, of the post office — on most of these topics the nation had rung with debate for years, but few traces of the wearisome arguments appeared in the convention. Most of them were adopted without prolonged discussion, some with no discussion at all.

But certain matters that had not stirred the national consciousness so deeply did cause the widest divergences.   The convention was not a uniformly harmonious body; at times it was a fairly passionate one; once it seemed likely to break up in futility; but the greatest difference of opinion centred mostly on one general issue.   The question that almost disrupted the proceedings and nearly sent its members home to report failure was as to the nature of the proposed Union.   Was the Federal organization to be comprehensive, possessing jurisdiction over the people, or were the states to exist as all-powerful sovereignties, virtually independent nations? In 1787, it must be kept in mind, there was an American Union; there was even a sovereignty known as the United States of America.

The prevailing notion that the American Union was created by the Constitution of 1787 must be dispelled. The statesmen who most angrily denounced the "new plan of government" were foremost in protesting their love for the "Union" and the necessity of permanent coöperation among the states. In reading the history of this period one must be constantly on guard in the use of terms. Thus the word "Federalist" had a meaning different before the adoption of the Constitution from that attributed to it afterward — a significance, indeed, practically the reverse. It came to be the word used to describe the political party formed under Washington and John Adams, a party which stood for centralized power, in distinction to that which laid chief emphasis on the states. That was not the sense in which it was used by those who framed the Constitution. By "Federalist" these statesmen described a confederation, or, as the Southern states called it in 1861, a Confederacy, such as the "Union" that existed from 1781 to 1787. Two words were constantly on the lips of debaters in 1787 — "National" and "Federal" — and the point at issue was whether the new government was to be a National or a Federal one.

By National government was understood a government built on national lines, with minor emphasis upon the states. In the proposed legislature both houses were to be chosen on a national basis, or on "proportional representation," as it was called. State boundaries, in its selection, were thus to be disregarded. To Americans to-day, a Senate composed, not of two members from each state, but of men elected, precisely as is the House of Representatives, in proportion to population, seems the strangest of anomalies, but that was the conception in 1787 of the proponents of a National government. One of the most powerful men who favored this plan, James Wilson, of Pennsylvania, suggested that there be one Senator for every 100,000 inhabitants. Had this proposal ruled and prevailed until the present time, the Upper House would now contain about 1250 members. Had the maximum number of Representatives provided for in the Constitution — one for every 30,000 people — survived until 1936, we should have a House of Representatives of not far from 4000 statesmen! The chief argument in its favor, one hundred and fifty years ago, was that such a method would enhance the "democratic" character of Congress. It would make that body truly National — responsible directly to the people. But those who upheld the Federal plan desired something different. Their demand was that the national legislature consist of a single chamber, in which the states should be represented as states, not as people, and that each state should have a single vote. That the states might have more than one representative was freely granted, but these state representatives, when it came to casting ballots in the proposed Congress, should each hold a little election within themselves, to determine what the state vote should be. This was the Federal plan, so far as the formation of Congress was concerned. Rhode Island — so unpopular for its commercial self-ishness that it had come to be known as "Rogues' Island" — would have precisely the same weight in the new nation as the largest state, Virginia. The Federal plan, of course, was the same as existed in the Articles of Confederation, and the persistence with which its friends insisted on its perpetuation produced almost a lethal rift in that hot summer of 1787.

The proposal for a National government represented a complete revolution in the American political form. Madison pithily described the difference between the two systems when he explained, for the benefit of his convention associates, that a Federal government operated on those impersonal entities known as states, while a National government operated directly upon flesh-and-blood human beings. The present income tax is the perfect expression of the National idea, as applied to the collection of revenue. And the legislation of Franklin Roosevelt — his attempt to make Congress paramount over all industry and agriculture — may be taken as Nationalism in extreme form, far more extreme than anything contemplated by Hamilton, Madison, or the other advocates of the Nationalistic conception of 1787. For the Rooseveltian purpose is the utter annihilation of state lines and that "consolidation" of the central government which so frightened the State-rights democrats of 1787. Had Richard Henry Lee, the great Virginia opponent of "consolidation" in 1787, foreseen anything resembling the present activities of his political descendants, he would have regarded Hamilton as the mildest of Nationalists.

That such a change in the government would produce sharp alignments in the convention was to have been expected. The division of sentiment, however, followed different lines from those our subsequent national history would lead one to expect. The Federal idea, based upon the supremacy of the states, suggests that theory of State rights which played so important a part in the conflict of succeeding years; while the National idea, subordinating state concerns to the interest of the country as a whole, brings to mind the doctrine afterward upheld by such statesmen as Webster and Lincoln. If one turns to the record of the Constitutional Convention, however, expecting to see South and North drawn up in opposing camps on this issue, he will be disappointed. The demarcation then did not follow sectional lines. In general the advocates of what afterward became known as State rights were the small states, while the champions of National government were the large ones. And another surprise appears when the large and small commonwealths are arranged in groups. In 1787 big and little states were something different from those of the present time. The census of 1790 shows that the largest were Virginia, Pennsylvania, North Carolina, and Massachusetts, in the order named. With these four usually — though not constantly — voted South Carolina and Georgia; these were not yet "big states," but their population was increasing so rapidly that, in a short time, they were expected to achieve this rank. Indeed, one of the hallucinations of the convention, frequently expressed, was that in a comparatively short time the Southern states would exceed the North in population. The contemporary New Yorker — in 1787 denizens of this state were known as "Yorkers" — will be humiliated to discover that in 1787 his commonwealth, now majestic in size, ranked, if not as a "small state," at least as a moderately sized one. It took its appropriate place, in this grand division, alongside New Hampshire, Rhode Island, Connecticut, New Jersey, and Maryland. And the separation on this question of a National or a Federal government followed these lines. The foremost advocates of the plan for a scheme that, to a great extent, would obliterate state boundaries and consolidate the Union were Virginia, Pennsylvania, and Massachusetts; the most outspoken champions of state independence were Connecticut, New York, New Jersey, and Maryland. All histories of the Continental Convention say much of the two plans before the delegates — the "Virginia plan" and the "New Jersey plan"; the great difference was that the Virginia plan provided for a government on national lines, the New Jersey for a government that left the state supreme. The whole thing, to modern eyes, seems topsy-turvy. "Do you mean to abolish the state government altogether?" Charles Pinckney asked Edmund Randolph after he had introduced his Virginia plan. Of course Mr. Randolph intended nothing so drastic, but he and his Virginia and Massachusetts associates did advocate a national system, one that made the states, even proud Virginia and Massachusetts themselves, insignificant agencies in the comprehensive scheme.

IX

The leaders of National Union were Madison, James Wilson of Pennsylvania, and Rufus King of Massachusetts, while the foremost contenders for State rights were William Paterson of New Jersey, and Roger Sherman and Oliver Ellsworth, of Connecticut. In many ways James Wilson was the most powerful intellect and strongest moral force in the convention. History has neglected him; he has provided the theme of no full-sized biography, and even contemporary references to the man are neither frequent nor revealing. Evidently Wilson's personality did not favorably impress his associates, or perhaps the misfortunes of his final days, when he fell one of the numerous victims of the time to land speculation, explain his eclipse. Yet few members figure so conspicuously in Madison's *Debates,* and few spoke so often or with such constant enlightenment. Wilson, from the most advanced, "progressive" point of view, seldom goes astray. Indeed, he was about the only member who consistently bespoke the interests of the "people." Some usually laid emphasis on what they called the "landed interest," others on the "monied interest" — that is, the holders of state and Federal bonds, almost the only form of investment securities known at the time; still others on the commercial "interest" — that is, the business of shipping; but Wilson's was almost the only voice lifted in behalf of the masses.

It is interesting that at least two of the greatest minds at Philadelphia were foreign born — and Scottish at that; but Wilson derived more immediately than Hamilton from Scotland, for he was born, of cotter stock, near St. Andrews, obtained his education in three Scottish universities, St. Andrews, Glasgow, and Edinburgh, and was led to emigrate to America at the age of twenty-three because of his love of free institutions. He reached his cherished goal at a critical time — 1765, Stamp Tax year — and fell into excellent hands, for he became a student of law in the office of John Dickinson, whose "Farmer's Letters" exposing the constitutional weakness of the British contention proved a powerful incentive to the American Revolution. In the succeeding ten years, "James the Caledonian" took a far more advanced stand on the British-American dispute than Dickinson. Parliament, he insisted, had no right to legislate for the colonies on any question; the colonies were Dominions of the British Empire, owing allegiance to the King, but self-sufficient for themselves in lawmaking. This, of course, is the conception underlying the present British Empire. His prominence in this great assize and his professional success made Wilson a marked man in Pennsylvania; when the early Tory delegates for his state to the Continental Congress were dismissed, Wilson was chosen as an advocate of independence, taking his seat in time to sign the Declaration. Naturally, as one of Pennsylvania's most forward men, he was sent to the Constitutional Convention. And here, in every issue that rose, Wilson was in favor of trusting the people and extending their power. That was the essence of the National plan which he at once took under his wing. He suggested that not only Representatives and Senators should be chosen by popular vote on a ratio based on "number of inhabitants," but the President also.

No one heaped greater scorn on the constitution of Pennsylvania, Franklin's favorite child, which that statesman asked the central government to take as a model — with its single-chamber legislature, its many-headed executive, its board of censors. What Wilson particularly disliked about this strange *mélange,* copied largely from the French, was that it had not been adopted by the people, but had been imposed on the state by the body that framed it. He insisted that there was such a thing as the American people; that they should be united, and, thus united, control the Union. Of state boundaries he made as little as Hamilton. "Is this government," he asked, "to be of men, or of imaginary beings called states?" Practically every illiberal idea proposed brought Wilson to his feet. Certain members, — the chief was Gouverneur Morris, — fearful of new states in the buckskin West, insisted that constitutional precautions be taken against granting them political equality with the more sedate Atlantic seaboard. Wilson insisted that such states, when admitted, should stand upon the same footing as the older communities. Gouverneur Morris — and others — were also constantly talking about the advantages of an aristocracy, and the small confidence that could be placed in the common people, asserting that the chief business of government was the "protection of property." "I do not agree," said Wilson, rebuking his Pennsylvania colleague, "that property is the sole or primary object of government. The cultivation and improvement of the human mind is the most noble object" — a sentiment that puts Wilson almost in the class of the most advanced democrats of the present time.

Naturally Wilson became the foremost champion of the National conception — of an organization built on the political power of the average man. He did not find his opponents in Virginia, or South Carolina, but in New England. The most uncompromising advocates of localism, in 1787, were the gentlemen from Connecticut. This small state, next to Virginia, had the ablest delegation — at least the most influential — in Philadelphia. It consisted of only three members, but all three were men of keen intellect, personal force, large experience and information — vigorous-minded Yankees, who knew precisely what they wanted and stuck unerringly to the point until they obtained it. Dr. William Samuel Johnson, son of the president of Columbia College, who himself, on retiring from Philadelphia, acceded to the same position, was one of America's most learned men; in his residence in England before the Revolution, as agent for Connecticut, his intellectual attainments had been recognized by an honorary degree from Oxford and the friendship of great Englishmen, including his namesake, Dr. Samuel Johnson of the Dictionary.

Yet Johnson, weighty as was his work at Philadelphia, yielded precedence to another statesman of much more homely flavor. The most original character in the convention was Roger Sherman. He was a spectacle so strange to the eye that the planters of the South hardly knew what to make of him. "Mr. Sherman," wrote William Pierce of Georgia, "exhibits the oddest shaped character I ever remember to have met with. He is un-meaning and unaccountably strange in his manner. But in his train of thinking there is something regular, deep and comprehensive; yet the oddity of his address, the vulgarisms that accompany his public speaking, and that strange New England cant that runs through his public as well as his private speaking make everything that is connected with him grotesque and laughable; and yet he deserves infinite praise — no man has a better Heart or a clearer Head. If he cannot embellish he can furnish thoughts that are wise and useful. He is an able politician and extremely artful in accomplishing any particular object; it is remarked that he seldom fails." A fellow New Englander, John Adams, contributes further details to this rustic portrait. "Sherman's air is the reverse of grace; there cannot be a more striking contrast to beautiful action than the motion of his hands; generally he stands upright, with his hands before him, the fingers of his left hand clenched into a fist and the wrist of it grasped with his right. But he has a clear head and sound judgment; but when he moves a hand in anything like action, Hogarth's genius could not have invented a motion more opposite to grace; it is stiffness and awkwardness itself, rigid as starched linen or buckram."

Silas Deane said that Roger Sherman was as fitted for a polite dinner party "as is a chestnut burr for an eye-stone," mentions the "odd questions he asks" and "the countryfied cadence with which he speaks." In the statue of Roger Sherman which Connecticut has placed in the Washington Capitol as one of her two greatest men, these physical traits are considerably softened, but contemporary paintings, particularly that of Ralph Earle, quite substantiate the likenesses sketched above. Externally indeed Sherman appears native and rough-hewn. The gnarled and corrugated face, the hair hanging unkempt and listless on collar, the sharp protruding nose, the shrewd but dreamy eyes, the suggestion of untidiness in the clothes, the erect frame and upraised hand, firmly grasping a goose quill — hardly any place except the New England hills could have produced a figure like this, and in all Sherman's moral aspects and political principles the New England nature was deeply bred. Adams called Sherman "an old Puritan, as honest as an angel." Surely his protest, in the Continental Congress, against ferry travel on the Sabbath; his suggestion that, in the quarrel with England, Americans abstain from horse racing, cockfighting, and play-going — evidently as a means of propitiating divine grace; his desire that Connecticut should enact an excise on rum in order to discourage its use, and his unavailing plea for daily prayer at the Constitutional Convention, bring out the more obvious traits of the Puritan character. Yet Patrick Henry said that the three greatest men in the Continental Congress were Washington, Richard Henry Lee, and Roger Sherman, and that Sherman and George Mason were the greatest statesmen he had ever known. He was an early exemplar of that type of American public man, unschooled and rough working, who was destined to become a conspicuous figure in the new America whose foundation he did so much to lay.

Born in 1721, near Boston, the son of a shoemaker, Sherman was himself at the age of ten apprenticed to that same craft. His early days were Franklinesque. As he toiled at the bench there was one object as invariably present as his last and tools: always spread before the young man was a book, on which his eyes continually strayed from his labor. The shoemaker's manner Sherman apparently never lost; his famous gesture in speaking, someone remarked, resembled a shoemaker drawing a thread. And as Franklin amid his type and printing presses was able to acquire a substantial education, so Sherman, at his cobbler's bench, picked up a good store of miscellaneous learning, even of a specialized kind. How many university graduates of that or of the present day, for example, can calculate lunar eclipses — an act that this self-taught mathematician made his own? Soon, too, Sherman began to write on such practical topics as public finance and the evils of paper money. And just as Franklin abandoned Boston for another clime, so Roger Sherman, at the age of twenty-three, left the same neighborhood for what seemed the more prosperous land of Connecticut. With shoemaker's kit thrown across his back, he walked the whole distance to Litchfield County — a matter of almost one hundred and fifty miles; and here, beginning the study of law, he was soon a noted figure. Again like Franklin, Sherman became an almanac maker, and if his pages were not graced by the jewels of worldly wisdom that illumined Poor Richard's, they served for many years as a household mentor to those seeking accurate information on the behavior of the planets and the rise and fall of the tides, all calculated by the self-made astronomer. True Yankee that he was, Sherman mastered several trades: shoemaker, publisher, writer for the press, pamphleteer, lawyer, finally judge of the superior court; he was also storekeeper on a large scale, maintaining flourishing shops at New Milford, Wallingford, and New Haven. It was not by ingratiating acts that the man won his way to popular favor. He was as famous for stolidity of manners and unsociableness as for common sense. At a tea party he would silently stalk in, sit down and sip his refreshment, then rise and walk out of the room, not having spoken a word or bowed to a single member of the company. On the street he would solemnly march straight forward, never nodding his beaver-covered head to a soul. At church he insisted on occupying a back pew, preferably all to himself, and, having no ear for music, was visibly bored by the protracted psalm singing popular in that day. Yet, when he was so disposed, Sherman's conversational powers made him welcome in all classes.

Despite his lack of formal education, Yale College took him to its bosom, making him treasurer and giving him an honorary degree of M.A.; the town elected him to those successive offices — list taker, leather sealer, gauger, fence viewer, selectman — that signified things as substantial in this body politic as did ædile, quæstor, or prætor in ancient Rome. Whenever a boundary line was to be run, or a new highway laid out, the sagacious Sherman usually helped in performing the lofty task, and in that training ground of statesmen, the New England town meeting, his halting speech and awkward gestures always carried weight. He represented the town in the legislature, and here his wisdom served the colony so well that, when it came to select Connecticut's delegation to the Continental Congress, the choice of Sherman became a matter of course. He was no fire-eating patriot, disapproved riot and Liberty Boys as a method of broaching constitutional questions, but was prepared to eliminate the British Parliament from any influence in affairs American. He served on the committee of five to draw up the Declaration of Independence, and did important work in framing the Articles of Confederation. One day Thomas Jefferson, exhibiting to a friend the great figures of Congress, pointed to the ungainly figure. "That," he said, "is Mr. Sherman, of Connecticut, a man who never said a foolish thing in his life." Certain of his pithy phrases remind one of a Yankee President of recent times. Once, at the opening of a new bridge, Sherman was called upon impromptu for a speech. He walked critically over the structure, then, turning to his audience, delivered his oration: "I don't see but it stands steady." No man appreciated with more dry humor certain failings of the Continental Congress. When news came of the surrender at Yorktown, that body voted exuberantly to build a monument in honor of the event. Sherman, knowing the Congressional habit of indulging in grandiose plans which were never carried out, remarked: "The vote is the monument." The man's skill at managing legislative assemblies was much praised; how completely he had mastered the secret appeared from the rule that, first of all, directed his parliamentary career: "When you are in a minority, talk; when you are in a majority, vote."

The third member of the Connecticut triumvirate was as distinguished, though in a different way. For Oliver Ellsworth was as remarkable for personal grace and polished learning as his older colleague was for natural sense and wit. He was educated at two colleges, for, after an unsuccessful year at Yale, he abandoned New Haven, — not entirely without the acquiescence of the faculty, — betook himself to Princeton, and thus added further to the reputation of that seat of learning as a training ground for constitutional statesmen. Despite this aberration, Ellsworth was Connecticut from top to toe. "America," he remarked in old age, "is the best country in the world, New England is the best part of America, and Connecticut the best part of New England." Ellsworth gave voice to this contentment after a life in which he had filled many great positions and seen much of the world: leader of the bar in his native state, delegate to the Continental Congress and the Constitutional Convention, dominant figure in the first United States Senate, author of the Judiciary Act which still forms the basis of our Federal courts, Chief Justice of the United States Supreme Court, Minister to France, "main pillar" of Washington in Congress. In his general appearance Ellsworth suggested comparison with Washington. He resembled rather the Virginia giant than the spare New Englander of tradition. A portrait painted in Paris brings out distinctly Washingtonian characteristics — the large head set straight on shoulders, high forehead, rectangular face, big eyes, big nose, and big mouth, the whole expression friendly, but inquiring and noncommittal. "Tall, dignified, and commanding," so the first Timothy Dwight, president of Yale, describes the jurist he admired. Though six feet two in height, Ellsworth's figure was slim and sinewy; in his early days as a lawyer he had eked out his fugitive practice by chopping wood, and the athletic qualities developed in this way remained. There is another charming portrait of Ellsworth and his wife, showing them in old age, in the quiet of their Connecticut home, suggesting, in its high breeding, domestic satisfaction, composure, and dignity, nothing so much as similar representations of the lord and lady of Mount Vernon. Here was a man conscious of his strength and in full command of it. Ellsworth once said that as a young man he had made an important discovery about himself. He lacked imagination. There was nothing left, therefore, but to develop less showy gifts — a capacity for work, for grasping fundamentals, for developing a mind first of all precise. The same Timothy Dwight quoted above, however, insisted on qualities that Ellsworth denied himself. He found the man's oratorical images "glowing," and his "sentiments noble"; his mind was "ardent, bold, intense, and masterly," and following the custom of the time in finding similarities to classic heroes in contemporary favorites, Dwight compared Ellsworth to Demosthenes, "frequently pouring out floods of eloquence which were irresistible and overflowing."

Ellsworth's favorite as a public man was that associate, Roger Sherman, to whom he bore so slight a visible resemblance; he had taken Sherman as his model, and in later days never came to New Haven without paying a visit to Sherman's grave. The friends were perfectly agreed on the theory of the new Constitution, whether it should be National or Federal. On this, as on the general principle of popular or class rule, they were at one, and better teamwork

ROGER SHERMAN

OLIVER ELLSWORTH

TIMOTHY PICKERING

JAMES WILSON

in debate no two leaders ever exhibited.   Neither was a democrat in the modern sense of the word.   "The people immediately," said Sherman, "should have as little to do as may be about the government.   They want information and are constantly liable to be misled."   The ex-shoemaker apparently had little faith in the political wisdom of the class from which he had sprung.   And his colleague, this pre-Revolutionary rail splitter, was not more indulgent.   Both men, as befitted citizens of Connecticut, were champions of the small states.   The superiority of little over big communities was with them a conviction almost Jeffersonian.   "The people are more happy in small than in large states," said Sherman, with a glance at neighbor Massachusetts.   "The largest states are the worst governed," echoed Ellsworth, with a squint at Virginia. Perhaps in retaliation Madison remarked that Connecticut had not been overscrupulous in supplying her "requisition" to the Federal treasury.   Ellsworth was up in a flash.   If Connecticut had been delinquent in this regard, it was from "inability" — she was a poor state, "with little ready cash."   He appealed to her great exertions during the war in supplying both men and money.   The muster rolls would show that she had more troops in the field than Virginia.

But Ellsworth and Sherman on the one hand, and Madison and Randolph on the other, differed on more essential matters than the relative virtues of Connecticut and Virginia.   On the great issue before the convention they were at loggerheads.   The Virginians were for a National government, the men of Connecticut for a Federal one.   The Virginians, so far as representation in both House and Senate was concerned, would erase state lines; the Connecticut statesmen would preserve them.   The existing Confederation, with certain new powers given to Congress, was satisfactory to New Haven and Hartford County.   At an early day in the convention Ellsworth moved to have the word " 'national' stricken out as descriptive of the new government."   The convention should limit itself to amending the Articles of Confederation.   "He turned his eyes," Madison records, "for the preservation of his rights to the state governments.   From these alone he could derive the greatest happiness he expected in this life."   Neither did Sherman wish to see the existing Confederation broken up.   The new Constitution should not make "too great inroads on the existing system."   His preference was for a single-chamber legislature, like that under the Confederation, the members to be chosen, not by the distrusted people, but by the state legislatures; and in this each state should have, not necessarily one representative, but one vote.

He wanted these representatives paid by the home states, not the national Congress, and he argued that the new Constitution should be ratified by the state legislatures, not by the people in convention. Thus would he avoid that "We, the people" with which the Constitution begins, and make it read, "We, the states." The Connecticut ideal of the Union was about the same as that subsequently developed by Jefferson. In all matters of domestic government the states were to be supreme, the Federal government having to do only with relations with foreign nations.

These two Yankees, with some assistance from the third Connecticut delegate, Dr. Johnson, led the Federal cause. Others who played minor rôles on the same side were William Paterson of New Jersey, John Dickinson of Delaware, and Luther Martin of Maryland, sometimes known, from his quarrelsome manner, violent denunciation of opposing views, and constant interruptions, as the "Thersites" of the convention. Against them were pitted most of the Virginia delegation, led by Madison, by James Wilson and Gouverneur Morris of Pennsylvania, and, more feebly, Rufus King of Massachusetts. Alexander Hamilton's influence was cast entirely with the National men, but he cut little figure at Philadelphia and was absent a good part of the time. New York was on the state side, and had sent two other delegates, Yates and Lansing, whose vote negatived Hamilton's. Accordingly that advocate of powerful government left the convention in August, more or less in wrath, after submitting his plan, more National even than Virginia's. The opposing camps in the first two months were drawn sharply on National and State lines. And the battle raged over the composition of Congress — whether both branches should be elected on the basis of proportionate population. "Battle" is hardly too strong a word, for both sides held tenaciously to their point for six hot, exciting weeks. At times the bad blood that developed seemed to threaten the whole proceeding. "You see the consequences of pushing things too far," John Dickinson remarked to Madison, when Paterson of New Jersey introduced his Federal scheme. "Indeed," remarked Madison, "the eagerness displayed by the members opposed to a national government began now to produce serious anxieties for the result of the convention." Dickinson himself was one of the most defiant. The Delaware delegates had come "instructed" by their state to accept no constitution that did not give the small states the same power as the big, and these directions Dickinson and his colleagues sedulously adhered to. "We would sooner submit to a foreign power," he informed Madison, "than submit to be deprived, in both branches of the legislature, of an equality of suffrage, and thereby be thrown under the domination of the larger states." His associate, Gunning Bedford, made this threat in open convention. "The large states," he declared, in what Rufus King, who rebuked him for his un-American sentiments, described as "a vehemence unprecedented in that house," "dare not dissolve the convention. If they do the small ones will find some foreign ally, of more honor and good faith, who will take them by the hand and do them justice." That is, Delaware, Connecticut, New Jersey, and the rest would cast in their fortunes with Great Britain! "New Jersey," said Paterson, "will never confederate on the plan before the committee. She will be swallowed up. I had rather submit to a monarch, a despot, than to such a fate. I will not only oppose the plan here, but on my return home do everything in my power to defeat it there."

"If the small states," James Wilson retorted, "will not confederate on this plan, Pennsylvania will not confederate on any other. If New Jersey will not part with her sovereignty it is vain to talk of government."

"New York," said Lansing, "would never have concurred in sending deputies to the convention if she had supposed the deliberations were to turn on a consolidation of the states and a national government."

"I will never accede to a plan," bawled Luther Martin of Maryland, "that will introduce an inequality and lay ten states at the mercy of Virginia, Massachusetts and Pennsylvania."

Madison kept reminding the delegates that if the convention failed the Union would split up into several confederacies, all subject to foreign intrigue and ultimate extinction. Ellsworth used the same point as an argument on his side. Perhaps with a prophetic glimpse of future secession movements in New England, he intimated that, if the convention went to pieces, New York and New England would join hands and become an independent nation. "If the deplored event happen," Wilson replied, "it will neither stagger my sentiments or my duty. If the minority of the people of America refuse to coalesce with the majority on just and proper principles, if a separation must take place, it could never be on better grounds." The climax was reached when the brilliant Gouverneur Morris, one of the fiercest advocates of Nationalism, arose and shouted, — at this moment endowed, it would seem, with the gift of far sight, — "This country must be united. If persuasion does not unite it, the sword will."

Evidently Roger Sherman was obeying one half of his favorite political maxim, "When you are in a minority, talk." He and his small state group were certainly in a minority, as test votes showed; but talk did much to clear the air, present the problem in all its aspects and dangers, and prepare the way for the solution which he had hinted at several times. Whether Sherman or Ellsworth originated the device that has passed into history as the "Connecticut Compromise" has been much disputed. The fact that Roger Sherman, eleven years before, had met a similar *impasse* with a similar proposal would seem to point to him as the original begetter. When the first union of the United States was formed, under the Articles of Confederation, this same difficulty of representation arose. Should the vote in Congress be based upon the states or on population? The Connecticut representative on the committee surprised his colleagues at that time by suggesting that it be founded on both. How was that possible, when the congress of the Confederation was to consist of a single chamber? Let the states send delegates, said Sherman, in numbers proportionate to their inhabitants. Then let two votes be taken on every question. In the first, each state should have one vote, a majority of each delegation determining what that should be. In the second, Congress should vote as individuals. Unless the two votes coincided, the motion would be lost. It was an ingenious suggestion worthy of the Yankee mind, but it was not adopted. Now Sherman, in all the welter of recrimination, threats of secession, civil war, the gallows, and what not, came forward with a solution not unlike it; more workable in the present instance, however, because it was to be applied to a congress of two houses, not one. Madison, in a few lines, thus describes Sherman's intervention: —

"Mr. Sherman proposed that the proportion of suffrage in the first branch should be according to the respective numbers of free inhabitants; and that in the second branch, or Senate, each state should have one vote and no more."

It is hard to recall any words ever spoken in a deliberative assembly more momentous than these. For they made possible the Constitution of the United States and the establishment of a powerful American Union. Without them the convention, its nerves already strained to the breaking point, would have dissolved. Sherman had created one of the most famous legislative bodies in history, the United States Senate. Subsequently the assembly amended his proposal, by giving each state two Senators, instead of one; but the essential principle, that of the equality of the states in the upper chamber, was not altered.　Another change was made: instead of having the membership of the popular house apportioned on the number of "free inhabitants," the convention, at the insistence of the Southern states, agreed to include "three-fifths of all other persons" — that is, negro slaves.

Satisfactory as this compromise of large and small states seems to-day, in that distracted chamber it did not meet immediate acceptance from the larger communities.　Sherman made his motion in committee of the whole on June eleven, but not until a month afterward, on July sixteen, was the arrangement embedded in the Constitution.　One would like to have the secret history of that month — especially the meetings of coteries, the buttonholings, the private arguments and threats, even the "deals" that went to make the conclusion.　Madison, Wilson, Gouverneur Morris, and King — Virginia, Pennsylvania, New York, and Massachusetts — maintained their ground to the end.　The final vote, which they regarded as the extreme of injustice and as contrary to the principles of democratic government, seemed to them appalling.　They held a frantic conclave to determine on their course: should they withdraw from the convention — "bolt" — and thus reduce it to a nullity, or bow to the inevitable?　Rather than reduce the American State to utter chaos they decided to abandon their opposition.　It was, they concluded, a Constitution with a Senate composed of two members from each state, or no Constitution at all.　They therefore accepted defeat, and it is a tribute to their public spirit that, in the struggle for ratification which immediately followed, the Constitution had no more zealous defenders than the men who had so bitterly denounced its most important feature.　To Franklin is usually attributed a share in this "accommodation."　In order to assuage the big states, he slipped into the original compromise a stipulation that all bills for raising and spending money should originate in the House, and that the Senate, in considering them, should have only the right to approve or disapprove — not to increase or decrease appropriations. It is interesting at the present moment to note that, had this plan been incorporated, Congress would have started with something resembling the present budget system of Great Britain.　But it was finally whittled down to the requirement, still in effect, that "all bills for raising revenue" shall originate in the larger chamber.

X

Those looking for the hidden motives behind this accommodation should observe one enlightening fact — that North Carolina, though the third largest state[1] and sympathetic with Virginia throughout the convention, cast its vote for the "Connecticut Compromise." Up to the final moment this delegation had stood firm against the proposal; its sudden switch, however, made the Connecticut idea victorious by a vote of five to four — one of those five to four decisions which, when exercised by the Supreme Court in recent years, have stirred revolutionary emotions. Were there considerations secretly at work drawing together the two extreme sections of the Union, the "deep South" and New England? Such bonds of sympathy presently developed on another great topic of dissension, and this suggests that an understanding had already been formed. And here again the alignment completely reverses prevailing conceptions of American history. For the point on which the second, almost fatal, quarrel arose was the slave trade. The section that led in the antislavery movement in the forty years preceding 1861 was New England, but the abolitionists of that region could find little to stir their admiration as they looked back on the behavior of their representatives in the Constitutional Convention. Conspicuous among the apologists for slavery in Philadelphia were the Yankee delegates, while the state that took first place in denouncing slavery and insisting on its exclusion from the Constitution was Virginia.

From about midsummer to the end of the sessions the men of North and South Carolina and Connecticut displayed a strange unanimity on most disputed questions. South Carolina was constantly presenting the convention with ultimatums: certain things, she insisted, must be included in the new form of government or she would decline to become a member. She wished no export duties laid upon her cotton, rice, and indigo. The Connecticut delegates agreed that her demand was justified. The slave states proposed

[1] According to the census of 1790.

that, in apportioning representatives on the basis of population, three fifths of their negroes should be counted. This aroused great opposition, but Mr. Sherman and Mr. Ellsworth seemed to think the compromise should be accepted, and it was incorporated. Another disputed clause was that providing for the return of runaway slaves — one of the most troublous sentences in the Constitution. In agreement with this Southern demand Sherman used phrases that, at the present time, have an unpleasant sound. "He saw no more impropriety in the public seizing and surrendering a slave or a servant than a horse."

But it was the slave trade that caused a particularly exciting discovery. Virginia and Maryland had already outlawed what George Mason called this "nefarious traffic," but the states further south still felt the need of supplementing their labor supply by periodic descents on the African jungle. Any effort to give Congress power to end the business, declared these states, would mean their abstention from the Union. The remarks of their delegates were full of threats. "Religion and humanity," said Rutledge of South Carolina, "have nothing to do with the question. Interest alone is the governing principle with nations. The true question is whether the southern states shall or shall not be parties to the Union. If the northern states consult their interest they will not oppose the increase of slaves, which will increase the commodities of which they will become the carriers." Again the Connecticut compromisers agreed with the Southern brethren. "Mr. Ellsworth was for leaving the clause as it stood. Let every state import what it pleases. The morality or wisdom of slavery are considerations belonging to the states themselves." These remarks led to what was perhaps the most inspiring episode of the convention. For then George Mason of Virginia rose and delivered his famous oration against slavery, against the slave trade, and against Great Britain for its policy in the colonial period of cultivating the traffic and blocking all Virginia's attempts to abolish it. Emotions were tense as Mason turned towards the New England delegates and, in a few hot words, laid bare the reason for their tender attitude on the question. "He lamented that some of our eastern brethren had, from a lust of gain, embarked in this nefarious traffic."

That thrust naturally struck the Puritans on the raw and Ellsworth, in replying to the charge, became almost unparliamentary. Mason had emphasized the brutalizing effect of slavery on the slave owner. "As I have never owned a slave," Ellsworth began,

"I cannot judge the effects of slavery on character." This was a palpable hit, for Mason, despite his hatred of the institution, was himself a slave owner. If the matter "was to be considered in a moral light," continued Ellsworth, "we ought to go further and consider those slaves already in the country." And Virginia had a spot as vulnerable as New England's interest in shipping, which Ellsworth now proceeded pitilessly to explore. That state was already a breeder of slaves for sale in the plantations of the lower South. Here was the explanation, cried Ellsworth, for the Old Dominion's hostility to slave ships! The African traffic was hurting its business. The importation of slaves from a distant, foreign land was interfering with a prosperous home industry! "Slaves multiply so fast in Virginia and Maryland that it is cheaper to raise than import them, whilst in the sickly rice swamps foreign supplies are necessary. If we go no further than is urged we shall be unjust towards South Carolina and Georgia."

The speech was not a pretty one, especially as Mason had disclosed the secret of the unholy alliance already established between the lower South and New England. The preliminary version of the Constitution, which served as a basis for this debate, contained one provision, irksome to the ambitious shippers and shipbuilding interests of that section. It gave Congress power to regulate trade with foreign nations, but stipulated that no Navigation Act could be passed except by a two-thirds majority. Navigation Acts were those measures which kept the carrying trade an exclusive national monopoly. It was the old English Navigation Act, limiting commerce between the American colonies and Great Britain, that, in the economic belief of the day, had made England the world's premier mercantile country. New England wished an American Navigation Act that would similarly give her control of American commerce, which would naturally include the business of carrying slaves. The Southern "staple" states, having virtually no shipping of their own, and having no particular love for New England, did not wish to put their cotton and tobacco at the mercy of Yankees, and were prepared to turn over their cargoes to English shipmasters. But by the time this angry debate took place, the difference had been adjusted. The Yankee talent for a bargain had triumphed once more. It is no secret now and was not then — Madison positively states the fact — that New England and the lower South had come to terms: the clause requiring a two-thirds vote for a Navigation Act was to be stricken out, and the slave trade was to be permitted for thirteen years — afterward extended to twenty-one. And so it was voted. The complaisance of South Carolina — it fairly exuded honey towards New England — appears in the speeches of her delegates. Charles Cotesworth Pinckney complimented his acid Northern compatriots on their "liberal conduct towards the views of South Carolina. . . . I had prejudice against the eastern states before I came here, but I have found them as liberal and candid as any men whatever." And Pierce Butler, of the same state, said that he voted for New England on the Navigation Act because he "was desirous of cultivating the affection of the eastern states." The friendly understanding established on this basis had important results, for the section of South Carolina, conciliated by this bargain, remained for thirty years after the adopting of the Constitution a seat of high Federation, working hand in hand with New England on most of the political issues and political controversies of the time.

But Virginia was still unreconciled. Randolph declared that he would give up the whole Constitution rather than accept it with this slave-trade proviso. Mason, who a few weeks before had declared that he would "leave his bones" in Philadelphia if that were necessary to obtain a Constitution, now asserted that he would "cut off his right hand rather than put it" to that instrument. Both these Virginians, in fact, refused to sign the Constitution, and though Randolph changed his attitude, Mason became an irreconcilable opponent. The slave-trade proviso was one of the reasons for this Virginian's hostility to the Constitution.

XI

The charge, frequently made, that all was not idealism in the framing of this great organ of government is thus true enough. If one cared to scrutinize further, other motives might appear, not entirely acceptable to an age that has inherited a century and a half of steadily expanding democracy. The extent to which the claims of property "as the main purpose of government" were put forth by such admirable citizens as Dickinson, Gouverneur Morris, and most of the Southern delegates, even including George Mason, has already been indicated. But the fact is that the Constitution was a compromise between other things than the slave trade and methods of representation in Senate and House; the whole thing was a compromise between fundamental conceptions — that of the idealist seeking perfection and that of the practical genius in the search for the attainable. Roger Sherman said that it was better to have the slave trade for twenty-one years than to lose three states to the Union, and the practical shoemaker's conclusion expressed the views of most of his compatriots on the whole constitutional question. In their willingness to compromise, Sherman and Ellsworth and their Southern sympathizers represented the prevailing opinion that made the Constitution possible. That instrument is the best illustration American history affords of the great political principle laid down by Bolingbroke. "The true point of political wisdom consists in distinguishing justly between what is absolutely best in speculation and what is best of the things practical in particular conjectures." That was the guiding motto of the men who framed and those who made effective the American form of government. "The Constitution that is submitted," Washington wrote David Humphreys, "is not free from imperfections, but there are as few radical defects in it as could well be expected, considering the heterogeneous mass of which the convention was composed and the diversity of interests that are to be attended to." "The truth is that the plan," said Alexander Hamilton before the New York convention, "in all its parts, was a plan of accommodation." That concessions to a thing so odious in modern eyes as the slave trade were necessary to American union may be deplorable, but in this, as in other things, the Connecticut compromisers represented the spirit of Philadelphia.

That there were two types of mind at work in that convocation and in the state ratifying conventions that immediately followed is thus apparent. These may be called the mind purely philosophic and that chiefly statesmanlike; the mind that reasons and theorizes and the one that acts most advantageously in the circumstances at hand. Most of the leading personalities of 1787 can be divided into these two classes. They are the two types that are usually arrayed against each other in crises of the kind. They foreshadowed, in the Philadelphia assembly and the conventions summoned by the states to adopt or reject its handiwork, the two attitudes towards the Constitution that have been manifest from 1787 to the present day. America has always been divided, as it is to-day, between those who advocate the strongest kind of central government and those who lay emphasis on the states. These constitute also two schools of thought and action traceable in most public questions. One is the practical man, seeking the most attainable solution of pressing problems, and the other the uncompromising idealist, wedded to persistent theories of man and his government, seeking not so much the best way out of an existing situation as human perfection and absolute justice. These may be styled — not because the terms are exact, but because they embody definite conceptions — the statesmen and the philosophers. For the statesman is not always the idealist; he is rather the practical "executive," while the philosopher is first of all the thinker, more interested in abstract excellence than a realistic handling of the imperative task. The advocates of the imperfect instrument of 1787 can usually be described as workaday statesmen; its enemies were commonly — though not invariably — men accustomed more to reasoning on government than actively engaged in attempting to make it operate. In general the believers in strong centralized power were men of practical experience; the adherents of the state were the readers and the scholars, those who liked to discourse on the "state of nature," "natural rights," "social compacts," and the like. Many of the Nationalists had played parts in American affairs in the field, in diplomacy, and had thus learned at first hand the need of "energy," as Hamilton never tired of describing the chief requirement of the "new plan." The more hesitant champions of localism were the pamphleteers, the orators, whose public services had been largely hortatory. In the first classification are found such names as Washington, Hamilton, Franklin, Henry Lee, John Marshall, — the two latter not members of the convention, but active forces for ratification by Virginia, — men whose principles of statesmanship were based rather on experience than argument.   In the second are such men as Samuel Adams, Richard Henry Lee, Patrick Henry, George Mason, Elbridge Gerry, and Luther Martin, all of whom had lived through the Revolution, but had been orators, students, gadflies of public opinion rather than active participants. Most of the first group, for instance, had figured in the army, while none of the second had witnessed the struggle face to face.   One leader defies this kind of classification — Madison, who, though first of all a bookish man and never an able executive, as he was to prove in his Presidency, was an upholder of the National point of view.

This same spirit of accommodation is apparent also in the compromise made by the strongest men in the convention with the rising spirit of democracy.   That the Constitution, as it came from the convention, was not a "democratic" document in the twentieth-century understanding of that term needs no elaborate demonstration.   The lack of faith in popular rule and the belief in the right of the more "respectable" elements to guide national destiny expressed by such men as Hamilton, Madison, Gouverneur Morris, Dickinson, Sherman, Gerry, Mason, and many others, shock the present age.   So far as they thought it possible, these statesmen embodied their allegiance to "property" and the dominance of the "well-born" and the educated, in the Constitution.   The original Virginia proposals were extreme on this side: they provided for a Senate to be elected by the House of Representatives, itself to be chosen by the limited suffrage laws that then existed in most of the states; for an Executive to be chosen by Congress; and for a "Council of Revision" consisting of the Executive and the Supreme Court, which should have the right to approve or set aside laws passed by the state legislatures.   The underlying purpose was to keep political power, as far as possible, out of the hands of the masses.   But these "Bourbons" had one trait that was not Bourbon at all. They were wise practical men, capable of learning.   And the convention had not lasted many days before they realized that any plan of separating the people too completely from the control of their government could not succeed.   They had before them a more difficult task even than framing a constitution: the more difficult job was to get it ratified.   And the concessions gradually made to what to-day would be called the proletariat represented their ambition to establish a strong, effective government, and one that, at the same time, the propertyless, who then, as always, comprised the great majority of the people, would accept. And perhaps the greatest tribute to their genius as statesmen is that they succeeded in doing this.

The scheme that was finally, after long deliberation, framed for choosing the President exhibits the spirit of accommodation that guided many other parts of the work. The demand of the ultra-conservatives that the chief magistrate should be elected by Congress and serve during "good behavior" — that is, for life, in fact an elective monarch — was scrapped; so was the proposal of the lonely democrat, James Wilson, that he be chosen by popular vote. A clumsy contrivance, an Electoral College, to be elected as the state legislatures might direct, was established solely to choose the President. In this way a compromise between the aristocratic and the democratic demands was arrived at, but the arrangement was significant for another reason. It illustrates the flexibility of what too many regard as a rigid instrument, but the Constitution's greatest quality is that it is malleable and can be moulded to meet new requirements and new circumstances. The Electoral College, essentially as it left the convention, still "appoints" the President, but ways have been discovered to make it the spokesman of the democratic masses. And this possibility is inherent in the whole Constitution; that is the reason it has survived most other forms of government that existed in 1787. As it issued from the convention it was, in the main, a bulwark of property; its subsequent history has been its gradual "accommodation" to the demands and needs of the "people." This process, of course, is not yet complete. The great strength of the Constitution is that it was, as Oliver Wendell Holmes describes it, "an experiment, as all life is an experiment." It was a thing made for men, and took due account of the strength and weaknesses that constitute human nature.

One feature of this "bulwark" has been a matter of controversy from that day to this. The supervisory power of the judiciary over the Constitution has precipitated "constitutional crises," from the time of Jefferson to that of Franklin Roosevelt. The United States started life under the protection of something unknown up to 1789 — a written instrument delegating powers to the three branches of government, legislative, executive, and judicial. Since the metes and bounds of each division of the body politic were set, — or supposed to be, — by what mechanism were they to be kept within the allotted limits? No other nation had ever been called upon to establish such an empire, for the best of reasons: no other nation had operated under a written compact; no other had sprung suddenly into existence, artificially created, as it were, by a piece of sheepskin. Great Britain, whose organization most resembles the new United States, has never needed an outside agency to determine the constitutionality of laws, because Great Britain, in the American sense, has no constitution. Parliament is supreme; it could constitutionally repeal Magna Charta or the Bill of Rights to-morrow, just as an act of Parliament in recent times has radically curtailed the power of the House of Lords. Had Britain lived under a constitution, formulated and adopted by the people, only a constitutional amendment, or a revolution, could have so altered the structure of its government. But the fact is that Parliament makes up the British Constitution as it goes along. As someone has said, it can do anything, except make a man a woman and a woman a man. The American Congress possesses no such omnipotence; it can exercise only the powers set forth in a written agreement. Unless there is some impartial referee outside its own authority to determine whether it has observed these rules, the Constitution is automatically abolished. The powers granted by the people can be disregarded at will.

The statement, made above, that no nation had previously developed the necessity of a restraining force needs one qualification. There were several political societies, not nations, that had been familiar with a supervisory body for a century and a half. These were the thirteen American colonies that in 1776 declared their independence of Great Britain. The controversy over the powers of the United States Supreme Court assumes a certain simplicity if this fact is kept in mind. A Supreme Court was nothing new in American experience. The colonial legislatures from settlement had been accustomed to "judicial review." Their judgments had been subject to a revisionary body for precisely the same reason that the acts of Congress are to-day; they were acting under powers expressed in written constitutions. That is to say, "judicial review" came into existence at the very moment that written constitutions did; one was necessary if the other was to exist. In colonial times the constitutions were called charters. They were granted to the overseas dominions by the King and stipulated the powers the colonial legislatures were to exercise. If these colonial legislatures passed laws that violated charter provisions, such laws were "unconstitutional" and were declared null and void. The colonial courts passed on the question in first instance as our district and circuit courts do to-day. Their judgments could be appealed to the Privy Council in England. A subdivision of that body, called the Committee on the Privy Council for Appeals, performed the same function for the colonies that the Supreme Court now does for the United States. "It was," says Edward Channing, "the precedent for the Supreme Court of the newly modeled United States." In pre-Revolutionary days, the case of *Winthrop* vs. *Letchmere* was a famous precedent, as that of *Marbury* vs. *Madison* became in the nineteenth century. The Connecticut charter provided that the laws of its legislature "should not be contrary to the laws of England." In face of this Connecticut passed a law declaring that, in the division of estates, all children should participate on equal terms, except the oldest son, who should receive a double portion. But according to the laws of England, all property went to the oldest male heir. Had not Connecticut, therefore, passed an "unconstitutional" law? The "great case," as modern lawyers would say, came up on the disposition of the property of Judge Winthrop, descendant of the famous governor. A double portion went to the oldest son, and the remainder was divided among his brothers and sisters. Winthrop, after meeting defeat in the Connecticut courts, took his grievance to the Supreme Court of the day, the Committee of the Privy Council on Appeals. That body decided that the Connecticut law violated the Connecticut charter, — that it was "unconstitutional," — set it aside, and handed all the family patrimony to the engrossing oldest son. Such was the precedent established for many cases in colonial times.

Naturally this power of judicial review, resident in a transatlantic authority, went into the discard when the colonies declared their independence. But it was promptly assumed by the courts of the states. Assumed because it was inevitable that it should be, for the state constitution took the place of colonial charters, and, like them, required interpreters. Thus the questions as to whether the framers of the Federal Constitution intended that the final dictum in constitutionality should be exercised by the courts answers itself. They so expected because that was the only system they had ever known. If necessary, many quotations could be taken from Madison's *Debates* expressing this expectation.[1] One of them was uttered by Madison himself. "A law violating a constitution established by the people themselves," he said, "would be considered by the judges null and void." The whole matter is well summed

[1] Beveridge, in his *Life of John Marshall,* Vol. III, p. 115 (footnote), has assembled these excerpts.

up by Edward S. Corwin: "Nor can there be much doubt that the members of the Convention were also substantially agreed that the Supreme Court was endowed with the further right to pass upon the constitutionality of acts of Congress. The available evidence strictly contemporaneous with the framing and ratification of the Constitution shows seventeen of the fifty-five members of the Convention asserting the existence of this prerogative in unmistakable terms and only three using language that can be construed to the contrary. More striking than that, however, is the fact that these seventeen members include nearly three fourths of the leaders of the Convention, four of the five members of the Committee of Detail which drafted the Constitution, and four of the five members of the Committee of Style which gave the Constitution its final form. And these were precisely the members who expressed themselves on all the interesting and vital subjects before the Convention because they were its statesmen and articulate members." [1]

The three great heroes of ratification were Hamilton, Madison, and Washington. Hamilton's performance in the New York convention is one of the greatest episodes in American forensic history. For this man, almost by his unaided efforts, by the assertion of an indomitable power of will, persuaded an overwhelming majority to change its mind and follow his leadership. Both Madison and Hamilton were conspicuous illustrations of the spirit of "accommodation." These two statesmen are usually looked upon as the chief authors of the Constitution; Madison has even passed into history as its "father." But the fact is that the instrument which finally emerged did not embody the favorite principles of either of these men. That they accommodated themselves to the need of compromise is perhaps their claim to greatness. Their joint work presents one of the most successful partnerships in American annals — a partnership fruitful not only in statesmanship, but in political literature. Their journalistic association not only served the immediate purpose, — that of convincing doubters in all parts of the country of the wisdom of ratification, — but produced, as Frederick Scott Oliver, Hamilton's English biographer, calls it, "one of the great books of the world." Hamilton wrote the papers of the *Federalist* in fever-like haste, sometimes composing the later paragraphs while the printer was setting up the first, but the volume is to-day not only the indispensable guide to understanding the

[1] *John Marshall and the Constitution*, p. 11.

Constitution, but is an accepted classic everywhere in the literature of government. The eighty-five papers of which it is composed — about fifty are usually attributed to Hamilton, five to John Jay, and the rest to Madison — were passed from hand to hand until threadbare, and persuaded waverer after waverer. Even while the letters were appearing in the New York newspapers, Washington caused them to be reprinted in Richmond. He had read everything written, pro and con, on the Constitution, he wrote Hamilton, and "I will say that I have seen no other so well calculated, in my judgment, to produce conviction on an unbiassed mind as the *production* of your *triumvirate*. When the transient circumstances and fugitive performances which attended this *crisis* shall have disappeared, that work will merit the notice of posterity." And Jefferson, from Paris, wrote Madison that the *Federalist* had resolved his doubts and made him an endorser of the Constitution. A work that could exercise its influence on two such different minds as Washington and Jefferson must have possessed real persuasion.

And Hamilton and Madison, themselves both converts to the "new plan," continued their activity in their state conventions. The Virginia assembly gathered at almost the same time at Richmond as did the New York at Poughkeepsie. Madison was the giant in Virginia and Hamilton in New York. Anyone who wishes to preserve his illusions about certain Virginia statesmen should forbear reading the debates at Richmond. Patrick Henry, for example, makes a sorry spectacle on the printed page, whatever emotions his uttered words may have started. The great reputation of George Mason also suffers considerable diminution. His fine philippic against the slave trade, delivered at Philadelphia, is damaged by his complaint, in Richmond, that the proposed Constitution has not "secured us the property of the slaves we have already." Light Horse Harry Lee, whose business it was to make miserable the enemies of the Constitution, taunted Mason on this grievance: "The gentleman abominates [the Constitution] because it does not prohibit the importation of slaves and because it does not secure the continuance of the existing slavery!" Mason also objected to setting aside ten square miles as the national capital, under the jurisdiction of Congress. He seemed to think that all the rogues in the country would flee to this spot to get away from state courts. "This ten miles square," he exclaimed, in words that may possibly find an echo in the breast of certain pessimists of the present era, "may, like the custom of the superstitious days of our ancestors, become the sanctuary of the blackest crimes.

Here the federal courts are to sit." But most of Mason's more serious objections were competently handled by Madison, who was constantly on his feet, little suggesting the shrinking boy of ten years before. And at the same time Hamilton was vigorously assailing the foe in New York — a foe more dangerous since the Virginia statesmen were sincere, seeking the best interests of the country, while Hamilton's antagonist was George Clinton and his political machine, working against the new government because it would rob them of power. Hamilton's eloquence is said to have moved his audience frequently to tears, but it did something more to the point: it changed their votes. "Two-thirds of the convention," Hamilton wrote, "and four-sevenths of the people are against us." At first he made no impress on this solid wall. He went at it again and again; his admirers perhaps remembered his one military exploit, the assault on the British redoubt at Yorktown. Yet several ballots, taken on essential points, disclosed a hopeless majority — about forty-six to nineteen — against the Constitution. In the darkest moment a friend approached Hamilton; he was returning to New York City and would have to answer many questions on the prospects of the Constitution. What should he say? "God only knows," said Hamilton. "It appears they are two to one against us." The questioner was about to retire, thinking he had his answer, when Hamilton seized his arm and, eyes blazing and form straightening, declared: "Tell them that the convention shall never rise until the Constitution is adopted." This determination carried the day. One by one Clinton's majority departed, the climax arriving when an express, sent from New York on a swift horse, reached the convention hall with the news that Virginia had ratified. Hamilton turned this to fine oratorical profit, and in the final ballot the minority with which he had started, fourteen, was changed to a majority of three.

But perhaps the greatest triumph was achieved by the quiet statesman observing these transactions at Mount Vernon. Washington had not attended the Virginia convention, but he was in constant touch with Madison. His correspondence shows his concern for the fate of the Constitution and his exultation at the result. For his emotions during this period his letters are a perfect revelation. The traditional "inarticulate" Washington is here outspoken enough. There is even an unaccustomed anger in his reference to Virginia "characters" who are working against union. His first act on returning from Philadelphia had been to send a copy of the Constitution to the unsympathetic Patrick Henry, seeking his support, which Washington knew would be powerful. He warned Henry "that the political concerns of this country are suspended by a thread, and that the convention has been looked up to, by the reflective part of the community, with a solicitude which is hardly to be conceived; and, if nothing had been agreed upon by that body, anarchy would soon have ensued, the seeds being deeply sown in every soil." This latter alternative Washington insisted on again and again. "The Constitution is now before the judgment seat," he wrote Henry Knox, in October 1787. "It has, as was expected, its adversaries and supporters. The former, more than probably, will be the most active, as the major part of them will, it is to be feared, be governed by sinister and self-important motives, to which everything in their breasts must yield. . . . Is the Constitution, which is submitted by the convention, preferable to the government (if it can be called one) under which we live?" "There are some things in the new form," he wrote Edmund Randolph, "I will readily acknowledge, which never did, and I am persuaded never will, obtain my cordial approbation; but . . . I do now most firmly believe, that in the aggregation it is the best constitution that can be obtained at this epoch, and that this, or a dissolution of the Union, awaits our choice and are the only alternatives before us." Should the Constitution be adopted, he wrote the Marquis de Chastellux, "America will lift up her head again," and in a few years "become respectable among the nations."

The imperfections Washington discovered in the new charter caused him no real anxiety. That experience would present difficulties he also knew, but he was satisfied to leave these to the good sense of another age. Over and over again, when these contingencies are presented, he points to one clause that, in his judgment, safeguards the future. The Constitution provided for such changes as its use might demonstrate to be needed. His final word was given in a letter to his favorite nephew and heir, Bushrod Washington, himself afterward a judge of the United States Supreme Court : —

"The warmest friends and the best supporters the Constitution has do not contend that it is free from imperfections; but they have found them unavoidable and are sensible, if evil is likely to arise therefrom, the remedy must come hereafter. . . . I do not think we are more inspired, have more wisdom, or possess more virtue, than those who will come after us."

Thus Washington, like Oliver Wendell Holmes a century and a half afterward, believed that the Constitution was an "experiment" and could be adapted to the changing needs of time.

BOOK II

THE STRUGGLE FOR EXISTENCE

I

THE gentlemen who, armed only with a piece of parchment, started for New York in the early months of 1789 were about to engage in an enterprise for which history has no parallel. From nothing, and almost extemporaneously, they were expected to construct a living government for four million people. Not one of the foundations on which this government was to rest — executives, courts, houses of legislation — existed, even in elementary form. The merchants of New York were obliged to join hands and raise $32,000 for refurbishing the old City Hall in which the inauguration was to take place; the expiring government of the Confederation could not make these preparations, for the Treasury was empty of funds! Historians cannot trace the origins of European states; they go back too far into the past, they are too much the slow growth of generation following generation, their institutions are based so universally on tradition and precedent. The beginnings of even so familiar a phenomenon as the British Parliament are lost in obscurity. Yet the government under which 125,000,000 Americans live to-day began its life at a particular date, and its development, in all its ramifications, is an open book. Never before had a nation sprung full-blown into existence. When Washington, rich in land but poor in money, borrowed six hundred pounds from accommodating neighbors and started on that northward journey which, in the honors paid at every crossroad, not only represented the universal affection and esteem of all classes but echoed the popular rejoicing on the establishment of "a more perfect union," and when newly elected Senators and Congressmen mounted their horses or embarked on sailing vessels and proceeded to the little town at the tip of Manhattan Island, the nation over which they were to preside existed only on paper. Its one tangible foundation was that Constitution which a distracted people had not so much adopted as reluctantly accepted when forced upon them by the pressure of events.

But only a year after Chancellor Livingston, having administered the oath of office to the first Executive, advanced on the balcony of Federal Hall, in Wall Street, and shouted to the echoing populace, "Long live George Washington, President of the United States," the phantom government was physically organized and smoothly functioning.   More important, the new Constitution was fulfilling most of the advantages its advocates had foreseen.   By 1791 peace and prosperity had been brought to a disordered country.   The economic distress that had hung over the thirteen states since 1776 had given way to one of the most prosperous eras the nation has ever known.   The American ships which for years had lain languidly at their docks were now sailing the seas and even finding their way into India and China.   The yards of New England and the Middle states were daily adding to what was soon to become one of the world's great mercantile fleets.   Southern planters were again finding world markets for their tobacco, rice, and cotton; in the Eastern and Middle states manufacturing establishments were turning out goods that foreshadowed the vast industrial future of America.   With all this naturally came a new satisfaction with life and a new pride in an expanding nation.   The enthusiasm with which the people had hailed the outlook — the houses illuminated with candles, the bonfires and fireworks, the parades, of which the conspicuous figure had been the good ship *Constitution* — was quickly justified.   The success of the Constitution, says Edward Channing, was "immediate and great," and for a contemporary judgment no more unprejudiced witness could be consulted than Thomas Jefferson. "In general," Jefferson wrote to C. W. F. Dumas of Paris, in May 1791, "our affairs are proceeding in a train of unparalleled prosperity.   This arises from the real improvements of our government, from the unbounded confidence reposed in it by the people, their zeal to support it, and their conviction that a solid Union is the best rock of their safety, from the favorable seasons which for some years past have coöperated with a fertile soil and a genial climate to increase the productions of agriculture, and from the growth of industry, economy, and domestic manufactures; so that I believe I may say with truth that there is not a nation under the sun enjoying a more present prosperity, nor with more in prospect."

Significantly, Jefferson attributes the new day in America first of all to the Constitution and the loyalty which it inspired in all classes.   The troubles that presently arose should not obscure the general satisfaction and tolerance which prevailed.   Even the bitterest foes of the "new plan" seemed now inclined to give it a fair chance.   Samuel Adams, at first unfriendly, had bestowed his blessing.   Patrick Henry, the foremost enemy in Virginia, became a convert, and even the Clintonians of New York suspended warfare. Richard Henry Lee was one of the first two Senators from Virginia. That the Constitution itself was the chief agent in producing this new national prospect is susceptible of proof. That clause, as celebrated now as then, giving Congress control over commerce explains the sudden improvement in shipping. That same provision changed, almost overnight, the United States from a bankrupt nation into one famous, from that day to this, for the soundness of its credit. It was on the power to levy taxes on imports that Hamilton erected his great financial system. This "commerce clause" provided the money that made possible the funding of the Federal debt and the assumption of state debts — measures which aroused a great outcry at the time, the echoes of which can still be heard, but which gave the United States the highest standing in the markets of Europe. One can hardly imagine the effect when holders of American securities suddenly realized that they represented value, and not repudiated promises to pay. If present-day holders of Peruvian and Mexican bonds should awake some morning and discover that interest and principal had been provided for, they would experience sensations identical with those of holders of American obligations in 1790. American bonds at once began selling at more than par, and new American offerings, in London and Amsterdam, were readily marketed. Other developments of financial sanity exercised a similar influence. Now came an end to the floods of paper money sent forth by the states. The wisdom of that constitutional clause forbidding states to "coin money" or "emit bills of credit" impressed all beholders, even in the communities that had been most addicted to the demoralizing practice. Perhaps few single manifestations did more to foster the sense of nationality than the appearance of a new system of money. In place of the Spanish doubloons and pieces of eight, moidores and half-joes, most of them so worn and clipped that every commercial transaction proved to be a violent argument in value, the new gold eagles, shiny silver dollars and quarters and halves, gave the populace a feeling of American solidarity. Roger Sherman stirred the interest of his colleagues, in the debate on the tariff bill, by proposing a duty of "fifteen cents" a gallon on rum. In this way that since familiar denomination made its début in Congress. It had been determined on, Sherman explained, as the unit of the new coinage. "Ten of them," he informed his somewhat bewildered hearers, "make a dime and ten dimes make a dollar." The mathematical Yankee had himself been one of the originators of the scheme.

The more dignified position the United States had obtained was soon evidenced by the respect created in Europe. For the first time we entered into diplomatic relations with Great Britain. John Adams, who is usually regarded as America's first Minister to London, was in reality a diplomatic agent sent to England for a special purpose, the negotiation of a commercial treaty; his successor, Gouverneur Morris, had maintained a position even less important. No diplomatic status had existed between the United States and England and no British Minister had been accredited to the old Confederation. On this subject Britain had held aloof, regarding the United States, in a diplomatic sense, about as seriously as present-day Americans look upon Morocco. His Majesty had repeatedly said that he would never recognize revolted subjects in this honorable fashion; they would have to content themselves with a consular agent for such negotiations as could not be avoided. But the amalgamation of the states into one Union, the adoption of the Constitution, its success in transforming America from a bankrupt congeries of discordant communities into an honest, debt-paying sovereignty, as well as the country's expanding commerce and prosperity, caused George III to change his attitude and to appoint a resident minister in the new capital. In August 1791, Sir George Hammond, who had participated in the treaty negotiations of 1782–1783 that separated the colonies from the mother country, appeared as first British Minister to the United States. He soon symbolized the new spirit of coöperation by marrying a lady of Philadelphia. Thomas Pinckney of South Carolina in 1792 took up his abode in London as first minister to Great Britain. Pinckney's designation, in turn, was appropriate, for he had been educated at Westminster and Oxford and had lived much in England. It is true that British-American relations remained in an unsettled condition for several years and that neither Hammond nor Pinckney found his post particularly restful, but this new diplomatic association gave the American Republic a solid international position, and made complete that recognition of American independence by England that had been only partial in the treaty following Yorktown. In 1795 this same Thomas Pinckney went to Spain and negotiated a most successful treaty there, in which the navigation of the Mississippi was made free to Americans and the right of deposit at New Orleans secured. The United States was already diplomatically allied to France, Holland, Prussia, and Sweden; it had at last been admitted into fellowship with the world.

II

Satisfactory as these achievements were, and splendidly as the Constitution justified the expectations of its friends, its course in these early years was not plain sailing. No government ever came into existence painlessly, and the United States was not exempt from the troubles that accompany the process of nation making. Almost the chief satisfaction Jefferson had discovered in an instrument which, on the whole, met only with his qualified approval was that it had been created by "assembling the wise men, instead of assembling armies" — the process which had for centuries been the favorite one in Europe. Bismarck's formula for establishing empires, "blood and iron," ultimately became the means by which America's states were welded into union; and all the dangers that finally led to civil war appeared in the first quarter-century of the Constitution's life. This period, from Washington's inauguration in 1789 to the end of the second war with England, in 1815, may be taken as its time of infancy and adolescence. And despite the successful weathering of this early storm, the era proved to be a troublous one. All those unlovely human passions, hate, jealousy, selfish ambition, appeared side by side with the nobler motives that enabled the Constitution to survive; and all those disintegrating instincts, sectionalism, disloyalty, commercial greed, even treason, proved obstacles to the more statesmanlike qualities that at last made the document what, in an almost defiant clause, it had affirmed itself to be, "the supreme law of the land." And in this struggle for existence no state and no region can claim superiority in civic worth. Virginia regarded herself as the prime state in the Union; New England was even more convinced of eminence in everything that made America great; and both these communities, at different times, illustrated the best and the worst in the national spirit. Perhaps the thing that made the Constitution the object of affection and veneration it ultimately became was this very circumstance — that it was not the accomplishment of one man or group of men, or of any one section, but the joint production of all Americans and all states and the expression, incomplete perhaps, not always set forth in clear outline, of the American aspiration and purpose.

The difficulties with which the Constitution had to contend came from within and without. It was constantly assailed by its own people and by foreign enemies. From 1789 to 1815 there was hardly a year when some danger from one of these sources did not appear. Even at the start, when Americans as a whole were rejoicing over Union, the note of doubt and cynicism could be heard. The location of the "ten square miles" which the Constitution said should be set aside for a capital city was a matter of irreverent comment. "Why worry so much about the national capital?" it was suggested; long before the projected buildings could be finished, the nation would have expired. Connecticut had recently put up a fine new governmental structure in Hartford; this was regarded with distrust; was it really intended as the capital of that New England Confederacy which the disloyal Yankees had long been planning? At the end of the first session of Congress a resolution was offered, appointing a day to give thanks to God for granting the American people so beneficent a guide as the Federal Constitution. A crusty Virginian suggested that the demonstration be postponed until it was possible to learn just how much the people had to be thankful for. This sense of doubt lingered for a considerable time. Only the fact that Washington was to be first President, it was said, made the adoption of the Constitution possible, and it was predicted that the whole thing would go into the discard when he retired. Even as late as 1812 it was commonly declared that James Madison would be the last President of the United States.

From the first, internal divisions made wise men look with fear towards the future. Even before Congress came together, the first great fallacy of the Constitution had been made conspicuous. Its framers had failed to foresee the development of political parties. In fact several of its most important clauses, particularly that providing for the election of President, were constructed for a political Elysium in which parties should not exist. The oversight is the more remarkable since these parties were in process of formation in the very convention in which the Constitution was framed. In one respect the Anglo-Saxon political genius differs from that of other peoples, and it is a respect that probably explains the superiority of that race in government. Since the day when parties became the chief agencies of popular rule, the voters in the United States and Great Britain have aligned themselves in two camps. In other countries that have experimented with democracy and a liberal franchise, — France, Germany, Italy, and the rest of the Continent, — parties have been so numerous that orderly parliaments, at times, have been impossible. In France at the present time half a dozen parties are represented in the Chambre; at Germany's last election before the Nazi régime twelve parties appeared at the polls. But in the United States and England, — as well as in Canada, — from the day that party government became a fact, the nations, with certain temporary factional wanderings, have divided, almost in accordance with some biological law, into two congregations. These two parties appeared in the Constitutional Convention, and the great issue on which they split was essentially the same as that which divides them to-day. The Gilbertian ditty which insists that every man is born either a Liberal or a Conservative emblazons, for England and America, a profound political truth. And separation on this basis appears in Madison's *Debates*. One group took stand for a strong central government, in which the thirteen states, in national matters, should operate as a unit; the other desired a loose confederation, in which the states should preserve their independence, giving only carefully guarded powers to the larger organization. In the convention the first group were known as Nationalists, the second as Federalists. The curious change in titles that took place almost immediately on adjournment has already been pointed out. The Nationalists appropriated the name of the enemy and became Federalists. The other side could do no better than to adopt a negative designation and become Antifederalist. But this unsatisfactory appellation quickly disappeared, largely owing to the influence of Jefferson. That great statesman, fresh from the horrors of royal France, quickly discovered — or believed he had — that the leaders of the Federalist Party — Hamilton, John Adams, even Washington himself — were really monarchists at heart, and that the only Americans who believed in a republic were himself and his followers. Therefore he called his camp, who were, of course, the opposing group, Republicans — a name familiar enough, since the Civil War, as applied to an entirely different aggregation. Naturally this assumption that only Republicans were friendly to the Republic made the enemy rage, but Jefferson insisted to the end on this style. Sympathizers north of Maryland who believed in the Jefferson principle and acted in political coöperation with him called themselves Democrats, but it was a word which, as party designation, Jefferson never used. It did not sufficiently set off his aloofness from those "monarchists" and "monocrats" who figure so constantly in his correspondence.

The dissensions between these two armies — Federalists and Republicans — was one of the chief strains on the Constitution in its early, formative years. At times their differences seemed likely to wreck the whole structure. Even as early as the election of 1792, the South made a threat similar to that of 1860: if the Federalists gained a majority in Congress, she would secede. The frequency with which this word "secession" appeared in Congress and on the hustings appalls a contemporary observer. It was a word that had no terrors for our ancestors. In fact it was a favorite argument in debate. Whenever a particular section disliked a legislative proposal, the chronic threat was forthcoming that, if it passed, secession would follow — or "scisson" as Jefferson sometimes called it. One would think that the early United States resembled one of those primitive biological organisms in which division and subdivison are natural processes. If Hamilton's funding bill should be passed, the South would depart and disrupt the Constitution. If the Federal Government assumed state debts, Virginia would leave the Union; if the Federal Government did not assume them, New England would set up for itself. If the Federal Government should find its Capital on the Potomac, the North would secede; if on the Susquehanna or the Delaware, — or, most odiously of all, on the Hudson, — the Southern states would abandon the national cause. If Jay's Treaty became law, Republicans threatened to pronounce the Constitution at an end; the purchase of Louisiana almost persuaded New England and the "Yorkers" to cast that great charter adrift. The discovery was made, soon after ratification, that the Constitution had united two disharmonious countries, and that North and South, in history, manner of life, interests, and aspirations, were distinct communities. The trading instincts of New England codfishers, shopkeepers, and manufacturers hardly seemed, in Virginia's eyes, compatible with the gentlemanly character. James Monroe's protestation to the French Minister that all Americans were not "merchants, occupied exclusively with pepper and ginger," and that he himself had never known "what trade was," expresses a common Virginian disdain for the Eastern brethren, while the New England air was full of similarly depreciating views on slave-driving Southern planters.

III

The conflict over the permanence of the Constitution was one not only between section with section and interest with interest, but between ideas and between men. And the era of youthful experiment was an era of great Americans who, in addition to intellectual genius and statesmanlike capacity, had also the talent for disagreement. Their differences — amounting fairly to battles — over the document that had emerged from Philadelphia made the concluding decade of the eighteenth century and the first of the nineteenth one of the most personally exciting periods — and therefore one of the most engrossing — in our history. About the foes and the friends of this Constitution there was nothing of the pygmy, and they were also hard hitters and heroic haters — so much so that one wonders how, in the tense struggles that took place about its half-animate body, it succeeded in growing into vigor. Though there were many minor characters, the great influences in making strong the Constitution were Washington and Hamilton; and the men whose influence was largely directed to weakening it were Madison and Jefferson. The two latter figures should always be hyphenated, and the sixteen years, from 1801 to 1817, that composed their two Presidencies should be known as the Jefferson-Madison administration. For the thoughts that regulated American policy in this period were the same. That Madison, one of the men chiefly responsible for the Constitution, and in particular the advocate of Nationalism as opposed to state sovereignty, should have gone over to the Jeffersonian side indicates that the "grand lama of Monticello" was the stronger man.

One wonders just what would have happened to the Constitution had Jefferson been in America from 1785 to 1789, instead of in Paris. In that case he would undoubtedly have been a delegate to the convention, and would have sat restive during many of the speeches advocating what were to him obnoxious ideas. What would he have thought when such men as Elbridge Gerry, Roger Sherman, Rufus King, John Dickinson, and Gouverneur Morris were giving their views on the ignorant and unthinking populace — the "people" whom Jefferson regarded as the foundation of the state, the source of all power, with whose "consent" all government was formed and without which it possessed no sanction? Despite his own fondness for his acres, how would Jefferson have received the affirmations, so frequently made, that the safeguard of "property" was the main business of the state? And one can picture what his emotions would have been had he sat in the convention when Alexander Hamilton stalked angrily in, that hot August day, and made his speech proclaiming the British Constitution as his favorite form of government, advocating a Senate for life, a President who should serve during "good behavior," demanding vast power in the general government and all but obliterating state lines — including that of Jefferson's beloved Virginia. It is not likely that the "Virginia plan," though drawn up by Madison, would have pleased him more. For this also was full of odious ideas. Jefferson believed that the Articles of Confederation made a "good, old and venerable fabric, which should have been preserved, even as a religious relique"; but the Virginia plan, first of all, cast this into the wastebasket. Jefferson was a Federalist in the old sense of the word — that is, he believed in a Confederation, in the "compact" idea; but Virginia leaders proposed a scheme based on continental lines. There is little likelihood that Jefferson, in far-away Paris, knew anything of these discussions. Madison's letters to his friend contain no reference to them. After adjournment he sent Jefferson a copy of the Constitution, with a commentary on its principles, but of the angry discussion, the anti-democratic opinions expressed, the great struggle between Nationalists and State-rights men, nothing was said.

Jefferson's first impressions of the Constitution were unfavorable. Of the statesmen who formed it he had the most exalted opinion. "It is really an assembly of demigods," he wrote John Adams, and to C. W. F. Dumas he said, "The Convention holding at Philadelphia consists of the ablest men in America." But, as he studied the completed document forwarded by Madison, the demigods did not seem to have displayed supernatural wisdom. The frame of government they had elaborated was not Jeffersonian. It provided a strong central power; and this Jefferson did not like. "I own I am not a friend to a very energetic government. It is always oppressive." He was against the eligibility of the President to reëlection; that meant a President for life, a kind of Polish king, in the selection of whom foreign governments would constantly intrigue. The Constitution — and this in his view was an almost fatal defect — contained no Bill of Rights. There were sections that Jefferson did approve, such as the control of the House in originating appropriations, and the division of powers into legislative, executive, and judicial, but on the whole his lack of enthusiasm is marked. To other friends Jefferson expressed more emphatic disappointment. "As to the new Constitution I find myself nearly a neutral," he wrote Edward Carrington, December 21, 1787. "There is a great mass of good in it, in a very desirable form; but there is also to me a bitter pill or two." "How do you like our new Constitution?" Jefferson wrote John Adams, still residing in London. "I confess there are things in it which stagger all my dispositions to subscribe to what such an assembly has proposed." He inclined to accept the programme of Richard Henry Lee, George Mason, and other disapprovers; this was that another convention be called, to frame another charter, taking into consideration the many suggestions for "improvement" made in certain quarters. However, he finally adopted an attitude characteristically Jeffersonian: he thought it would be desirable that nine states should ratify and four reject, believing that the efforts made to persuade the hesitant into coöperation would result in the adoption of his favorite changes. In the Virginia Convention Patrick Henry and others insisted that Jefferson was against the plan, while Madison just as explicitly quoted his name in approbation. That both sides could claim Jefferson in support, and do so truthfully, is only another illustration of the man's nature, famous for its contradictions and suppleness.

The fact is that the document emanating from Philadelphia flew in the face of the Jeffersonian ideal of government. By this time his philosophy was completely formed. It was unfriendly to anything suggesting centralized power. The society of the American Indians — which, as he admitted, was no government at all — represented to Jefferson idyllic perfection; it was an idea with which his mind loved to play. The New England town meetings, in which the citizens as a mass came together for legislative purposes, "have proved themselves the wisest invention ever devised by the wit of man for the perfect exercise of self-government and for its preservation." The picture he liked to draw of America was one which hardly existed in his own time and certainly does not exist now. He saw the nation divided into a multitude of what he called "ward-republics": social and political organizations of minute size, each with a few hundred members whose exclusive occupation was to be agriculture and whose governmental activities were to be limited to supplying their joint but simple needs — roads, schoolhouses, the care of the decrepit and poor, if there should be any poor, and the establishment of such means of securing order and justice as an elementary society might require. The Jeffersonian system made no provision for cities; William Cobbett's description of London as a "great wen" completely pictured Jefferson's dislike of concentrated population. Neither did he like the things that accompanied cities, such as smoking chimneys of factories, trade and commerce; even the lovely ships turned out in New England yards neither aroused his artistic admiration nor represented a desirable human activity. Anything in government beyond his ward-republics Jefferson submitted to only as concessions to a world that insisted on being practical. The grouping of his wards into counties was permissible, and the assembling of these counties into states, for there were certain functions larger aggregations could perform better than the smaller entities. To go beyond this, and to mingle the states into a nation, was a necessity which he accepted most grudgingly. Jefferson's tombstone, for which he wrote the inscription, and which has found many admirers, can be interpreted as expressing his aversion to large governmental units. It describes him as the author of the Declaration of Independence, of the Virginia resolution for religious freedom, and as "father" of the University of Virginia. That he had served in Congress, had been Ambassador to France, and twice President of the United States, — all dignities associated with the nation, — are regarded as unworthy of attention. Even while he was President, Jefferson was inclined to minimize the importance of the Federal government. The true theory of the Constitution, in his view, reduced that instrument to simplicity itself; under it the centralized authority became a kind of Department of Foreign Affairs, for the benefit of those true sources of power, the states; its business was concerned only with foreign governments, while the real business of governing, in domestic affairs, was concentrated in the states. That the party "founded by Thomas Jefferson" should, in recent years, reverse all this, almost completely obliterate the states, and centralize all activities, great and minute, even to the details of personal life and outdoor relief, in that central government which Jefferson did not think worthy of mentioning on his tombstone is only one of those huge contradictions for which the Jeffersonian philosophy is responsible.

So far as the purposes of government are concerned, however, present-day tendencies to "liberalism," "progressivism," even the "abundant life," are all quite Jeffersonian. The second paragraph of the Declaration of Independence contains matter that is as significant of a new day as the assertion of the right to dissolve a worn-out political association. Eighteenth-century philosophers from whom the revolutionists of '76 derived their inspiration constantly harped upon one phrase. The business of government was to ensure to the individual the rights of "life, liberty and property." In incorporating this principle in his Declaration, Jefferson deftly inserted something new. He changed the word "property" to "pursuit of happiness." The duty of government, he thus made the new nation proclaim, was not only to make the citizen secure in life and liberty, but to make him "happy" — that is, to make him as large a participator as possible in the good things of existence.

That was Jeffersonism at its best. This article in a new political creed was an expression of the man's nature, which, despite its reticence and fastidiousness, was above all kindly and humane, always susceptible to pity, absolutely free from coarseness and vulgarity, desirous of making all his fellow creatures a part of the fine life to which he devoted his days. It is fashionable to describe Jefferson as "feminine," an adjective intended to suggest his persistence in gaining his ends, his intriguing unscrupulousness in attaining them, his habit of praising his friends in public and abusing them in private, his love of secrecy and indirection, even in large matters — traits which, whether feminine or not, were certainly Jeffersonian; and his hatred of war, his detestation of armies and of battleships, also belong to the same character, for he was our first great pacifist, a fact that has given him new vitality in an age when opposition to war is becoming universal. But Jefferson can be regarded as feminine in a finer way, for he was emotional, had a passion for popularity, yearned to be loved, had intense sympathy with suffering and injustice, aimed constantly to "meliorate" the lot of the person now known as the "common man." It would be difficult to find in all literature a more sympathetic and human letter than the one Jefferson wrote to Madison from Fontainebleau October 28, 1785, in which he described his walk and talk with a poor peasant woman whom he had met by chance. This opportunity to learn at first hand the condition of French laborers Jefferson characteristically seized, and the meditations that followed these revelations of misery not only reflect Jefferson's attitude towards injustice and suffering, but have a significance appropriate to present conditions. It was the problem presented by agricultural plenty side by side with want and unemployment! "I asked myself what could be the reason that so many should be permitted to beg who are willing to work, in a country where there is a very considerable proportion of uncultivated lands. . . . I am conscious that an equal division of property is impracticable. . . . But legislators cannot invent too many devices for subdividing property. . . . Another means of silently lessening the inequality of property is to exempt all from Taxation below a certain point and to tax the higher portions of property in geometrical progression. Whenever there is in any country uncultivated lands and unemployed poor, it is clear that the laws of property have been so far extended as to violate natural rights. The earth is given as a common stock for man to labor and live in. If for the encouragement of industry we allow it to be appropriated we must take care that other employment is provided to those excluded from the appropriation."

The French government of 1785 did not regard it as its province to worry about a French peasant woman, tilling the fields at a wage of eight cents a day when she could obtain any work at all, but Jefferson's personal interest in her troubles, and the reflections on the duty of government to which they gave rise, display the finest side of his character. They make him a man in tune with the best thought of the present day. Here was a compelling instance of that new function for which governments are instituted among men — "the pursuit of happiness." In his own day Jefferson regarded the distribution of Virginia's vacant lands among the poor, — thus assuring everyone a patrimony, — the construction of serviceable highways and other public improvements, public education at public expense, as illustrations of what he meant by this all-inclusive phrase. Such ends he believed could best be accomplished by those ward-republics that represented his democratic Arcadia. Afterward he became persuaded that the Federal government could engage in such improvements; anticipating events by nearly a hundred and fifty years, he recommended a programme of great public works — adding, however, one proviso, that an amendment to the Constitution would be a necessary preliminary!

Enough has been said to explain why Jefferson's mind should be in a state of uncertainty and hesitation on the proposed Constitution. Madison's letters and Hamilton's and Madison's *Federalist* turned the balance to the affirmative side. So, in September 1789, he left Paris, as he believed, on a six months' vacation, but, reaching America just before Christmas, found a letter from Washington enclosing a commission as Secretary of State in the new government.

Up to this point Madison had apparently been the main influence in Jefferson's attitude towards the Constitution; that was because Madison was on the ground, whereas Jefferson, in Paris, had no first-hand knowledge of events. As soon as the stronger character had been established in the new government and had gained some insight into the general prospect, this situation was reversed. Jefferson returned from Paris with an excited detestation of kings and arbitrary rule. His letters are full of the "government of sheep by wolves," as he described the European system, and his eye was morbidly vigilant for symptoms of such manifestations on his native soil. Jefferson's mind was subject to preconceived and fixed ideas; once a conviction had become lodged there, the most conclusive evidence in the contrary direction never carried the slightest weight. Despite the word "philosopher" traditionally applied to him, he lived by what his own generation called the "feelings" and we the "emotions," rather than by reason; and personal antagonisms exercised a powerful influence in directing his public life. There were two men, above all others, whom he came to hate, Hamilton and John Marshall, and it is absurd to deny that, in framing his attitude towards these statesmen and their policies, jealousy was an important element. The case of Hamilton, who first aroused Jefferson's hostility, was particularly to the point. Though Jefferson, as Secretary of State, was nominally the chief man of the cabinet, he quickly discovered that his rôle was secondary. Hamilton, on personal grounds, was Washington's favorite, and the Hamiltonian issues the great commander made his own. Hamilton's fiscal programme, the funding of the national debt and assumption, had restored national credit and launched the new nation on an era of prosperity, but these, as well as Hamilton's other measures, such as the National Bank, the promotion of commerce and manufactures, were most obnoxious to Jefferson, opposed as he was to the wide use of the Federal power. Washington sought both Hamilton's and Jefferson's advice on these policies — but in all instances followed Hamilton's. When war broke out between France and England, the question of American neutrality became the first great matter in foreign policy with which America had to deal; Jefferson was for throwing American influence on the side of France, while Hamilton insisted on maintaining an impartial attitude between the two countries. The issue belonged to Jefferson's department, not to Hamilton's, but Washington accepted Hamilton's judgment.

That this preference would gall such a proud and sensitive spirit as Jefferson's was inevitable.

Hamilton was equally obnoxious on grounds of principle. It would be difficult to imagine conceptions of the state more widely separated than those of Hamilton and Jefferson, and all the Virginian's abhorrence of "monarchists" and aristocratic rule naturally concentrated on a man who had noisily avowed his distrust of Jefferson's "people" and had expressed his preference for the British system, which Jefferson interpreted as meaning the monarchical system. John Adams's fussy fondness for high-sounding titles; his writings, expressing a preference for that same obnoxious British government; his use of phrases — phrases that plagued him for the rest of his life — about the "well-born"; the enthusiasm prevalent in large sections of New England society for Britain and the advertised dislike of many of its leaders for "democracy"; Washington's levees; his royal-like speeches to Congress; the debates on the address and the answer — here was clearly material enough in which a man whose mind was constantly brooding on the wickedness of kings could detect everywhere outcroppings of the desire in his native land. Washington, with his usual hard sense, told Jefferson bluntly that there were not "ten men in the United States whose opinions were worth attention" who had the slightest desire to establish an American monarchy. To-day the suspicion is looked upon as one of the two great delusions that controlled Jefferson's political career, the other being his belief that he could bring England and France to terms not with fleets and armies, but by "peaceable coercion," which meant excluding those countries from American commerce.

Yet even before Jefferson reached Monticello in late December, 1789, the word "monocrat" had become a favorite in his correspondence. Soon after his return it was applied not only to local plotters of monarchy, but to the upholders of the Constitution. By degrees the word also became a part of Madison's vocabulary. Almost the first American with whom Jefferson discussed politics was Madison, who came to Monticello immediately on his friend's arrival. For the next few months the men were in constant association, and there was established that personal alliance that was to endure for nearly thirty years. In that first wintry meeting at Monticello it may be confidently assumed that the Constitution figured in their talk. Just before Jefferson left France he had expounded in a letter to Madison one of his favorite ideas: that one generation had no right to commit another, in any matter; that one generation could not properly contract debts for its successors to pay; that similarly it had no right to adopt a Constitution that would be binding on its sons; that, therefore, every twenty years the existing frame should be revised or a new one constructed. This view Madison, whose feet were more firmly planted on the ground than his friends', gently but firmly opposed. In the succeeding two years, however, he came to accept most of Jefferson's ideas. Madison, a representative in Congress, accompanied Jefferson to New York in March 1790; in the Federal city they were constantly thrown together; and, after adjournment of Congress in May 1791, the two men made a month's journey through New England. A stenographic report of their conversations, on horseback rides through Vermont, or their evening sojourns at New England inns, would add much to the political history of the time. The purpose of the trip, as Madison declared, was "health, recreation and curiosity," but of course the nation, much interested in the excursion, regarded political intrigue as the real end in view. Significantly, a few months after their peregrination appeared the first number of Philip Freneau's *National Gazette*, in the establishment of which it is no secret that Madison and Jefferson coöperated.

The extent to which Madison's college mates at Princeton keep cropping out in the national story is suggestive; Henry Lee, Brockholst Livingston, Henry Brackenridge, all played a part in the political excitement of the time; and naturally enough when Jefferson discussed with Madison the founding of a newspaper in Philadelphia that should preach sound Republicanism and controvert the mischievous influence of Fenno's *Gazette,* the leading advocate of the Constitution and Federalism, Madison proposed his old Princeton friend. Philip Freneau occupies a more worthy position as a pioneer in American literature than as a political advocate. He was the first American poet who possessed originality and something approaching inspiration, but his political allegiance was not Washingtonian. Of French Huguenot descent, and thus a French sympathizer by natural right, his hatred of Britain had been heated to frenzy by cruel treatment received on a British prison ship in the war. A man of fiery conviction, intemperate eloquence, unrestrained in his controversial method, he had been from the beginning an enemy of the Constitution and of the "monarchical" propensities of the Federalist Party. That this man should have been assisted by Jefferson and Madison to publish a newspaper devoted to vitriolic attacks on Washington and his administration, at a time when Jefferson was a member of Washington's cabinet, has made the incident one of the most celebrated scandals in political history.   Madison, in recommending Freneau for this editorial post, spoke admiringly of "his character, talents and principles" — this the man to whom Washington, his phlegmatic temper stirred to rage by the galling attacks to which he was subjected, always referred as "that rascal Freneau."

But the chief importance of the Freneau episode in the present connection is its bearing upon Madison's attitude towards the Constitution.   It evinces how completely he had fallen under the Jeffersonian spell.   For the real purpose of the new paper, in Hamilton's words, was "to sap the constitution."   That he should find Madison enrolled among the supporters of such an enterprise was a saddening disillusion.   From 1781 to 1790 Madison had been Hamilton's closest associate in struggling for the new plan of government.   They had worked together at the Annapolis Convention, and, after Philadelphia, had joined hands in producing that *Federalist* which Jefferson had eulogized in words already quoted.   Madison had been the main influence in persuading Virginia to accept the completed instrument, and Hamilton had accomplished the same result, almost single-handed, in New York.   When Hamilton entered on his new duties in Washington's administration he had counted on Madison's coöperation; had he not felt sure of this, Hamilton always declared, he would never have assumed this task. That Madison should take the lead in opposing Hamilton's measures for establishing the national credit was thus a surprise and a disappointment — especially since, so Hamilton insisted, these proposals were Madison's own.   In the days before the Philadelphia Convention no man had taken a stronger stand for the payment of the national debt than Madison; his speech in the old Congress of the Confederation denouncing Virginia for her refusal of the impost, the money from which was to be used for this purpose, seemed a definite commitment.   Other addresses of Madison could be cited that seemed to approve, in advance, the Hamiltonian view. For Madison to ally himself with the Republicans, another name for those Antifederalists whom he had so successfully defeated, seemed, in Hamilton's eyes, rank apostasy.   Madison might maintain that he was still a constitutionalist, but the view of the Constitution he was now upholding was quite a different one from that he had championed in the Convention.   There he was a leading Nationalist — an advocate of strong government, of placing the states in a subordinate position to the central power, of obliterating the "compact" theory from discussion. But now he had transferred his allegiance to the Jeffersonian system, which sought to curb the Nationalistic conception and — in Hamilton's view — set up again the feeble organization from which Madison had done so much to rescue the country. He now joined Jefferson in a faction "dangerous to the Union" — and one outcome of this coöperation was Freneau's paper, pursuing a course "generally unfriendly to the United States." In a letter to Edward Carrington, Hamilton set forth his grievances at length. "Mr. Madison has always entertained an exalted opinion of the talents, knowledge, and virtue of Mr. Jefferson. The sentiment was probably reciprocal. A close correspondence subsisted between them during the time of Mr. Jefferson's absence from this country. A close intimacy arose upon his return. . . . Under the influence of all these circumstances the attachment to the government of the United States, originally weak in Mr. Jefferson's mind, has given way to something very like dislike in Mr. Madison's. . . . In almost all the questions, great and small, which have arisen, since the first session of Congress, Mr. Jefferson and Mr. Madison have been found among those who are disposed to narrow the Federal authority. . . . This kind of conduct has appeared to me the more extraordinary, on the part of Mr. Madison, since I know, for a certainty, it was a primary article in his creed, that the real danger to our system was the subversion of the national authority to the preponderancy of the state government. All his measures have proceeded on an apposite supposition."

One of Jefferson's most serious objections to the Constitution had been remedied by the first session of Congress. The complete document forwarded by Madison to Paris had contained no Bill of Rights. In the Convention itself this lack had aroused most unfavorable comment. In the conventions called for ratification, the failure to include in the body of the instrument the immemorial rights and privileges of freemen — freedom of speech, of the press, of assembly, of religion, of petition, immunity from unlawful seizure, trial by jury, security of life, person, and property, and the like — had given force to the arguments of men like George Mason and Patrick Henry against acceptance. These men and others had suggested that another convention be called for correcting this and similar omissions. North Carolina had adopted a resolution virtually declaring its refusal to ratify until this Bill of Rights should be added. There was no hostility, in the Philadelphia

Convention or outside it, to making these historic immunities part of the American system. To most of the statesmen of that convocation, however, a positive declaration seemed superfluous. Most of the state constitutions contained the Bill of Rights, thus assuring all the privileges in question to their citizens. Why, therefore, load down the organ of the central government with similar declarations? There were other reasons for exclusion that went deep into the principles of scholastic law and the nature of sovereignty, which need not be detailed in this place. But any idea that the failure to repeat the guarantees in the Constitution masked a deep-laid plot at public liberties no one believed at the time or has believed since.

Since the matter had given a handle to the enemies, however, Madison and other practical statesmen believed that amendments, in accordance with the programme set forth in Article V, should be added, incorporating all the privileges obtained by Englishmen at Runnymede and wrung from the Crown in succeeding centuries. The first ten articles of amendment were the result. Madison introduced the subject on June 8, 1789, about three months after the first Congress had assembled; on September 25 the articles in their present form passed the House and Senate by the necessary two-thirds majority, and were referred to the legislatures of the several states. In nine months states enough had ratified to make these emendations part of the Constitution. The whole proceeding has an interest for the present generation beyond that involved in the intrinsic merits of the changes themselves. One of the strongest of existing delusions is that the Constitution is rigid and inflexible, almost impossible to amend. This has never been the case. Whenever the popular will has demanded additions or alterations the process has been found simple and rapid. It is only on a question concerning which public opinion is unformed or divided that modification moves more slowly. This, of course, is precisely what the founders intended and what sound policy demands. How responsive is Article V to the public will the very first year of Congress showed. In about a year after the United States Government had been organized, ten amendments were added to the Constitution.

IV

The year 1794 marked one of the greatest crises in the early days of the Constitution. Again its enemies were both foreign and domestic. A considerable element at home and abroad expected an early dissolution of the government. Washington, it was believed, would go down in history as a great man, but also as a great failure. He had assembled the disorganized energies of a frontier people and succeeded in wrenching the states from an ancient allegiance, had caused them, for a brief period, to reconcile their angry differences and establish a paper government which, subjected to the exacting test of experience, was destined to an early disintegration. The spectacle presented by the American frontier substantiated, in large degree, this discouraging forecast. The American domain, between the Mississippi and the Alleghenies, was in a military sense in the possession of Great Britain, and, so far as British plans were concerned, seemed likely to remain there indefinitely. In the peace treaty of 1783 Britain had promised to surrender the military posts that controlled this region "with all convenient speed," but now, ten years after that agreement, they were held more firmly than ever in British possession. A reference to the map discloses the vice in which the maternal foe held her aspiring offspring. At the head of Lake Champlain, at Pointe-au-Fer and Dutchman's Bay, were stationed British forces that controlled the route from Vermont into Canada and northern New York. On the St. Lawrence the post of Oswegatchie dominated both banks of the St. Lawrence River. Forts Niagara and Oswego placed Lakes Erie and Ontario entirely within British domination. Detroit and Michilimackinac, then possessed by British redcoats, transformed Lakes Superior, Huron, and Michigan into exclusive British seas. Moreover, British plans contemplated the exclusion of the United States from all the territory north of the Ohio River. This expanse was to be converted into a so-called barrier state under British "protection," and was to be set aside as a happy hunting ground for Indian tribes, from which all Americans already settled were to be expelled and all ambitious new pioneers denied admission.

A great strip in western New York, comprising about half of the
present Empire State, was also to be sliced off and transformed
into British soil.   Part of the purpose of this plan was imperialistic,
its aim being to increase the British domain and strangle the
development of the American Republic; a more immediate end was
commercial, for this contemplated dominion would entirely surround the Lakes and the St. Lawrence, control the water system of
the Northwest, and ensure the permanent British possession of the
fur trade, then the greatest source of American wealth.

At the same time England was planning to oust decadent Spain
from the Mississippi River, including the territory to the west, and
install herself in Spain's place.   Thus the two great trade routes
into interior America, the Mississippi and the St. Lawrence, — and
water transportation was the only kind that mattered then, — as
well as the land north of the Ohio River and Louisiana, would
have become permanently British.   Besides this, British trade
policies had reduced the Atlantic states to commercial dependency.
Thus east, west, and north the new struggling Union could feel
destruction approaching.   Verily the work of the Revolution and
of the Constitutional Convention seemed about to be undone.   But
the British programme extended even further.   The likelihood that
the one-time colonies, or at least a portion of them, would drift
from Federal allegiance never ceased to preoccupy British statesmen.
The sad part of the story is that much encouragement was derived
from certain factions in the United States.   New England regarded
itself, from the standpoint of race, religion, political instincts, and
mores, as part of the ancient land.   Despite hostilities and hatreds
the innate feeling for Britain was strong.   Especially was Vermont's
enthusiasm for the Federal Union tepid.   Before 1791, when the
"New Hampshire grants" were finally erected into a state, the
"Green Mountain boys" were inclined to look upon their country
as an independent nation and were uncertain whether to join the
United States or to become a province of Canada.   A pro-British
party, including Ethan Allen himself, — once, at Ticonderoga, joint
spokesman of "the Continental Congress and the great Jehovah," —
actually sent a deputation to London to discuss a possible return
to the old allegiance.   The explanation for this strange action was
that "interest" which, as the realistic Washington had declared,
would determine whether sections would be loyal or disloyal to the
Constitution.   The prosaic fact is that it was much easier for the
"Vermontese" to transport their goods to market by way of Lake
Champlain, the Richelieu River, and the St. Lawrence, than across
the Green Mountains and deep-mired roads to Atlantic seaports.

Practical considerations like this frequently have more to do with the development of nations than political ideals.

All along the Appalachian border, from Vermont to Mississippi, similar forces were at work. In 1794 actual rebellion, to be presently described, broke out in western Pennsylvania. British intrigue was busily at work, attempting to separate Kentucky from the Union. That these plotters had a fertile soil was shown in the Virginia Constitutional Convention. The delegates from Kentucky, then a part of Virginia, were most outspoken against ratification; the new government, they feared, would pay little attention to the ultramontane country; there were no eastward transportation routes to the Atlantic and their economic future would lie with the nation — whether Spain, France, or England was not clear — that finally controlled the Mississippi River. The same situation prevailed in Tennessee and Mississippi.

And just as that "unimaginative leader" George Washington had foreseen these problems, so he proved to be the statesman who solved them. The matter entered the critical stage in 1794, and Washington, more than any force, reduced these separative tendencies to unity and saved the Constitution. In doing so he reached not only the highest peak of statesmanship, but of moral character; for he took the course before which smaller men quail — he faced an enraged multitude, steadfastly insisted on a policy that made him odious in the eyes of the populace, and never even momentarily swerved from the course on which, he was convinced, the future of the Union and of the Constitution hung. There is no intention to rehearse again in this place the story of Jay's Treaty; that exciting episode has been told many times. But it is essential to point out the issue involved in that contest. It was the fundamental one: Was the Constitution to survive? All the town meetings, parades, newspaper vilifications, tar-and-featherings, hangings in effigy, and other forms of argument that flourished in that discussion should not be permitted to obscure this fact. Had Jay's Treaty not been ratified, the United States would have ultimately lost her land beyond the Alleghenies and been cabined and confined to the thirteen states along the Atlantic fringe. The little new Republic — little, at least, in comparison with its present extent — would have been surrounded by a hostile England in the West, a hostile Spain and France beyond the Mississippi. Under these circumstances the new nation, subject to foreign plottings and domestic disturbances, would inevitably have been split up into smaller units, and finally absorbed by European powers. The Union and the Constitution would have vanished after a few brief inglorious years. The danger was dramatically

set forth in the House of Representatives by Fisher Ames, chief
orator on the Washington side, in the debate upon the treaty in
April 1795. The speech was the kind popular in a turgid age, and
Fisher's enfeebled condition gave it the essential touch of pathos.
Indeed his declaration caused almost as many tears to flow, almost as
many men to rage and women to faint, as Sheridan's harangue at
the impeachment of Warren Hastings. "Not a dry eye," John
Adams writes, "was in the House, except some of the jackasses who
had occasioned the necessity of the oratory. These . . . smiled
like Foulon's son-in-law, when they made him kiss his father's dead
and bleeding head." It was the tremulous speaker's final words
that brought the climax. "When I come to the moment of deciding
the vote I start back with dread from the edge of the pit into which
we are plunging. In my view even the minutes I have spent in
expostulation have their value, because they protract the crisis and
the short period in which alone we may resolve to escape it. Yet
I have perhaps as little personal interest in the event as anyone here.
There is, I believe, no member who will not think his chance to be
a witness of the consequences greater than mine. If, however,
the vote should pass to reject and a spirit should rise, as it will, with
the public disorders to make confusion worse confounded, even I,
slender and almost broken as my hold on life is, may outlive the
government and Constitution of my country."

That was the real matter at stake in Jay's Treaty — whether the
Constitution should vanish and the new nation dissolve into a multitude of parts. That was the reason Washington had sent John
Jay to London, and that was the reason why, obnoxious as in many
ways the treaty was, he put all the force of his character behind it.
Those who believe, as most historians now do, that the ratification
of the treaty saved the nation from impending destruction should
render thanks to Washington, for, without his determined support,
the measure would have failed. Few defenders as the treaty, on
its merits, has had, in 1795 or since, the fact remains that its alternative was war. And that war, at this time, would have meant
the dissolution of the United States and the fruition of Britain's
territorial plans is an unavoidable conclusion. Admiral Mahan has
said that the mere negotiation of a commercial treaty between the
United States and Great Britain was an "epochal event"; the attitude
which Britain maintained towards the infant nation is no matter
of pride to Americans to-day or of satisfaction to the descendants
of the England of that time.

The final change in her policy represented by Jay's Treaty signalized a new status for the despised Republic. So far as commercial advantages were concerned, little was gained. The chief complaint was that American ships did not secure free access to the British West Indies. The principle of "free ships free goods" was not acknowledged — in fact "the freedom of the seas" still represents an unrealized ideal in maritime warfare. Despite these and other disappointments the Jay Treaty obtained one concession of the utmost consequence — one that, in Washington's eyes, redeemed its most glaring defects. Britain surrendered the Western posts and thus secured American possession of its great estate. This clause made certain the development of the United States on its present lines, saved it from becoming a fringe of weak and helpless states along the Atlantic Coast, surrounded by encroaching nations on north and west, limited, for its western barrier, to the Allegheny Mountains, and dependent, for trade and prosperity, on such favors as its neighbors might vouchsafe. England has always had the annoying habit of settling herself, at strategic points, on the doorsteps of other nations, and already in American territory half a dozen little Gibraltars had been established, which were causing great trouble at the time and would have caused an infinity of trouble in the future. One startling surprise produced by reading these debates to-day is the general failure to appreciate the importance of the West. Only Washington and Hamilton, of our great men, saw far into the future. Madison, then a Representative in Congress, bitterly fought ratification. The only value of the Western country, he declared, was the fur trade. Jefferson, though destined in the Louisiana Purchase to become the greatest Western expansionist of them all, pillories Jay's Treaty as "an execrable thing," "an infamous act," "a treaty of alliance between England and the Anglo-men of this country," and called upon Congress to reject it as something not "to be quoted, or looked at or even mentioned." Events have justified the foresight of Washington and Jay, and dealt harshly with the prognostications of Jefferson and Madison. The Indians and their peltries have long since vanished from the Northwest, and in their place have developed such states as Ohio, Indiana, Illinois, Michigan, and Wisconsin, and such cities as Buffalo, Toledo, Detroit, and Chicago. What led Washington to accept the Jay Treaty was his conception of his country as a great nation; even injustice could be disregarded so long as the one great need of any nation, its territory, was made secure; whereas his fellow Virginians opposed the result because their minds had not encompassed this Nationalistic ideal.

V

And in this same year, 1794, the danger which Washington feared above all — of national disintegration — was concretely shown. And again it was his alertness and determination to protect the Constitution which prevented its success. Even while Jay was negotiating with Lord Grenville the treaty that was to put an end to separative tendencies in the West, the most formidable of many agitations of the kind had reached its height. This outbreak in the part of Pennsylvania which lies west of the Alleghenies has passed into history as the "Whiskey Rebellion," but this colloquial description conceals the importance of the issues at stake. For the Whiskey Rebellion concerned far more than what was then, in the West, the great national beverage. Above all, it had an important bearing upon the Federal Constitution. It was really a battle between the Democrats, as the followers of Jefferson and Jeffersonian ideas called themselves in Pennsylvania, and the Federalists, between the parties that would curb the Constitution, perhaps destroy it entirely, and those who would uphold it in all its strength. And the country involved comprised more than the four Western counties of Pennsylvania. That was merely the northernmost limit of a region of disaffection that included the land extending west of the Alleghenies and reaching as far south as Tennessee. This fertile valley, lying between two Appalachian ranges, is one of the most interesting in American annals. It was settled, much of it in the eighteenth century, by the Scotch-Irish race — a people who brought with them, in addition to the virtues of the pioneering spirit, many of the traits which had distinguished their forbears in the highlands of Scotland. Even to-day they are famous for their "feuds" — undoubtedly a survival of the animosities that characterized life in the old clans north of the Tweed. Like the Macgregors and Campbells of old, the highlanders of Pennsylvania, of the Shenandoah and the Watauga, were a fierce and independent people, a law unto themselves, not easily brought under the control of an external government, especially one so weak and distant as that formed by the Constitution. Any outside interference with their customs was fiercely resented. The life which these frontiersmen preferred was the life of the clan, making its own laws, enforcing its own elementary notions of justice, maintaining its own standards of conduct and morals. With the Hamiltonian system that established the United States on a firm economic basis this almost exotic section of America had little sympathy. Above all, the system embodied one provision that infuriated the whole country. To pay the national debt Congress had been forced to levy an excise on spirituous liquors. The exciseman had never been a popular figure in the highlands of Scotland, and his visits proved no more welcome in the corresponding precincts of the Western country where, even at the present writing, "moonshining" is not unknown. These mountaineers could not understand then, as, in many cases, their descendants cannot understand to-day, why they should not be permitted, unmolested by the tax gatherer, to distill their grain into a liquid which served them almost as a staff of life, and which was their chief export, as tobacco was in more civilized America. That they were thus contributing to the support of the new government made no impression on a people who had little interest in outside government of any kind. Thus, from 1791 to 1794, attempts to collect the excise in western Pennsylvania, Virginia, and North Carolina had caused an almost perpetual pandemonium.

Under the leadership of certain Democrats this opposition soon took on an Antifederal and anti-constitutional aspect. The Jeffersonians had made great progress in these border settlements, especially in western Pennsylvania. A conspicuous leader was a young Swiss immigrant, whose foreign accent while discussing American problems afterward was to enrage the advocates of "Americanism," but whose labors as Secretary of the Treasury were to place him high among American financiers and statesmen. Albert Gallatin's début in American politics was not so praiseworthy as his subsequent career. His sympathies naturally inclined to France in the dispute that was then ravaging Europe, and when, with the arrival of the French Minister Genêt, the United States was transformed into a battleground on the same issue, Gallatin joined that American party which championed the French side. The section in which he had settled, western Pennsylvania, offered promising opportunities for the exploitation of Francophile partisanship. The excise law had already aroused the whole region against the Federal government. Those "democratic societies" which were the bane of Washington's life, organized on the model of the

Jacobin Clubs of Paris, had here gained great ascendancy. But the spectacle of the sans-culottes of trans-Alleghenia, wearing the red cockade of revolution, dancing around Liberty poles, and holding hot disputations in the taprooms of taverns, was not pleasing to the pro-British Federalists of New England. For these societies, not only in Pennsylvania but in most parts of the nation, became bulwarks to the Jeffersonian party.

In western Pennsylvania the leader was David Bradford, who sought to combine the "whiskey boys" into an army directed not only against the payment of an unpopular tax, but against the Constitution and the new government. Bradford himself was not a person of much consequence; he was loud-talking, vain, given to cheap display, and, as it developed, cowardly; but he had the gift of representing all the disorderly and subversive influences that were rampant in an undisciplined country. That he was stirring up the mob against the Federal government was his boast, and his plan involved ideas upheld in more respectable quarters, such as the principle afterward widely acclaimed as state nullification of hated Federal laws. Secession from the Union, and the transformation of the four western counties of Pennsylvania into a little republic, under the protection of a European power, — that is, Great Britain, — also figured in his orations.

England was then seated in the military posts of the West, and that she would soon bring this whole country under her control Bradford took for granted. Just as the Vermont seceders of 1791 were debating whether to join themselves to a power that would furnish access to market, so the whiskey insurrectionists under Bradford were looking longingly to an alliance that would make available the great water highways of the Northwest, ultimately the Mississippi. Gallatin never sympathized with these extreme plans of separation, but in the early days of the whiskey disorders he participated in a scheme that gave his enemies a subject of recrimination for the rest of his days. In August 1792, at a meeting of protest in Pittsburgh, Gallatin had served on a committee of three which drew up resolutions advising the people to refuse payment of the excise, and to treat with contumely and resist the officers sent to collect. For this act, which indeed came pretty close to sedition, Gallatin afterward made a public apology, admitting that the resolution had been "violent, intemperate and reprehensible," and, when the disturbances attained really alarming proportions, he played a public-spirited part and exercised all his influence to reduce the country to quiet. For unhappily the people had promptly acted on the recommendations of this Pittsburgh meeting. For nearly two years the whiskey country was in a state of insurrection. Revenue collectors were assaulted and murdered; their houses and offices were burned; an army of 7000 malcontents had assembled at Braddock's Field to resist the Federal government, and finally Washington had been compelled to send a force of 15,000 men, under command of Light Horse Harry Lee, to reduce the district to submission. This it did without firing a shot, the embattled "whiskey boys" taking to the mountains at the first appearance of these well-equipped troops.

Jefferson and his party associates ridiculed Washington's whiskey army and the rebellion it had been sent to suppress. For such outbursts he had no condemnation. Occasional rebellions Jefferson had long regarded as desirable processes in a well-regulated republic. His comments on the performances of Daniel Shays have been frequently quoted. "I hold it that a little rebellion now and then is a good thing and as necessary in the political world as storms in the physical. . . . It is a medicine necessary for the sound health of government." These sentiments he expressed freely, once in a letter to a person so pious and well-behaved as Abigail Adams. And to Ezra Stiles, the president of Yale College, he had become even more graphic. "If the happiness of the mass of the people can be secured at the expense of a little tempest now and then, or even of a little blood, it will be a precious purchase." This was only one of many Jeffersonian opinions with which Washington had no sympathy. The President regarded the Pennsylvania outburst not as a "riot," as Jefferson called it, but as the test of a great constitutional question. The uprising kept Pennsylvania in a state of excitement for two years, during practically all of which time the authority of Congress had been defied. The "riots" were spreading into Maryland, Virginia, and North Carolina; unless they should be checked, Washington believed that the whole Western country would be in a blaze and that Federal power would be brought to an end. The contempt into which the "whiskey boys" were bringing the Constitution was the really appalling danger; unless they were subdued, the whole American people would lose respect for their government. A modern point of view is that of Edward Channing, who thinks the Whiskey Insurrection "was no unmixed evil, although it occurred at a very critical time in our relations with Great Britain, because it enabled the federal government to show its power and to prove that it was no mere rope of sand that could be easily dissolved." Washington expressed his apprehension when he asked several members of his cabinet for their opinions as to the proper course to be pursued. "The government can no longer be a passive spectator of the contempt by which the laws were treated," he said. Randolph, Secretary of State, was the only member of his cabinet who hesitated at armed suppression. This rather timorous adviser evidently believed that such action might have far-reaching consequences. "The moment is big with a crisis," he wrote Washington, "which would convulse the eldest government and if it shall burst upon ours, its extent and dominion can be but faintly conjectured." What was disturbing Randolph's peace was the same fear that haunted so many minds in the season of Jay's Treaty. Military operations against the insurrectionists, he warned Washington, might result in war with England and "a severance of the Union." The French Ambassador, Fauchet, in reporting to his government the mysterious behavior of Randolph at this time, gives an unforgettable picture of his distracted state. "All his countenance was grief," wrote Fauchet. "'It is all over!' he said to me. 'A civil war is about to ravage our unhappy country.'"

The very consideration that made Randolph hesitate was the one that impelled the President to effective action. The Constitution itself was in question. "Actual rebellion against the laws of the United States exists at this moment," he wrote Charles M. Thruston. "What may be the consequences of such violent and outrageous proceedings is painful in a high degree even in contemplation. But if the laws are to be trampled on with impunity and a minority (a small one too) is to dictate to the majority, there is an end put, at one stroke, to Republican government, and nothing but anarchy and confusion is to be expected hereafter. Some other man or society may dislike another law and oppose it with equal propriety until all laws are prostrate and everyone (the strongest I presume) will carve for himself." A letter to Henry Lee, commander of the expedition, contains a thrust at Jefferson and Madison, with whom the President's patience had been strained almost to the breaking point. "This insurrection is viewed with universal execration and abhorrence, except by those who have never missed an opportunity, by side blows or otherwise, to aim their shafts at the general government." "The real purpose," Washington wrote Lee, referring to the Democratic societies which he deemed responsible for the rebellion, was "to destroy the best fabric of human government and happiness that has ever been presented for the acceptance of mankind." In his proclamation Western troubles were described as the outcome "of combinations against the Constitution and laws of the United States," and he named the forces placed under Lee's command the "army of the Constitution."

These Democratic societies were one of the few phenomena that could disrupt Washington's placidity; they filled a position in his consciousness, indeed, not unlike that of the "monarchists" and "monocrats" in Jefferson's. He could not even keep them out of his address at the opening of the December session of Congress. The Western insurrection had been quelled; the leader, David Bradford, was in flight beyond the Mississippi; the collection of the excise was proceeding in orderly fashion; yet Washington believed that more disturbances of this sort were inevitable so long as the Jacobin Clubs instituted by Genêt existed. That such an organization had lately risen in South Carolina, named the "Madisonian," did not strike the President as a hopeful sign. "I should be sorry," he wrote Randolph, "if Mr. M——n from any cause *whatsoever* should get entangled with them on their politics." This aversion found place in Washington's speech opening the session of Congress in November 1794. After expressing satisfaction on the general happiness and prosperity, the President spoke of his regret "that some of the citizens of the United States have been found capable of insurrection." Chief blame was laid upon "combinations of men" who disregarded truth and "disseminated, from an ignorance or perversion of facts, suspicions, jealousies, and accusations of the whole government." For the successful riding of the storm "let praise be given to every description of citizen, but let [the people] persevere in their affectionate vigilance over that precious depository of American happiness, the Constitution of the United States. Let them cherish it too for the sake of those who, from every clime, are daily seeking a dwelling in our land."

VI

Both the excitement over Jay's Treaty and the Western insurrection brought Jefferson and Madison in opposition to Washington and his constitutional views; Jefferson, writing from Monticello, referred to Washington's attack on the "self-created societies" as "one of the extraordinary acts of boldness of which we have seen so many from the faction of monocrats" — a group in which he now apparently enrolled the President; while Madison, in the "debate on the address" in the House, attempted to have the obnoxious phrase eliminated. Other events, involving fundamental interpretations of the Constitution, drew the General and his one-time coworkers still further apart. Disagreement as to the nature of that document reached the critical point in the years 1798–1799, in the administration of John Adams. The doctrine that lay at the bottom of the Virginia and Kentucky Resolutions — papers that gave the course to American politics for the next seventy years — struck at the very root of the Federal government. It was the same question that had figured so generously in the Constitutional Convention — the one that had arraigned the little states against the big. Was the new plan organized like the Confederation of 1781? Was it, like the Continental Congress, a body in which the states had supreme power, or one which, for all Federal purposes, represented a "consolidated government"? That the outcome of the convention was a "consolidated" government, and not an association of independent and still sovereign states, was the claim of such men as Patrick Henry, George Mason, and Richard Henry Lee, who had opposed its adoption for that very reason. In that convention and in his papers in the *Federalist,* Madison had argued that it was a "national government" superior, along the lines in the Constitution itself, to the states. The specific question that puzzled the early generation and which, even after one hundred and fifty years of experience, arises now was: who shall decide whether laws passed by Congress are constitutional? That laws not authorized by the Federal Charter are null and void — on this point there has been no disagreement, in those days or at the present time; but the vital question still remained: who was to decide the question of constitutionality?

Such was the issue involved in those famous documents, the Virginia and Kentucky Resolutions. The purpose of proclamations was to magnify the state and cast down the general government; to deprive the Supreme Court of the right to decide constitutionality and to give it to the states. They involved also the principle of nullification that lay at the basis of the lethal philosophy of John C. Calhoun and of that secession which finally resulted in war. That Jefferson should have written the Kentucky Resolutions is not surprising, for they accorded well with his ideal of preëminent localism in government; that Madison should have written the Virginia Resolutions is not so understandable, for they made necessary a complete departure from his past. Both men had come much under the influence of a political scholar of the most authentic Virginia breed, who is not particularly well known to the present generation. John Taylor of Caroline was one of those Revolutionary characters, like Carroll of Carrollton and Daniel of St. Thomas Jenifer, whose names popularly carried territorial titles which seemed hardly in keeping with the rigid democratic principles for which they stood. Taylor was an ornament of the political and social existence of Caroline County, on the Rappahannock, the proprietor of a splendid estate cultivated by a multitude of slaves — or rather of several estates, for, like most of the contemporary Virginia advocates of simplicity in government, like Jefferson and Madison themselves, he was of the "landed interest" and came from the oldest Virginia lineage. Taylor fought in the Revolution, became a member of the Virginia House of Delegates, and succeeded Richard Henry Lee in the United States Senate, a body in which he figured for many years. It is not as a statesman, however, that John Taylor of Caroline is remembered — when he is remembered at all; he belonged to that class whom Virginians of his time liked to describe as "philosophers." As a "Plato" of government, he was the author of many expansive volumes, all setting forth, in most crabbed and un-Platonic style, those political theories which formed the groundwork, first of Jeffersonian State rights and afterwards of Calhoun's principles of nullification. Taylor's scheme of things outdistanced even Jefferson; in his latter phase, indeed, the philosopher of Caroline looked askance at the neighboring academies of Montpelier and Monticello. Centralization never had a more uncompromising foe. The dominance of the Supreme

Court on constitutional issues fairly embittered the man's life. To him New York and Massachusetts were "foreign nations"; John Marshall and John Adams, false prophets leading Americans to destruction. America's most odious political character, in Taylor's eye, was Alexander Hamilton. Funding, assumption, the bank, the excise, the national revenue based mainly upon a tariff, the Army, the Navy, and the Constitution itself, so long as it was interpreted as favoring a National or Federal government and not a "compact," were all noxious evils springing from the New Yorker. Such doctrines would lead to civil war! Jay's Treaty and practically all measures of the Washington and Adams administrations Taylor regarded as insidiously aimed to establish monarchy. Washington himself fell under the Taylor ban. He fought a Virginia resolution praising Washington's first administration and was pacified only when the word "country" was changed to "native state." He favored the secession of North Carolina and Virginia in 1798 and the creation of a separate republic, and when the rest of the Union refused to accept the Kentucky Resolutions he wrote Jefferson that he gave "up all for lost." Unless changes should be made in the Constitution to conform to his State-rights views "I will bid adieu to politics and eat my potatoes and cabbages, whatever king shall reign."

Taylor is an influential man in constitutional history, for he, more than any writer, controlled the mind of John C. Calhoun, and thus must be held responsible for a stirring epoch. Before this, however, he had gained a mastery over Jefferson. "Colonel Taylor and myself have rarely if ever," Jefferson wrote, "differed in any political principle of importance." And in 1798 these three statesmen — Madison, Jefferson, and Taylor — came to strike the harshest blow that had ever been leveled at the Constitution up to that time. In the summer Taylor and Jefferson spent much time together, consultations in which Madison must have joined, for Taylor many years afterward revealed, in a letter to Thomas Ritchie, a secret that had been previously kept under cover. "Mr. Madison wrote John Taylor's resolutions," he said, meaning the paper which he, as a member of the Virginia House of Delegates, had sponsored in that body.

The three men, Jefferson, Madison, and Taylor, formed the great triumvirate of State rights, and their literary labors were intended to usher in a new day. The crimes of New England were the measures that have passed into history as the Alien and Sedition Laws. More than anything else this legislation accounted for the political wreck of President John Adams, and destroyed, like a tornado, the once all-powerful Federal Party. The Alien Laws were passed in response to a public emotion that is not unfamiliar to the present generation. The nation was full of foreigners — in this case mostly Frenchmen — accused of plotting against American institutions and seeking to make Americans the slaves of foreign peoples. There was the great Volney, for example, ostensibly indulging in an American journey for purely botanical purposes; was his real aim in exploring the West to examine its flora and fauna, or was he seeking to stir up a separatist movement in the interest of France and its rising star, Napoleon Bonaparte? The remedy for such foreign incursions was the same that is proposed to-day: the "deportation" of such revolutionary characters. The Alien Laws gave the President power to ship out of the United States denizens of Europe whom he regarded as injurious to the nation. The Sedition Laws offended more seriously, for these seemed to strike at the freedom of the press and thus to violate the recently adopted and much cherished First Amendment. Particularly did the clause threatening direful things to the scribe writing disrespectfully of the President seem a faint harbinger of the coming Mussolini and Hitler.

Were these measures constitutional? Many doubted it, but the doubters proposed to solve that problem in different ways. This was precisely one of those cases, the constitutionalists urged, that had been foreseen by the Philadelphia Convention; and the question whether Mr. Adams's pet measures conflicted with the Federal Charter could properly be referred to the courts. But Jefferson, Madison, and Taylor believed that this issue gave an ideal opportunity for their views on constitutional interpretation. All this was before the time of John Marshall, and before the Supreme Court had set aside a law of Congress as violation of the basic charter. Had the protesting trio succeeded in their aim, a principle would thus have been introduced contrary to that established by the great Chief Justice. The Jefferson-Madison-Taylor pronouncements asserted that the states, in their legislatures or in conventions called for the purpose, could determine the constitutionality of acts of Congress. The idea had many variations: Jefferson took the extreme stand that each state, all by itself, could nullify a Federal law, which then, so far as that state was concerned, became "void." Madison did not go quite so far; he declared that a state could "interpose" when a law seemed to contravene the "compact," but precisely what form that "interposition" should take was not specified.

Taylor, of course, went to the Jeffersonian extreme. Much has been written about the Virginia and Kentucky Resolutions, but these were the points at issue. Madison, in his latter period, when Calhoun took up the nullification idea, attempted to explain away his Virginia Resolutions and to prove that they implied something different from nullification, but in this he never succeeded. The father of the Constitution was also one of the men who sowed the seeds of secession and civil war.

John Taylor of Caroline resigned his seat in the United States Senate in order to enter the Virginia House of Delegates and press the new doctrine. For Kentucky an equally aggressive, but less "philosophic" spokesman was selected. This was a member of the famous Nicholas family of Virginia — a son of that Robert Carter Nicholas who was for years head of the Virginia bar, a reluctant adherent of revolution, and an opponent of Jefferson in many of his reforms. The elder Nicholas died in 1780, and his widow moved with her family to Albemarle County, not far from Monticello; thus the talented sons came under the influence of Jefferson, whose Declaration of Independence the father had refused to sign. Two of these sons, Wilson Cary and George, were enlisted in the Jefferson service at the crisis of the Virginia and Kentucky Resolutions. The whole proceeding illustrated one of Jefferson's least desirable characteristics — his fondness for working anonymously. His correspondence on this subject with the Nicholas brothers, outlining the plan, cautions the utmost secrecy, his associates even being enjoined to burn his letters. Nor was Jefferson's agent in the Kentucky legislature so honorable a figure as the John Taylor who represented Madison at Richmond. George Nicholas had already served an apprenticeship in secession. The freedom from restraint that seems a natural part of the frontier spirit had already led him into schemes antagonistic to the federated power; in particular he had become involved in the last plot of Spanish intriguers to detach Kentucky from the Union and affiliate it with the Spanish Empire. The bait, as always, was the navigation of the Mississippi River, plus a cash consideration of $100,000 and reimbursement of such emoluments as might be lost by departure from American loyalty. Nicholas and his crowd, in the words of the Spanish Governor Carondelet, were "immediately to exert all their influence on impressing on the minds of the western country a conviction of the necessity of withdrawing themselves from the Federal Union and forming an independent government." It was this Nicholas and his brother Wilson Cary who, with Jefferson, led the Kentucky contingent supporting the Kentucky Resolutions. The man selected to serve as personal spokesman in the legislature, John Breckenridge, was of more moderate views than either Jefferson or Nicholas. The form in which the pronouncement was handed Breckenridge proved too strong meat for his more Unionist soul. The Jeffersonian draft, declaring "null and void" several acts of Congress, including the Alien and Sedition Laws, was much toned down. Instead of asserting in so many words the principle of unabashed nullification, the censored Kentucky Resolves merely called upon Kentucky's Senators and Representatives to "use their best endeavors" at the next session of Congress to secure their repeal. But the other states to which the Resolutions had been sent for concurrence understood the real motive at work. Not another commonwealth joined in this interpretation of the Constitution. South Carolina and Georgia never replied to the Kentucky-Virginia invitation, and others sent refusals of varying emphasis. But an idea completely destructive of the Constitution had been introduced into American politics.

This effort to weaken the Constitution served at least one good purpose, for it gave Washington a final opportunity to testify his allegiance to that instrument. The Kentucky and Virginia Resolutions also brought another early patriot to Washington's side — that Patrick Henry who had refused to attend the Constitutional Convention and had nearly persuaded Virginia not to ratify its achievement. Modern writers who enjoy picturing Patrick Henry as a foe of the Constitution overlook the last days of his life when he threw himself upon its side and, with his virtually dying breath, called on all good Americans to come to its support.

As was to be expected, Washington, now spending his last year at Mount Vernon, saw the danger. He had already parted with Jefferson. The letter Jefferson had written Philip Mazzei in 1796 was published in 1797. In this Jefferson pictured the veteran of Yorktown as one of those monarchists who were seeking to bind the nation to Great Britain. Never had Jefferson exercised his "felicity" at phrase-making so disastrously. One can imagine Washington's feelings as he read the lines that were destined to a wretched immortality: "It would give you a fever were I to name you the apostates who have gone over to these heresies,[1] men who were Samsons in the field and Solomons in the council, but who have had their heads shorn by the harlot England." Washington never wrote or spoke to Jefferson after reading that sentence. But

[1] That is, the advocates of monarchical rule.

there came one solace in these final years in a new companionship with Patrick Henry. The last episode in the lives of these two great Revolutionists discloses them ranged side by side in opposition to the Jefferson-Madison programme of nullification. Patrick Henry's hostility to the "new plan" underwent a change as a result of its administration under Washington. All the dreadful consequences of adoption that Henry had foreseen in the Virginia Convention had not come true. The President had not been transformed into a Nero, or even into a "Polish king"; America had entered on a new period of prosperity; nor had liberty vanished from the land. The adoption of the first ten amendments had done much to reconcile Henry to the "new form." The affectionate and loyal man was also much offended by the attacks of Jeffersonians on his old Virginia friend, and he detested the Democratic societies as cordially as did Washington himself. Though many attempts, engineered by Light Horse Harry Lee, to attach the orator officially to the Washington administration failed, — "Most assiduous court is paid to Patrick Henry," wrote Jefferson to Monroe; "he has been offered everything they knew he would not accept," — the declinations were framed in words that disclosed a most friendly attitude towards the Federal Party. "I should be unworthy of the character of a Republican," Henry wrote, October 16, 1795, refusing to become Secretary of State, "if I withheld from the government my best and most zealous efforts because in its adoption I opposed it in its unamended form. And I do most cordially execrate the conduct of those men who lose sight of the public interest from personal motives." Though unable, from ill-health and advancing years, to accept a post, a crisis might arrive, he intimated in a letter written in 1795, that would call him again into public service. "If my country is destined in my day to encounter the horrors of anarchy, every power of body and mind which I possess will be exerted in support of the government under which I live and which has been fully sanctioned by my countrymen."

"The horrors of anarchy," Washington believed, would be the necessary outcome of the Virginia and Kentucky Resolutions. That the Antifederal forces would bring them forward again in the next session of the Virginia House of Delegates was well understood. In searching for ways of circumventing the enemy, Washington's mind turned to this promise made by Patrick Henry three years before. Here was his chance to redeem it. On the fifteenth of January, 1799, Washington therefore wrote Henry one of the most vigorous letters of his life, and one of the most denunciatory. It was a fierce arraignment of the Jefferson party and its attempt to emasculate the Constitution. "It would be a waste of time," the letter began, "to attempt to bring to the view of a person of your observation and discernment the endeavors of a certain party among us to disquiet the public mind with unfounded alarms — to arraign every act of the administration — to set the people at variance with the government — and to embarrass all its measures. Equally useless would it be to predict what must be the inevitable consequences of such a policy, if it cannot be arrested." What a spectacle, Washington said, their Virginia then represented! Their delegates in the state legislature and in Congress were seeking to destroy the Union! "Torturing every act of their government by constructions they will not bear, into attempts to infringe and trample upon the Constitution with a view to introduce monarchy!" "When measures are systematically and pertinaciously pursued, which must eventually dissolve the Union . . . ought characters who are best able to rescue their country from the pending evil to remain at home? Rather, ought they not to come forward, and by their talents and influence, stand in the breach which such conduct has made in the peace and happiness of this country and oppose the widening of it?" Therefore, would not Patrick Henry stand as candidate for the Virginia General Assembly at the coming elections so that, on the floor, he could fight these measures? "My fears that the tranquillity of the Union is hastening to an awful crisis" was Washington's explanation for making this appeal to a man who, as all Virginians knew, was then on the brink of the grave.

The response to this appeal came at Charlotte Courthouse in early March, 1799. A huge crowd gathered, for Patrick Henry had announced that he would address his fellow citizens on that day. After declining to be Secretary of State and Chief Justice of the United States, he had acceded to Washington's request, and was about to ask his neighbors to elect him to the state legislature. Excitement was intense, for Madison, William Giles, John Taylor, and George Nicholas, knowing what a struggle this portended at Richmond, had announced their candidacies, in order to pit their united strength against the man whom Jefferson had described as "the greatest orator who ever lived." The hero worship bestowed by the crowd on Henry that morning indicated the importance of his intercession. When the speaker arose, his weakness was manifest. His face was colorless and careworn, his whole frame shaky, his voice, at the beginning, cracked and tremulous.

In a few minutes, however, the Henry of the old Virginia House of Burgesses sprang from this emaciated shell. The Virginia and Kentucky Resolutions were denounced with all the vehemence that had once been visited on King George. These proceedings filled him "with apprehension and alarm . . . they had planted thorns upon his pillow . . . the state had quitted the sphere in which she had been placed by the Constitution . . . in daring to pronounce upon the validity of Federal laws she had gone out of her jurisdiction." All the old-time gesticulations were once more pressed into service. Just as, in the Richmond speech of 1775, Henry had dropped on his knees, raised his palms to heaven, and cried, "Give me liberty or give me death," so now again he clasped his hands and waved his body back and forth, the audience unconsciously swaying in unison. "Let us trust God," Henry declaimed, "and our better judgment to set us right hereafter. United we stand, divided we fall. Let us not split into factions which must destroy that union upon which our existence hangs." Charlotte Courthouse, where this speech was made, is situated less than thirty miles from Appomattox, and from this spot, seventy years afterward, were heard the guns that forced Lee's surrender. Patrick Henry seemed to have divined all this as the inescapable outcome of the Virginia Resolutions. "Such opposition on the part of Virginia" — this was his parting message to his countrymen — "to the acts of the general government must beget their enforcement by military power," and this would produce "civil war."

At the end of his oration, Henry literally fell into the arms of bystanders and was carried almost lifeless into a near-by tavern. Two months afterward he was dead. He was overwhelmingly elected to the House of Delegates, but was never able to take his seat. And Washington, in December, also died. Thus the last act of these two leaders of 1776 was a joint effort to preserve the Constitution. Washington's final word was not so sensational as Henry's, for his style of writing and speaking was less impassioned, but it was as emphatically to the point. The injunction is found in his farewell address. "You have improved upon your first essay, by the adoption of a Constitution of Government, better calculated than your former for an intimate Union and for the efficacious management of your common concerns. This government, the offspring of your own choice, uninfluenced and unawed, adopted upon full investigation and mature deliberation, completely free in its principles, in the distribution of its powers, uniting security with energy, and containing within itself a provision for its own amendment, has a just claim to your confidence and your support. Respect for its authority, acquiescence in its measures are duties enjoined by the fundamental maxims of true Liberty. . . . The Constitution which at any time exists till changed by an authentic and explicit act of the whole people, is obligatory on all. . . . Let there be no change by usurpation; for though this, in one instance, may be the instrument of good, it is the customary weapon by which free governments are *destroyed*."

VII

So far this narrative has been rehearsing the several attempts to modify or destroy the Constitution that had their origins in the West and South. But it is doubtful whether these regions were the greatest sinners. The true birthplace of secession was not the land of the Cavalier but of the Puritan. The period from 1789 to 1800 was the time of Northern ascendancy in the Union. Washington, as President, represented New England ideals rather than Virginian, and it is likely that he was more popular in the land of Hamilton and John Adams than in that of Jefferson and Madison. During this period, therefore, New England remained loyal to the national government. But the Jeffersonian era, beginning in 1801, brought in a new day. Then, according to the gospel of the new President, the American Republic was founded. The principles of his own Declaration of Independence, trampled on by the monocrats and aristocrats of the Washington and Adams administrations, were at last to become the foundation stones of a new nation. But the Northern section did not interpret events this way. To the Federalists of New England the triumph of Jefferson in 1800 was as odious as was the election of Abraham Lincoln to the South in 1860, and in the minds of extreme Federalists Jefferson's inauguration seemed to justify secession from the Union, just as did Lincoln's to the deep South in 1861. The most orthodox exemplars of New Englandism regarded this modern Marat and Robespierre (for these were the mildest of the names affixed to Jefferson) as embodying every political ideal, every principle of conduct, which was repellent to respectable government. New England divines searched the Old Testament for odious characters with whom their President could be compared; they assailed his deism, his democratic theories, his so-called demagogic political methods, his constant advocacy of the supremacy in statecraft of the masses, his hostility to England and partiality for France. His whole conception of economics and government was felt in New England as not only a political but a personal affront.

It is hard to say whether New England esteemed as more atrocious Jefferson's friendly attitude towards Tom Paine or his ceaseless preachings on the superiority of the agricultural life and the degrading influence of manufactures and commerce. For Jefferson's whole conception of ward-republics, deriving their sustenance directly from the soil and subsisting with as little government as could be endured, ran foul of the New England system. His rather condescending reference in the first inaugural address — intended to conciliate the North as well as the South — to "the encouragement of agriculture and of commerce as its handmaid" caused fierce resentment in every New England town. Commerce as merely the handmaid of agriculture! New England shipping respectable only as a means of transporting Virginia tobacco to its European market! The new President could not have hit New England in a more sensitive spot. If there was anything of which this Northern promontory of the American continent was proud, it was her seamen and her ships. New England yards were turning out the most beautiful sloops, schooners, and brigs then sailing the seas, and her mariners were already famous for the hardiness and skill that, in the War of 1812, made them the superiors of British tars. Even so acrid a soul as Timothy Pickering could become fairly poetic in his references to New England, "whose farms are on the ocean and whose harvests are gathered in every sea."

Virginians who thought of their state as the indisputable Paradise of America were at times astonished to discover that New England was even more arrogantly convinced of her preëminence. John Adams, observing his surroundings during the first Continental Congress in Philadelphia, commented that this city, after all, "was not Boston. The morals of our people are much better; their manners are more polite and agreeable; they are purer English; our language is better; our taste is better; our persons are handsomer; our spirit is greater, our laws are wiser, our religion is superior, our education is better." There spoke New England. A generation later, George Cabot, who regarded popular rule anywhere as the negation of nature, did not believe that it could succeed "even in New England where there is among the body of the people more wisdom and virtue than in any other part of the United States." And this was the underlying reason why New England's "wise and good" distrusted Jefferson. He was the preacher of democracy, of the rule of the majority. Cabot called him an "anarchist," a disbeliever in government of any kind. That he had "sold" the American nation to the French, that he received the British

Minister dressed in dirty corduroy breeches and slippers minus heels, that at state banquets the rule of pell-mell existed and guests were not seated according to rank, that he opposed building a navy and organizing an army, even that his maritime policy reduced the North to utter ruin — these were serious offenses but, after all, minor vices. The real Jeffersonian crime was popular rule. "We are full of errors," to quote again George Cabot, "which no reasoning could eradicate if there were a Lycurgus in every village. We are democratic altogether and I hold democracy in its natural operation to be the government of the worst."

Such was the scourge, in the judgment of the Ultrafederalists of New England, that Jefferson had substituted for the happy rule of Washington. So hopeless did Cabot and his kind regard the Republic that they thought it useless to attempt any improvement. Let Democracy — or Jeffersonism, the same thing — run its rake's progress, and bring to America the political and social chaos it had brought to other countries; then "the wise and the good and the rich" would be called upon to piece together again the fragments of a nation. But there were more impatient souls who advocated immediate action. From 1804 to 1815 these prophets made no less than four aggressive attempts to destroy the Constitution, to separate the Northern and Eastern states from that body of death, the Federal Union, and to organize a New England Confederacy. The man who most completely embodied this determination was that Timothy Pickering whose apostrophe to New England commerce is quoted above. Pickering was not only the most inveterate champion of disunion, — no Southern fire-eater in 1860 quite approached the fervor of his antagonism to the central government, — but by far the ablest. To the present generation he seems an unpleasant figure, full of that sectional prejudice which disfigures the most worthy character, — "the hatred of Pickering for Jefferson," says Henry Adams, "was the hatred of Cotton Mather for a witch," — yet this should not make us blind to the integrity of his nature or the sincerity of his motives. For Pickering represented the Puritan character in its best as well as in its least attractive aspects. His hostility to the Constitution as it stood was a conviction religious in its depth and zeal. To eliminate it as the bond of sections that should never have been united he regarded as a lofty form of patriotism. Pickering was a religious man, and that Puritan conception of life as merely a transitory affair, a period of probation for the hereafter, was his rule of conduct. He also shared the Puritan's ill opinion of the human race and personal responsibility for its chastisement and reformation. "How little virtue," he would exclaim, "is there among mankind?" It was the deism of the French Revolution that made it in Pickering's estimation a shameless and evil thing, and its American supporters, among whom were classed Jefferson, Gallatin, and their Democratic followers, were regarded as despoilers with whom New England should have no fraternity. The call to arms against them was thus a call to war against Satan. Pickering's chief argument for secession naturally was drawn from Scripture: "Wherefore come out from among them" — this quotation was constantly on his lips — "and be ye separate, saith the Lord, and touch not the unclean thing." And Pickering's devotion to New England was all a part of this Puritan fervor. The descendant of frugal but educated New Englanders, the man had absorbed the directness of speech and action, the ability to struggle best when faced with difficulties, the adherence to principle and the disregard of amenity, and the taste for hard work which seemed inherent in New England soil. And his feeling for his region — or his "country" as he called it — was like that of Oliver Ellsworth, already quoted. Shocked at proceedings in other states, he comments: "Such events would not have happened in New England." He made no profession of being, first of all, an American. His allegiance was frankly sectional. He once arranged his loyalties of location in precise regimentation: "Not that every part of the Union is alike to me; my affections still flow in what you will deem their natural order — towards Salem, Massachusetts, New England, the Union at large." "His mental outlook," one commentator says, "was always that of a citizen of Salem, facing the ocean."

In appearance, as well as in the directness of his conversation, Pickering was all New England. His dislike of pretense and artificiality is evident in his portrait, one of the finest achievements of Gilbert Stuart. "While all sorts of people are greased with pomatum and whitened with powder," he remarked, "my bald head and lank locks remain in *statu quo.*" This is the figure that looks out from the Stuart canvas, and with it should be coupled that of Pickering's wife, dignified, erect, her thin-featured, narrow face gazing almost winsomely beneath the white lace cap, the whole full of gentleness and character. Pickering himself is a more formidable portent, with high forehead, long, sharp, Roman nose, severe, questioning, and doubtful eyes, seeming to search his observer for those evil qualities he regarded as the inheritance no man could escape. The long narrow face, tight-shut lips, sharp-pointed chin, and sombre dress strengthen the impression.   Here was a man who, as Secretary of State, — a post to which he would seem ill-adapted, for a less diplomatic person never lived, — would not hesitate to call His Catholic Majesty's Minister to the United States a "Spanish puppy," to send home gleefully the romantic, intriguing Adet, representative of the French Republic, and to write the most humiliating reprimand to James Monroe, American Minister in France, for the kiss and hug he had so rapturously received from the monsters of the French Revolution.   This quality of forthrightness was perhaps the thing that made Pickering a favorite with a man of very dissimilar attributes.   But Washington had tested this Yankee admirer under severe conditions.   Recently graduated from Harvard, the young man had entered zestfully into the Stamp Tax disputation with England, distinguishing himself as drafter of petitions and pamphleteer; and from literary labors he joined the army at the first sign of warfare.   He fought with Washington at Long Island, White Plains, and in the campaign in the Jerseys, his abilities so impressing the Commander in Chief that he was appointed Adjutant General.   Pickering's skill in scraping together food and tents for men and fodder for horses at Valley Forge, and afterward for the Yorktown campaign, were precisely the traits that made the Puritan dear to Washington, who was more amused than offended by his less engaging personal traits.

After the war Washington was therefore glad to welcome Pickering into his administration as co-worker.   Here his honesty of character and justice made him a favorite with a part of the population who were excellent judges of such traits, the Indian tribes, for whom he became the favorite negotiator.   The same quality appeared when, almost alone among Revolutionary patriots, he protested against the treatment measured out to loyalists.   Washington made him Postmaster General in 1791, — at that time not a cabinet office, — advanced him to Secretary of War in 1795, and — much against Pickering's will — to Secretary of State on the downfall of Randolph.   In all the disturbing events from 1791 to 1800 — Jay's Treaty, the cavortings of Citizen Genêt, the Jefferson-Hamilton feud, French and British piracies upon American commerce, diplomatic imbroglios with the French Directory, the resulting war with France in 1798, the Alien and Sedition Laws — Pickering proved one of the strongest pillars to the Federal cause. At an early date he identified himself with the Hamilton wing, accepting all the Hamiltonian measures and all the fundamental Hamilton doctrines.   Nothing so incensed his irascible temper as the enhancement of French prestige in the United States. He was convinced — and in this the facts were probably on his side — that the incorporation of America in the Bonapartist system was part of the French imperial policy. Just as the conqueror had seized Holland, Spain, Switzerland, and a large part of Germany and Italy, and converted them into agencies for winning the mastery of the world, so the United States, unless it resisted successfully the Francophile influences at work, would become another subject province. It was on this issue that Pickering turned against John Adams, in whose cabinet also he served as Secretary of State. He had never liked Adams and opposed him openly even while a member of his cabinet, but when Adams, after maintaining for two years a hostile attitude to France, suddenly changed his policy, sent an embassy to the Directory, and did this without consulting his cabinet, — even his Secretary of State, — Pickering made warfare against his chief with all the violence of his nature. Adams, in his own phrase, "discharged" his Secretary of State, who immediately joined Hamilton in the movement to defeat the President for reëlection. These two men were thus largely responsible for the break-up of the Federal Party and the triumph of Jefferson.

In all this much could be said for Pickering's point of view, but he soon passed into activities that were subversive and, in fact, bordered on treason. That Massachusetts did not resent his fight against Adams became apparent in 1804, when Pickering was elected United States Senator — a seat he occupied until 1812. These eight years were occupied largely in assaults upon the Constitution and the Union. The mere circumstance that by splitting the Federalist Party he had become responsible for the advent of Jefferson did not diminish Pickering's loathing for this "unclean thing." There was only one way, he insisted, by which salvation could be attained. New England, perhaps in association with New York and Pennsylvania, should sever the bonds that united her with the Jeffersonian South. Thus Washington's chief anxiety for his country, its division into small confederacies, came to realization in the plans of one of his favorite statesmen. Pickering's letters disclose that, in advocating a New England republic, he was thinking mainly of New England's soul. Only by cutting itself loose from the Jacobins could his native "country" preserve its greatest treasures, "its religion and its morals." The matter came to a crisis in 1804, after the purchase of Louisiana. Most Americans to-day see in this tremendous coup of Jefferson his greatest achievement as a statesman; and as we complacently regard the thirteen prosperous

American states that have been carved from the domain, we can hardly understand the hostility the purchase aroused in New England. But to the constitutionalists of Boston the acquisition of Louisiana meant the dissolution of the Union. The Constitution, they insisted, was an agreement adopted by the people who occupied the territory as it existed in 1787; the acquisition of a new empire — for Louisiana was greater in extent than the whole American domain of 1787 — not only violated, but brought to an end the compact. This view received its most memorable expression in 1811, when a bill was introduced to admit a small section of the purchase as the State of Louisiana. In the ensuing debate Josiah Quincy, Representative from Massachusetts, afterward president of Harvard, startled his hearers with a declaration which had been the conservative New England view since 1803. "If this bill passes," he said, "it is my deliberate opinion that it is virtually a dissolution of the Union; that it will free the states from their moral obligation; and, as it will be the right of all, so it will be the duty of some, definitely to prepare for a separation, — amicably if they can, violently if they must."

The Federalists based their antagonism to Louisiana on what to-day seems a fantastic contention — that the Constitution comprised only the American territory of 1787. The fact is that they had unquestionable grounds for pleading unconstitutionality in the specific terms of that document itself. There is no question that the purchase, with its agreement to admit the citizens of Louisiana to American citizenship and to incorporate the province as an American state, was without specific constitutional warrant. The contented inhabitants of present-day Iowa, Nebraska, the Dakotas, and indeed all the states of trans-Mississippi America, little realize that their standing as American citizens runs foul of the much valued Tenth Amendment. "The powers not delegated to the United States by the Constitution, nor prohibited by it to the States, are reserved to the States respectively, or to the people." Nothing is more certain than that the Constitution "delegates" no power to the Federal government to acquire foreign territory. One of the fascinating aspects of Jefferson's mind was its complexity and its ability to disregard a profoundly held philosophy when practical contingencies arose; this resiliency was one of the elements in his greatness; and not the least of the contradictions his career presents is that the strict constitutionalist should have violated, on a scale unknown then or since, its hard-and-fast stipulations. He recognized this fact himself, said again and again that the purchase of Louisiana was unconstitutional, and almost abjectly pleaded with the American people to adopt an amendment that would make the transaction legal. But no such amendment was adopted, and the power to acquire extrinsic territory, afterward exercised in land obtained from Mexico, in the purchase of Alaska and Hawaii and the conquest of the Philippines, must be regarded as part of that unwritten American constitution which has grown up, by precedent and acts of Congress, alongside the formal document.

It is unlikely, however, that constitutional difficulties formed the real reason for New England's resistance. The Louisiana territory was obnoxious for definite New England reasons. Had Jefferson, instead of purchasing Louisiana from the French, purchased Canada from the British, there would have been no perturbation in Hartford or Boston. The real objection was that the purchase of Louisiana was a Southern measure and that it would vastly enhance the political strength of the South and thus unsettle the American "balance of power." Out of it New England could already perceive a dozen states created — states that would be exploited by Southern planters and their slaves, each possessing two votes in the Senate and corresponding power in the Electoral College. The result would be a perpetual Virginia majority in Congress and an unassailable Virginia dynasty in the White House. The fires of abolitionism were already beginning to flame in the North. That compromise, without which there could have been no Constitution, giving three fifths of the slaves representation in Congress was working like a poison. By 1804 there were fifteen members of the Lower House whose constituents were those whom the Constitution calls "other persons" — that is, negro slaves. This was what Pickering meant when he declaimed against "negro Presidents and negro congressmen"; was the North to submit to new states that would steadily add to this kind of representation? To such a nation Pickering and his sympathizers had no desire to belong. New England and the North had never displayed much interest in the Mississippi; their ships had unbounded access to the sea without sailing a thousand miles of a murky and tortuous river! Uriah Tracy, Senator from Connecticut, echoed the prevailing New England opinion when he opposed the acquisition of Louisiana as "vicious," adding that "this would be absorbing the northern states and rendering them as insignificant in the Union as they ought to be if by their own consent the measure should be adopted." Thus Pickering had plenty of material for the proposed revolution that was taking shape in his mind. The New England masses were not so excited, but that did not greatly matter; they had no right to busy themselves in momentous issues; what was important was that the "wise, the good and the rich" regarded the time as ripe. To a degree Pickering did not exaggerate the case. Most of the great men of New England, at least those in high office, except John Quincy Adams, were numbered among the secessionists. Both the Connecticut Senators, James Hillhouse and Uriah Tracy, and the most important Connecticut Congressman, Roger Griswold, were deep in what it is no exaggeration to call the "plot." Senator Plumer of New Hampshire, though he afterward did penance for "the greatest mistake of my life," was secretly among the conspirators. He has left on record an account of an evening walk in the environs of Washington with Pickering, when that Catiline of the Puritan gentry guardedly broached the subject. "He thought," Plumer quotes Pickering as saying, "the United States were too large and their interests too variant, for the Union to continue long, and that New England, New York and perhaps Pennsylvania might and ought to form a separate government. He then paused and looking me fully in the face awaited my reply."

Before Plumer's eyes rose the figure of the American who had been largely the engineer of the Constitution. "Was not the division of the states," he asked, "the object which General Washington had most pathetically warned the people to oppose?"

"Yes," answered Pickering, "the fear of it was a ghost that for a long time haunted the imagination of that old gentleman."

But certain of the "best and wisest" Pickering did not draw into his net. The ultra-conservative Essex Junto did not favor his plan. George Cabot believed that separation would be a desirable change but that it did not hit the really grievous evil. The enemy was Democracy — the rule of the worst! Destroy that and New England's troubles would be over! Cabot lacked the deadly seriousness of Pickering and looked upon his efforts with an airy and amiable cynicism. "Why can't you and I," he said, "let the world ruin itself in its own way?"

But Pickering found more aggressive opposition in another quarter. In his mind the adhesion of New York State was essential to success. New York was no longer placed among the "small states" as it had been in the Constitutional Convention, and indications were plentiful enough in 1804 that at an early day it would become the largest and richest of all. Moreover, the leader of the Federalist Party in New York was also its leader in the nation — more than any man its founder; and although Hamilton had retired from public life in 1795 he had maintained an ascendancy not only in Federalist councils, but in the administration of Washington and, until the great schism arose, in that of John Adams. His contempt for Jeffersonian principles and his antagonism to unmitigated majority rule were things of which he made no secret. That Hamilton's personal ambition was unbounded there had been signs in plenty; he had been made — after a prolonged party squabble — second in command to Washington in the projected military operations against France, and had been disappointed in his desire for military glory, with consequent political aggrandizement, when John Adams truckled — so it was called — to Bonaparte. The Pickering crowd had therefore confidently decided on Hamilton as the leader of such military adventures as their plan might entail. But they had mistaken their man. Hateful as the Jeffersonian system was to Hamilton, his emotion had not reached the height of treason. That he looked upon the whole plot as a harebrained conception, necessarily doomed to failure, may be assumed; yet the main fact was that Hamilton's loyalty to the Union which he had done so much to establish was unassailable. All approaches from the Pickering cohorts, therefore, were received coldly. "The session of Congress closed on the 4th of March, 1804," wrote reminiscent John Quincy Adams in 1828, "and I shortly afterwards returned to spend the summer at my father's residence at Quincy. On my way thither I was detained several days in New York, during which I frequently visited Mr. Rufus King, who had then recently returned from his first mission to England. On the 8th of April I called and passed a great part of the evening with him in his library. I found there, sitting with him, Mr. Timothy Pickering, who, shortly after I went in, took leave and withdrew. As he left the house, Mr. King said to me, 'Colonel Pickering has been talking to me about a project they have for a separation of the states and a northern Confederacy; and he has also been this day talking of it with General Hamilton. Have you heard anything of it in Washington?' I said I had, much, but not from Colonel Pickering. 'Well,' said Mr. King, 'I disapprove entirely of the project; and so, I am happy to tell you, does General Hamilton.' I told Mr. King that I rejoiced to hear that was his opinion; and was equally gratified to learn that it was that of General Hamilton; that I was utterly averse to the project itself and much concerned at the countenance I had heard it was receiving at Connecticut and at Boston. It was the acquisition of Louisiana which had been the immediate incentive to the plan."

Failing to entice Hamilton into their scheme, the Pickering

conspirators now resorted to an alliance that indicated the despera-
tion of their cause. They turned, for a leader, to Hamilton's great
enemy, Aaron Burr. Though Burr was a Democrat, ostensibly a
member of the Clinton machine in New York, and at that time Vice
President of the United States, the Yankee disunionists selected him
as the most available man to head the Federalists in New York in a
secession movement. Burr had indeed become a political mendicant,
a man who had reached the end of his tether so far as political
preferment from the Democrats was concerned, and was prepared to
accept any new allegiance that would give scope to his restless and
unscrupulous ambition. And so he eagerly accepted the invitation
to head the separatists. His mind fairly leaped to the grandiose
plan. Why not make an arrangement with Great Britain and add
the Canadian provinces to the new confederacy? Why not revive
the several plots for the secession of trans-Alleghenia and give his
Northern republic this vast area for expansion? Roger Griswold
wrote to Oliver Wolcott that the "views" of Colonel Burr "extend
much beyond the office of Governor of New York. He has the
spirit of ambition and revenge to gratify and can do but little with
his 'little band' alone." This sentence discloses the details of the
Burr-Pickering programme: it was to make Burr the Federalist
candidate for governor of New York; his election — which was
fatuously taken for granted — was expected to redeem him as a
political force and fortify the leadership necessary to success in the
larger enterprise. But the result proved a disappointment.

Hamilton, disgusted both with the onslaught on the Constitution
and by the elevation of a discredited Jeffersonian to the command
of the Federal Party, exerted all his influence against Burr's election.
But it was the common man who really destroyed the scheme. The
outcome proved that the rank and file whom Pickering so despised
were still faithful to the Federal government. The projected rebellion was an exclusive affair; its membership was limited to the
aristocracy, and a rather small segment of that. "I do not know one
reflecting Nov-Anglian [that is, New Englander] who is not anxious
for the great event at which I have glanced." So wrote Pickering,
and that had been his mistake, in depending only on the upper social
classes for success. The elections of 1804 were probably regarded
by George Cabot as completely justifying all the gentle vituperation
he had leveled against democracy. The whole nation, including
New York and most of New England itself, went in one great
wave for Jefferson. The President who had entered the White
House in 1801 by the narrowest margin was reëlected in 1804 by

an overwhelming majority. A cry of triumph was sounded from Monticello. The last enemy had been conquered. New England Federalism had fallen in ruins before the rush of the Republican Party. Of all the New England states, lonely Connecticut remained faithful to Federalism and that by the slightest of majorities. "I sincerely congratulate you," wrote Jefferson to a New England friend, "on the return of Massachusetts into the fold of the Union. This is truly the case where we may say, 'This our brother was dead and is alive again; and was lost and is found.' It is but too true that our Union could not be pronounced entirely sound while so respectable a member as Massachusetts was under morbid affection. All will now come to rights."

But the rebellion of 1804 was not entirely bloodless. There was one battle, and in this the Pickering Federalists were successful. It took place one July morning on the heights of Weehawken; the outcome was the death of the greatest of Federalists, who paid with his life for his opposition to the conspiracy. For the Hamilton-Burr duel was the direct result of this unsuccessful effort to destroy the Constitution. The bad blood that had been generating for years between Hamilton and Aaron Burr reached its most violent state in the New York campaign of 1804. The defeat which Burr suffered in a campaign that, he believed, was to make him head of a new nation he attributed chiefly to the force and ability with which Hamilton had fought him. For Hamilton's methods had not been at all suave. He regarded Burr as the most odious influence in American public life and was determined to end his career, once for all. And he succeeded. Hamilton, always at his best at social gatherings, had expressed opinions of Burr that, in that vindictive gentleman's standard, could be atoned for only in one way. That in challenging Hamilton to what was called in those days an "interview" he was deliberately seeking the death of his rival is the judgment of most historians. In such an encounter the experienced Burr must certainly be victorious, and there was no political or social career for the humiliated adventurer so long as Hamilton lived to block his way. Hamilton's acceptance of the challenge was immediately related to the constitutional danger. Just before going to the dueling ground he explained, in writing, why, his moral objections to dueling being what they were, he regarded himself as having no choice but to meet his antagonist. "The ability to be in future useful, whether in resisting mischief or effecting good, in those crises of our public affairs which seem likely to happen, would probably be inseparable from a conformity with public prejudice in this particular." That is, to decline a meeting would so stamp him with cowardice that his character would be ruined in popular estimation, and his value as a leader in the "crises" he knew to be impending would be destroyed. And the greatest of these "crises" would be such attempts to destroy the Union as the Burr-Pickering effort of 1804; and even that had not been utterly silenced, for summons to a meeting in Boston in the fall, to consider further action, had been issued. In Hamilton's last political letter, addressed to Theodore Sedgwick, he refers to this peril, as well as again sets forth that distrust of popular rule which remained an ultimate conviction. "I will here express but one sentiment," he wrote, July 10, 1804, the day before the duel, of which end the message seems to carry an intimation, "which is, that dismemberment of our empire will be a clear sacrifice of great positive advantages, without any counterbalancing good; administering no relief to our real disease, which is Democracy." And thus Hamilton's last injunction to his countrymen was to hold fast to the Constitution, largely, it would seem, as a protection against the excesses which he believed to be inherent in a system of popular rule.

VIII

But Hamilton's death, though it definitely ended the conspiracy of 1804, did not destroy the secession movement in New England. The Pickering-Burr attempt at separation proved to be only the first of several outbreaks that followed in the next ten years. And the demonstrations of 1809–1812 and 1814–1815 were more formidable than the ill-digested scheme of 1804 for the reason that the earlier revolt was really a palace revolution, a secret plot hatched by self-designated leaders, while the subsequent disaffections had a great popular following. The elections of 1804 indicated that Jefferson was almost as well-favored in the North as in the South, but one of those violent reactions in public favor so common in American politics presently set in, with the result that Jefferson, when he left the White House in 1809, was, in the judgment of New England, an "unclean thing" indeed. The foreign policy that followed his triumph in 1804 quickly made him an object of execration in every New England village. For his philosophy of foreign relations had a practical expression that affected this region in its most sensitive spot. Thomas Jefferson sincerely believed that he had solved the greatest riddle of civilization, had evolved a plan for ridding mankind of what had been its greatest scourge for ages. Modern philosophers, such as William James, have fondly toyed with some idea that would provide a "substitute for war"; this substitute Jefferson was convinced he had discovered. In his system of statecraft it is figured as "peaceable coercion." Properly handled commerce and trade could become as effective in battling the national enemy as ships of the line, fortifications, and armies. The policy rested upon the conviction that American products and American ships were indispensable to the very existence of Europe, especially of England, and the way to meet foreign aggression and injustice was to withhold these advantages until the enemy should be brought to terms. Jefferson therefore deprecated the preparation of shot and shell in the face of looming danger, reduced rather than enlarged the feeble American navy, almost disbanded the army, and took strong stand against relying upon the common material means of upholding American rights. If the situation should become tense, and even if war should threaten, the withdrawal of all American ships from the ocean, the shutting of all American ports to the aggressor, would, he insisted, accomplish far more than all the armies and navies in Christendom.

The statesman's purposes represented a noble effort to abolish bloodshed as a method of asserting the rights of America, but bore with a practical severity on New England, and, indeed, on all sections of the country, including tobacco-growing Virginia. It all but destroyed the Constitution, all but drove the Northern country out of the Union. There is no intention of rehearsing again in this place the often-told story of Jefferson's embargo — the cessation of all American commerce with the outside world that represented the attempt, made in 1807–1809, to compel Great Britain and France to end their depredations against American ships, their impressment of American sailors, and all the injuries against neutrals that accompanied the life-and-death struggles of the two empires. It is interesting, in this connection, as presenting perhaps the greatest threat to the Constitution that had appeared up to that time. Had Jefferson not seen the error of his programme in time, disunion would have come in 1808 instead of 1861, and been led by New England instead of the South. For the sight of their loved ships rotting at the wharves, of idle sailors loafing in the streets, of farmers raising produce for which there was no market, of fishermen prohibited from making their profitable trips to the Grand Bank, of vacant ships, yards, and jobless workmen, of the multitude of industries dependent on commerce without occupation, started Yankeeland into a blaze of fury, all poured forth against the central government. Pickering, still the leader of separation, now had what he had lacked in 1804, a strong public sentiment behind his cherished New England confederacy. And in seeking allies he was not forced this time to rely on so fragile an aid as a discredited adventurer like Aaron Burr; this time he really did become a traitor, for he aspired to enlist the aid of Great Britain. His correspondence clearly proves his conniving with the British cabinet. A New England confederacy that should include Canada, backed by close alliance with the British Crown, was the scheme taking form in the Ultrafederalist mind. A Canadian agent, sent by the British Governor General of Canada, was in constant association with many of "the best and wisest" in Boston; town meeting after town meeting in New England passed resolutions breathing the strongest sympathy with Britain; a meeting in Faneuil Hall, denouncing the embargo, recalled in its intensity gatherings in the same place held in Stamp-Tax days; James Hillhouse, Senator from Connecticut, was proposing amendments to the Constitution which, if adopted, would have destroyed the fabric erected by the Philadelphia Convention; while its governor, Jonathan Trumbull, — that "brother Jonathan" so dear to Washington, — was preaching nullification with a fervor that suggested the excitement of the Alien and Sedition Laws. "The Federalists in 1801," says Henry Adams, the historian of this period, "were the national party of America; the Federalists of 1808 were a British faction in secret league with George Canning" — Canning, the Foreign Secretary of Great Britain.

Only one thing saved the nation from disunion — the repeal of the embargo and the admittance again of throttled New England commerce to the sea. But the interval lasted only three years. In 1812 the separatists became active once more. The outbreak of war with Great Britain — a war on the brink of which the United States had hung for fifteen years — gave the signal for a new secession. When Pickering sought the assistance of the cynical George Cabot in 1804, that foe of popular rule and of Jefferson replied that the time was not ripe, Democracy had not sufficiently reaped its harvest of evil, but that it would in due time force upon the nation some great evil that would make separation the only resource of New England. "A war with Great Britain, manifestly provoked by our rulers," would be such a fateful calamity. That had now come, and with it came also the desire for casting adrift the rest of the nation that Cabot had foretold. And, significantly, leadership in this latest attempt at "scisson" passed from the hands of Pickering and into the control of such aristocrats as Harrison Gray Otis and Cabot himself. Pickering, indeed, did participate in all the perturbations that led to the Hartford Convention, but it was rather as critic than as leader, an extremist who regarded that assemblage as a halting and tepid affair. No proceeding in American history has been the subject of more lively debate. Ever since the twenty-six delegates closed their secret session in January 1815 it has been assailed on one hand as a gathering of traitors engaged in separating the Northern region from the nation, and, on the other, as a pious convocation of patriots, heroically and successfully laboring to forestall that very result. Harrison Gray Otis, its master spirit, spent the larger part of his days writing apologies, seeking to prove that the accusations of disloyalty to the Union leveled at him were calumnies, and that the Hartford Convention was actually the agency that saved the nation from falling to pieces. Here again is another tangled story which it would be unprofitable to seek to unravel in this place. On the face of it there was some virtue in Otis's explanations. The Hartford Convention certainly did not advocate separation from the Union — at least separation at that time. But to estimate accurately the rôle of the convention in American history it must be considered as merely one episode in the attitude of New England and the North towards the second war with England. That attitude is one to which New Englanders can look back with no satisfaction. It is possible to point out great contributions made by this section in men and money — probably the most creditable performances were of the navy, and that was the work of New England seamen; on the other hand, the behavior of New England from the beginning was hostile, and certain overt acts actually tended to help Great Britain and impede American operations; while all through the war the spirit of secession was rampant.

The leaders of the Hartford Convention, especially Otis, had been leaders also of this disloyalty, and the meeting of the delegates was the final episode in a long course of hostility to the Washington government. In December 1814, when George Cabot, as president, called the convention to order, it is said that at least half the people of New England favored secession. Apologists have claimed great credit for this body because, in face of such a popular attitude, it refused to recommend a departure from the Union. But there are countervailing facts involved. The report of the convention expressed the view that, although the time was not ripe for separation, that time might soon arrive. "A sentiment prevails to no inconsiderable extent that the time for a change is at hand. Those who so believe regard the evils which surround them as intrinsic and incurable defects in the Constitution. They yield to a persuasion that no change, at any time, or on any occasion, can aggravate the misery of their country. This opinion may ultimately prove to be correct." This can hardly be regarded as a strong defense of the existing Constitution.

Especially appalling was the statement that the Hartford Convention was really a preparation for a larger gathering of all the states for the revision of the existing form of government. That is, it was to be regarded as a kind of Annapolis Convention, a mere preliminary to another comprehensive national assembly like the Philadelphia Convention of 1787. That any constitutional convention brought together in 1815 could have agreed upon a new Federal Union is inconceivable; the result would have been the destruction of the existing Constitution and the creation of several inharmonious confederacies. But the measures recommended by the Hartford delegates to meet the immediate crisis practically all contained the seeds of disunion. One of them was nullification, of the Madisonian brand. In Madison's very words, it asserted the right of a state to "interpose its authority" to protect itself from the "infraction" of the Constitution. At the time this right was insisted on in the Connecticut capital the original author of the phrase was a woebegone figure, residing in the Octagon House in Georgetown, the White House from which he had recently fled being a charred ruin, the handiwork of British incendiaries. One wonders if he found much satisfaction in this echo of his principles of 1798 in far-off Hartford. Just as the Virginia legislature that year had used his doctrine to declare invalid the Alien and Sedition Laws, without waiting for the judgment of the Supreme Court, so the Hartford Convention, in 1815, wished to set aside any Federal legislation that enrolled state militia in the national forces or made any movement towards conscription. It was the subsequent claim of Otis that the main purpose of the Hartford Convention was to provide for the defense of the New England states by themselves against an expected British attack. A government in which the component parts raise their own armies and conduct separately their military operations flies even in the face of Jeffersonian State rights, for common defense, in his view, was the one great reason for federation. The Hartford Convention wished to have money raised by Federal taxation in each state revert to the state for this national defense. The openly proclaimed right of secession could no more strongly have signified the break-up of the Union than such a system of finance. Thus as the measures recommended by this body are examined they practically all strike at the Constitution, even though, in the same breath, the convention advised against formal departure from the Union.

There is little doubt that, had the war lasted a year longer, the separation foreshadowed at Hartford would have become the New England programme. But hardly had its labors been concluded when news from Europe turned American thoughts in another direction. The treaty of peace had been signed at Ghent and the war was over. A week or two afterward came news of Jackson's great victory over Wellington's veterans at New Orleans. In the outburst of national enthusiasm that followed, even in New England, the Hartford Convention lost any influence it may have had in directing American policy and became an odium which its participants tried vainly for the rest of their lives to live down. The Constitution was still to face many crises of this kind, but New England, from that day, ceased to be a rallying point for disunion.

IX

It is apparent that the chief impediment to the Constitution during the period under review was the absence of a national spirit, of any widespread realization that the United States formed a nation. This failure was manifest both at home and in Europe. In America it explained the many outbreaks of disintegration and secession. In the twenty-five years following the Philadelphia Convention there was scarcely any time when the Western frontier, in whole or in part, from Vermont to Louisiana, was not in danger of separating from the new government. That the territory over which the Constitution should reign — if it survived in any form — would be limited by the area between the Atlantic and the Alleghenies became every day more likely. Great Britain would reclaim the land north of the Ohio and east of the Mississippi which had been ceded to the new republic in 1783. France would recover Louisiana, and establish west of the Mississippi an American Napoleonic empire. Had these plans succeeded, the remnant of the United States, fringing the Atlantic Coast, would quickly have passed under the influence, which would presently have become the domination, of a European power, probably Great Britain. During these years no European government treated the new republic with anything that suggested equality. None of them really looked upon the nation as independent, or a power that was likely to endure. A large element in America held no more exalted view. The Jeffersonian party rested on the theory that the United States were *not* a nation, but a league of independent sovereignties. Up to 1800 two American statesmen had been foremost in maintaining the other view: in their opinion the country was a nation, and only as a nation could survive and maintain its liberties. Washington died in 1799, and Hamilton — who was to perish five years afterward — ceased to be a strong political force. Madison had long since abandoned the Nationalistic principle. Had another champion of enlarged conception not appeared to carry on and complete Washington's and Hamilton's work, the American states would have presently disintegrated into an assortment of South American republics, warring among themselves, constant victims of European intrigues and aggressions, finally vanishing as an independent people. That a more imposing fate was reserved for them is the debt the American people owe John Marshall.

In many ways Marshall was personally the most attractive figure among the early constructors of the Republic. At least he had one quality which most of these great men lacked — a sense of humor. We miss this desirable trait in Jefferson, Madison, Hamilton, even in Washington, but it is apparent in all the contemporary impressions of John Marshall that have survived. It is said that Gilbert Stuart, making his first attempt at a portrait of Washington, was so over-awed and unnerved by the man's physical dignity that the painting was a failure. He would have suffered no such embarrassment had Marshall been his subject. Instead he would have been perpetually entertained by light and gossipy conversation, by an endless flow of witticisms and anecdotes. One specimen of this talent is worth preserving for its suggestion of subsequent history. On Marshall's elevation to the Supreme Bench Jefferson politely made a call of congratulation; not finding the new appointee home, he left his card, on which had been hurriedly scribbled regrets that he had been so "lucky" as not to find the enemy at home; then, correcting the lapse, he changed the message to read "un-lucky." "That is the first time," Marshall remarked, glancing at the pasteboard, "that Jefferson came *near* to telling the truth."

Marshall's gayety, drollery, whimsicality, and fondness for story-telling figure in contemporary recollections; and his friends' informal sketches of his personal appearance indicate a carefree, happy-go-lucky nature. Jefferson, forgetting that his own habit of sitting on one hip had occasioned widespread criticism, objected — among other things — to Marshall's "lax lounging manners"; manners that served to remind the public of what was the fact, that Marshall, in origin and training, was a frontiersman, child of that "Hollow" in the side of the Blue Ridge Mountains, a section which then represented Virginia's farthest West. Whether Marshall appeared at an assembly at Yorktown, shocking the gold-laced gentlemen by his own backwoods raiment — not shocking, however, the elaborately gowned Virginia beauties present at the same gathering, for Marshall, despite his neglect of adornment, was always liked by women; or as one of the few cheerful optimists at Valley Forge, lightening the gloom by his laughter and stories, and by his athletic prowess, for he was the fleetest of all that crowd in foot races,

INDEPENDENCE HALL

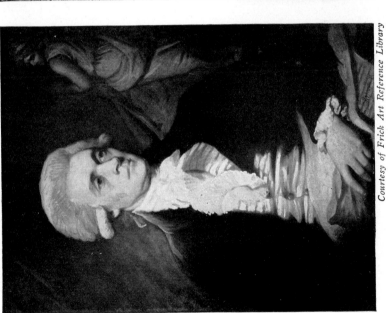

THOMAS JEFFERSON

JOHN MARSHALL

which he ran in stocking feet, the white patches on the black whirl-
ing far ahead of all competitors, giving him the nickname of "Silver
Heels"; or as an attendant of Wythe's law lectures at William and
Mary, scribbling in his notebook references not only to Blackstone
and Coke, but to Polly Ambler, the girl on whom Marshall had
fixed his heart; or as the wooer of that lovely lady, reading to her
from the English poets; or as a member of the Virginia Constitutional Convention, where, according to Grigsby, the young lawyer,
conspicuous with blazing black eyes and black, straight hair, looked
"more like a poet than a statesman"; or as the leader of the Richmond bar, walking bareheaded along the main street, his hat, full
of cherries, held in front, from which he rhythmically conveyed the
fruit to his mouth, the picture is always the same, that of a man
natural, plain, genial, direct, elemental, and simple. His swarthy
face, his long legs, his six feet and more of height, his powerful lithe
frame, also suggest the frontier. A writer much praised in the early
nineteenth century for pen portraits was William Wirt, one of the
lawyers whose constant appearance before the Supreme Court in
Marshall's time contributed to its prestige. He describes the Chief
Justice as "in his person, tall, meagre, emaciated; his muscles relaxed
and his joints so loosely connected as . . . to destroy everything
like elegance and harmony in his air and movements. Indeed in
his whole appearance and demeanor, dress, attitude, gesture, sitting,
standing or walking, he is as far removed from the idolized graces
of Lord Chesterfield as any other gentleman on earth. . . . His
head and face are small in proportion to his height; his countenance
has a faithful expression of great good humor and hilarity, while
his black eyes — that unerring index — possess an irradiating spirit
which proclaims the power of the mind that sits enthroned within.
His voice is hard and dry; his attitude, in his most effective orations, often extremely awkward; as it was not unusual with him to
stand with his left foot in advance, while all his gesture proceeded
from his right arm, and consisted merely in a vehement perpendicular
swing of it from about the elevation of his head to the bar behind
which he was accustomed to stand." Justice Story gives a portrait
somewhat more dignified, but similarly human. The man had
one blessed gift not particularly common among the rather sombre
public characters of the time. "I love his laugh," writes Story,
"it is too hearty for an intriguer; and his good temper and un-
wearied patience are equally agreeable on the bench and in the study."

In early surroundings at least Jefferson should have found Marshall a sympathetic figure, for the Hollow in Fauquier County, in

which his antagonist was born and spent his boyhood, came pretty near to being one of those ward-republics Jefferson regarded as the basis of an idyllic commonwealth. The few log cabins that composed it, with the one-story-and-a-half frame shack in which Thomas Marshall and his fifteen children lived, almost reproduced that "state of nature" which, in the political lingo of the day, approached perfection. Here there was little government and little need of any; the denizens scraped a living from a not too friendly soil, supplementing it from the game and fish in which the primeval hills and brooks abounded. One feature which Jefferson regarded as indispensable to his wards Marshall's place of nativity did not enjoy — there was no primary school in the Hollow, and for education the future jurist had to depend on his parents and neighbors. His finest tutor was his father, a man of ability and prominence, representative of Fauquier in the House of Burgesses. Marshall afterward acquired a considerable amount of Latin from one of those Scottish clergymen who had so much to do with forming the pre-Revolutionary mind of Virginia. Books were not common in this remote region, but there was one volume that Marshall conned. Pope became his absorbing delight; at the age of twelve, he says, he had transcribed the whole of the *Essay on Man* and parts of the *Moral Essays* and memorized a large part of them. Warburton's edition of Pope (1751) contains the *Essay on Man* and the *Moral Essays* bound in the same volume, and it is undoubtedly this book that had strayed from London to the Blue Ridge. This enthusiasm suggests an interesting literary, as well as constitutional study. To what extent did the fundamental ideas of Pope seat themselves in the mind of the growing boy? To what extent is the *Essay on Man* responsible for his approach to constitutional interpretation? Does this classic explain in part the sense of order and licensed liberty which the Constitution has implanted in the American mind? The influence of a single volume on adolescent intellects is easy to exaggerate, but the fact that Marshall pondered Pope at such an impressionable age, and so constantly and diligently, must not be disregarded. For the *Essay on Man* is full of ideas and sentiments — many of them have passed into common English speech — which lay at the basis of the American charter. "Order is heaven's first law" — and Marshall, like Washington and Hamilton, became a devotee of system, precedent, stability in life as well as institutions. Existence to them, as well as to Pope, was "a mighty maze but not without a plan." The poet's description of the "first cause" that "acts not by partial but by general laws" is itself a fair summation of the

American Constitution, and the frequent appearance of the capitalized words ORDER and REASON and SUBORDINATION proved excellent discipline for a boyish mind that was to accentuate these principles in explaining the American system of government. What keeps in subjection the evil tendencies inherent in the selfish human race? "Government and Laws!" the poet responds, elaborating the dictum by a sentiment as Jeffersonian as "the pursuit of happiness" — for the end of government "is the good not of one, but of All." And, in order to produce this universal blessing, government must be subjected to restraints. Only coöperation and majority rule can safeguard mankind from its selfish and exploiting instincts, or what Pope calls "self-love." "All join to guard what each desires to gain." The well-ordered empire founds "the private on the public good" and thus arises "the ascending music of a well-mix'd state." What better motto could the prospective United States adopt than Pope's lines: —

> Such is the World's great harmony, that springs
> From Order, Union, full Consent of things.

The picture of the twelve-year-old Marshall, in his backwoods home, copying painfully these maxims and committing great stretches of the poem to memory, should be remembered in properly understanding the judge who afterward gave the Constitution the interpretation it has borne ever since his day. For Marshall, certain legal pundits insist, was not a great lawyer — not a learned judge, in a technical sense; his opinions contained few citations or references to precedents; always his mind was fixed on great principles: the principles of order, system, harmony, justice, the necessity of subordinating the rights and privileges of the individual to the good of the mass — all of which excellent ideas are set forth, frequently in undying phrase, in the didactic poem that found its way into his early home. So much for poetical theory; the time presently came when Marshall learned the same lesson in more prosaic way. One of his father's close friends was George Washington, whose surveying expeditions frequently brought him to the frontier country of the Blue Ridge. In the ten years of disputation that preceded the Revolution the elder Marshall followed Washington's view, and, when his leader assumed command of the American army, at once enlisted for the war. In the Third Virginia regiment, which presently joined Washington's forces, the Marshalls were well represented: Thomas Marshall was major, and his son John, in 1775 twenty years old, captain. Though the younger

Marshall fought well at Brandywine, Germantown, and Monmouth, the lessons derived from this experience were not chiefly military. What the war really taught him was the need of national union. In the army, this Virginian afterward recorded, "I was confirmed in the habit of considering America as my country and Congress as my government." These conceptions were not widely prevalent at the time. Marshall must be classified as one of the immortal triumvirate — the other two being Washington and Hamilton — whom the miseries of Valley Forge taught the need of national organization. And Nationalism, even at this callow stage, became with Marshall a mental habit, and in the events that followed the Revolution, the conviction increased in strength.

When he entered the Virginia House of Delegates in 1782 the roughly clad member from Fauquier felt real embarrassment, for he found himself surrounded by many of the greatest American statesmen. The twenty-seven-year-old Revolutionary veteran hardly felt at home in a company that included Patrick Henry, Thomas Jefferson, James Madison, Richard Henry Lee, George Mason, and Edmund Randolph. Yet the question disturbed Marshall, as it was disturbing Washington and Madison, as already set forth: why were these great men serving in their state legislature instead of devoting their talents to the recently established United States? Did not statesmen of this calibre, he insisted, belong in Congress instead of in the Virginia Assembly? Not only that, but the interests engaging them showed that local selfishness, even provincialism, was more congenial to their taste than the fulfillment of patriotic duty as Americans. Debts owed by Virginia to Great Britain formed the great topic of the hour. In the war Virginia had passed laws "sequestrating" — polite name for "repudiating" — these debts, but the treaty of peace with England had provided for their payment. That was one of the things that made the treaty, and the united government which had negotiated it, so unpopular in Virginia, and it is melancholy to relate that the activities of these great statesmen — though not of all — in the Virginia legislature during Marshall's service were used in seeking to find ways of evading their obligations. Marshall was one of the most consistent of America's statesmen and jurists, and just as, in the Revolution, he stood forth as a Nationalist, so, in the Virginia legislature, he set forth the view on the inviolability of contracts which he was afterward to embody in judicial decisions. Marshall also felt outraged by the disrespect shown on all occasions by these lawmakers towards the confederated government. Their backing and filling on the subject of giving Congress power to levy the 5 per cent impost he regarded as an argument for enlarging its prerogatives. The Nation! The Nation! — this was the conception always in the front of his mind. The "harmony" of "the whole," about which his favorite poet had had so much to say, was then, as afterward, his incentive in public life.

Naturally the movement for a Federal Constitution had no more earnest champion, nor, when the work of the Philadelphia Convention was finished, did there appear any more determined advocate of adoption. Between 1782 and 1788 Marshall had made his way to the world. He had only six weeks' preparation for the bar, and, at first, clients came reluctantly, for they could not take seriously as a legal light a man so uncouth in his attire and so awkward in his manner. Soon, however, it was demonstrated that this backwoodsman was far more effective before judges and juries than most of the silk-breeched graduates of the Middle Temple who sought haughtily to oppose him. Marshall showed in his marriage how little he had in common with Tidewater. "Family and fortune" was the quest of most Virginia gentlemen in matrimony; even Washington had an eye to the main chance in his selection of rich widow Custis as his bride; but Marshall, when, after a three-year courtship "dearest Polly" became his wife, was indulging only his heart. "Family," indeed, he did incidentally obtain, for the Amblers ranked among Virginia's best, but they were very poor, and the rising lawyer and his wife began housekeeping in elementary fashion. But Marshall's professional progress was rapid. This was shown in 1788 when, although only thirty-three, he was elected a member of the Virginia Constitutional Convention, the most distinguished body ever assembled in Virginia then or since, and one of the greatest America has ever known. It had been gathered to answer the question with which all America was ringing, the one that comprehended all America's future: should the largest and most influential state ratify the new national "plan"? Again the consistence of Marshall's beliefs appeared; again the teachings of "Mr. Pope" found expression. The part of this youthful jurist in the deliberations is an important one. Probably it seems more important to the present generation than to his fellow debaters. Among those experienced giants Marshall was not a spokesman of first rank, and his speeches, respectfully as they were received, did not seem to them, as they do to the reader to-day, an epoch in American history. Yet the young man's orations proclaimed the doctrine that has made the United States a unified country. Only as a nation, he maintained, could the United States survive. Everywhere there were threats of "European intrigue" and of internal dissension. "Foreign powers are pleased with our disunion. If we invite them by our weakness to attack us, will they not do it? If we add debility to our present situation, a partition of America may take place." He pledged his faith to "Democracy," but it was to be a democracy safeguarded by restraints self-imposed, or, to use Marshall's own expression, "well regulated."

Nothing could seem more appropriate, in view of Marshall's subsequent career, than that, in the Convention, he should have given his best efforts to the judiciary. He had studied the question profoundly, and had come to the conclusions which remained with him to the end of his days. Here again his life, from beginning to end, was all of a piece. That George Mason cut a poor figure at the Virginia Convention has already been noted, and this white-haired and black-eyed veteran displayed himself most unfortunately, perhaps, in his tilt with the youthful Marshall. No limitation, Mason cried, had been placed upon the Federal courts! They would drive the state courts out of existence! Their jurisdiction was apparently unhampered! "The judicial power," he quoted, "shall extend to all cases in law and equity arising under the Constitution." This prospect appalled him. "What objects," he asked, "will not this expression extend to? . . . The effect of operation" of the Federal courts "will be utterly to destroy the state governments. . . . To what disgraceful and dangerous length does the principle of this go? . . . There are many gentlemen in the United States who think it right that we should have one great, national, consolidated government and that it was better to bring it about slowly and imperceptibly than all at once. . . . To those who think that one national, consolidated government is best for America, this extensive judicial authority will be agreeable; but I hope there are many in this Convention of a different opinion and who see their political happiness resting in their state governments." Madison rather excitedly interrupted to proclaim that he was not one of those who desired to use the courts for this imperial purpose. Significantly, however, Marshall made no disclaimer. He did repudiate Mason's idea that, under the Constitution, state courts would cease to exist; by showing how each judiciary, Federal and state, had precise spheres of operation, he inferentially disposed of the apprehension that the new government would be a "consolidated one" — that is, one in which state lines would disappear; but the National conception — National in the powers delegated to Congress — had always represented his ambition. He believed that it was the business of the courts to protect authority, even against Congress itself. "To what quarter will you look for protection from an infringement of the Constitution if you will not give the power to the Judiciary? There is no other body that can afford such a protection." "Can they [Congress] go beyond the delegated powers? If they were to make a law not warranted by any of the powers enumerated, it would be considered by the judges as an infringement of the Constitution which they are to guard. They would not consider such a law as coming under their [that is, Congress's] jurisdiction. They would declare it void."

X

Such was the principle Marshall, aged thirty-three, upheld in the Virginia Convention; and such remained the ideal to which the rest of his life was devoted. Added reputation came to the man who had so brilliantly bearded Mason and other great men in 1788. Public office he could have had on his return in plenty; but the champion of what was now known as Federalism preferred to exercise his influence as a private citizen. In Virginia, Marshall became virtually the leader of Federalism, and the ever-alert defender of Washington against the Virginians — who were probably the majority — that opposed the new administration. He combated the French pretension to affiliate the United States with the new Republic, and was one of the few conspicuous Americans in either party who had a good word for Jay's Treaty, only because, should that agreement fail, his hopes of the United States as a nation would reach an end. His greatest service, the achievement that made him a national hero, came when, on the solicitation of the new President, John Adams, he finally accepted a public appointment and was sent to France, with two other commissioners, to adjust numerous difficulties with that nation. In many ways this is the most celebrated diplomatic embassy in American history. Certainly few have been the object of such excited public emotion and probably none have accomplished so much in stimulating that national consciousness which Marshall regarded as the path to salvation. To become the hero of a crisis in which the chief performer is insulted and his country treated with contempt seems almost a contradiction in terms, but that was the outcome. The story of XYZ, long, tedious, and complicated, forms a large chapter in all American histories and need not be repeated here. Marshall and his associates, Elbridge Gerry and Charles Cotesworth Pinckney, found themselves face to face with one of the most conscienceless and diabolically adroit scoundrels who ever served as foreign minister to a great nation. "A silk stocking stuffed with filth," was Napoleon's description of Talleyrand, and no one has ever improved on it. Before they could be even recognized as ambassadors and admitted to Talleyrand's presence, the Americans were informed that they must give him

$250,000 as a personal bribe and that the American government must make a large "loan" to reënforce the depleted French treasury. The vigor and skill and dignity with which Marshall repulsed these advances marked him as one of the foremost Americans of his day. The United States answered the insult by making war on France; Washington came from retirement and assumed command of the army; the American navy assailed so successfully French men-of-war and French commercial ships that the French government, after a year's hostilities, notified the United States that a new American embassy would be received with pleasure and treated on a basis of equality and respect.   Thus, as with every episode in which Marshall played a part, the effect was to enhance national feeling and promote national coöperation.

No man viewed with more satisfaction the progress Marshall had made and the vigorous stand he had taken in face of these French insults than his old commander at Brandywine and Valley Forge. The attitude the one-time junior officer held on the Constitution increased the favor with which he was regarded at Mount Vernon. Washington, in the last two years of his life, was maintaining an especially vigilant eye on the fortunes of the charter for which he had sacrificed so greatly, for that period was a particularly dangerous one.   His summoning of Patrick Henry to stand for the Virginia Assembly in 1799, that he might lead the fight against the Jefferson-Madison resolutions, has already been described.   But it was not only in the Virginia legislature that the onslaught was in course of preparation.   The enemy was planning his campaign in Congress as well.   There the Constitution needed its ablest champions.   Who could be more useful than the lawyer and diplomat with whose praises America was then ringing?   One day in September Marshall received an invitation to Mount Vernon.   Another rising Virginian was summoned at the same time — that favorite nephew of the General, Bushrod Washington, who became his heir and who served afterward for many years as an associate justice of the Supreme Court, on the same bench with Marshall.   The elder Washington now thought that both these *protégés* should enter Congress, to meet impending attacks on the Constitution.   "The temper of the people of the state," he wrote Bushrod, "is so violent and outrageous that I wish to converse with General Marshall and yourself on the election which must soon come."   Years afterward Justice Story related the details of this meeting, obtained from Marshall himself.   The discussions took place on the piazza of Mount Vernon and were continued three days.   They represented only the final of many constitutional discussions that had been held at the same mansion, the first of which had been the meeting of the Virginia and Maryland commissioners in 1785 which had led to the Philadelphia Convention. Bushrod quickly accepted his uncle's proposal that he stand for Congress, but Marshall needed persuasion. His personal affairs were demanding attention; his law practice could not be neglected; besides, what could he do that others could not do equally well? But Washington grew more and more insistent. "There are crises in national affairs which make it the duty of a citizen," Washington said, "to forgo his private for his public interest. The country is now in one of these crises." Look at himself! He had retired from the Presidency, after delivering a farewell address to the country, yet, at the new danger of war, had come out of retirement and accepted the generalship of the army. "My resolution," Marshall afterward said, "yielded to this representation."

How great this final service was to prove to the nation Washington, who died two months afterward, never knew. For the really significant outcome was not Marshall's brief career in Congress, but his appointment as Chief Justice of the United States. Marshall's independence in the Federal legislature made him almost the leading man of his party, — especially after Hamilton's defection, — and, appropriately enough, when Adams "discharged" Timothy Pickering as Secretary of State he put the Virginian statesman in this place. Soon afterward advancing years forced Oliver Ellsworth to retire as Chief Justice. Adams had already tried unsuccessfully to appoint Marshall to the Supreme Bench. His chief reason for this selection is to the point; it was because Marshall stood so high as a defender of Nationalism. Speaking of Marshall's work as envoy to France, Adams said: "He has raised the American people in their own esteem, and if the influence of truth and justice, reason and argument, is not lost in Europe, he has raised the United States in that quarter of the world." Yet, in January 1801, the question of the vacant Chief Justiceship was not arousing much public interest; the one exciting event of that year was the fight that was tearing the Federalist Party to shreds. The President first offered the Chief Justiceship to John Jay, who had resigned the same post in 1795 after six years' service. "Jay was yesterday nominated Chief Justice," Jefferson wrote to Madison, December 19, 1800. "We were afraid of something worse." When news arrived that Jay had declined the honor and that John Marshall had been chosen in his stead, Jefferson probably believed that his worst forebodings had been realized.

XI

The reason that Marshall's selection caused no nation-wide interest was that the Supreme Court itself was held in no high esteem. "John Jay," commented the Jeffersonian *Aurora* when that gentleman was nominated, "after having through decay of age become incompetent to discharge the duties of Governor [of New York], has been appointed to the sinecure of Chief Justice of the United States. That the chief justiceship is a sinecure needs no other evidence than that in one case the duties were discharged by one person who resided at the same time in England and by another during a year's residence in France." Both Jay and Ellsworth had indeed treated this dignity in rather casual manner. Jay's relationship to the first place in the new American judiciary can be taken as a fair illustration of the slight consideration it received at that time. He served only a brief time when, without surrendering the post, he became candidate for governor of New York. Failing in that ambition, he resumed his judicial duties, only to be detached by Washington for his work in England as negotiator of the treaty. Landing in New York in 1795, he found that in his absence the Federalists had again nominated him for governor; still retaining the Chief Justiceship, he engaged in a hurly-burly campaign, this time successfully. Though first Chief Justice, Jay's reputation does not rest upon his work in that office, for little happened during his incumbency and little was done to elevate the courts to their eminent work of constitutional interpretation. More humiliating than Jay's goings in and out were the constant refusals of conspicuous "characters" to accept judicial office. Robert Hanson Harrison declined appointment by Washington, and Charles Cotesworth Pinckney and Edward Rutledge both evaded the honor; they preferred to remain members of the South Carolina legislature! Alexander Hamilton put aside the Chief Justiceship; his growing law practice in New York could not be sacrificed. Among the many opportunities of service in the administration refused by Patrick Henry was the same position. That Washington held the bench in high esteem and had a prevision of its destiny is indicated by the calibre of the men he tried to appoint, and a constant disappointment was the difficulty of persuading his candidates to accept the place.

But, as a whole, the government treated the Court with scant respect. In 1800, the new capital city was established on the Potomac. Here quarters had been prepared for the executive and legislative departments, but the Supreme Court had been overlooked. No building and no chambers were provided for the third coordinate branch. A committee of the House, in 1796, had recommended that a building be constructed for the Federal Court — a recommendation not carried into effect until 1935, when the present sumptuous temple, defiantly confronting that Congress with which the institution has been battling for one hundred and forty years, was exclusively dedicated to its use. So obscure was the meeting place in Marshall's early years that the antiquaries have had some difficulty in definitely placing it. Mr. Charles Warren, modern historian of the Supreme Court, after exhaustive researches, concludes that a room on the first floor of the Capitol, twenty-four by thirty feet, then known as the Senate Clerk's office, in recent years the office of the Marshal of the Court, was the one graciously assigned by Congress for the convocations of Marshall and his associates.

If the Supreme Court was not treated with too much deference by the public or its coördinate branches, a certain part of the blame belongs to itself. In early days the Court was not an extremely august body. Politics were conspicuous, not only in appointments, but in judicial behavior. Jefferson was justified in regarding it as a part of the Federalist political machine. The present generation, which frowns upon political activities by judges, is shocked at the unabashed party performances of judges in Marshall's time. On circuit they usually opened each session with speeches — frequently unbecoming harangues — in the interest of the Federalist candidates. Charges to grand juries were sometimes little better than stump orations. The instance that figures largest in history is that of Justice Chase, who constantly edified the Court with his wild deliveries from the bench, in which he lauded the Federalists and their principles, and denounced, in best ward-politics fashion, the Jeffersonians and all their works. In August 1800, this judicial luminary abandoned the bench altogether, leaving it without a quorum for that time, in order to engage in a vituperative political tour in behalf of Adams's Presidential campaign. The most grotesque of these early judges was John Rutledge of South Carolina, who, on Jay's resignation as Chief Justice, solicited the office for himself. He had already been associate justice, and now thought a brief period as head of the Court would form an excellent cap to his career. As he was a distinguished and able lawyer and a man of great reputation in the South, Washington acceded to his request. But news presently reached the administration that South Carolina was burning Jay in effigy and that Rutledge was engaging in untempered denunciations of the treaty. One newspaper report declared that the prospective Chief Justice had appeared "mounted upon the head of a hogshead, haranguing a mob assembled to reprobate the treaty and insult the executive of the Union . . . insinuating that Mr. Jay and the Senate were fools and knaves, duped by British sophistry or bribed by British gold, prostituting the dearest rights of freemen and laying them at the feet of royalty." Rutledge's friends denied the accuracy of this report; another explanation is that Rutledge, hitherto a most dignified and learned judge, had suddenly gone mad; not unnaturally the Senate refused to confirm his appointment.

Few decisions of supreme importance had been delivered before Marshall's accession. During this pre-Marshall era not many suits of any kind came up for adjudication. For the first three years almost no litigants appeared, and the Court met only to adjourn. The real business of the judges was performed on circuit, and the hardships of this life were one of the reasons why the service was unpopular. The country was divided into three great circuits — Southern states, Middle, and Northern; each had its circuit judge with whom, making a body of three, sat two members of the highest tribunal. This meant that a Supreme Court justice spent most of his time traveling, and no commercial salesman of the present day experiences such hardships as came to his lot. Life in filthy inns, transportation in lumbering stages that frequently sank in mud to the hubs, made existence one prolonged horror. To be overturned in a stagecoach or to lend a helping hand in pulling it out of the mire was one of the commonplaces of judicial life. John Marshall himself suffered a broken collarbone in one of these mishaps, and so numerous did they become that Gouverneur Morris remarked that not legal learning, but the "agility of a postboy," was the main qualification for service on the highest bench.

Despite these inauspicious beginnings, circumstances, in 1801, combined to presage a new dignity for the judicial branch. The year 1801, like the year 1933, was expected to introduce a "new deal." When Thomas Jefferson left Mrs. Conrad's boarding house in the morning on that fourth of March, and walked, unattended by the military panoply which, even in democratic America, had previously accompanied Presidential installations, American history, in Jefferson's eyes, began anew. The simplicity of that occasion, as well as the informality of White House etiquette that accompanied it, was intended to symbolize this change. Then followed one of the most dramatic confrontations in American annals. Jefferson arose to take the oath; facing him, to administer it, stood John Marshall, who for one month had occupied the office of Chief Justice. Here, in one man, was embodied the incipient Revolution, and, in the other, the jurist who was to apply those "regulations to democracy" which he had advocated in the Virginia Convention. Jefferson himself would have phrased it differently. In his Virginia compatriot he visioned those forces of evil that had so far guided American affairs, and in himself the prophet of righteousness who was to start it on a new path. Washington may have wrenched thirteen colonies from the British yoke, but Jefferson was to be the real founder of the Republic. For ten years the Virginia statesman had been engaged in warfare to one end: he had organized a political party for the express purpose of expelling the "monocrats" from the national citadel, and placing Republicans in charge. On that March morning, as he glanced around, the magnitude of his triumph appeared on every side. In the Senate and House the Federals had been reduced to a minority and Republicans reigned supreme. In the executive department everything was safe in Jeffersonian hands. John Adams was wending his way to retirement in Braintree, Massachusetts, and his cabinet had been scattered to the winds. That only men sacredly devoted to the new dispensation would attain important office for at least four years to come was something the new President could reasonably guarantee.

However, the triumph was not complete. The presence of Marshall, solemnly administering the oath of office and smilingly congratulating the new President, was a reminder of that fact. After all, the American government did consist of three, not of two, parts; Jefferson and the Republicans controlled the executive and the legislative, but not the judiciary. That was the one ominous cloud on the horizon. John Adams, with crafty Federalist foresight, had robbed Jefferson of complete victory. Though the popular elections of the preceding November had swept the Federalist Party into an obscurity from which it never emerged, Adams had salvaged the judiciary. Jefferson was convinced that this was no accident. He believed that Adams had deliberately reformed the judicial department as a Federalist bulwark against untrammeled Republican-

ism, and he was undoubtedly right. A law had been rushed through
Congress at the last minute, enormously strengthening the courts.
This stipulated that the Supreme Court judges should no longer
perform duties on circuit, but confine all their attention to the
Supreme Court. Sixteen new circuit-court judges were provided
for and to these new posts — with an accompanying small army
of marshals, attorneys, and clerks — only Federalists were appointed.
As all members of the Supreme Bench belonged to the same party, and
as all Federal judges held office for life, this meant — and such
was the intention — that this branch of the government would
indefinitely remain in the hands of the party that had just lost the
election. And the Adams plot was more than a scheme for reward-
ing sound Federalists with warm jobs. They were placed in these
strategic posts, Jefferson insisted, in order to ensure the permanence
of Federalist — that is, "monarchist" — principles. What the party
had lost at the hands of the people they were thus to regain at the
hands of the machine, in the final moments of its expiring power.
For the new judiciary law, and the appointment of the new judges,
had been almost the last of Adams's acts as President; the tradition
grew up that the names had been hurried through in the last hours,
just as the day was dawning on Jefferson's administration, and from
this impression — which was not far from the truth — they have
always been known in American history as "the midnight judges."

This was an unpleasant fact facing Jefferson as Marshall administered the oath. Courteous as was the behavior of both men
on this occasion, there were no two Americans then extant who
detested each other more. "The morals of the author of the letter
to Mazzei cannot be pure," was Marshall's summation, referring
to the missive in which Jefferson had furtively attacked Washington as a monarchist. Jefferson reciprocated by declaring that Marshall's "mind was of that gloomy malignity which will never let
him forgo the opportunity of satiating it upon a victim." But
personal aversion was not the important matter in either case. The
two men standing amid the smelly new stone and mortar of the
unfinished Capitol personalized two conflicting ideas concerning the
American realm and the Constitution. That Marshall was a Nationalist, a man determined to link the states together by chains
of steel, and was prepared to use to this end all the power of the
Supreme Court — this made him odious in Jefferson's eyes. That
Jefferson was the author of the Kentucky Resolutions which, carried into practice, would reduce the judiciary almost to a nullity
was, in Marshall's view, the irreconcilable offense. The ultimate

issue, which both men understood and for which both were prepared to do battle to the death, was simply this: should the Constitution, as a power of centralization, survive, or should it be reduced to a feeble bond, gathering in the weakest association a mass of disorganized and inharmonious states?

Thus the matter at issue was not even primarily judicial: it was a problem of statesmanship, or, if the term is preferred, of politics. That the Supreme Court could ever be a lofty body, dwelling apart from the political world, is an absurd conception. Certainly Marshall understood that he was engaged in political warfare — in a struggle, that is, in which public questions, even political questions, would be involved, and in which forms of government were the issue. Since practically all the disputes coming before the Court involved questions that had formed the subject of fierce political debate in the press, on the stump, and in Congress, naturally the decisions augustly handed down would have political interest. Nor did Marshall hesitate to ponder the political aspects of these problems, or in his judgments introduce subtly political considerations. That is, he was more than a hair-splitting judge; he was a statesman, and a statesman wedded to ideas which he was determined to make prevail. His task was to protect the Constitution against the attacks that were everywhere being leveled against it; to make that document the dominant force in the establishment of a new nation. That was a political question; it had formed the subject of lively political debate for ten years and furnished the issue on which the great political parties had been formed. In the first case in which Marshall set forth his conception of union, Jefferson himself had started the discussion. This was the one created by the Kentucky Resolutions. That Congress had the right to pass laws only in accordance with powers granted by the Constitution was a point on which both Marshall and Jefferson agreed. Otherwise of course there would be no Constitution, for there was no Constitution if Congress could disregard it at will. Jefferson always proclaimed his allegiance to the Constitution, "properly understood." But the vital point still remained: who was to say when the Constitution had been violated and that the laws so passed were "null and void"? The states themselves, replied Jefferson, acting through their legislatures. If Congress adopted a measure which the Virginia or New York legislature believed a violation of the national charter, then the legislature could set it aside, — just as the Supreme Court does to-day, — and the law, so far as that particular state was concerned, no longer would encumber the statute books. But to Marshall that meant the end of the nation. Can you have a nation in which laws are laws in one part, and not laws in another? To which Jefferson replied that the United States were not a nation, but a federation made for limited purposes, joined together by a "compact" which was to be the ruling authority only when the states regarded it as convenient that it should be. Such was the basis of the great Marshall-Jefferson argument.

As a first blow, Jefferson decided to destroy the judicial structure the Federalists had so artfully put together. Inasmuch as the new administration controlled both branches of Congress, this was readily accomplished, though the debate was heated and protracted. The whole proceeding was ostentatiously political. The merits of the new judicial system devised by Adams were not the point at all. Whether an increase in business made necessary an enlarged judiciary; whether relieving the Supreme Court judges of their "post boy" duties and enabling them to remain in Washington engaged in their most important work was a desirable improvement — matters like these were worthy of discussion, but had little to do in deciding the question. Federalists everywhere made no mistake in interpreting the repeal as an attack on the organic law, a Republican effort to minimize the national power and to aggrandize the states. Hamilton was right when he wrote that the repeal of the Judiciary Act was "a vital blow to the Constitution," and so was Gouverneur Morris when he asserted that the Jeffersonian triumphs had "battered down the great outwork of the Constitution. The Judiciary has been overthrown." Jefferson himself would have agreed with these statements. His purpose was to destroy the judiciary and to drive the Federalists from their last citadel of power. The mere repeal of the new judiciary system did not quite secure this result; it was only the first step in a programme that aimed at annihilation. The reorganization of the courts accomplished by Adams had gone into the discard, and a large army of Federalist circuit judges, Federalist district attorneys, Federalist marshals, and other impedimenta of the new mechanism had lost their jobs; but the Supreme Court and the inferior courts established in 1789 were still intact. More important, John Marshall was still Chief Justice, as the country was presently to learn.

The circumstances of the epochal decision which now issued from Marshall fairly portrayed the close association that had always existed between political events and the judgments of the Court. The debate on the judiciary repeal had again forced to public attention the always vital question of constitutionality. The pretended right of the Supreme Court to annul invalid legislative acts was the ghost that haunted the entire discussion. Ever present in the Jeffersonian mind was the likelihood that the Court might set aside the very measure then under consideration and thus rob the Republicans of their victory. Again and again did the Federalist orators assert that repeal of the Judiciary Act was unconstitutional and would be so declared by Judge Marshall's court. The heaviest debaters on the Jeffersonian side, John Breckinridge of Kentucky, John Randolph of Virginia, James Jackson of Georgia, aimed their fiercest attacks on this apprehension. Breckinridge was that same leader who, in 1798, had introduced Jefferson's resolution in the Kentucky legislature, but now he took a new stand. The Jeffersonian view expressed in those rescripts, that each state legislature could nullify acts of Congress, had given place to another Jeffersonian idea. Each department of government had the right to interpret such laws as directly affected itself — such was the new doctrine. Thus the President could decide the constitutionality of measures that affected the executive, the judges the laws that affected the judiciary, Congress itself such enactments as affected the legislature. This rather intricate new philosophy Breckinridge, doubtless under coaching from the White House, now expounded in Congress. But the real point on which emphasis was laid was a denial of any prerogative of the Supreme Court on constitutionality. Jefferson and his party were not interested so much in determining where this mighty power lay as in challenging any inclination John Marshall might evince to assume it. It was merely one detail in the struggle then being waged for power. Just who Jupiter Tonans was could be postponed for future decision; the all-important fact was that he was not a body that met twice a year, huddled in a small and almost inaccessible corner of the Federal Capitol.

Marshall picked up the gauntlet, but did it so quietly, so adroitly, — even, it almost seemed, so humorously, — but with such judicial dignity that the episode is worthy of admiration merely as a work of art. When William Marbury, a gentleman otherwise unknown to fame, was nominated by John Adams on March 3, 1801, to be justice of the peace in the District of Columbia, he hardly realized that he was to become the vital bone of contention in a great political battle, as well as to precipitate an historic constitutional crisis. The only reason the selection of such humble officials as justices of the peace became a Presidential duty was that the District of Columbia, possessing no sovereignty of its own, was more or less — as it is still — the ward of the national government. President Adams appointed nineteen of these petty officers, but only fifteen of them received commissions, the delivery of the other four, of which Marbury's was one, having been overlooked in the hurry incident to the President's last day in office. The executive responsible for this oversight, strange to relate, was John Marshall himself, then Secretary of State. As his first official act, on entering the Presidency, Jefferson swept into the wastebasket all the unfinished business of his predecessor, and poor Marbury's commission as justice of the peace, lying undelivered on the table, went into the general rubbish heap. Yet this commission had been executed in due form, the hateful signature of President Adams had been attached, and the great seal of the United States had been solemnly affixed. Was it not absurd, therefore, that the mere failure of John Marshall to place the document in Marbury's hand should render it invalid? Marbury thought so, and asked the new Secretary of State, James Madison, for his commission; and when it was refused brought suit. The case came up in the December term of the Supreme Court, 1801, and Chief Justice Marshall issued what the lawyers call a "rule to show cause." "Mandamus" is a Latin word meaning "we command." It is the legal description of a writ, issued by a court, directing a person to perform a specific act. Marshall's "rule" was a notification to James Madison, Secretary of State, to appear in court on an indicated date and give satisfactory reasons why a mandamus should not be issued ordering the delivery to William Marbury of his commission as justice of the peace in the District of Columbia. Unless Madison's reasons should convince the Court that such a mandamus would be unjustified in law, the command would be forthcoming.

The word "mandamus" became an active one in political discussions of the next two years. "This mandamus business," as it was called, largely filled the public press and private argument. The mysterious legal term acquired importance because, according to Jefferson, it had become the symbol of judicial arrogance. The Supreme Court had assumed the right to instruct the executive department on its duties — to tell the Secretary of State what he could and could not do! In reality Marshall's writ was regarded by Jefferson as an attack on the President. In the exciting Congressional debates Mr. Marbury had become one of the most conspicuous of Americans. He had grown into the agent by which the Supreme Court was to magnify itself into the dominant force in government. "The present suit," said Breckinridge, "is leveled at the dignity of the first Executive Magistrate and the Senate is bound to protect that dignity." What was the end to be? Could the courts order the Executive to do things at will? "In this inquisitorial capacity," shouted Randolph of Roanoke, "the Supreme Court may easily direct the Executive by mandamus in what mode it is their pleasure that he should exercise his functions." In Jefferson's view, his prophecy of the designs of Federalism had been fulfilled. That party, having lost control of the legislative and executive branches, had, by the grace of John Adams, barricaded itself behind the courts and from this vantage ground it proposed to retain control of the government and make its policies prevail. The proposed mandamus, said Breckinridge, "is the most daring attack that the annals of Federalism have yet exhibited."

Thus popular interest was inflamed as it can be only when a bitter personal contest is involved. Marshall understood all this, for few men gauged public feeling so accurately. Jefferson and his friends enjoyed the prospect; enjoyed it because they regarded a triumph as certain. Whether or not the Supreme Court issued its commands, victory, they believed, would perch on their side. That Marshall would issue the mandamus when the case came up — that is, that he would order Secretary of State Madison to deliver his commission to William Marbury — they took for granted, as did all observers. In this way would Marshall deliver the Supreme Court into their hands! For the Jeffersonian strategy was decided on. The administration would ignore the instructions, pay no attention to the order, still withhold from Marbury his right to act as justice of the peace — an honor, by the way, to which Marbury, by two years' waiting, had become indifferent. Then what would Marshall do? "John Marshall has made his decision; now let him enforce it," said Andrew Jackson many years afterward; and Jefferson's and Madison's programme was to anticipate this attitude. Unlike the President, the Supreme Court had no army and navy to compel obedience; Madison therefore would ignore its ukase; Marshall would thus, after all his thundering, be simply left to wring his hands in rage, while the whole country laughed.

On February 12, 1803, after much argument by attorneys who never touched on the real issue, Marshall gave his decision. It came so unexpectedly that the Jeffersonians were stunned. For the Chief Justice had decided the argument in Jefferson's favor! Madison was informed that he need not deliver the commission to Marbury; so far as the Supreme Court was concerned, that gentleman would have to go to his grave without becoming a justice of the peace. That Marbury was entitled to the honor the Chief Justice indeed did proclaim. After all, Marshall did read his "lecture" to the executive department, denouncing the Secretary of State as a violator of the law, as a man who had neglected his clearly evident duty. But the Supreme Court had no intention of issuing a mandamus directing him to perform the abominated act.

And the reason why Marshall did not issue the mandamus is what has made this decision immortal. Marbury's attorneys had asked for it, basing their contention on a certain section of the Judiciary Act of 1789. This gave the Supreme Court power to issue "writs of mandamus . . . in cases warranted by the principles and usages of law, to any courts appointed or persons holding office, under the authority of the United States." Oliver Ellsworth, great lawyer that he was, had apparently made a serious mistake when he wrote that sentence. For Congress had no right to extend such power to the Supreme Court of the United States. That body, as set forth in the Constitution, was an appellate court. It was, that is, the court to which appeals were taken from the decision of the lower departments of the bench. In legal phrase, it was not, and was never intended to be, a court of "original jurisdiction." The Constitution made only two reservations to this general rule. "In all cases affecting ambassadors, other public ministers, and consuls, and those in which a State shall be party, the Supreme Court shall have original jurisdiction."

Thus the issuance of a mandamus to a public official is not one of the functions over which the Supreme Court has this "original jurisdiction." In other words, Congress, in passing this section of the Judiciary Act, had violated the Constitution. The enactment on which William Marbury had asserted his right to such relief was thus "unconstitutional." Marshall now set it aside as "null and void" and decided that Marbury should take his plea to the proper tribunal. Thus the judiciary for the first time, after fourteen years of national existence, declared the right to set aside laws of Congress that violated the Constitution. Marshall had silenced Jefferson by giving him a cheap victory — the President had won his fight so far as Marbury was concerned; but at the same time he administered the worst defeat Jefferson had so far suffered, for he had destroyed the main support of the Jeffersonian structure. Thus poor Marbury was sacrificed, but a constitutional principle of vast significance was made the bedrock of the American system. The point has already been indicated that Marshall possessed a keen sense of humor.   That he enjoyed the sardonic aspects of this situation may be well believed.   Had Jefferson not withheld Marbury's commission, — had the President simply handed to him an insignificant piece of paper and let him quietly start an obscure and scantily paid career as justice of the peace, — the great opportunity of Marshall's life would not have come, at least not at that time.   The fact that he so deftly seized it, and used it as the occasion of asserting this principle, shows that he was not only a great judge, but a statesman.

Since then the prosaic words *"Marbury* vs. *Madison"* have taken on in the American story an imaginative quality almost Shakespearean.   It was the Jeffersonian idea that the courts were to have nothing to do with the ultimate interpretation of constitutionality. That was to be the prerogative of the states, or perhaps, in some fashion never precisely defined, of the coördinate branches themselves.   The Jeffersonian contention did not die, but the Marbury decision has prevailed up to the present time.   The recent work of the Supreme Court, in outlawing the structure of the Rooseveltian "new economic order," rests upon this litigation of 1803.   The cashiering of the NRA, the AAA, and other legislation goes back historically to John Marshall's decision refusing a commission as justice of the peace to William Marbury.   All these judgments rest upon the same principle — the right of the judiciary to set aside laws for which the Constitution gives no warrant.   A vast literature has accumulated on this decision; books have been written about it; lectures delivered without end; it has formed a subject of debate from that day to this.   Learned legal authorities have picked it to pieces over and over again.   Numerous flaws have been detected.   Marshall's declarations as to Marbury's rights have been objected to as superfluous, as *obiter dicta,* and out of place.   If the Court had no jurisdiction, why discuss the matter in question?   It has even been urged that the clause of the law of 1789 which Marshall ruled to be a violation of the Constitution was not a violation at all. Historically these contentions have little importance.   The outcome of the decision was the creation of a new department of government.   It was also to contribute a new idea to the science of democratic self-rule.   It was the introduction into the American system of that "regulation" which Marshall, as a young man in the Virginia Convention, had asserted was necessary to the just working of democracy.   The existence of an impartial umpire to safeguard constitutional rights and to prevent lawmaking bodies from using powers which the Constitution has not given them is generally regarded as America's great contribution to this difficult art of self-government. When Lord Salisbury spoke of America's "magnificent institution of a Supreme Court," which gives "a stability to the institutions of the country which, under the system of vague and mysterious promises here, we look for in vain," it was this power established by John Marshall that he had in mind.

BOOK III

THE RISE AND FALL OF NULLIFICATION

I

THOUGH Jefferson accepted the Marbury decision, the Supreme Court still remained his favorite aversion. The position it attained as interpreter of the Constitution aroused his bitter antagonism. In the Supreme Court, he asserted, the Federal Party had entrenched itself for the purpose of destroying his Republican system. That had been his idea in 1801, when he ascended to power; that was his conviction in 1809, when Madison succeeded him in the Presidency; and that persuasion persisted for the seventeen years he lived in ostensible retirement. His last letters are full of such recriminations. The experiment in Republicanism had failed, largely because the judiciary was usurping the highest functions of government. "The great object of my fear," Jefferson wrote in 1821, "is the Federal Judiciary. That body, like gravity, ever acting with noiseless foot, and unalarming advance, gaining ground step by step, and holding what it gains, is engulfing insidiously the special government into the jaws of that which feeds them." "It is a very dangerous doctrine to consider the judges as the ultimate arbiters of all constitutional questions. It is one which should place us under the despotism of an oligarchy. . . . The Constitution has erected no such single tribunal." And to Edward Livingston, a few months before Jefferson's death, the same foreboding was expressed: "This member of the government [the Judiciary] was at first considered the most helpless and harmless of all its organs. But it has proved that its power of declaring what the law is, *ad libitum,* by sapping and mining, slyly, and without alarm, the foundations of the Constitution, could do what open force would not dare to attempt."

These are the words of a defeated man. And, so far as the Constitution was concerned, Jefferson had fought a losing battle. Many of the Jeffersonian ideas had passed into forgetfulness by the time of his death, and into the general discard had gone his belittlement of the judiciary. In writing his final abjurations Jefferson had in mind the completeness of this failure. In particular, the figure of John Marshall loomed large in memory — the man who, at every step, had stood athwart the Jeffersonian path. The famous decisions in which his fellow Virginian, in Jefferson's last years, still further erected the structure of national life only strengthened the fabric he had begun in the early days of the century. George Mason, it will be recalled, anticipated, in the Virginia Convention, this slow, patient, but resistless process of "consolidation." This would be the work, Mason declared, of the judiciary department. To a degree that prognostication had been fulfilled. The struggle was not ended; Nationalism and State rights were to provide the issues of American public life for the next forty years — indeed the two conflicting views are a most pressing problem of the present moment; but the function of the Supreme Court as the protector of the Constitution had been established.

The several stages of this process form a long and complicated story. All methods, political and judicial, had been used to lessen Marshall's importance. Jefferson himself, after the Marbury decision, — a decision which, at first, disturbed him more for the pretended right of the Court to issue "orders" to the Executive than for the assertion of judicial review, — had attacked the new tribunal in several ways. The repeal of Adams's judiciary system — a system which, in the opinion of Charles Warren, represented a much needed reform — has already been described. In the same general assault the sessions of the Supreme Court were cut from two to one a year. For fourteen months, from December 1801 to February 1803, the highest tribunal, though the calendar was clogged with cases, — for the time when this body met only to adjourn had long since disappeared, — ceased to function. But the most destructive blow ever leveled at this object of Jefferson's detestation was the attempted impeachment of Justice Chase. This is as vital an event in American history as the impeachment of Andrew Johnson sixty years afterward. In both cases the purpose and the motive were the same. In both instances the end aimed at was the removal of a public officer obnoxious to the forces uppermost in politics; the method utilized, in 1805 as in 1868, was political pressure. The failure to remove Chase from the Supreme Court Bench because his manners and decisions were distasteful to the Jeffersonian party did much to solidify the Supreme Bench in the national system; similarly the collapse of the plot to displace Andrew Johnson because his policies did not agree with those of the radical leaders in the Reconstruction era exerted an incalculable influence in safeguarding the chief magistracy from partisan attack. The discomfiture of the destructionists in both instances was a triumph for American common sense and patriotism.

That Samuel Chase, in his own or the present time, represented the highest ideal of a judge would not be maintained. He was insolent, vulgar, irascible, totally lacking in dignity or in any sense of the proprieties of his office. His advocacy of the Federalist Party on the stump, his speeches from the bench denouncing Jefferson, his tyrannical treatment of counsel in open court, his brawlings and browbeatings — all these things have given him an unenviable notoriety in judicial annals. When the Jeffersonian party sought to remove him from the bench, however, they were engaging in an enterprise for which the Constitution gave no warrant. That document carefully specifies the causes of impeachment of "all civil officers." These are "treason, bribery or other high crimes and misdemeanors." Chase's personal behavior had been outrageous; he had offended many highly placed men — including Jefferson and his cohorts; but no evidence was produced that he had committed any of these crimes. Indeed it was hardly pretended that he had; the motive for the proceedings against him was almost frankly political. Again this impeachment reflects that maze of contradictions which formed Jefferson's political character. He was the great "strict constructionist" — the man who insisted on the technical interpretation of the Constitution, of keeping to its letter and never seeking to expand its spirit; yet in this instance his aim was to use impeachment for a purpose never contemplated by the fathers. In the Jeffersonian vocabulary "impeachment" was another word for "removal." The plan was, by commanding a majority in the House and a two-thirds vote in the Senate, to use this impeachment clause of the Constitution to get rid of any judge whose place was desired by the predominant power. In 1805 this meant all but one of the six judges then making up the Court. Had the impeachment of Chase succeeded, it was intended to free the bench of all Federalists, including Marshall himself. By the Jeffersonian party this programme was frankly avowed. Jefferson's spokesman in the Senate, who had charge of the Chase proceedings, was William B. Giles of Virginia. "Mr. Giles gave us his theory of impeachments under the Constitution," John Quincy Adams writes in his diary for December 20, 1804. "According to him, impeachment is nothing more than an inquiry, by the two houses of Congress, whether the office of any public man might not better be filled by another.   This undoubtedly is the source and object of Mr. Chase's impeachment, and on the same principle any officer may easily be removed at any time."

Next day Senator Giles unfolded his ideas even more directly. After adjournment of the Senate, "sitting by the fireside," Adams records, "I witnessed a conversation between Mr. Giles and Mr. Israel Smith, on the subject of impeachments, during which Mr. John Randolph came in and took part in the conversation.   Giles labored with excessive earnestness to convince Smith of certain principles upon which not only Mr. Chase, but all the other judges of the Supreme Court, except the one last appointed, must be impeached and removed.   He treated with the utmost contempt the idea of an *independent* [1] judiciary — said there was not a word about such an independence in the Constitution, and that their pretensions to it were nothing more nor less than an attempt to establish an aristocratic despotism among themselves.   The power of impeachment was given without limitation to the House of Representatives; the power of trying impeachments was given equally without limitation to the Senate; and if the judges of the Supreme Court should dare, AS THEY HAD DONE, to declare an act of Congress unconstitutional, or to send a mandamus to the Secretary of State, AS THEY HAD DONE, it was the undoubted right of the House of Representatives to impeach them, and of the Senate to remove them, for giving such opinions, however honest or sincere they may have been in entertaining them.   Impeachment was not a criminal prosecution; it was no prosecution at all. . . .   A trial and removal of a judge upon impeachment need not imply any criminality or corruption in him.   Congress had no power over the person, but only over the office.   And a removal by impeachment was nothing more than a declaration by Congress to this effect: You hold dangerous opinions and if you are suffered to carry them into effect you will work the destruction of the nation.   *We want your offices* for the purpose of giving them to men who will fill them better."

"I perceive," was Adams's gloss on this conversation, "that the impeachment system is to be pursued, and the whole bench of the Supreme Court to be swept away, *because their offices are wanted.* And in the present state of things I am convinced it is as easy for Mr. John Randolph and Mr. Giles to do this as to say it."

Jefferson's control over Congress was strong, but not powerful enough to carry into practice this conception of impeachment. Senators in sufficient number, of his own party, rejected the idea,

[1] Italics and capitals in this quotation appear in the original.

and insisted that only evidence of an indictable offense would warrant Chase's removal. That destruction would have followed had this view prevailed needs no demonstration. Impeachment would have become merely a means for that "recall of judges" of which much has been heard in recent times. Under this Jeffersonian procedure, the treatment of all unpopular judges, then and in crises since, would have been simple. A vote of Congress would have sufficed to retire them all to private life. The judiciary, as a mechanism for interpreting the Constitution and distributing justice with independent and untrammeled hand, would have disappeared. How simple would be Franklin Roosevelt's problem at the present writing with disliked justices had Jefferson's theory of judicial impeachment become the established order!

But Jefferson did not abandon his warfare on the judiciary. Failing in this attempt, he resorted to another method — a method which has found imitators in modern times. In the quotation above, Mr. Adams notes that only one member of the Supreme Court was to be permitted to hold his seat. That was Judge William Johnson, Jefferson's recent appointment from South Carolina. An upholder for many years of good Republican doctrine, a foe to extreme Federalism and Federalist interpretation of the Constitution, Judge Johnson apparently met all the Jeffersonian qualifications of an upright judge. Appointment should be made on strictly political grounds — such was the conviction that constantly appears in Jefferson's writings. Not only should the nominee be a strict party man, of long-tested loyalty, but his views should be identical with those of the administration in power. Considerations of this kind had led to Johnson's selection. In 1810, when the judge whom Jefferson rather irreverently calls "old Cushing" died, he advocated a successor of Republican breed. "At length," wrote Jefferson, "we have a chance of getting a Republican majority in the Supreme Judiciary. For ten years that branch has braved the spirit and will of the nation, after the nation had manifested its will by a complete reform in every branch depending on them." Jefferson might have been writing in 1937! He therefore called upon Madison, now President, to "appoint a democratic Republican, with nothing equivalent about him." But both Jefferson and Madison were to learn that attempts to "pack" the bench do not always succeed. Johnson, Jefferson's Republican choice, turned against his chief in embargo matters, and displayed a complete independence that furnished a model for future generations. Similarly the "Democratic-Republican" Madison so carefully picked as "old Cushing's" successor turned out to be Joseph Story, one of the greatest jurists America has ever known, as famous for his *Commentaries* and other juristic writings as for the high standards and complete independence maintained through thirty-four years on the highest court. Some kind of ichor evidently enters the blood of Supreme Court judges which, irrespective of partisanship displayed in private life, converts them into wonders of impartiality and high honor once they are promoted for life to this exalted station. "Packing the bench" has been shown to involve fundamental misunderstandings of human nature.

Thus, by repealing circuit laws, by limiting to one year the sessions of the Supreme Bench, by impeaching judges, by attempting to make them elective for comparatively short terms and removable by Congress and the President, finally by appointing only good party men who were expected to interpret law in a way sympathetic to the administration, Jefferson waged his war on the judiciary. But failure met him on every hand. For during the years when this programme was being pursued, Marshall and his associates were steadily increasing judicial power. Decision after decision, extending the national ideal, made miserable the great philosopher's final years. "The slipperiness of the eels of the law" was only one of many characterizations hurled at the Supreme Bench from Monticello.

The more far-reaching decisions came in the last years of Jefferson's life. In 1819 two pronouncements fixed principles which are still vital in the American system, but which were as odious to Jeffersonian doctrines as the case of William Marbury. The Dartmouth College suit, as celebrated for the plea of Daniel Webster as for Marshall's decision, asserted the determination of the Federal government to enforce the sanctity of contracts. The case of McCulloch against the State of Maryland gave finality to a principle that had figured in all ratification debates in 1788, and which ran foul of the most precious philosophy of the State-rights school. Could the states, by the simple process of passing contradictory laws, nullify legislation of Congress? Could they destroy, by such legislation, institutions which the national government had erected, relying upon those "implied powers" regarded as conferred by the Constitution? Congress had established a United States Bank. In many communities this was immensely unpopular. The wranglings it set loose against the Federal government form a lively episode in American history. In order to rid themselves of the obnoxious corporation, certain states passed laws that taxed its branches. Maryland, desiring to destroy the Bank in Baltimore,

proceeded to levy a tax that would have made its operation unprofitable. No secret was made of the real purpose in view. The
Democratic majority in the legislature hated the Bank, the creation
of Alexander Hamilton and his Federalist Party, and resorted to
this method of driving it out of existence. In other words, a state
was making war upon an institution chartered by the Federal government, presumably in accordance with authority residing in the
Constitution. It is not difficult to see where the Constitution would
end if this proceeding were to rest unchallenged. That instrument would be reduced to nullity and the State-rights school would
rise triumphant. The fiery discussion that accompanied the plead-
ings — the assertion of state independence emanating from John
Taylor of Caroline, Thomas Jefferson, John Randolph, Spencer
Roane, and all the other spokesmen of the familiar doctrine, with
counterblasts from upholders of centralization — shows that this
fact was well understood. The law in question had been passed
by the "sovereign state" of Maryland. Had the Supreme Court
the right to set aside a state law on constitutional grounds? In
Marbury vs. *Madison* it had annihilated a law of Congress; that was
bad enough, according to John Taylor and his associates, but to
reach its hand over a state legislature and declare void one of its
measures, on the ground that it violated the Federal Charter, was
infinitely worse. Again there rose threats of secession, should the
Supreme Court presume to invade State rights in this high-handed
fashion. Such a decision, said Jefferson and Taylor, would mean
the end of the states and the final emergence of that "consolidated
government" against which they had been preaching since 1789.

Marshall met the challenge in his usual intrepid fashion. His
opinion in this case, *McCulloch* vs. *Maryland,* ranks next to Marbury
in its influence on the Nationalistic ideal. That the Supreme Court
could quash state laws conflicting with the Federal Constitution he
took for granted. Does not the document itself proclaim that "this
Constitution and the laws of the United States which shall be made
in pursuance thereof . . . shall be the supreme law of the land"?
How then can a state legislature pass legislation which violates it?
And that the Maryland law taxing the United States Bank did
run foul of the Constitution Marshall proceeded to show, in an
opinion as notable for its logic and statement of constitutional principles as for its sparkling, lucid English. It contains phrases that
have passed into current speech. In developing the famous doctrine
of "implied powers," Marshall answered, once and for all, the
question of the authority of Congress, under that section which

permitted it to pass "all laws which shall be necessary and proper for carrying into execution" the prerogatives enumerated. "Let the end be legitimate, let it be within the scope of the Constitution, and all means which are appropriate, which are plainly adapted to that end, which are not prohibited, which consist with the letter and spirit of the Constitution, are constitutional." Had the Federal government power to establish a bank? That was denied by State-rights advocates then — a denial that looks a little absurd in this day of Federal Reserve Systems, farm loan banks, Home Owners' Loan Corporations, and countless other Federal corporations of similar type. It was Marshall's ruling that made possible this modern use of Federal control. And if the Federal government had the right to establish a bank, certainly no state had the right to demolish it. Could any more effective way of reducing the Bank to ruins be devised than taxation? "The power to tax is the power to destroy." And so the Maryland law and other similar measures in other states vanished from the statute books. The Supreme Court had crushed them.

The decision itself was calamity enough, in the eyes of the State-rights adherents; an especially bitter phase of the matter was that it was unanimous. And the Supreme Court Bench was in 1819 overwhelmingly Jeffersonian. Of the seven members only two were Federalists. The Jeffersonian plan of freeing that tribunal of political opponents had succeeded; five of its members had been appointed by Jefferson, Madison, and Monroe, famous as the "Virginia dynasty." Yet all these men, supposedly upholders of the Virginia school, had joined their Federalist brothers in negativing this act of the Maryland legislature. William Johnson, whom Jefferson, after a patient search for a man of sound Republican principles, had elevated to the bench, supported Marshall's contention.

But Jefferson was to suffer another even more destructive blow to his conception of Republican rule. It came in 1824, when the author of the Declaration of Independence was eighty years old, and gave the final impetus to his pessimistic views of his country's future. But in considering the "Steamboat Case," as it was popularly known, we do not think so much of Jefferson, in his last days at Monticello, watching his constitutional ideas falling in ruins, as of Washington at Mount Vernon, in 1785, entertaining those commissions from Maryland and Virginia who had gathered to settle conflicting claims on the navigation of the Potomac. We think also of Hamilton and Madison at the Annapolis Convention in 1786, laying plans for the greater assembly at Philadelphia in 1787. For the problem that brought the commissioners to Mount Vernon and the delegates to Annapolis and Philadelphia was not solved until John Marshall, in 1824, delivered that judgment that figures in constitutional annals as *Gibbons* vs. *Ogden*. The purpose that had been aimed at in all these meetings and in the Constitution itself was, first of all, the regulation of commerce between the states. That issue was not definitely settled until Marshall's decision. The fact that the lawsuit in question was known as the "Steamboat Case" shows that America had passed into a new age. Members of the Philadelphia Convention of 1787 did have a faint glimpse into the future, but, so far as history records, none foresaw its meaning. On an August day the delegates were invited to view the launching and operation of a new water craft, propelled by a steam engine, the work of the unlucky Connecticut Yankee who has passed into history as "poor John Fitch." No one apparently suspected that this contrivance was to accomplish more than any single agency in knitting the American states into a nation and presenting their descendants with one of the greatest problems in constitutional interpretation.

The delegates, after witnessing the Fitch boat progress slowly up the river, by virtue of power imparted by strings of paddles along the side, moving back and forth by some invisible force, returned to the convention hall, and, in due course, adopted that clause in the new Constitution which gives Congress power "to regulate commerce with foreign nations, and among the several States, and with the Indian tribes." Whether the delegates appreciated the connection between this phrase and the scene they had witnessed on the Delaware is not recorded. Probably they saw no association, for the new clause produced little discussion and went into the Constitution almost automatically. The question at issue had been actively debated for years, and the evils to be corrected were glaring; the convention, in fact, had assembled largely for the purpose of giving the Federal government this power. Neither did the state legislatures, for many years, perceive any relationship between this grant over interstate commerce and John Fitch's steamboat. In 1807 Robert Fulton succeeded in doing what John Fitch had never accomplished — he established a successful commercial steamboat service on the Hudson. And now one circumstance disclosed how far the commerce clause of the Constitution had been forgotten. Fulton had formed a partnership with Robert R. Livingston, and Livingston, it appeared, had secured from the New York legislature a monopoly of steamboat traffic on the Hudson. Livingston was a powerful citizen, both politically and socially, and it is a simple matter to attribute this special privilege to his personal influence. Nevertheless the legislators who voted the monopoly hardly believed that they were doing him great service. The whole thing was regarded as a joke. If a New Yorker at the present time should ask the exclusive right to transport passengers and freight to the planet Mercury the request would arouse the same response as did Livingston's appeal in 1798. But Livingston was familiar with Fulton's experiments in France and rated the privilege more highly.

And so, when the *Clermont* began chugging noisily up the Hudson, increasing its freight and passenger traffic with every trip and rapidly developing into a treasure chest for its owners, the discovery was made that only Fulton and Livingston had the right to use the river for that purpose. Any other citizen presuming to engage in the business was forced to depend upon the winds for motive power. Steam was a monopoly reserved for these two farsighted gentlemen. They had been even more forehanded, for they had secured the same exclusive right to navigate the Mississippi. Had their position continued unchallenged, all the picturesque river traffic for which the Mississippi subsequently became so famous could have come into existence only by paying tribute to these citizens of New York. Other monopolists obtained identical rights on the Ohio and many of its tributaries. Lake Champlain soon became a closed sea except to a certain group of capitalists. The Connecticut River, so far as steam was concerned, became the property of other sons of fortune — and undoubtedly of politics. Naturally there were forward-looking souls in those days who opposed these engrossing tactics. But they met opposition at every turn from the entrenched beneficiaries of monopoly. Their frequent appeals to the courts were coldly received. Even so great a judge as Chancellor Kent, of New York, decided that Livingston's grant was unassailable. No one, except by making terms with the triumphant combine, could run even a steam ferryboat from Jersey City to Manhattan Island. A particularly daring adventurer sought to establish a regular steamboat line from Elizabethtown, New Jersey, to New York. But when his vessel touched the waters of New York Bay it was seized and confiscated, under a law recently passed. The old-fashioned Jeffersonians thought that this was all as it should be. It was a legitimate exercise of State rights. Were not the harbors and rivers of a state the exclusive property of the state in question? Had it not the privilege of prescribing regulations for their use? For a "foreign" country — New Jersey was a foreign country to New York from this point of view — to intrude with its vessels on a state that insisted on exclusion was to enter territory where it did not belong.

After about twenty years of hermit-like policy, a growing spirit of public hostility began to lend support to those constitutionalists who had been insistent from the first that these principles violated their cherished instrument. What did the Interstate Commerce clause mean? Anti-Livingstonians insisted that it made all watercourses, for purpose of navigation and commerce, open to all vessels of the nation at large, irrespective of motive power; that Connecticut could freely send its steamers to New York and that New York could send hers to Virginia and South Carolina. It certainly meant, they persisted, that not the individual states, but Congress, could fix the terms on which these watercourses could be used. In modern days of open intercourse, of the greatest coasting trade known to the world, of railroads running freely from state to state, of bus and airplane traffic, — of a huge nation, to the extent of three thousand miles, completely at the disposal of anyone who wishes to use its transportation routes, — it seems strange that much breath was wasted in so obvious an argument. Had the opposing view prevailed, the states of the American Union would have become individual entities indeed, constantly shutting out each other's citizens, engaging in everlasting commercial war; and the greatest privileges of civilized countries, those of transportation and of intimate, easy circulation, would have remained the monopoly of a few powerful groups. That all these restrictions were broken down and the whole nation, in the matter of commercial and personal intercourse, made a unit was the achievement of another of Marshall's decisions — probably the most potent of all so far as its nationalizing effect is concerned.

That was the meaning of *Gibbons* vs. *Ogden*. It proved to be, as the historian of the Supreme Court has called it, "the emancipation proclamation of American commerce." It is the base of all the interstate commerce acts, Sherman anti-trust laws, measures for regulating telegraphs, telephones, and other utilities which are now so permanently embedded in the American system. Yet to the lay reader of the present day this is not one of the most interesting of Marshall's outgivings, chiefly because it proves so exhaustively contentions which, to the modern mind, scarcely call for proof. It is almost impossible for us to transport ourselves back to the era when the constitutional right to regulate commerce needed so exhaustive a demonstration, and when there existed a large body of thought which insisted that this was the right of the states. Only when the events of that period are reviewed, and the outburst of public emotion that followed the decision is considered, does the event stand out in its true proportions. For seldom has a court decision so stirred popular emotion. The monopoly grants to steamboats were hated everywhere, even in the states that gave them. The Livingston empire on the Hudson River was as much detested by New Yorkers as by New Jerseyites, for it excluded all New York citizens from the dominion asserted by this influential family. The celebrations that followed Marshall's judgment recall the rejoicings caused by the repeal of the Stamp Act and the Declaration of Independence, to which events, indeed, it had a certain resemblance. A few days after the pronouncement the steamboat *United States,* from New Haven, sailed into the waters of New York Harbor. It was decorated in high colors and a large company of passengers cheered furiously as the ship proceeded to the dock, unimpeded by harbor officials of New York. On the wharf stood a considerable population, welcoming the one-time intruder with huzzas, and the festivities that ensued reflected the utter lack of enthusiasm for the restrictive laws. All along the Atlantic Coast similar scenes took place. Vessels arriving from "foreign" states were met by salvos of friendly guns, by bonfires, fireworks, and public banquets. American commerce was at last free; the aspirations of Washington and his compeers had been made a fact. America, so far as its rivers and harbors and navigation were concerned, had at last become a nation.

The vast enhancement of trade and navigation that followed *Gibbons* vs. *Ogden* demonstrated its effect in unlocking the resources and enterprises of the American people. A new day was dawning, a time that had not been foreseen in the philosophies of John Taylor and his disciples. It was a time in which the Jeffersonian principles of localism could not possibly endure. This year of the commerce decision, 1824, may be taken as the dividing line between the old and the new. A section little known to the Revolutionary generation, a section feared as a menace to American stability and to the Constitution, was coming into national consciousness — a region that, in ideas and in leadership, was to perform its share in cementing the nation.

II

New names now come to the front in the constitutional story. These are men who had no part in the Revolution and the political events that followed. Several of the founders — Jefferson, Madison, Monroe, John Adams — lingered for a time, but in the retirement of their country homes. The year 1824 witnessed a change in leadership no less revolutionary than 1800, a change that involved more than a mere alteration in personal forces. The West, which, until the second war with Britain, had been a threat to national union was now developing a loyalty whose effects the most farsighted scarcely foresaw. By the West was understood the new states beyond the Alleghenies — Ohio, Indiana, Kentucky, western Virginia — as well as the "backlands," or uplands of western North Carolina and Tennessee. This area now comprised a fairly homogeneous country, as distinct in its characteristics as New England, the Atlantic midland states, and the tidewater South. And its quality, socially and politically, had little in common with the region of original settlement. The predominant race was Scotch-Irish; the predominant religion the Presbyterian; the predominant occupation old-fashioned agriculture; the predominant form of labor the independent, free yeoman farmer. The difficulty with which the Constitution had made its way in this distant American world has already been described; it was the land of whiskey rebellions, of British and French and Spanish intrigues, of a population whose economic outlook flowed not eastward to the Atlantic Coast, but southerly through the Mississippi Valley. The purchase of Louisiana, and the War of 1812, made the Mississippi forever an American highway, and so established the allegiance of the trans-Allegheny country by the strongest of all bonds, that of economic interest.

And from this time forward this Western frontier was to wield a powerful force on the side of union. The war had brought to the front a group of extremely able young men — men in every way competent to carry forward the work of the Constitution makers of 1787. It is true that the greatest of the quartet which for the fifty years following the War of 1812 directed constitutional history was a New Englander of unassailable breed, but Daniel Webster was also a frontiersman; he was born and spent his early life in Salisbury, New Hampshire, itself a log-cabin country, farthest north of American settlements.   But his associates — Henry Clay of Kentucky, Andrew Jackson of Tennessee, John C. Calhoun of upland South Carolina — represented the new Western country.   This latter trio, reaching Washington during the excitements caused by Orders in Council and Milan Decrees, became the "war hawks" of the second contest with England, and, when this was finally settled by the Treaty of Ghent in 1814, proceeded to engage in battles almost as sanguinary in the politics of the day.   The war, as wars so commonly do, had created a new country.   Certain military aspects of that struggle were not flattering to national pride, but the last martial engagement, in which an army of raw, underdisciplined troops, inferior to their adversary in numbers, training, and equipment, outgeneraled and outfought that adversary, composed in the main of Wellington's veterans of the Peninsula, completely discounted all the humiliations of earlier campaigns.   The performance was symbolic of the new day, for both the general in this campaign and the forces under his command came from that Western frontier which had now wholeheartedly cast in its lot with the Union.   It indicated how completely America was separating from its past.   Already the discerning had grasped a fact of historic import — that the reign of Virginia in American public affairs was coming to an end.   Another Virginian, the one eligible survivor of the Revolutionary group, assumed the Presidency in 1817, but everyone knew that James Monroe would be the last of that company to head the nation.   Hardly had he taken office when the scramble for the succession began.   This struggle involved not only the break-up of parties, but the forming of new alignments, the launching of new public issues, the creation of loyalties and convictions that formed the substance of American public life for the next fifty years.   Virginia had furnished the President for twenty-eight out of the thirty-six years from 1789 to 1825, and the realization that someone not elected from the Old Dominion could guide the affairs of America gave a new aspect, as well as a new commotion, to political life.   And the transition was a permanent one, for since 1825 no man chosen from Virginia has occupied the Presidential chair.[1]

---

[1] John Tyler, it is true, became President in 1841, but he was not elected to the office, succeeding as Vice President on the death of President Harrison.   Other Presidents, born in Virginia but elected as citizens of other states, were William Henry Harrison of Indiana, Zachary Taylor of Louisiana, and Woodrow Wilson of New Jersey.

Two of the most influential statesmen of this day were born in the same year, 1782, just as the Revolution was coming to an end. Daniel Webster was the son of pioneering New England farmer stock, and John C. Calhoun, of the upland county of Abbeville, South Carolina, was the son of Scottish Covenanters who, settled in Ireland in the time of Cromwell, found their way to the Shenandoah Valley in the early eighteenth century, and thence, by oxcart and horseback, advanced through the Watauga and Waxhaw country of North Carolina into the rich land of the Savannah River. Thus Webster was no more the descendant of that rich commercial and professional aristocracy dominant in New England in the early century than was Calhoun an offshoot of the cotton and rice grandees of the South Carolina seaboard. Both men, however, were in due course to become identified with the predominant elements in their respective communities. And both manifested, in all their strength, the characteristic virtues of their sections. No two faces, if we except Washington and Lincoln, are so indelibly impressed on the American consciousness. One is struck, comparing surviving portraits of these men with the representations of American leaders of the last fifty years, with a certain power, unusualness, pungency, and individuality in the lineaments of the early nineteenth century. Where to-day do we find anything in the human countenance as masterful as the piercing, sunken eyes, lofty cranium, and tight-lipped mouth of Webster, or the glowering, uncompromising features of Calhoun? These faces are history in themselves. The portrait which has most deeply seized the American mind is Webster, both because he fought on the winning side and because his nature, with all its inexorableness, had a greater human warmth than did that of his Southern rival and found expression in glowing orations that have survived as literature still vibrant with national ambitions; while to open the bulky writings of Calhoun is like excavating a dead city, so full are they of conceptions that now form the American political museum.

In devotion to the Constitution, Webster's life presents a model of consistency. Love of the Union was his earliest allegiance. In him that dictum attributed to the Jesuits, "Give us the child until his seventh year, and we don't care who has charge of his training afterward," finds a perfect confirmation. For the human mind, in this plastic period, absorbs fixed ideas, not only in religion, but on political principles and loyalties. And the ideals constantly held before this keen, impressionable boy were Washington and the Constitution. Ebenezer Webster, the father, was outwardly a plain New England farmer, not particularly different from thousands of others in that

New Hampshire country where he had set up his home. He was rough-mannered, unschooled, hard-working, of deep religious faith, patriotic in primitive, fervid fashion; and his soul similarly burned with zeal for Washington and for the Constitution. Both these enthusiasms he had acquired by authentic experience. Ebenezer had been one of the first of those Minutemen who were roused to enlistment on the news of Bunker Hill; he had fought at the siege of Boston, at Long Island and at White Plains, as well as in most of the campaigns of the Revolution, finally reaching colonel's rank. More important were his several meetings with Washington, which he loved to describe to the admiring Daniel. At West Point, on the eve of Arnold's treason, Ebenezer was selected by Washington as officer of the guard, and Washington's commendation on that occasion, "Captain Webster, I am sure I can trust you," was, as Daniel Webster afterward said, the finest inheritance his father could have left him. Indeed it was almost the only one, for the Webster family was poor, the soil from which it derived sustenance was of the traditional rocky New England type, and the upbringing of a large family was an unending struggle. But most of what Daniel Webster became is traceable to this father. His very appearance — a tall, erect figure, dark complexion, raven hair, piercing eyes — foreshadowed the future orator. He was as great a failure in practical matters as his irresponsible son, and that same primary interest in public affairs and the intellectual life that, in Daniel Webster, did so much to shape the nation's history was similarly marked in the father.

Ebenezer Webster never realized his highest ambition, which was to represent his district in Congress, but he did become a judge, served in the New Hampshire legislature, and in the convention called by New Hampshire to consider the new Federal Constitution he exercised a decisive influence. His work in that body was the episode in which his son took the greatest pride. It probably exerted a greater influence than any single early experience in shaping the man's career. So much weight did Webster himself attach to his father's work in the Constitutional Convention of New Hampshire that he carefully told the whole story to George Ticknor Curtis, with the request that he should make it public. The sentiment of New Hampshire when Ebenezer Webster entered the convention was opposed to ratification. Like most of the other delegates he had been sent to Concord under instructions from his town to vote against the "new plan." This, however, did not accord with his private views and, taking advantage of a recess in the deliberations, Webster went

HENRY CLAY

JOHN C. CALHOUN

Courtesy of Frick Art Reference Library

SALMON P. CHASE

Courtesy of Frick Art Reference Library

DANIEL WEBSTER

home, pleaded with his constituents, and finally obtained permission to vote in accordance with his judgment. The speech the father made on that occasion, which Daniel as a boy committed to memory and in after life frequently repeated to his friends, probably had a greater educational effect than all the volumes subsequently studied. In it is found the germ of his career, as lawyer and statesman. "Mr. President, I have listened to the arguments for and against the Constitution. I am convinced such a government as that Constitution will establish, if adopted — a government acting directly on the people of the states — is necessary for the common defense and the general welfare. It is the only government which will enable us to pay off the national debt — the debt which we owe for the Revolution and which we are bound in honor fully and fairly to discharge. Besides, I have followed the lead of Washington through seven years of war, and I have never been misled. His name is subscribed to this Constitution. He will not mislead us and — I shall vote for its adoption."

Herein are found, or at least implied, certain of the ideas to which Webster's life was to be devoted. The government was one directly acting on the "people" — that is, a national government, not a loose confederacy of states; it was to be a strong one, able to maintain national honor, fulfill national obligations, protect the country from foreign foes, and — the phrase is significant in view of the interest ever since attached to it — "promote the general welfare." The elder Webster's advocacy may have had a greater influence upon history than appears in the record. New Hampshire was a "pivotal" state. It was provided that the constitution should go into effect when nine states had ratified; and the affirmative vote in this far-away region was the ninth and thus put the new charter into effect. News of its action reached Richmond when Madison and his friends were fighting a hard battle in the Virginia Convention and gave an impetus the cause desperately needed. At this time Daniel Webster was a child six years old, being taught to read by his older sisters, the Bible serving as textbook, but from that day to his death the Constitution was almost a daily companion. One of his earliest recollections, which he always liked to tell, was purchasing for a few pennies a cotton handkerchief from the country store, on which the Constitution was printed; the treasure remained in his possession for several years and thus the period that the boy of the present time devotes to detective stories Webster spent conning the several articles and sections which he was afterward to expound in Congress and before the Supreme Court. Another piece of literature picked up in this fugitive fashion was that same classic, with its capitalized admonitions to Union, Order, Harmony, and Subordination, which had done so much to frame the adolescent mind of John Marshall. "I remember," writes Webster, in his fragment of an *Autobiography*, "that my father brought home from some of the lower towns Pope's *Essay on Man*, published in a sort of pamphlet. I took it and very soon could repeat it from beginning to end. We had so few books that to read them once or twice was nothing. We thought they were all to be got by heart." Another volume absorbed on the same basis was the Bible. "I do not remember when or by whom I was taught to read; because I cannot and never could recollect the time when I could not read the Bible. I suppose I was taught by my mother or by my elder sisters." In after years Webster was famous for his ability to repeat verbatim chapter after chapter of the Old Testament. He similarly exercised his juvenile talent for memorizing on the poetical works of Dr. Watts. "By far the greater part of Dr. Watts' Psalms and Hymns I could repeat *memoriter* at ten or twelve years of age."

Thus the Constitution, the *Essay on Man*, the Bible, and Watts's *Hymns* seem to have been the literature on which this childish mind mainly fed. The collection is significant, for Webster, from youth to age, was intellectually the simplest of souls, his conceptions being the fundamental ones of primitive evangelical religion, of reverence for tradition, belief in property and law as its protector, veneration of the American Revolution and what, he ever reiterated, was its greatest product — the organic law of 1787. His early orations, delivered when a student at Dartmouth and a rising lawyer at Portsmouth, New Hampshire, have been assembled and preserved amid the nineteen volumes that now constitute his works. They would be worthy of study, even though the speaker had not outgrown the tawdry rhetoric they disclose and become one of the greatest orators of all time. For they mirror the thoughts and emotions of the New England that was emerging from the eighteenth into the nineteenth century — a New England that was Protestant to its core, that despised "Papists" and Voltaire, that literally accepted the Bible, regarded Thomas Jefferson as Antichrist, and idolized Washington and John Adams as the pillars of the state. All this was Webster; he was elemental, traditional, the inheritor and propagator of Anglo-Saxon conceptions of life, impervious to innovation, a solid rock of convictions accumulated and sanctified by time. "The man is a little cathedral in himself," explained Sydney Smith, gaining his first glimpse of Webster. Smith was vastly impressed by the American's appearance, as were all Englishmen with whom he was thrown in association, but the phrase might be also applied to Webster's spiritual side, for he was as solid and conservative as a cathedral, as much the creation of minds and racial ideas of the past. All this stands out exuberantly in these early speeches. His first appearance on the scene is in the character which also belongs to the childhood of the nation — the Fourth of July orator.

In style these speeches hardly foreshadow the dignified and restrained enthusiasm that became the quality of Webster's mature manner; but in conviction, in national ideals, even in constitutional interpretation, the coming American prophet stands revealed. His oration at Hanover in his eighteenth year, while still an undergraduate, was so highly esteemed that it was published in pamphlet form. Evidently the young man's glowing faith in the Constitution struck a responsive chord. Only eleven years had passed since the new government had started operations; during all that time the Federalist Party had directed the destinies of the nation; John Adams was still President, and the election that was to install the Jeffersonians in power and cause so pessimistic a revulsion in New England had not yet taken place. Afterward the lifelong constitutional debate between Webster and Calhoun turned on one point: was it a popular government, established by the people, or an impersonal, rigid confederation of independent states? The point was one that became familiar enough in the discussions of the next fifty years, but it had not reached a critical stage in 1800. Yet Webster's boyish speech contained the germ of his subsequent attitude. "In the adoption of our present system of jurisprudence, we see the powers necessary for the government voluntarily springing from the people, their only proper origin, and directed to the public good, their only proper object." This sentence not only sounds the doctrine of the whole Websterian course, but is a precocious foreshadowing of the Gettysburg Address. Webster's whole declamation, indeed, — and the statement is true of other Fourth of July performances in the next few years, the period he spent studying law and making his beginnings in practice, — is a glorification of the Constitution. "Glorification" is the descriptive word, for his expressions are flamboyant, uncritical, juvenile, quotable only as making emphatic his predominant bent. Search history for six thousand years, and nothing will be found so perfect, so just, so fertile in human happiness, as the social and political prospect of America at that time! British justice and even British intellectual life were every day becoming inferior to those of the United States! France was bleeding under the heel of a "supercilious Directory, a gasconading pilgrim of Egypt" — Bonaparte's adventure on the Nile had recently come to a lamentable end. And what was the reason America stood so superior to everything in Europe or Asia? Its form of government, its Constitution! It is "the greatest approximation towards human perfection the political world has ever yet experienced"; it will "forever stand in the history of mankind without a parallel"; its "advantages are utterly incalculable." And much more of the same sort.

Let it be repeated that Daniel Webster was eighteen years old when he thus exhilarated the citizens of his college town in words which, he subsequently wrote, "were in very bad taste; I had not then learned that all true power of writing is in the idea, not in the style." It was a lesson he grasped much more quickly than most of the orators of that blowsy age. Before he was thirty, speeches were issuing from the Webster rostrum clothed in reasonable expression and full of digested conviction. These disclose him as a New England man, deeply imbued with all the New Englander's love of the sea and commerce, all its worship of Washington, all its respect for property and social castes, all its belief in strong, centralized government. That is, Webster was a Federalist — not, however, a Federalist of the Timothy Pickering brand. Afterward, Webster's attitude during the War of 1812 was constantly thrown in his face; he opposed that war with Federalist fervor, but the worst accusations hurled against him, that he had advocated secession and was favorably disposed toward the Hartford Convention, were not true. In many eminent New England characters love of the Constitution did not survive the embargo and the Jefferson-Madison diplomacy; but Webster remained faithful to the ideas absorbed in his boyhood days. He deprecated the war, regarded the administration's conduct as a disgrace, but openly proclaimed his loyalty. The evils taking place in the government were transitory and could be remedied when the Federalist Party should be restored to power, but the Constitution was fixed, and the youthful Webster remained liegeman to that and to the government it had established.

Not that the views of this country lawyer, from 1800 to 1812, caused widespread reverberation; Webster was accepted as a fine, clean-living young man, already marked out by a striking personal appearance and by cleverness as an advocate in modest litigation, but he was too inexperienced and too humble of origin to exercise great influence. In 1812, however, Webster had reached his thirtieth year; he had made steady progress at the Portsmouth bar; and again he was asked to perform his now familiar rôle of Fourth of July orator. The speech delivered on this occasion is, in substance and style, that of a mature man. So great an impression did it make that Webster suddenly found himself elected to Congress. The mere fact that he had settled in Portsmouth intensified his political convictions. He came there in 1807, a year that proved to be the most critical in the town's existence. That was the year the embargo prostrated New England's shipping and all the commercial existence depending upon it. Portsmouth was one of the greatest of New England's ports — celebrated not only for the fleets sailing to the Grand Bank, but as a headquarters of the carrying trade and shipbuilding. Naturally this devastation visited on the town by the war formed the imagery of the young man's castigations. These criticisms, however, were framed in temperate, dignified language; in fact the speech is really a dissertation on the Constitution, especially in its relation to commerce. The Washingtonian and the Jeffersonian methods of dealing with the same international situation are subjected to comparison most unfavorable to the statesman of Monticello. Washington had declared no embargo; of two enemies, both of whom had assailed and insulted the nation, he had not singled out one as a foe against whom to declare war, making a virtual ally of the other, whose injuries were even greater. Washington had not neglected national defense, dismantled such navy as we had, and refused to construct an adequate one, but was constantly building up our military strength. He had not cherished one section of the nation and reduced the other to ruin, but had done all in his power to develop the agriculture of the South and the commercial and industrial greatness of the North. What, after all, had been the chief reason for framing the Constitution? It was adopted, said Webster, "for no single reason so much as for the protection of our commerce." And now followed a eulogy on that commerce and all that it had done for the United States. It "has discharged the debt of the Revolution. It has paid the price of independence. It has filled the Treasury and sustained the government from the first moments of its existence to the present time. The interests and the habits of a vast proportion of the community have become interwoven with this commerce, in a manner not to be changed and that no government has the power of changing. To call upon us now to forsake the seas, to forget the virtues of the magnet, to lose even the observance and guidance of the stars, is to summon us to repeal at once, as well the constitution of civilized man and the laws of nature, as the Constitution of the country."

Yet war had been declared; it was now the law of the nation and "resistance and insurrection form no part of our creed. The disciples of Washington are neither tyrants *in* powers nor rebels *out*. If we are taxed, to carry on this war, we shall disregard certain distinguished examples and shall pay. If our personal services are required we shall yield them to the precise extent of our constitutional liability." But "by the exercise of our constitutional right of suffrage, by the peaceable remedy of election, we shall seek to restore wisdom to our Councils and peace to our country." The right of protest New England also reserved, and under young Webster's leadership proceeded to use it. For Webster was the author of the Rockingham Memorial, adopted at an out-of-door meeting at Brentwood, on August 5, 1812; it was another dignified but not unimpassioned state paper, addressed personally to James Madison, President of the United States, rehearsing all the arguments against the war, describing the evils in which it was engulfing the nation, and demanding that it be brought to a close. So far as the record shows, the President did not pay the Memorial the tribute of acknowledgment, but it had one historic result: it solidified the sentiment created by Webster's recent Fourth of July address in favor of sending this brilliant young man to Congress that he might act further as a gadfly on the Madison administration. It was clearly the case of office seeking the man, for Webster at first resisted the invitation; he had married happily, had two children, had already reached the leadership of the Portsmouth bar and was looking forward to a great professional career. However, as he mused over the situation, the possibility arose in his mind: why could he not be both, a constitutional lawyer and a statesman? Washington was the seat not only of Congress but of the Supreme Court. In this day Americans would look a little doubtfully on legislators practising before the Federal courts, but in Webster's time it was almost inevitable that they should. Poor transportation made it difficult and expensive for lawyers to travel to Washington to plead before the final tribunal; litigants were therefore obliged to retain counsel living near the capital. In a time when the ablest lawyers were commonly selected to represent districts and states in Congress or the Senate, desirable advocates for important cases were usually already on the ground. Thus there was no incongruity or impropriety in Webster's adoption of this dual career. From the moment almost of his arrival in Washington, in May 1813, he became a defender and expounder of the Federal Constitution in three chambers of the raw, unfinished Capitol — in the House of Representatives, afterward in the Senate, and in that crowded little room directly under the latter hall that had been grudgingly set aside for the Supreme Court.

III

One of the first acquaintances made by the thirty-one-year-old Webster was that South Carolinian, of precisely the same age, who was to be his chief legislative rival for the next forty years. Though the two men struck fire at their first meeting, on personal grounds they had many points of sympathy. In fact, though they differed on practically every question that arose, especially questions involving the Constitution, intellectually they maintained cordial relations, based on a mutual respect that lasted undiminished to the end. But the Calhoun of 1813, both in appearance and in opinion, was a different man from the one who remains fixed on the historic landscape. Tall, — more than six feet, — thin, even rangy, his hair not yet having attained the horrendous appearance of subsequent portraits; the face smooth, long, full, unmarked as yet by those high cheekbones which afterward gave it a cadaverous aspect; the features sharp and clear-cut; the gleaming eyes suggesting, at this early stage, eager ambition rather than frustration and disappointment — here was a man, interested in books, in the historic and social phases of public questions, given to personal intercourse and conversation, one to whom chronicles of the day freely ascribed "charm" and "winning manners," an ornament of the best dinner tables of Washington and a friendly gossip in lobbies, whom the New England man readily found companionable. In a certain sense Webster and Calhoun had much in common. Both men, as already stated, came from a log-cabin civilization. Calhoun must not be identified with that glamorous South Carolina that still exercises its spell: the South Carolina of Rutledges, Laurenses, Pinckneys, Lowndeses, and the like; of rice plantations, stately mansions, and splendid gateways — in a word, the South Carolina of Charleston and the adjacent coast. His South Carolina was as distinct from this as though it had been anchored far beyond the Allegheny Mountains. Two streams of settlement had founded this colony and state, one coming by sea and building up the coast line, the other coming overland from the Northern mountains and preëmpting the rich, loamy, upland soil.

To this latter stock belonged Calhoun. His birthplace was a farm in the Abbeville district, almost on the line dividing the state from Georgia. This region was not only distinct, in religion, politics, ways of life, from the sea-island country, but extremely hostile to it. So raw and uncivilized was northwestern South Carolina considered by urbane Charleston that it was shut out from participation in state affairs. It thus developed a kind of local autonomy, living apart from those agencies of government usually deemed essential to orderly life. It was the country in which the "Regulator" for a long time reigned supreme. In the administration of criminal law this term is synonymous with Judge Lynch. Indeed, social investigators looking to-day for the origin of Ku-Klux Klans and similar extralegal institutions could profitably study the upland regions of the lower Southern states in the eighteenth century, in which impossibility of communication with older communities, the ostracism that kept them separate from courts and lawmaking chambers, forced the growth of "Regulation," a system of government based not on constitutions and laws, but on *mores* and tribal conceptions of justice.

Conditions were not quite so rough in Calhoun's boyhood, but the spirit prevailed and did affect him in those impressionable early years. Thus Calhoun's circumambient ideas were diametrically different from Webster's. While the child of New Hampshire was studying the Constitution from a cotton handkerchief picked up in a country store, and listening to the glowing admonitions of his father, his contemporary on Lone Lane Creek near the Savannah was absorbing views that were antinational. The prominence achieved by Charleston in the secession of 1861 has obscured the truth of its earlier history. The South Carolina seaboard, for nearly fifty years following the Revolution, was as intensely Federal as New England itself. The great South Carolinians whose spirit Webster invoked to his reply to Hayne — the Laurenses, the Rutledges, the Pinckneys — were all Federalists, all undeviating champions of the Constitution. The candidate on whom the Federalists united, in 1800, as Vice-Presidential candidate was Charles Cotesworth Pinckney of Charleston. With these seaboard Carolinians, as they called themselves, superbly ignoring the existence of North Carolina, high Federalism was not only a political, but a social creed. Jeffersonians here, as in the best circles of New Haven and Boston, were atheistical and disruptive nobodies whom good people would not meet at the dinner table. This attitude in itself would have made the South Carolina upland Jeffersonian, for that quarter inevitably became everything that the snobs of Charleston were not; and there were other reasons for their Republican views. A region that cared nothing for its own state would naturally have little interest in the nation. A community that was virtually excluded from representation in the state legislature would have no enthusiasm for a Federal Congress and Senate, nor would one that depended largely on "Regulation" for the punishment of murderers and horse thieves have much understanding of the United States Supreme Court, even when presided over by an Oliver Ellsworth or a John Marshall. The mere fact that Calhoun's county belonged to the Federal Union was, in its own eyes, a measure of its political debasement. It had opposed ratification of the Constitution with all its native energy; Calhoun's father was as fierce an enemy of that paper as was Ebenezer Webster its worshiper; its hostility, however, amounted to nothing but vociferation — the thin but wealthy coast line of Federalism, much smaller in population than the Western land, monopolized political power and rushed the state into approval.

Thus in his childhood and boyhood days, from father, neighbors, schoolteachers, — such as they were, — the sensitive ears of Calhoun heard nothing but imprecations on the central government. Until his nineteenth year the future statesman received little education; his training in reading and writing was so rudimentary that he developed habits of bad spelling which remained for life; his career was fairly marked out — he was to be a rough, untutored planter, with a few acres and a few negroes, to marry a rustic wife and rear a large family of rustic children. But about this time changes appeared in himself and in the attitude of relatives and friends. The domestic circle slowly began to realize that this nineteen-year-old boy had a mind — that mentally, as well as in body, he was extremely vigorous, well-informed, able to hold his own in disputation with the most keen-witted neighbors. His pious mother entertained the usual ambition Southern women of her class cherished for promising sons: he might grow up to be a Presbyterian minister! At any rate the sentiment now became general among Calhoun's parents, sisters, brothers, uncles, and cousins: "John should be educated." And an even wilder hope dawned in the family aspiration — why should he not go to Yale? This remote New England college was then the favorite with Southern youth, especially from South Carolina, and to Calhoun it represented the ultimate Valhalla in the higher learning. Up to his nineteenth year Calhoun had never opened a Latin grammar or gazed upon an algebraic formula; in two years, however, by the intensest concentration, he mastered enough of this preliminary matter to enter the junior class at Yale. Interested as he had become in Cicero and Homer, he could hardly have selected surroundings more alien than New Haven; he might as well have placed himself in Charleston! Connecticut was the most Federalist region in the Union; it was the only New England state which never went over to the Jeffersonian side; and the archpriest of the creed was the first Timothy Dwight, then president of Yale. Legend has preserved stories of the conflicts of this unyielding "Pope of Federalism" with the rawboned rebel from South Carolina. All the heresies Calhoun had absorbed in childhood were now visited upon this pedagogue who, in addition to other duties, was professor of moral philosophy. Their disputations frequently kept the lecture room in a state of excitement, and they were renewed in private talk — for that was the happy day when association was constant between teacher and pupil. Out of these gymnastics one fact has survived — the tremendous respect Dwight acquired for Calhoun's mentality. The young man, he declared, had qualities that would fit him for any career; he might even some day be President! This prognostication — uttered of most promising young men then and since, just as at Eton an exceptional youth, even now, is hailed as a future Prime Minister — entered deeply into Calhoun's consciousness and ultimately took on the form of an obsession. But Calhoun's two years at Yale — he was graduated in 1804 — were educative in more subjects than appeared in the curriculum.

Connecticut in that period was a kindergarten in a science at which Calhoun subsequently became an adept — that of secession. The state was a leader in the Pickering attempt at separation in 1804; both her Senators, James Hillhouse and Uriah Tracy, were subterraneous forces in that conspiracy. Evidently the Connecticut atmosphere was not uncongenial, for, after receiving his Yale degree, Calhoun did not follow the usual practice, return to South Carolina and study law in a lawyer's office, but adjourned to the only law school then in operation in the United States, that at Litchfield. The presiding genius was Tapping Reeve, whose wife was Aaron Burr's only sister and whose correspondence discloses that he also was active in the Pickering plot. That the future Democratic champion of secession should have circulated in his early life among Connecticut Yankees whose grandchildren subsequently went to war to suppress Southern attempts at disunion is a biographical fact not to be ignored. Calhoun, despite the political divergences of subsequent years, was always devoted to Yale, and Yale has always venerated the memory of her rebellious son. One of the beautiful

Gothic quadrangles recently built in New Haven bears the name of Calhoun College.

Returning to South Carolina, Calhoun advanced by the usual steps, as did Webster, to a seat in Congress; he was a lawyer and a good one, a Fourth of July orator, a member of the state legislature, and, at the age of twenty-nine, a representative of the Abbeville district in the Lower House. The session of 1813 reminds one again that the present age is not the only period when youth has had its day. In that Congress the most brilliant and influential members were the Speaker, Henry Clay, aged thirty-six, Calhoun, Chairman of the Committee on Foreign Relations, — the most important of all when the nation is at war, — thirty-one, and Webster, of the same age. The second struggle with England was not a Northern and Eastern war, it was the pet measure of the South and West; its main proponents in Congress were Clay, "Harry of the West," — the West in this case being Kentucky, — and John C. Calhoun. On this issue Webster and Calhoun had their first difference, for Webster opposed the war in Congress, as he had outside, while Calhoun, fierce and passionate, was its fiery spokesman. But the difference is more significant, for Calhoun's first appearance is as a Nationalist, keen for the nation's honor and interest, while Webster seems to be speaking for a narrow sectional interest, the shipmasters of New England. And this same broader outlook Calhoun maintained for nearly twenty years. His career, from the standpoint of the Constitution, is divided into three parts: from his earliest conscious days until about 1812 he was the Jeffersonian advocate of State rights, of strict construction, of concentrating great powers in localities, not in the Federal government. From 1812 until about 1828 his position was exactly the reverse: his horizon was national, he stood for everything that extended national powers; sectionalism had apparently vanished from his philosophy. About 1828 he veered again, returned to the conceptions of his youth, and developed into the most tragic expounder of sectionalism in history. In the period now under consideration his expansive opinions ruled his career.

Into the new United States that succeeded the peace of Ghent in 1815 no statesman entered with more eagerness than Calhoun. His favorite description of the war, in his speeches in Congress, was "the second war for independence"; he accepted the result for what it was, the ultimate creation of an American nation, finally — as then it seemed — rescued from internal dissension and foreign encroachment. The three great issues that supervened were all Nationalistic; their purpose was to strengthen the nation as a unit, and of all three

Calhoun became the champion.   The first was the Bank.   The war left the Federal treasury bankrupt, in default in its bonds, and with no currency except worthless paper in circulation; only the resurrection of the United States Bank, whose charter had expired in 1811, could rehabilitate national finances.   Though the party to which Calhoun belonged was traditionally opposed to this institution, Calhoun worked hard and successfully for its recharter.   The second Nationalizing force was the tariff.   The United States had been shut out from European manufactures for fifteen years, owing to the Napoleonic Wars; as a result Americans had started manufacturing for themselves and had become, from Pennsylvania north, a flourishing industrial nation.   Should Europe, especially England and France, be permitted to flood the American market with their products and thus destroy what Americans had so painfully constructed?   No, said Calhoun, taking his stand alongside Henry Clay as an advocate of protection.   The third weakness demonstrated by the war was the lack of internal communication.   The disasters of the Canadian campaign were the result not only of military incompetence; the difficulty of moving men, equipment, ammunition, and food thousands of miles over a forest country that had no roads made the task an impossible one from the start.   Never had a nation received so disastrous a lesson in the need of internal improvements. The oxcart movement of immigrants into the new West also pointed out the necessity of highways into that region.   Already work had started on the Cumberland road, a noble enterprise beginning at Cumberland, Maryland, thence extending to Wheeling, West Virginia, and ultimately into Ohio.   Already the trek of pioneers into the West had reached considerable proportions.

In these days of Federal activities in banks, road building, and other national works, it seems a little ludicrous that all such extensions of Federal power were regarded by the Democratic Party as unconstitutional.   Reluctantly President Madison signed the Bank Bill of 1816, only on the ground that thus could the government get money enough to pay its current bills, including the salaries of its servants; but his successor, James Monroe, in 1822, vetoed an appropriation for the Cumberland road, on the ground that it violated the Constitution.   Yet on all these three issues — the Bank, the tariff, and internal improvements — Calhoun broke with his party. And he did so on grounds of Nationalism!   He supported these extensions of Federal power because they would more closely knit the Union.   In this period Congress had no more outspoken champion of state amalgamation.   A strange passage — strange in view of after events — appears in the *Reminiscences* of J. A. Hamilton, son of Alexander. "Sir," he quotes Calhoun saying to him in 1824, "I have a clear conviction, after much reflection and familiarity with the history of our country and the working of our government, that his [Alexander Hamilton's] policy as developed by the measures of Washington's Administration, is the only true policy of our country." Evidently the young man who had so doggedly upheld Jeffersonism at Yale had, in this mature period, adopted the Nationalizing tenets of his enemy. The quotation would be difficult to believe did not certain Nationalizing passages stand out in Calhoun's own speeches of the same time. He endorsed a protective tariff that would foster manufactures because it "is calculated to bind together more closely our widely spread Republic. It will greatly increase our mutual dependence and intercourse and will, as a necessary consequence, excite an increased attention to internal improvements — a subject every way so intimately connected with the ultimate attainment of national strength and the perfection of our political institutions." At the same time he described "Disunion" as "a new and terrible danger. This single word comprehends almost the sum of our political dangers, and against it we ought to be perpetually guarded." At this time Calhoun's views were exceedingly unpopular in the South and brought a reprimand from that unbridled champion of Jefferson and John Taylor — Randolph of Roanoke. His speeches, exclaimed the irreconcilable Virginian, exalted the national government at the expense of the states. His principles "prostrate the state governments at the feet of the national government."

What is the explanation of Calhoun's attitude during this middle period — the sixteen years from 1812 to 1828? The answer involves the moral problem presented by Calhoun's career. His political enemies of the day had no difficulty in explaining this change of view, and unfriendly historians since have found the issue simplicity itself. James A. Hamilton, to whom Calhoun had entrusted his conversion to the Hamiltonian views, cynically adds that he was expected to report the tidings to his Federalist friends, whose support in the pending Presidential election the South Carolinian desired. The crusty John Quincy Adams entered similar suspicions in his Diary. The South Carolinian, he says, was constantly seeking public favor; Adams reports General Brown as speaking of "his excessive thirst of turning everything into instruments for the promotion of his own popularity." "His opinions," Adams writes at another time, "are the sport of every popular blast," and he "veers round to be always before the wind and makes his intellect the pander of his will." Few men ever coveted the Presidency as did Calhoun. His nature, ambitious and intense, was early fixed on this prize. His rise in American life was lightninglike; and no position, after a single term in Congress, seemed beyond attainment. The prophecy uttered by Timothy Dwight at Yale was repeated by countless admirers in Washington and in the South. The election of 1824 was to be a free-for-all; there was really only one party, the Democratic-Republican; by talents, force of character, personal dignity, few men seemed so well fitted for the office. Supporters appeared in Virginia, South Carolina, Pennsylvania, even in New York. Yet as the time drew near for the election, in the fall of 1824, it became apparent that the Presidency was not for Calhoun. Not only was the "Virginia dynasty" to be swept from power, but everything for which it stood. Virginia Republicanism was passing; the day of Western Democracy had arrived. Government, which up to that time had been the privilege of the "educated" and the "well born," was henceforth to be the right of the masses. A new portent, embodied in the person of the "hero of New Orleans," had appeared in the West. There were five dominant candidates for the office — Calhoun, Crawford, Henry Clay, John Quincy Adams, and Andrew Jackson, and of them all Jackson was the only one who had a huge and passionate popular following. The others were candidates of political leaders. Jackson was the idol of the rural and urban mob. When Pennsylvania unceremoniously dropped Calhoun and uproariously adopted Jackson, the South Carolinian knew that his Presidential dream was all but ended. The ambition did not die, and on various occasions for the next twenty years flickered into life, but the possibility of Calhoun's attaining the White House was quashed, for all time, in 1824.

On this disappointment is founded the unpleasant picture so frequently painted of Calhoun — that of a fierce, frustrated man, seeking to rend limb by limb the Union which had denied him its greatest honor. This view makes him about the most sinister figure in American annals. But the explanation is too simple and obvious. Probably, had Calhoun attained the goal, his extreme sectional "philosophy" would not have reached fruition; but the fact is that America was changing, and the changing relationship of North and South might well account for alterations in a statesman's attitude. Calhoun's most careful biographer, William M. Meigs, — a Northern writer, — presents dates and facts to prove that Calhoun adopted his new course while his chances for the Presidency were still bright. Such an elaborate defense is scarcely necessary. The dispute on which national destiny turned after 1816 was the tariff, and the economic situation, after the passage of the act that year for which Calhoun voted, was something quite different from what it had been previously. At that earlier time there was a likelihood that the nation might develop symmetrically; that South and North would each be both agricultural and industrial; woolen manufacture had started in South Carolina as well as Massachusetts, and that fact had much to do with Calhoun's first emergence as a protectionist. By 1824, however, still more so by 1828, when the tariff came up for revision, this expectation had vanished. The North was growing tremendously in wealth and population; the South was falling behind. The North was developing a rounded civilization, agricultural, industrial, commercial, rural and urban, the whole based upon capitalism and free labor; the South was almost exclusively a land producing staple crops — tobacco, cotton, rice, indigo — with slave labor and farming methods that were primitive and wasteful. Its economy had changed little from that of Virginia in the eighteenth century. Then the planters raised their tobacco and sent it to England; in return no money was received, but instead came the manufactured articles — clothes, farm and household utensils, luxuries, and all things needed for the plantation existence. This was the system which the whole South, after a brief experimentation with Clay's "American system," wished to resurrect. Manufactures from the North, stimulated to lively production by the tariff of 1816 and those that followed at regular four-year intervals, were found more expensive than those that could be obtained from Great Britain. There was an even greater difficulty, in which the present generation has been schooled: the South's market for its staples, especially cotton, was not the Northern states, but Europe, predominantly England. Sound exchange demands that one buy where one sells; there seemed every likelihood, therefore, that unless the South took British manufactures, the British would cease, of necessity, to buy the Southern cotton crop. The truth is that the South was still economically part of the British Empire, not of the United States. The way in which the North was using its power to pass tariff acts that forced Southern planters to purchase manufactures from the Yankees, to whom they sold practically nothing, instead of acquiring goods at much lower prices from the English, to whom they sold the whole output of their plantations, seemed to Southerners little less than tyranny.

Such was the cause of the constitutional crisis that now took place. And it was this developing situation, every day becoming more intense, that caused Calhoun to abandon his policy of broad-minded Unionism and become the apostle of section.   South Carolina was the most obstreperous centre of disaffection, and Calhoun was more and more its spokesman.   The North increased tariff duties in 1820 — against Southern protest; it further increased them in 1824, against increasing cries of anger; in 1828 it passed the most oppressive act of all, enshrined in history as the Tariff of Abominations. and South Carolina broke out into what was little less than rebellion. Public meetings were held all over the state, in which the one note was resistance — and not passive resistance; the words "secession," "war," "nullification," echoed from one end of the state to the other.   By this time Charleston and the lowlands had outgrown the Federalism that had marked the days of the Rutledges and Pinckneys, and was as full of hostility to the Union as the upper country.   "It is time to calculate the value of the Union" was the much-quoted statement of Dr. Thomas Cooper, one of Carolina's leading pamphleteers. Calhoun had undergrown a transformation quite as complete.   He was now Vice President, having accepted this solace on the failure of his larger hope, and his office kept him from much public participation in debate, but behind the scenes he was the focus of opposition. His home, Fort Hill on the Savannah, became the vantage ground of all the men most active in the cause.   From it issued, in August 1828, the first of Calhoun's great state papers, which, circulated at public expense by the thousands, became the new Southern declaration of independence.   This was the "South Carolina Exposition," a document consisting of two sections, one setting forth the tariff grievance and the other proposing a remedy.   Once more the word "nullification" looms in the constitutional story.   For Calhoun went back to the teaching of Jefferson and Madison in the Kentucky and Virginia Resolutions of 1798–1799.   It was not the prerogative of the Supreme Court, he insisted, to pass on the constitutionality of laws.   Any state, in its legislature or convention summoned for the purpose, could set aside an act of Congress which, in its judgment, contravened the fundamental law.   South Carolina was now urged to take such action and declare "null and void" the tariff of 1828, to cease buying the articles forced on it by the North and trade with its natural customers, the British.   Only Calhoun did not like the word "nullification"; he preferred the softer Madisonian term and always called his cure "interposition."

And thus the conflict of interpretation was elevated to a height it had never attained hitherto, for the new stage was the United States Senate and the new disputants John C. Calhoun and Daniel Webster.   Until the resurgence of the doctrine in 1828, nullification had been little more than a constitutional theory; it had received qualified endorsement in the Virginia legislature of 1798 and had been held forth as a threat by the anti-embargoists of Faneuil Hall, but no state had attempted to resort to it in practice. Now the question was translated from the realm of discussion and reduced to a policy. At last a state was to attempt to set aside a law of Congress, defy the officers of the Federal government entrusted with enforcing it, even to raise an army to resist the power of the Union. However, the first battle in this new struggle was of words — and splendid words. In the development and strengthening of the Constitution that had followed the war with England, Daniel Webster had been a power almost coördinate with John Marshall. The decisions that had seemed to destroy, for all time, the Jeffersonian idea and to make the nation an "indissoluble Union" had really been the work of the two men. Webster, before the tribunal, arguing the greatest of constitutional questions, and Marshall, from the bench, rendering the decisions that transformed the states into a nation — this is the personal aspect of the change that was taking place. Webster's admirers go even further, insisting that most of the principles enunciated by Marshall appear in the arguments and briefs of the Massachusetts lawyer. The Dartmouth College case had made Webster leader of the American bar, especially in matters involving the Constitution. It also made him Senator from Massachusetts — for he had started the practice of law in Boston in 1814, soon after retiring from the Lower House of Congress. Thus for the next thirty years Webster alternated between the two chambers, arguing a constitutional case before the Supreme Court one day, appearing on the floor of the Senate the next. A mob of listeners, of both sexes, followed him from one scene to the other, for his power of oratory increased with the years. In the two greatest cases following that of Dartmouth College, — *McCulloch* vs. *Maryland,* establishing the supremacy of the Federal Constitution over that of the states, finally making real the document's own assertion that it was "the supreme law of the land," and *Gibbons* vs. *Ogden,* upholding the right of Congress to regulate commerce, — Webster had been the counsel for the plaintiff. His rôle as orator on great occasions — in Plymouth in 1820, celebrating the two hundredth anniversary of the Pilgrims, at Bunker Hill in 1825, laying the cornerstone of the monument — had made him the expounder of Nationalism and the one American, next to Marshall, who represented in his own person that devotion to a strong, centralized Union which, in the view of a large majority of the American people, had been established by the Constitution.

IV

The discussion over the tariff had been proceeding for more than a year, in and out of Congress, when an unexpected event brought it suddenly to the attention of the Senate. Samuel Foot of Connecticut was not an important legislator, and probably no one was more surprised than himself that his resolution, introduced in the latter part of 1829, precipitated the greatest debate which the Senate has ever known. This proposed an inquiry on the disposition of the public lands. The sale of the Western domain had been proceeding at the rate of 1,000,000 acres a year; more than 70,000,000 acres had already been surveyed and set aside for public entry; Senator Foot mildly suggested a holiday in surveys and a possible temporary suspension of the surveyor's office. The motion was one ostensibly in the interest of economy, of which much was then being said, but the fact that the proposer was a New Englander presently gave the discussion a sectional basis. Why was New England so desirous of seeking a halt to Western settlement? For several weeks the resolution was debated, but in desultory fashion, arousing almost no public interest. In early January, however, things began to take a more lively turn. Senator Thomas Hart Benton of Missouri led in a general onslaught on the proposal. The purpose, he said, was obvious. New England had always been hostile to the settlement of the West. That region feared that her citizens would abandon their own unproductive soil and seek new homes in the teeming lands of the Mississippi Valley. New England wished to keep the people home, cram them in cities, herd them to work in factories, and build up those big industries for which the new tariff was to lay the basis. What Mr. Foot and his selfish partisans really wished was "to check the growth of these new states and territories and to deliver large portions of them to the domain of wild beasts." Even Benton's harangue aroused no great attention. Though Southern born, he was first of all a Western man, one of the most powerful pillars of the Federal Union, and his eagerness for settlement in the Northwest and in the Louisiana country was the expression of his virile Americanism. Recriminations from him, therefore, even when they assumed a sectional bias, were, after all, the criticisms of a friend, and were patiently endured. But when the Senator from South Carolina, Robert Young Hayne, arose on January 19, 1830, and at once proceeded to enlarge on the Benton cue, the atmosphere became tense.

Hayne was then in his fortieth year, one of the youngest members of the Senate as well as one of the most brilliant and attractive. In history he lives chiefly as the man who provoked Daniel Webster's greatest oration, and in this history has been unjust, for Hayne was a man able, sincere, full of courage and of public spirit. The term applied to him by John Quincy Adams, "the malignant Hayne," is no fair description of his nature. For the last quality Hayne possessed was malice. Neither was he the typical South Carolina aristocrat, arrogant, bullying, disdainful, living in the narrow world of his own state, without imagination so far as the greater life of the nation was concerned. Hayne was of good, but not distinguished family; from early boyhood he had made his own way, had received slight educational advantages, and had reached his position as Senator from South Carolina through native genius, high personal character, and the patronage of John C. Calhoun. His portrait — one of the works of Samuel F. B. Morse — little suggests those vituperative qualities now associated with his name. It is not that of the Southern fire-eater; it is rather feminine in character. The face is soft, full-featured, even gentle; the eyes mild, distant, dreamy; the cupid's mouth almost sensuous. Clearly this man was a child of the sentimental South, not of the browbeating type that figured so conspicuously in Congress in the decades preceding the Civil War. All contemporary appreciations emphasize these characteristics. His nephew, the poet Paul H. Hayne, describes him as "a reflective studious youth of gentle bearing and amiable manner." Thomas Benton not only admired his talents but loved the man. "Nature had lavished upon.him all the gifts which lead to eminence in public and to happiness in private life. His person was of the middle size, slightly above it in height, well proportioned, flexible and graceful. His face was fine — the features manly, well formed, expressive, and bordering on the handsome; a countenance ordinarily thoughtful and serious, but readily lighting up, when accosted, with an expression of kindness, intelligence, cheerfulness, and an inviting amiability. His manners were easy, cordial, unaffected, affable, and his address so winning that the fascinated stranger was taken captive at the first salutation." That Hayne had a measure of eagerness, fire, and love of combat — even of "chivalry" — was also true; this was perhaps a legacy from his mother, Elizabeth Peronneau, of French extraction; it is also true that Webster, in a eulogy paid Hayne on his early death, signaled out, as his conspicuous trait, "sincerity." Perhaps a more eloquent tribute to both men is that, even after their two weeks' battle in the Senate, they continued to be good friends and that Hayne was for several days Webster's guest in the latter's country home at Marshfield, Massachusetts.   It was probably these personal charms which explain much of the man's success; significantly, though not himself of Carolina's bluest blood, both his wives were, the first being a daughter of Charles Cotesworth Pinckney, the second — who brought the young widower riches as well as position — Rebecca Motte Alston, of the famous South Carolina family.

By the time of his second marriage Hayne had reached a high position not only at the bar, but in public life.   In 1814 he was chosen a member of the state assembly and at his first session became its speaker.   His intelligent zeal subsequently attracted the attention of South Carolina's leading statesman, then Secretary of War in the cabinet of James Monroe, and already involved in the contest for the Presidential succession.   It was perhaps this latter fact, rather than Hayne's sympathetic tariff views, that accounts for Calhoun's interest.   The Senatorial term of William Smith of South Carolina was to expire in 1824; that celebrated gentleman was opposing the Calhoun candidacy, favoring the pretensions of Crawford of Georgia; in consequence Smith failed of reëlection and was chagrined to discover that his successor in the United States Senate was the antitariff expounder, Robert Young Hayne, at that time only thirty-two years old.

The new Senator was thus inevitably a Calhoun man, representative not only of Calhoun's political aspiration, but of his political views.   In the Presidential election of 1824, none of the five candidates had a majority in the Electoral College.   The House of Representatives, neglecting Andrew Jackson, although he had led all contestants, chose John Quincy Adams — another insult to the South, for Adams was not only a minority candidate, but was the exponent of opinions, both on the tariff and on slavery, that were becoming more and more unpopular in the land of cotton, rice, and indigo. Calhoun, as already noted, accepted the Vice Presidency — a position that, as presiding officer of the Senate, excluded him from participation in debate.   Thus his young disciple became spokesman of the Calhoun philosophy, especially on the tariff and State rights.   And as such, on January 19, 1830, he rose to give his views and those of

South Carolina on the Foot resolution concerning the public lands. The speech, as one reads it to-day in the musty debates of Congress, does not at first seem unduly provocative. Yet, studied more closely, it does contain sentiments that would excite the New England conscience. It is a restrained and carefully reasoned argument against national policy in the allotment of the public lands. The lands had been sold to the highest bidders, Hayne protested, and the receipts accumulated as a huge fund in the Federal treasury. The intelligent policy, he insisted, should be to dispose of them in the way that would best promote their settlement — to give them away if necessary to the upbuilding of great American commonwealths, rather than to use them as a source of national revenue. So far his speech seems wholly statesmanlike, but it was the reason for his objection to the existing method that aroused his Northern compatriots. Hayne objected to a large national revenue because that tended to erect a powerful centralized nation! Certain of his sentiments on this point have contemporary interest, for they illustrate how far his present political descendants have departed from the opinions on the use of the Federal treasury for local purposes expressed by this Democrat just about one hundred years ago. "I distrust the policy of creating a great permanent national treasury, whether to be derived from public lands or from any other source. If I had, sir, the powers of a magician and could, by a wave of my hand, convert this capital into gold for such a purpose, I would not do it. If I could, by a mere act of my will, put at the disposal of the Federal Government any amount of Treasure which I might think proper to name, I should limit the amount to the means necessary for the legitimate purposes of the government. Sir, an immense national treasury would be a fund for corruption. It would enable Congress and the Executive to exercise a control over States, as well as over great interests in the country, nay, over corporations and individuals — utterly destructive of the purity and fatal to the duration of our institutions. It would be equally fatal to the sovereignty and independence of the States. Sir, I am one of those who believe that the very life of our system is the independence of the States and that there is no evil more to be deprecated than the consolidation of this government. It is only by a strict adherence to the limitations imposed by the Constitution on the Federal Government, that this system works well and can answer the great ends for which it was instituted."

Though the debate had been under way for nearly three weeks, Webster had shown little interest in it. In fact he had attended few sessions, for he was busy with one of his most important cases before the Supreme Court. Just before Hayne rose and expressed these sentiments, however, Webster had casually strolled into the Senate and taken his seat. He was tired and somewhat disheveled, for his day spent in the chamber below had been a fatiguing one; under his arm he carried a bundle of court papers. That Hayne was to speak and that his remarks were to touch the vital point of localism versus Nationalism he did not previously know. As the Senator went on, however, Webster's deprecating colleagues gathered around him. The speech, they insisted, must not go unanswered; the Northern point of view must be set forth, and Webster was the man to do it. "I did not like the Hayne speech," Webster said afterward, "and my friends liked it less." At its conclusion he took the floor, but the hour was late and, at the suggestion of other members, Webster agreed to defer his remarks till the next day. Though the whole proceeding had an atmosphere purely accidental, Thomas Hart Benton always insisted that Webster's programme, from the first, was deliberate. He liked to refer to Webster's speech as one "of which he was lying in, to be delivered of." According to his explanation, the New Englander had been awaiting his opportunity for several months. He had kept careful note of the disunion meetings in South Carolina; had heard of secret convocations by Hayne, Calhoun, and others in Washington, planning schemes for Webster's humiliation and fall; knew that nullification was every day gaining converts and would soon result in rebellion. He thus feared that the Constitution was in imminent danger of being overthrown. His rejoinder to the South Carolinian's first speech was not intended, says Benton, to be Webster's real effort. Hayne had said nothing about nullification; that doctrine had never been promulgated on the floor of Congress; but Webster was lying in ambush in hope that the matter would be raised. When he rose in the Senate on January 20, therefore, it was not his plan to fire his heaviest artillery; his purpose was to goad Hayne to fury, in the expectation that the Southern speaker would reply in kind and lay bare the whole disunion programme.

If this was really Webster's strategy, it admirably succeeded. Southern writers have always insisted that Webster's first speech was extremely challenging — more so than the one to which it was a reply — and that the ferocity of Hayne's second attack was completely justified. Certainly Webster's rejoinder did contain sentences and even paragraphs most irritating to the Southern ear, and yet it never once exceeded the bounds of good taste and even courtesy. In places it was ironical; in others it touched South Carolina's most sensitive wounds; it eloquently sounded the praises of all that New England had accomplished for the settlement of the West; the speech was steely, cold, and insidiously cutting, but it was always parliamentary. The behavior of "some persons in the part of the country from which the honorable member comes," their comments and acts in deprecating the Union, their habit of magnifying "all the evils, real and imaginary, which the government under the Union produces"; the comparison of Ohio and Kentucky, the one prosperous, well-kept, happy, and the other down-at-heel, the population for the larger part engaged in a wretched struggle for existence, — the explanation being that Ohio was a state of free white men, while Kentucky was given up to negro slavery, — sentiments such as these were not likely to fall gently on the Southern spirit. At any rate, Webster's criticisms angered the ordinarily genial Hayne — which, according to Benton's theory, was precisely the effect Webster intended. An obviously angry man opened Senatorial proceedings the next day. Hayne abruptly — in a manner which, Webster's sympathizers insist, was "offensive" — refused to postpone his remarks. Webster had an important engagement before the Supreme Court and asked for a brief interim before the discussion should be resumed.

Hayne declined the request. Such requests were not unusual, and to accede to them was Senatorial etiquette; the refusal from the urbane gentleman from the South indicated the extent to which his feelings had been aroused. The Senator from Massachusetts had said things, Hayne replied, that "rankled here" — touching his breast. "The gentleman has discharged his fire in the face of the Senate. I hope he will now afford me the opportunity of returning the shot."

Webster rose. "Let the discussion proceed," he said; "I am now ready to receive the gentleman's fire."

Hayne spoke for nearly four hours. The speech was far more intemperate than Webster's of the previous day. The man's personal anger and sectional feeling appeared in almost every sentence. Never indeed had the sectional spirit so flamed in the Senate. "Little did I expect," Hayne began, "to be called upon to meet such an argument as was yesterday urged by the gentleman from Massachusetts. Sir, I questioned no man's opinions; I impeached no man's motives; I charged no party, or state, or section of the country with hostility to any other; but ventured, I thought in a becoming spirit, to put forth my own sentiments in relation to a great national question of public policy. . . . The gentleman has thought proper to

strike the South through me, the most unworthy of her servants. . . .
He has crossed the border, he has invaded the state of South Carolina, is making war upon her citizens and endeavoring to overthrow her principles and her institutions. Sir, I meet him at the
threshold. I will struggle while I have life, for our altars and our
firesides, and, if God gives me strength, I will drive back the in-
vader discomfited. If the gentleman wants war, he shall have war.
Nor shall I stop there. I will carry the war into the enemy's territory and not consent to lay down my arms until I have obtained
indemnity for the past and security for the future."

The speech that followed this defiant introduction consisted of
four parts: an attack on Webster, an attack on New England, a defense of slavery and of nullification. On the first two points the
invective was excellent and, despite the fierceness of tone, did not
exceed the privileges of debate. Webster's attitude on the tariff,
like Calhoun's, had been vacillating, though the two men had always
been on opposite sides. In 1816 Webster was a free trader and
Calhoun a protectionist; from 1824 Webster had espoused high
tariff, whereas Calhoun had preached tariff exclusively for revenue.
Inconsistency is always a favorite point of attack in political discussion, and Hayne paraded his opponent's contradictions effectively.
His eulogy of Webster as the instructor of South Carolina in the
blessings of free trade was really a masterpiece of irony. But New
England had taught the South more than the true path in fiscal policy;
it had been its preceptor in nullification also! Where had the gospel
been preached more effectively than by Senator Hillhouse of Connecticut — whose disloyal remarks in the War of 1812 were quoted
— and the meetings of Boston's intellectual aristocracy in Faneuil
Hall? Even Mr. Webster's own skirts were not entirely clear.
"At that awful and melancholy period of our national history, the
gentleman from Massachusetts who now manifests so great a devotion to the Union and so much anxiety lest it should be en-
dangered from the South was with his brethren in Israel! He saw
all these things passing before his eyes; he heard those sentiments
uttered all around him. I do not charge the gentleman with any
participation in these acts or with approving these sentiments. But
I will ask why, if he was animated by the same sentiments which he
now professes, if he can 'augur disunion at a distance and snuff rebellion in every tainted breeze,' why he did not that day exert his
great talents and acknowledged influence with the political associates by whom he was surrounded (and who looked up to him for

guidance and direction) in allaying this general excitement, pointing out to his deluded friends the value of the Union?"

Webster had given Hayne perhaps his most telling opportunity by mentioning Nathan Dane and holding him forth as the author of the Northwest Ordinance of 1787, excluding slavery from this region. "Sir, I doubt not," said Hayne, "that the Senator will feel some compassion for our ignorance when I tell him that so little are we acquainted with the great men of New England that until he informed us yesterday that we possessed a Solon and a Lycurgus in the person of Nathan Dane he was only known to the South as a member of the celebrated assembly known by the name of the Hartford Convention." The speaker seized a book from his desk which he brandished in Webster's direction. It was a report of the proceedings of that convention, and Hayne proceeded to read extracts from the pamphlet — extracts which hardly breathed loyalty to the Federal Union or Western expansion. Then, throwing the book on the table and looking with flashing eyes at Webster, he concluded this part of his speech: "So much for Nathan Dane, of Beverly, Massachusetts!"

Hayne's contrast of the devotion of South Carolina to the Union in the Revolution and New England's course of opposition in the War of 1812 was set forth in much lurid detail. And now New England — such was the tenor of his discourse — had the effrontery to accuse South Carolina of disloyalty! Most of New England's representatives squirmed during this part of the discourse, but Webster sat impassive, occasionally scribbling notes on a sheet of paper. Friends thought they even detected a gleam of satisfaction in the latter half of this Southern oration. For Hayne, dropping personalities, proceeded to deliver what was little less than a eulogy of slavery and nullification. On slavery the speech almost took the ground afterwards enunciated by Calhoun — that it was not an evil, but a good. New England's profit from the slave trade; the unhappy fate of free negroes in Northern cities; the effect of Northern agitation in stirring up negro discontent, even insurrection — all these points and many more, commonplaces in the discussions of the next thirty years, now came to the front. The concluding sections of the address were undiluted Jeffersonism. They consisted largely of extracts from the writings of Jefferson and Madison — all upholding the state as the arbiter on constitutional questions. The right of the Supreme Court to pass on constitutionality was denounced, supported by abundant quotations from the third President.

Jefferson, recently dead, was proclaimed the leader of the South in this doctrine.

All America now realized that a great moment had arrived in the nation's history. Foot's resolution had been introduced December 29, 1829; the debate had already lasted long enough for the news to reach most large centres of population. The South, represented by Hayne, and the North, represented by Webster, were deadlocked in the greatest discussion that had ever taken place in the upper chamber. The subject in dispute was the most momentous of all subjects — the meaning of the Constitution and the nature of the American Union. Matters which for a generation had formed the topic of argument in newspapers, pamphlets, private letters, and the hustings had at last reached the most portentous forum — the Senate, a body which, in the genius of its membership and prestige, had reached the highest peak of its history. A procession of interested citizens had been under way towards Washington for nearly a week, eager to be on hand at this tremendous forensic battle. All the hotels in Washington were filled, and early in the morning of January 26, 1830, when Webster was to deliver his reply to Hayne, great crowds started towards the Capitol. Business in Washington, official and unofficial, came practically to an end. Government offices were deserted; foreign diplomats joined in the rush for favored places; no quorum could be obtained in the House of Representatives, Congressmen having congregated in a mass in the Senate chamber. That chamber could hold only a fraction of the crowd pressing for admission. It was a small apartment — the same room that, until a recent day, was occupied by the Supreme Court. Into it the mob now penetrated in such numbers as to make it practically one solid mass of humanity. Outside, the audience filled all the corridors and staircases. The presence of women dressed in highest fashion — gay bonnets, many-colored gowns, the whole lightened by eager, animated faces — made the scene a brilliant one. The ladies filled all the galleries and even encroached on the floor of the Senate, in many cases the lawmakers having surrendered their own seats to the visitors. They added not only to the liveliness but to the emotions of the gathering. Those were the days when audiences made no effort to conceal their feelings, and Webster's oratory was frequently accompanied by the sobs of women and the tears of men, while strangers, at particularly excitable moments, did not hesitate to clasp each other's hands.

In all this excitement only one person seemed completely calm. That was Webster himself. Despite the anxiety of friends, he had remained imperturbable. In the wave of discouragement that swept over his supporters on the conclusion of Hayne's speech, the intended victim displayed no uneasiness. The South Carolinian's attack was recognized, by foe and friend alike, as a splendid one. The South was jubilant, the North downcast. Hayne's position, Southern advocates insisted, was unassailable; even Webster must remain helpless in the face of such hard-hitting rhetoric and such impregnable arguments; and even Northern admirers could not see how their champion could meet the onslaught. What appalled them, above all, was the little time Webster had had for preparation. Hayne had concluded at about four o'clock the preceding day; Webster was scheduled to pick up the gauntlet at noon the next. In that brief time how could even the greatest of speakers compose his rejoinder? The answer, of course, is that he could not. Webster's reply to Hayne fills seventy-five pages of his works — about 30,000 words. So far as phraseology was concerned, — and such phraseology had never been heard before in the Senate and has never been heard since, — the oration was extemporaneous. In his scant time for consideration Webster had scribbled on a few sheets of notepaper some of the points of his discourse; these rested on his desk, but he scarcely looked at them for the four hours he was speaking. In after life, when asked what preparation he had made, he usually replied: "My whole life had been a preparation." His career, almost from childhood, had been given to the study of the Constitution. For fifteen years he had been arguing vital points in several places — before the Supreme Court, in formal addresses, in political campaigns, in letters and in private discussion; thus his convictions, and the indicated answers to Hayne's contentions, were at his fingertips. A few New England friends, alarmed at the forcefulness of Hayne's presentation, called on Webster that evening to proffer assistance. Edward Everett, afterward president of Harvard, said that he had somewhat shared in the apprehensions of New England men that "it was impossible for Mr. Webster to answer that speech." In this fear he dropped in upon his friend. "Mr. Hayne has made a speech," he began. "Yes," replied Webster, "he has made a speech." "You reply in the morning?" "Yes, I do not propose to let the case go by default, and without saying a word." "Did you take notes, Mr. Webster?" The Senator drew from his vest pocket a piece of paper, about the size of a man's palm, on which a few pencil marks were visible. "I have it all; that is his speech," said Webster. Soon afterward Justice Story called, offering to spend the night looking up material for his friend to use the next day. "Give yourself no uneasiness, Judge Story," Webster answered, "I will grind him as fine as a pinch of snuff." The truth is that Hayne's argument had given Webster great satisfaction. It was precisely the speech he had hoped for. "When Hayne made that attack upon me and upon New England," he said later, "I was already posted and had only to take down my notes and refresh my memory. In other words, if he had tried to make a speech to fit my notes, he could not have hit it better."

As Webster strode up the Capitol steps to the Senate chamber, there was a faint suggestion of the naïve Homeric hero — not only in his somewhat arrogant walk and high-poised head, but in his self-confidence and even boastfulness. As he passed Senator Clayton, that gentleman asked, "Are you well charged?" "Seven fingers!" replied Webster, holding up his index member — seven fingers of powder in one of the muzzle-loading shotguns of that time being as much as the weapon could hold. Senator Bell of New Hampshire met him in the cloakroom. "It is a critical moment," said Bell, "and it is time, it is high time, that the people of this country should know what this Constitution is." "Then by the blessing of Heaven," Webster replied, "they shall learn this day, before the sun goes down, what I understand it to be." A few moments later he rose before that solemn, half-hysterical company. A few feet to Webster's right sat Hayne, now in his habitually pleasant mood, conscious of his triumph the day before, presently taking notes of his adversary's remarks. Yet Hayne, despite his prominence in the debate, was regarded, neither by Webster nor by the audience, as the real enemy. In the chair sat the thin-faced, silent, unimpassioned Vice President of the United States, John C. Calhoun. Webster necessarily, because of his position, was compelled to confront him and to him address his remarks; but more than the courtesy of parliamentary procedure demanded this. Everybody present knew that Hayne had been Calhoun's mouthpiece; from him the younger man had learned his lesson, to him he owed his very seat in the Senate, and it was generally believed that Calhoun had coached him for the attack on Webster. Thus Webster concentrated the glare of his fierce eyes upon the real father of nullification. In one moment he even, without naming the author, quoted from one of Calhoun's speeches in favor of internal improvements. This brought from the Vice President his one interruption. His question was intended to imply that he had not changed his mind upon the subject.

But in reality there was only one visible figure in the Senate chamber that morning. Probably no man quite so completely filled any room in which he was placed as Daniel Webster. Though he was not unusually tall, — five feet ten inches, — his massive head, broad shoulders, and bulky figure conveyed an impression of great stature. Webster's cranium is a part of biological history; weighed after his death, it proved to be the largest, except Cuvier's, in scientific records. It was also splendidly shaped, with lofty brow, surmounted by coal-black hair — "raven" hair was the favorite expression of his time — and lighted by coal-black eyes; for Webster, in 1830, was only forty-eight, without a trace of age. Probably the best description is the classic one of Carlyle, who met the American on his visit to England and sent his impressions to Emerson. "Not many days ago I saw at breakfast the notablest of your notables, Daniel Webster. He is a magnificent specimen. You might say to all the world, 'This is our Yankee Englishman; such limbs we make in Yankee-land.' As a logic fencer, or parliamentary Hercules, one would incline to back him at first sight against all the extant world. The tanned complexion; that amorphous crag-like face; the dull black eyes under the precipice of brows, like dull anthracite furnaces needing only to be *blown;* the mastiff mouth accurately closed; I have not traced so much of *silent Berserkir rage* that I remember in any man." This impressive figure now rose, clad in the blue "swallow-tail" coat of the period bedecked with shiny gold buttons, buff waistcoat, high white stock that was then the badge of statesmanship, tight-fitting trousers — brilliant garments that have long since vanished from legislative chambers. This day Webster's olive skin — so dark that in youth he was commonly known as "Black Dan" — was sufficiently touched by a glowing red to suggest the fire burning within. Yet it was a glow not of excitement, but of earnestness. Outwardly Webster was calmness itself. His very first words, uttered quietly in his harmonious voice, which was a deep bass, put the audience at ease. "Mr. President. When the mariner has been tossed for many days in thick weather and on an unknown sea, he naturally avails himself of the first pause in the storm, the earliest glance of the sun, to take his latitude and ascertain how far the elements have driven him from his true course. Let us imitate this prudence; and before we float farther on the waves of this debate, refer to the point from which we departed, that we may, at least, conjecture where we now are. I ask for the reading of the resolution before the Senate."

The personal features of his address: its defense of New England as the friend, not the enemy, of Western development; its statement of the Northern position on slavery — its willingness to leave that system undisturbed in those states of the old South in which it represented an ancestral inheritance and could not be displaced without bringing probably greater evils than slavery itself, but its inflexible opposition to extension into territories where it had not previously existed; the neatness with which the orator turned Hayne's tart criticism of the Hartford Convention against himself and South Carolina — accepting, as Webster did, all the harsh things Hayne had said of that convocation, but pointing out that New England had long since abandoned its disloyal teachings, whereas South Carolina seemed to have adopted them as its present rule of action; Webster's skill in replying to Hayne's abuse of New England by delivering a superb eulogy on South Carolina, and holding up its behavior in the Revolution and afterward as a model for the whole nation to follow; the references to Massachusetts ("there she stands. Behold her and judge for yourselves") which became the favorite declamation of millions of American schoolboys — all these things, breathlessly as they held the attention of his auditors, were really secondary matters to the orator. Webster had entered the debate — perhaps even provoked it, as Hayne's partisans asserted — for one supereminent reason. He had risen to expound and defend the Constitution. His business was to exalt the Nation above the State. Especially had Webster come to unhorse that doctrine of nullification which Calhoun and his lieutenants were every day, with increasing vehemence, preaching as the safeguard of State rights. Webster's purpose was to defend the Supreme Court as the arbiter of constitutional points and to proclaim the Union as the one salvation of American future.

Repeatedly did the speaker quote, with an ironical curve of his lip, Hayne's reference to New England as "the enemy's territory." It was a phrase which Webster pretended not to understand. As a Massachusetts man, he insisted, he was aware of "no enemy's territory" within the confines of the Republic. Certainly he did not hold that attitude towards South Carolina. Why should he? Had he not gone frequently to South Carolina and its statesmen for lessons in national policy? Had South Carolina not been his teacher in the very matter under discussion at the moment — the tariff? Was not South Carolina, in 1816, when Congress had entered on that protective system which now threatened to split the Union, a leader in its adoption? No sarcasm could have struck quite so effectively, for Calhoun, the presiding officer of the Senate at the very moment of this debate, had been one of the most eloquent promoters of protection in 1816. In another question that now aroused South Carolinian wrath, internal improvements, South Carolina, Webster pursued, had also taken the lead. Everybody knew that the prime apostle of internal improvements — of the use of Federal money for building roads, canals, the support of education, and the like — was the able statesman then seated in the presiding officer's chair. And here was Mr. Hayne turning his back on this Carolinian policy — chiefly because it established a bond of union between the states, the same reason for which he opposed a national debt and national taxation.

A question put the day before by Mr. Hayne gave a perfect understanding of the difference in the present attitudes of South Carolina and of New England towards the Union. " 'What interest,' asks he, 'has South Carolina in a canal in Ohio?' Sir, this very question is full of significance. It develops the gentleman's whole political system, and its answer expounds mine. Here we differ. I look upon a road over the Alleghenies, a canal around the falls of the Ohio, or a canal or a railway from the Atlantic to the western waters, as being an object large and extensive enough to be fairly said to be for the common benefit. The gentleman thinks otherwise, and this is the key to his construction of the powers of the government. He may well ask what interest has South Carolina in a canal in Ohio. In his system, it is true, she has no interest. In that system Ohio and Carolina are different governments and different countries, connected here, it is true, by some slight and ill-defined bond of union, but in all main respects separate and diverse. In that system Carolina has no more interest in a canal in Ohio than in Mexico. The gentleman therefore only follows out his own principles; he does no more than arrive at the natural conclusion of his own doctrines. . . . Sir, we narrow-minded people of New England do not reason thus. Our *notion* of things is entirely different. We look upon the states, not as separated, but as united. We love to dwell on that union, and on the mutual happiness which it has so much promoted, and the common renown which it has so greatly contributed to acquire. In our contemplation, Carolina and Ohio are parts of the same country, states united under the same general government, having interests common, associated, intermingled. In whatever is within the proper sphere of the constitutional power of this government, we look upon the states as one. We do not impose geographical limits to our patriotic feeling or regard; we do not follow rivers and mountains, and lines of latitude, to find boundaries, beyond which public improvements do not benefit us. We who come here, as agents and representatives of the selfish men of New England, consider ourselves as bound to regard with an equal eye the good of the whole, in whatever is within our powers of legislation. Sir, if a railroad or a canal, beginning in South Carolina and ending in South Carolina, appeared to me to be of national importance and national magnitude, believing, as I do, that the power of government extends to the encouragement of works of that description, if I were to stand up here and ask, 'What interest has Massachusetts in a railroad in South Carolina?' I should not be willing to face my constituents. These same narrow-minded men would tell me that they had sent me to act for the whole country and that one who possessed so little comprehension, either of intellect or of feeling, one who was not large enough, both in mind and in heart, to embrace the whole, was not fit to be entrusted with the interest of any part."

Superb as was the restrained irony and scorn of this passage, it was even exceeded when Webster dissected what he called the "Carolina doctrine" just set forth by his opponent — the doctrine that any state could defy and set aside a law of Congress which it deemed unconstitutional. That was the ghost Webster had stalked into the Senate that morning to lay. After he had set forth, in a few sentences, what he took the doctrine to be, Hayne arose in his seat and read the much-quoted paragraph from Madison's Virginia Resolutions of 1798: that "in case of a deliberate, palpable and dangerous exercise of other powers" not granted by the Constitution, "the states who are parties thereto have the right, and are in duty bound, to interpose, for arresting the progress of the evil, and for maintaining within their respective limits the authorities, rights and liberties appertaining to them." That, Hayne said, was his "proposition." Webster admitted that citizens and states, in extreme contingencies, had the right to defy laws of Congress. But it was not a right they possessed under the Constitution; it was the right of revolution, which free people always held in reserve. Senator Hayne rose and interrupted once more. "I do not contend," he said, "for the mere right of revolution, but for the right of constitutional resistance. What I maintain is, that in case of a plain palpable violation of the Constitution by the general government, a state may interpose; and that such interposition is constitutional."

Webster now assailed, as it had never been assailed before, the whole fabric so painfully constructed by Jefferson, John Taylor, and Calhoun. In striking at its base, he approached again, as he had in his sophomoric Fourth of July address of 1800, the ideas, and used almost the very words of, the Gettysburg Address. Liter-

ally he took the words with which the Constitution begins, and
which had so affrighted Patrick Henry in the Virginia Convention.
"We, the people of the United States." There is the authority,
there is the creator, of the national government. The view that
certain abstractions, known as states, were the makers of the Constitution led to the "absurdity" that the new nation was "the servant
of four-and-twenty masters [1] of different wills and different purposes, and yet bound to obey all. . . . It is, sir, the people's Constitution, the people's government, made for the people, made by
the people, and answerable to the people. The people of the United
States have declared that this Constitution shall be the supreme
law. We must either admit the proposition or dispute the authority. The states are, unquestionably, sovereign, so far as their
sovereignty is not affected by this supreme law. But the state legislatures, as political bodies, however sovereign, are not yet sovereign
over the people. So far as the people have given power to the
general government, so far the grant is unquestionably good, and
the government holds of the people and not of the state governments.
We are all agents of the same supreme power, the people."

And the idea that these states, as states, could pass on the constitutionality of the laws the people's representatives had made was the
conception that Webster now proceeded to refute. There was a
power, he insisted, instituted to settle constitutionality, and this
power was "independent of the states." If that is not the case,
"is not the whole Union a rope of sand? Are we not thrown back
again, precisely, upon the old Confederation? . . . Four-and-
twenty interpreters of constitutional law!" Mr. Hayne had drawn
comfort from New England's behavior at the time of the embargo.
Its heavens had rung with denunciation of that law as unconstitutional, and for that reason not entitled to respect or obedience. He
had quoted a statement to this effect by James Hillhouse, once a
Senator from Connecticut. Mr. Hillhouse, then in his seventy-
sixth year, was one of the most absorbed listeners to the Webster-
Hayne debate. Webster gracefully acknowledged his attendance.
"The honorable and venerable gentleman is now favoring us with
his presence. . . . The Connecticut Senator is a constitutional
lawyer of sound principles and enlarged knowledge; a statesman
practiced and experienced, bred in the company of Washington and
holding just views upon the nature of government." There was
nothing in his opinion, so ostentatiously quoted by Hayne, that gave
the slightest support to his "Carolina doctrine." Of course Senator

[1] There were twenty-four states in 1830.

Hillhouse had regarded the embargo as unconstitutional; so had practically all of New England. Of course he had thought an unconstitutional law should not be obeyed; was there anyone, then or since, who did not think so? But that was not the point; the point was, who was to decide whether the law was unconstitutional? Did the legislatures of the New England states attempt to set the laws aside, and then proceed to disregard them, as Hayne now proclaimed to be the constitutional procedure? Not at all! They took their grievance to the tribunal the people had provided for that purpose — the Supreme Court of the United States. They engaged the most brilliant of New England's lawyers, Samuel Dexter, to whom Webster paid a eulogy. "He put into the effort his whole heart as well as all the powers of his understanding. . . . He argued the cause; it was lost and New England submitted. The established tribunal pronounced the law constitutional; and New England submitted. Now, sir, is this not the exact opposite of the doctrine of the gentleman from South Carolina? According to him, instead of referring to the judicial tribunals, we should have broken up the embargo by laws of our own; we should have repealed it, *quoad* New England; for we had a strong, palpable and oppressive case."

And thus Webster had reached the apex of his discourse, the point to which his whole exposition had been tending — and a point perhaps even more interesting to the present generation than to his own. On that subject on which contemporary constitutionalists become so vehement — the right of the Supreme Court to pass on constitutionality — Webster had no doubts whatsoever. Moreover his attitude was not apologetic. He did not rest it on the theory that the right was "implied" and rose from the nature of the case; that it was not explicitly granted by the Constitution itself. For Webster insisted that there were two clauses in the Constitution which conferred the power of judicial review. The first was the declaration that "this Constitution and the laws of the United States . . . made in pursuance thereof . . . shall be the supreme law of the land . . . anything in the Constitution or laws of any State to the contrary notwithstanding." The second was the provision that "the judicial power shall extend to all cases" arising under the Constitution and laws of the United States. "These two provisions," Webster said, "cover the whole ground. They are, in truth, the keystone of the arch! With these it is a government; without them it is a confederation. In pursuance of these clear and express provisions Congress established, at its very first session,

ROGER BROOKE TANEY

OLD SUPREME COURT CHAMBER

WEBSTER REPLYING TO HAYNE

in the judicial act, a mode for carrying them into full effect, and for bringing all questions of constitutional power to the final decision of the Supreme Court. It then, sir, became a government. It then had the means of self-protection; and but for this it would, in all probability, have now been among things which are past."

Webster's whole oration was restrained, though vigorous in expression; it was an appeal to the intellect, not the emotions; there was nothing pompous or inflated in the style; even in this sophisticated age we can read it with no affront to our sense of good taste; it is still as fresh as when it first fell from his lips. Not till the end did he let himself go and indulge in a flight of impassioned oratory. The passage, of course, is one of the most famous in American literature, but no account of the speech that aims to convey its spirit and epitomize its nationalist purpose would be complete that ignored it. "I profess, sir, in my career hitherto, to have kept steadily in view the prosperity and honor of the whole country and the preservation of our Federal Union. It is to that Union we owe our safety at home and our consideration and dignity abroad. It is to that Union that we are chiefly indebted for whatever makes us most proud of our country. That Union we reached only by the discipline of our virtues in the severe school of adversity. It had its origin in the necessities of disordered finance, prostrate commerce and ruined credit. Under its benign influence these great interests immediately awoke as from the dead and sprang forth with newness of life. Every year of its duration has teemed with fresh proof of its utility and its blessings; and although our territory has stretched out wider and wider and our population spread farther and farther, they have not outrun its protection and its benefits. It has been to us all a copious fountain of national, social and personal happiness. I have not allowed myself, sir, to look beyond the Union, to see what might be hidden in the dark recess behind. I have not coolly weighed the chances of preserving liberty when the bonds that unite us together shall be broken asunder. I have not accustomed myself to hang over the precipice of disunion, to see whether, with my short sight, I can fathom the depth of the abyss below; nor could I regard him as a safe counsellor in the affairs of this government, whose thoughts should be mainly bent on considering, not how the Union may be best preserved, but how tolerable might be the condition of the people when it should be broken up and destroyed. While the Union lasts, we have high, exciting, gratifying prospects spread out before us, for us and our children. Beyond that I seek not to penetrate the veil. God grant that, in my day at least, that curtain may not rise! God grant that on my vision never may be opened what lies behind! When my eyes shall be turned for the last time to the sun in heaven, may I not see him shining on the broken and disordered fragments of a once glorious Union; on states dissevered, discordant, belligerent; on a land rent with civil feuds, and drenched, it may be, in fraternal blood! Let their last feeble and lingering glance rather behold the gorgeous ensign of the Republic, now known and honored throughout the earth, still full high advanced, its arms and trophies streaming in their original lustre, not a stripe erased or polluted, nor a single star obscured, bearing for its motto no such miserable interrogatory as 'What is all this worth?' or those other words of derision and folly 'Liberty first and Union afterwards'; but everywhere, spread all over in characters of living light, blazing in all its ample folds, as they float over the sea and over the land, and in every wind under the whole heavens, that other sentiment, dear to every true American heart — Liberty *and* Union, now and forever, one and inseparable!"

One of the first to approach and grasp Webster's hand in congratulation at the conclusion of the reply to Hayne was a Senator from the South. "Mr. Webster," he said, "I think you had better die now and rest your fame on that speech!" Hayne was standing near and heard the remark. He turned to Webster: "You ought not to die," he said; "a man who can make such speeches as that ought never to die." That same evening the two men met at the President's reception. "Well, how are you to-night?" was Webster's good-natured greeting. "None the better for you, sir!" replied Hayne. This fairly epitomizes the impression made by this oration both North and South. Whatever one might think of the contending views, the reply to Hayne emblazoned the truth that, in Webster, America had produced an orator qualified to rank with the greatest of all times, ancient and modern. Possibly the scholarly Edward Everett's praise was extravagant, but it represented the judgment of contemporaries and has been echoed by commentators of more recent date. "It has been my fortune to hear some of the ablest speeches of the greatest living orators on both sides of the water, but I must confess I have never heard anything which so completely realized my conception of what Demosthenes was when he delivered the oration on the Crown."

The reply was printed in many editions and circulated by the hundreds of thousands. It found its way into every American farmhouse and into practically every American city dwelling, and in a brief period had become the textbook of the new Americanism. Ideas which up to that year had been the matter of formal reasoning before courts of law or dry discussion in legal treaties suddenly became the topic of debate with the common man. The Constitution, which had previously been a distant abstraction, a piece of paper, venerated it may be but hardly realized as a personal possession, entered, almost as a living thing, into the consciousness of the people. That conception of Nationalism which had been its dominating note now rose defiantly to challenge the disintegrating forces still working for the reëstablishment of the ancient system. "It turned the attention of the public," said Chancellor Kent in his remarks at a dinner given Webster by the citizens of New York in honor of his reply to Hayne, "to the great doctrine of national rights and national Union. Constitutional law ceased to be wrapped up in the breasts, and taught only by the responses of the living ranks of the law. Socrates was said to have drawn down philosophy from the skies and scattered it among the schools. It may with equal truth be said that constitutional law, by means of these Senatorial discussions and the master mind that guided them, was rescued from the archives of our tribunals and the libraries of our lawyers, and placed under the eye and submitted to the judgment of the American people."

V

This debate took place in January 1830; the America to which it was addressed was a new America, in which forces were at work that would have seemed strange and wild, even dangerous, to the statesmen of 1787. One need only to glance at the gaunt figure occupying the White House, and watching, with somewhat quizzical interest, proceedings at the other end of the avenue, to realize that new political and social influences had seated themselves in power. Gouverneur Morris and others had expressed a desire to curb the growth of the West; that desire had found expression in the recent debate; and in the White House at that moment sat the triumphant frontiersman who embodied all the apprehensions they had feared. For the first thirty-nine years of the new government the President had signalized wealth, social caste, good manners; several of the Presidents had been highly educated men; the predecessor of Andrew Jackson, John Quincy Adams, was probably the man of greatest intellectual attainments who has ever filled that office. But to qualities of this kind Jackson made no claim. He was the product of something new, not only in America, but in the world. Both Calhoun and Webster, as has been indicated, were in a sense frontiersmen, but they, and others of similar origin, had softened this rough beginning with academic education and the love of books and study. Jackson had shown no interest in these things, either as boy or as man. No well-worn edition of the *Essay on Man* had intruded in his cabin home. Almost the only literary allusion his biographers have unearthed is a predilection for *Scottish Chiefs* and admiration for Sir William Wallace as a "model for the young." The partiality is significant. The love of combat, the championship of the oppressed, the devotion to one's native soil, the faith in elemental justice, combined with a personal dignity and even chivalry of deportment — these were traits that Jackson had in common with the primitive heroes of his allegiance.

And it was a loyalty to which he had a natural claim. For Jackson belonged by birth to the Scottish clans — by way of Ireland.

Though his place of American origin, the Waxhaw district of South Carolina, was primitive, it did not prove sufficiently rough-hewn for Andy Jackson. Of that early boyhood in northwestern Carolina vivid recollections in plenty have been handed down. Mr. James Parton, in many ways still Jackson's best biographer, spent much time on his native soil gathering first-hand reminiscences, and the figure constructed from them is not inconsistent with the statesman who subsequently occupied the White House. A tall, lanky, athletic youth, thin-legged, narrow-bodied, with a long, indented face, steel-blue eyes that always looked straight at persons and objects, red hair that rebelliously rose from a lofty, noble forehead, a spirit violent, quarrelsome, ready momentarily to fight, with gun and fists, and seemingly always alert for insults to be avenged — it is precisely the same image we frame in thinking of the soldier who drove the British from New Orleans and the President who raided the Civil Service in the interest of his friends and swept to destruction the most powerful financial institution of his day. With the boy and young man, hates and affections, loyalties and aversions, devotion to right and justice, were all instinctive — just as they were subsequently with the public man. "Do what is right between these parties; that is what the law always means" — such was Judge Jackson's favorite charge to juries from a backwoods bench in Tennessee, and in this direct and simple fashion, ungraced by refinements and abstractions, did he always go to the core of any question. And that same magnetism and personal likableness and respect which explain his popularity as a statesman were also manifest in his early days. The girls of the Waxhaw region felt that Andy was "something" as a boy; the Creole ladies of New Orleans, after looking disdainfully at the soiled garments in which the general entered the city, presently found themselves captivated by his dignified deference and reserved charm, just as did all classes in Washington twenty years afterward. Yet on the whole this early Jackson is a rather disturbing figure. His mother, like Calhoun's, perceiving his superiority to most boys of the neighborhood, early marked him for the Presbyterian ministry. Others less prejudiced observed certain disqualifications. That Andrew, as a fifteen-year-old boy, was one of the best judges of horseflesh in the region; that, instead of poring over books, he spent most of his time in the stable, fraternizing with its occupants, or in card playing and dice throwing; that he was much given to cockfighting and personal pugilism — these traits were not incompatible with the clerical career, for the age was a robust one; but the boy's facility at loud swearing, the freedom with which, in conversation, he handled the first and second Persons of the Trinity, were out of character, even in that frontier atmosphere.

Hardly had Andrew reached his teens when his fame spread far and wide as a duelist — and this also was an avocation that accompanied him almost to the Presidential chair.   And education? It was most fragmentary.   Jackson, in a technical sense, was an illiterate man through life, yet, like many forceful souls, his writings had something that might almost be called style.   His paragraphs were a sad jumble of misspelled words, of sentences telescoping one another in wildest abandon, yet there were in them frequently thought and power, and, when tidied up by secretaries, they were sometimes clarionlike in appeal.   His most famous state paper, the Nullification Proclamation, was, in its present state, the work of Edward Livingston, but the memorandum on which it was based survives, in Jackson's rapid slanting scrawl — and it has an eloquence and patriotic fervor that the polished final draft hardly attains.

All this was the natural person that Jackson was; not the man of ideas, but of passions and prejudices — not of thought, but of supreme will.   And to the creation of this embodied force the more civilized side of American life contributed practically nothing. Calhoun was born in a frontier country, moved on to civilization, liked it, and became more and more its denizen and spokesman. Jackson, child of the backwoods, emigrated as a youth to Charleston, disliked it, and plunged deeper into the wilderness.   A grandfather, dying in Carrickfergus, Ireland, — natal place of the Jackson tribe, — left Andrew a legacy of three or four hundred pounds. In those days that was really a fortune; it would have put the young man through college and established him on a Carolina plantation. Instead the harum-scarum invaded Charleston, where the money rapidly vanished; just how it was spent no one knows, but in view of the young man's fondness for horse racing and card playing, the problem is not absolutely mysterious.   So, leaving the uncongenial soil, Jackson started in the direction of the Blue Ridge, crossed the Watauga Gap, tarried for a brief period at Jonesboro, then settled amid the few log cabins that figured on the map as Nashville, Tennessee.

At this time Jackson was twenty years old, having been born in 1767; the year was the momentous one 1787, the time of the Constitutional Convention.   There are no signs that Jackson had much interest in the deliberations of Philadelphia.   The man who was to become so strong a defender of the Constitution had at that time little national feeling. He was a true representative of the trans-Allegheny section, not only in appearance, occupation, and temperament, but in disregarding the process of nation making then at the beginning. He had in himself all the makings of a "whiskey boy," and felt no allegiance to the new, distant, central governing power. Tennessee, like the rest of the Scotch-Irish expanse west of the Alleghenies, was deep in Spanish intrigue. Certain telltale letters of Andrew Jackson show that he was not opposed to some kind of understanding with the power that controlled the Mississippi, and therefore the Cumberland River, on which he had staked his fortunes. When he arrived at Nashville, that section of America was known as the Western District. But presently it blossomed out as the Mero District — a change in name that graphically shows the political currents of a shifting, uncertain era. "Mero" is simply a backwoods transliteration of Miro — and this was the name of Don Esteban Miro, Spanish governor of Louisiana, with whom these frontier statesmen, including Jackson, were then intriguing. Indeed, the active question at this moment was whether the Nashville community should join themselves to Spanish Louisiana or rise as an independent nation. The idea of paying taxes to those whom Jackson called the "neebobs" of Philadelphia — a government that could furnish no access to a market for their cotton and grain — was too fantastic for serious consideration.

Almost the same sentiments prevailed in the convention held in Nashville in 1796 to erect the territory into a state. Jackson had so advanced in the estimation of his fellows — that "presence," that "something about him," immediately forced him to the front — that he was one of the dominant members of the body. Tradition says that his suggestion gave the new state its name of Tennessee — almost a claim to immortality, at a time when Jefferson was naming the new Western commonwealths *Metropotamia, Polypotamia, Chersonesus, Polysipia*. However, Andrew was not a good constitutionalist, not even, in the present acceptance of the word, a good American. Spain had admitted Americans to the navigation of the Mississippi, and there was still a feeling that the friendship of the Don was more useful to the new community than allegiance to the Federal administration. The Spaniard could protect Western settlers from the Indians more effectively than the new Constitution. One of these hard-fisted epistolary attempts of Jackson's early period shows that he shared this view. Indeed at times the question laid before the log-cabin convention held in Knoxville seemed to be whether the new Tennessee should be an independent state or one in intimate alliance with the Spanish Empire. That Britain was negotiating for its friendship was also no secret, but Andrew Jackson did not love England. His hand and his forehead bore large white scars, mementoes of his conflict, at the age of thirteen, with one of Tarleton's troopers — and Jackson carried to his grave not only these gashes, but the permanent anti-British emotion they had aroused in his adolescent spirit. The Tennessee Convention, however, solved its international problem in a way of its own; it adopted a constitution and proceeded graciously to annex itself to the new Federal Union. That was a little dash of frontier irregularity, for Congress, in the Constitution, had retained the right to form new states, and therefore presumed to look this new gift horse in the teeth. There were other things about this new Tennessee that made the conservatives of Philadelphia somewhat hesitant. Its constitution justified many of the apprehensions certain framers of 1787 had entertained of the West. The democracy that, in the person of President Andrew Jackson, thirty-five years afterward, seized supreme power in the nation now raised its shameless head. In this constitution appeared the spectre of universal suffrage, of general qualification for public office irrespective of education or extensive property holdings. President Washington was still riding on state occasions in his princely coach, drawn by four cream-white horses; levees, in full military dress, were still the great occasion in the Federal capital, and the possibility of democratic Tennessee, clad in buckskin, bursting upon this sedate complacency was something not to be lightly entertained.

However, that is what happened. Tennessee, despite its disregard of constitutional etiquette, gained admission, and sent, as its first Congressman, — it was entitled to only one, — the very type of frontier statesman Virginia and Massachusetts had feared. More than this, the new representative was that horse-racing, cockfighting, gun-toting, dueling, and cursing Andrew Jackson, whose early fame had already crossed the Alleghenies. His appearance shocked even the Democrats, who were then reviling Washington for his imitations of monarchy. Albert Gallatin, himself an inciter of Western Whiskey revolutionists, balked at first view of the new lawmaker. The horrific image never faded from Gallatin's memory; in after years he described his latest colleague as "a tall, lank, uncouth looking personage, with long locks of hair hanging over his face, and a queue down his back tied with an eel-skin; his dress singular, his manners and deportment those of a rough backwoodsman." Thomas Jefferson, the ink on his Mazzei letter scarcely dry, was similarly shocked by this incarnation of his new Democratic ideal. "His passions are terrible," Jefferson afterward remarked to Daniel Webster. "When I was president of the Senate he was Senator and he could never speak on account of the rashness of his feelings. I have seen him attempt it repeatedly and as often choke with rage." Jefferson's recollections refer to the brief period, in 1798, when Jackson had been promoted by Tennessee to the upper chamber; but there are indications that his tendency to wrath showed itself as Representative. He did not like Philadelphia or the Federal government. Even President Washington fell under the Jacksonian ban; the gentleman from Nashville demanded his impeachment! He wished the father of his country so treated because of his part in Jay's Treaty. That Washington preferred this peaceable settlement to war did not impress Jackson, still mindful of his boyish encounter with British redcoats. He was prepared to fight England at a moment's notice. That same treaty he denounced as the "insulting, cringing and ignominious child of aristocratic Secracy." At the conclusion of Washington's service as President, the House drew up an address, felicitating him especially on his "wise, firm, and patriotic administration." Several super-Jeffersonians objected to this phrase and demanded its exclusion — a change that would have put the House on record as censuring Washington's work as President. A disgraceful debate followed, after which sixty-seven members rallied to Washington's side, while twelve voted for this uncomplimentary emendation. Among the twelve was Andrew Jackson. His zeal for Democratic simplicity also flared in a vote against appropriating fourteen thousand dollars for furnishing the President's house in the new national capital then rising amid the swamps on the Potomac. The fact is that Jackson's one term in the House plays no more important part in his biography than did Lincoln's, forty years afterward, in his; neither did his even briefer service as Senator, which followed it. He was elected in 1797 for a six-year term; he spent one sad session in Philadelphia. So little did he appreciate his toga, however, that, after this short experience with it, he resigned and returned to Nashville, to become, of all things in the world, a judge of Tennessee's highest court.

Thirty years after this departure from the capital, the backwoodsman — essentially a backwoodsman still — returned, to take the oath of office as President of the United States. Webster, horrified at the earliest suggestion of Jackson's candidacy, denounced it as a "nomination not fit to be made." In this the new Executive did not greatly differ with him. "I can command a body of men in a rough way," he said, "but I am not fit to be President." Circumstances, however, had made his elevation inevitable; that new popular force in America, public opinion, increasingly demanded this highest honor for its man. If ever an American citizen reached the White House without the aid of politicians, but at the persistent call of the people, that man was Andrew Jackson. The fact is that since his departure in 1798 from participation in the Federal government and his arrival in 1829 to become its head, Jackson had shown the qualities of a great man. In the Christmas season of 1814–1815 he performed a military service that redeemed all the mistakes of the War of 1812 and made the country west of the Mississippi part of the permanent American domain. It is well enough to say that the battle of New Orleans was fought after the signing of the treaty of peace and did not influence the result. The fact is that Britain sent Pakenham to Louisiana in order to conquer that territory and make the country west of the Mississippi a new American empire. Had she once gained lodgment there it is too much to expect, treaty or no treaty, that she would have politely withdrawn. It was the lank major general from Tennessee that frustrated this design. And his triumph was an expression of his own character. It was his supreme determination, his will to crush the foe, that superseded all obstacles and carried the day. The lesson that Americans gained from this achievement was that a new force of nature had appeared among them. Jackson was no more learned, no more given to thought, in this new aspect than in his early days. He was still a mass of feelings, hates, affections, and loyalties. But once he had fixed on a goal he went at it with a terrific will that crushed all obstacles. His goal, after New Orleans, was not the Presidency, though, as the idea became familiar, the crown was not thrust aside; nothing, after New Orleans, could have kept him from the White House. Jackson had raised the almost paralyzed spirit of his people, given them a new self-respect, and made them proud to be Americans. That is, he had shown himself to be a great leader, and nothing was more to be desired in the Presidential chair at that time.

In one respect Jackson, by 1829, had undergone a change. The frontiersman of 1789, listless in his Nationalism, had become an impassioned devotee of the Constitution. Devotee is the word, for here, as in all things, his loyalty was one of the emotions. That same fierce energy with which he had gone to the defense of Louisiana he now bestowed upon the American Union. The hatred that he had felt, as a boy, for the soldiers of Cornwallis he now felt for those who would lay hostile hands on the fundamental law. In his hostility to the foremost of these, in 1830, John C. Calhoun, personal abomination gave edge to his sentiment. For Hayne the President personally had an affection, but, as with Webster in the debate, his attitude was really concentrated on his fellow South Carolinian. Jackson distrusted Calhoun as a public citizen and hated him as a private man. He thought his championship of nullification dishonest in motive and his personal conduct treacherous. The quarrel between these two men is a celebrated episode in personal politics and need not be rehearsed in detail. Calhoun had sinned against Jackson in his two most sensitive spots: by secretly assailing Jackson in the most questionable part of his career he had irretrievably wounded his pride; by championing nullification he had run afoul of the love for the Union and the Constitution that came nearest to his heart. Jackson, after his victorious course in Louisiana, had been sent in 1818 by the Monroe administration to subdue the Seminole Indians of Georgia and Florida, then menacing American settlers in the Southeast. The intrepid commander, as always a law unto himself, and as hostile towards the Don as in his apprentice days he had been conciliatory, transformed the Indian raid into a campaign to expel the Spaniard from Florida. He seized Pensacola, to the vast indignation of the Spanish Minister in Washington and to the consternation of the Monroe cabinet — to all of it, that is, except the Secretary of State, John Quincy Adams, who accepted the performance as a *fait accompli*, refused to move the American soldiers from the fort, and, in fact, adroitly used the "incident" as a means of forcing Spain to sell Florida to the United States. The other cabinet officers insisted that Jackson had exceeded his instructions — as he undoubtedly had — and demanded a disavowal. Calhoun was the most severe; he argued that Jackson should be arrested and court-martialed. This was bad enough, but the circumstance, as Jackson always insisted, that Calhoun had kept his animosity secret, and had led Jackson to believe that he had always approved his Spanish tactics, was what made his anger blaze into fury. Twelve years after the Seminole campaign, Jackson, then President, learned the true story of Calhoun's attitude in this crisis. Then the usual avalanche of epithets, the usual rapidly scrawled letters of denunciation, burst from the White House upon the Vice Presidential culprit. When he first heard of Calhoun's "treachery" in the Florida matter, Jackson wrote, "It smelled so much of deception that my hair stood on end for an hour."

And Jackson, always seeing public policy in its personal

embodiments, concentrated on Calhoun's favorite doctrine that same hatred that he felt for the man himself. Calhoun meant nullification and nullification meant Calhoun; on the two the despot of the White House fell with an intensity that boded well for the safety of the Constitution, however unpleasant its other aspect might be. Some Southern critics, indeed, insist that Jackson never became the outspoken foe of State rights until his break with Calhoun. On the other hand it is true that his love for the Union and the Constitution had been ardent for many years. When he exclaimed "I will die for the Union!" Jackson — South Carolinian though he was — meant just that. And on April 13, 1830, three months after the Webster-Hayne debate had made the question a household topic, the President gave public testimony to his consecration in words that flew into every corner of the nation and which have since been engraved on most of the monuments erected to "Old Hickory's" memory. April 13, it will be observed, is Jefferson's birthday. The time-honored practice of celebrating this festival had started as early as this, only four years after the statesman's death. Expectation was on tiptoe on that April 13 of 1830, for it was known that at the Jefferson dinner in Washington not only would the advocates of nullification, Calhoun and Hayne, be on hand, but President Jackson himself. What would be the consequence of such a gathering at a banquet in honor of the man who had devised the nullification doctrine? Functions of this kind, a hundred years ago, indulged in a ceremony that the present age would regard as appalling. That was the ritual known as the "toast." This "toast" — sometimes consisting of only a sentence or two — was really a miniature speech of praise, blame, apprehension, or warning, occasionally of congratulation or covert threat. But what astonishes the weary addict of public dining to-day is the number of these sentiments. A hundred toasts were not unusual. At the Jefferson banquet of April 13, 1830, one hundred and twenty succinct orations of the kind enlivened the proceedings.

That Calhoun and the nullifiers would propose such toasts was a matter of course. But what could the President say? For this was in reality a nullification banquet, and only sententious outgivings that lauded this policy would obviously be in order. The spirit in which Jackson advanced to the Jeffersonian and nullification dinner table has been described by his henchman and successor, Martin Van Buren. "We repaired to the dinner with feelings on the part of the old Chief," he writes in his *Autobiography*, "akin to those which would have animated his breast if the scene in this preliminary skirmish for the defense of the Union had been the field of battle instead of the festive board." After Hayne had made a long and eloquent speech, deifying nullification and its author, a slight commotion became apparent in the neighborhood of the Presidential chair. Jackson's toast was a "volunteer" one — that is, it was not part of the regular programme, and was not printed on the card placed at each cover. But the President, while Hayne was speaking, was seen to be scribbling something on the back of his list, and, when the right moment came, he rose and read the inscription, in a voice that reached the utmost recesses. "The Union — it must be preserved!"

Calhoun sought to quiet the consternation by a "voluntary" offering of his own, but it lacked the terseness of Jackson's, and had that element of qualification not conducive to good literary effect. "The Union! Next to our liberty most dear; may we all remember that it can only be preserved by respecting the rights of the states and distributing equally the benefit and burden of the Union." This was really an essay in constitutional law, whereas Jackson's was a rallying cry — not only for that moment but for the next thirty years. Jackson had really transformed an elaborately staged demonstration in honor of State rights into a resounding *Te Deum* for the Union, and the applause with which his intercession was received, both North and South, showed that he was a dramatist of genius. It was a great moment in the history of the Constitution.

VI

The result was especially disappointing to the "nullifyers" — as Jackson described them in his letters — because this Jefferson Day banquet had been most painstakingly planned as the first gun in the battle on which they had now definitely engaged. It similarly appeared that Jackson's toast was only the initial blow in the operations of the old campaigner. And again he demonstrated that he was a man not of thought, but of action. Of fine constitutional disquisition Jackson knew little, but he did know that there was a Union, and for this he was prepared to fight to the end. And soon reports came from the White House that the venerable, now white-haired President was threatening to hang any man who attempted to interfere with governmental machinery. The statesman for whom he seemed to be preparing a particularly lofty gallows was Calhoun. Jackson's position had been tremendously strengthened since the Jefferson birthday dinner. At the election of 1832 he had been returned to the White House for another four years by one of the largest popular votes on record. His enemy, Calhoun, had lost the Vice Presidential nomination and was therefore about to be retired to private life. Political exigencies in South Carolina, however, had offered Calhoun a new rôle. Two months after the nation had manifested this renewed confidence in its anti-nullifying head, South Carolina took the step it had been threatening for several years. A state convention called for that purpose at Columbia assumed the prerogative which up to that time — and in fact ever since — had been regarded as the exclusive right of the United States Supreme Court. The two or three hundred laymen assembled on that occasion took under advisement the most momentous of all functions: was the tariff act of 1828 constitutional or had it been passed in violation of the fundamental "compact"? The convention, by an overwhelming vote, — there was nothing suggesting a five to four decision from this tribunal, — decided the issue in the negative. It declared the tariff law of 1828 "void and no law," informed South Carolinians that they need not obey it, and prohibited revenue officers of the Washington government from collecting duties on imports into the state. It handled the Supreme Court with a contempt the most modern denunciator of that august institution could not surpass. No case involving a nullifying ordinance should be permitted to reach that tribunal. Any lawyer or litigant who presumed to take such an appeal was to "be dealt with as for contempt of court." If the Federal government presumed to disregard the ordinance and persisted in its attempt to collect duties under the outlawed tariff act, "the people of this state will thenceforth hold themselves absolved from all further obligation to maintain or preserve their political connection with the people of the other states and will forthwith proceed to organize a separate government and do all other acts and things which sovereign and independent states may of right do." The legislature promptly passed the legislation necessary to put these sentiments into effect. A volunteer army of ten thousand was authorized. Thousands of citizens responded in a way that foreshadowed the behavior of the same people thirty years subsequently. Men, women, and children appeared decorated with the blue cockade of revolution, and medals were struck, with the inscription "John C. Calhoun, First President of the Southern Confederacy." It is said that on certain buildings in Charleston the flag of the United States appeared hanging upside down.

Here, then, the administration was apparently facing something that resembled civil war. There was one considerable difference, however, from the situation that arose in the same state in 1860, for South Carolina at this earlier time stood alone; her sister Southern communities showed no inclination to follow her lead; even Virginia, which had originated the nullification doctrine, showed a discouraging listlessness when faced with this opportunity of putting her favorite principle in action. Another difference was that a man occupied the White House in 1833 of a very different type from the James Buchanan who held the executive power in 1860. Perhaps the best definition of nullification is found in one of those toasts so popular at the time: "Nullification, anarchy reduced to a system"; and it is significant that the author of this criticism was a South Carolinian. It easily represented the opinion of most Southern statesmen. It certainly set forth the idea of the South Carolinian who was then filling the executive chair. Yet Jackson behaved with a poise that rather astounded his intimates. This too was characteristic. Like many men of violent passions, Jackson was likely, in the face of great excitement, to act with soberness and deliberation.

He showed this quality — a quality of true greatness — at New
Orleans, and exhibited it again in a crisis almost as alarming.   That
he was in dead earnest is evident from his private correspondence.
Calhoun and his co-workers were "treators" engaged in a "rebelous"
conspiracy.   The Presidential determination to "nullify the nullifyers" was expressed again and again.   "The wicked madness and
folly of the leaders, the delusion of their followers, in the attempt
to destroy themselves and our Union has not its parallel in the history
of the world.   The Union will be preserved."

Visitors to the White House obtained an occasional glimpse of
the grizzled veteran, sitting in shirt sleeves at his desk, corncob
pipe in mouth, furiously writing memoranda and notes which, when
finished, would be tossed into his huge beaver hat reposting at his
side — manuscripts as jumbled in expression as those that formed
the basis of Livingston's polished Proclamation.   Despite these
evidences of the old Jackson, his letters disclose also that he weighed
every step and continuously kept his head.   He sent secret emissaries
to Charleston to spy out the facts and make confidential reports;
he provided for supplying and provisioning the forts in Charleston
Harbor — one thinks of '61; he moved General Scott and details
of the army to the neighborhood of South Carolina; he announced
his desire to command in person the army of "volunteers" springing
up, North and South, in his support.   One morning the fashionable
residents of Charleston's "Battery" — most of them nullifiers —
discovered, anchored in a semicircle in the harbor, the guns pointing
at their beautiful homes and gardens, seven revenue cutters and the
warship *Natchez*.   Unlike General Lee and other Virginians in
1861, here was a chieftain who would not hesitate to make war
on his native state if that should be necessary to curb "treason."

That Jackson was ready to put the issue to the test is clear
enough, but more timid souls in Congress were not so inexorable.
The situation was precisely the kind to enlist the intervention of that
Kentucky statesman already famous as the great "compromiser."
In early January, Henry Clay and other leaders of both parties were
busy seeking some middle way out of the *impasse*.   The new South
Carolina system was to go into effect on February 1, 1833, but that
date came and went, Federal customs officers at Charleston continued
to collect duties under the "unconstitutional" tariff act — the ordinance, pending negotiations in Congress, was simply allowed to lapse.
The nullification leaders were faced with more troubles than a
determined President and an unacquiescent South.   There was a
large minority in South Carolina opposed to their procedure, and

the likelihood was strong that, if the ordinance were persisted in, civil war would break out within the confines of their own state. Still, it must be granted that, in this struggle, the Calhoun-Hayne contingent did obtain concessions that, if not amounting to a victory, at least gave them the chance to retire from the conflict with dignity. This was not the work of Jackson, but of Clay and his group in Congress. A bill was passed providing for a gradual but substantial decrease in tariff duties. Whether this measure cut down the tariff to a revenue basis, abandoning the protective system, is a point on which economists disagree. But it did give the South Carolina malcontents an excuse to call another convention and repeal their nullification ordinance, on the ground that the abuse against which it had been adopted was now rectified. An interesting complication was that Jackson was himself a low-tariff man and sympathized with South Carolina in its complaints, energetically as he opposed the method it had adopted for redress. Despite this, he was not pleased by the "compromise," preferring to fight the issue to a decision. When the bill came to him, however, he signed it, as it was the work of an overwhelming majority in Congress. The South Carolinians promptly put up the claim that they had won, — that nullification had justified itself, — and echoes of this cry are still heard. But history proved that they had lost. They did obtain for the moment — and only for the moment — a more satisfactory tariff bill, but nullification was dead. Andrew Jackson had killed it. It never reared its head again. A state convention, as the tribunal for passing on the constitutionality of laws, had no second trial. South Carolina and other states had grievances in plenty in the next thirty years, but did not attempt to gain redress in this way. Hayne had declared, in his debate with Webster, that nullification was a right under the Constitution; Webster had retorted that there was only one way in which a state could defy Congress — that was the way of revolution. South Carolina justified the Websterian dictum in its next violent disagreement with the powers of Washington. It did not attempt to nullify: it made the appeal to arms.

One of the most tragic figures in this crisis has so far not appeared in the nullification episode. The man on whose teachings the nullifiers mainly relied, and quotations from whose writings filled all their speeches, was still living. James Madison, in 1833, was eighty-two years old, living in solitude, almost unknown to that excited generation, in his Montpelier home. What were the emotions of this "father of the Constitution" when, at this advanced age, he beheld his fellow Democrats angrily tearing into shreds the web of the Philadelphia Convention, and doing so in his name? Madison's letters of the time picture his state of mind. He almost frantically denies that there is any connection between his doctrines of 1798 and those of the rampant South Carolinians. The "anarchical principle," he calls nullification, which "has the effect of putting powder under the Constitution and Union and a match in the hand of every party to blow them up at pleasure." He clearly foresees what it will lead to. It would eventually result in national disintegration. Some day "popular leaders, aspiring to the highest stations and despairing of success on the Federal theatre," will "unite the South, on some critical occasion, in a course that will end in creating a new theatre of great though inferior extent. In pursuing this course, the first and most obvious course is nullification; the next secession; and the last, a farewell separation." That his own and Jefferson's preachments in the days of the administration of John Adams had been adopted as a gospel by these disrupters of the nation haunted his last years. To refute the assumption became almost a mania. It filled his conversations and writings from the day of the first tariff dispute, in 1824, until his death in 1836. His letters, denouncing the nullifiers and denying all responsibility for their heresies, were published in the leading newspapers and magazines. From his invalid's chair the old man, almost blind, utterly deaf, so racked by rheumatism that his hands could not hold a pen, sent constantly forth his anathemas on the South Carolina statesmen. Yet those statesmen had drawn their constitutional ideas from the Madison of thirty years before. Into all his delicate web of differentiation and qualification, attempting to draw subtle distinctions between the Virginia and Kentucky Resolutions and the Hayne-Calhoun philosophy, it is not profitable to go. The fact is that he and Jefferson had first propounded the doctrine that states could upset legislation of Congress that they deemed unconstitutional, and that was the basis of the great dispute in question. It took a stronger hand than Madison's to undo the original mischief, and that is the work for which history is indebted to Andrew Jackson.

BOOK IV

THE GREAT FAILURE OF THE CONSTITUTION

I

STRANGE perturbations marked the theory of State rights in the first half of the nineteenth century. The limits to which the logic of Calhoun could carry its votaries was almost ludicrously illustrated in March 1837. For several hours the Senate debated an appropriation of $30,000 to purchase and publish the records of the Constitutional Convention left by James Madison, who had died, at an advanced age, in the preceding year. Since 1787 these priceless documents had lain in Madison's private archives. Only a few political intimates, such as Jefferson, had ever caught a glimpse of them. The nation, as a whole, scarcely knew of their existence. Discussions of the Constitution for the first fifty years after its adoption thus present an anomalous spectacle; statesmen, lawyers, editors, jurists, had been solemnly arguing its meaning, though none of them had access to the evidence that gives insight into the minds of its framers and explains their hopes and intentions. The bill now presented to Congress provided $30,000 for the purchase of that constitutional classic ever since known as *Madison's Debates* — the day-by-day record which the industrious Virginian had kept of the motions and speeches of the founders. The plan was to publish an edition under Congressional authority, with the idea of enlightening American lawmakers and the American people on the origin of their government.

In modern eyes few enterprises would seem more important or more within the jurisdiction of Congress. Should these documents be scattered to the four winds, — a positive danger, in view of the carelessness of that age with manuscripts, — or should Congress preserve for all time these essential records of its own creation? One Senator arose, however, to oppose the measure. Calhoun was now well advanced in the second phase of his career as the obscurantist defender of State rights. The use of public money for such a purpose, he declared, was "unconstitutional." An appropriation from the Federal treasury to purchase Madison's papers would really insult the memory of that great statesman. Such a transaction would be "a plain and palpable violation of that rule in the interpretation of the Constitution which Mr. Madison had himself laid down." Did the Senate really wish to pay tribute to Madison's fame? Then throw out this unconstitutional bill! "It would honor the memory of Mr. Madison far more to regard that rule than to purchase his manuscripts."

Thus spoke Calhoun, now become the strictest of the strict constructionists. Congress could exercise no power not specifically enumerated in the Constitution. Point out the clause that authorized the use of Federal money for the purchase of manuscripts! Look again to the Tenth Amendment! Not being a right granted the Federal government, such a function must necessarily be one of those "reserved to the States or to the people." Only one phrase, Calhoun insisted, could be tortured into conferring such a prerogative upon the general government. That was the dubious provision which had already risen several times to plague lawmakers and jurisconsults, which was to arise many times in the future, and which even disturbs the present age. It was the phrase which gives Congress the right to levy taxes "for the general welfare." What did that mean, asked Calhoun, as thousands of puzzled questioners have demanded since. What better authority could be cited, in the present instance, than President Madison himself? The Bible of nullificationists and of State-rights devotees was Madison's celebrated report on the Virginia and Kentucky Resolutions, prepared for the Virginia legislature in 1799. So Calhoun instructed the clerk to read the passages in this document that gave Madison's interpretation of the "general welfare" clause. The clerk obediently intoned the paragraphs. The recitation gave little comfort to those who understood the clause in the comprehensive sense that certain "latitudinarians" attributed to it. It did not mean, said Madison, that legislation could be passed for anything regarded as "promoting the general welfare." That would have made all the rest of the Constitution so much waste paper. The ways in which public money could be used to advance the "general welfare" were specifically set forth in the document itself. Beyond these Congress could not depart. The acquisition of literary muniments did not appear among the "enumerated" powers. To purchase manuscripts, now asserted the triumphant Calhoun, even manuscripts so valuable as those left by Mr. Madison, was clearly not within the purview of the Senate. The "generous scheme" devised for the benefit of the "amiable and distinguished lady" in the case — the now aged and decrepit Dolly Madison — was made impossible by her husband's own interpretation of the instrument he had been one of the most influential in framing. To pass the bill would thus be a flaunting of his memory. His shade, called from the depths, forbade it.

But Webster, Clay, Crittenden, Benton, and others laughed the interpretation to scorn. In this opinion, there was no need of invoking the "general welfare" clause. The Constitution had created Congress, and Congress, by the very fact of its existence, had the right to purchase such furniture and papers as would enable it to function in orderly and efficient manner. Had Congress not established a library, to diffuse information and stimulate intelligence among its members? If so, could it not purchase books and manuscripts that advanced such desirable ends? And could it not collect materials that formed a part of its own history? Did not the Constitution require Congress to keep a record of its proceedings, and were not these Debates, in a sense, part of that record — at least a record of the events that led to its establishment? Where, asked Senator Crittenden, did the Constitution in set phrase give Congress power to erect the ornate building in which it was then holding its sessions? In what clause was specifically found, the same orator demanded, pointing to a large object on the wall, authority to purchase that portrait of the father of his country? After long discussion the Senate decided that Calhoun's constitutional point was badly taken; the appropriation passed by an overwhelming majority, and the precious records were deposited in the Library of Congress, where they repose in safety to-day.

Perhaps, unconsciously enough, Calhoun was fighting for his own constitutional principles when he opposed paying Dolly Madison $30,000 for her husband's literary remains. The publication of these documents hardly helped his cause. The authors of that Constitution which Calhoun professed to revere lent little support to those doctrines to which the rest of his fierce Messiahship was to be devoted. In them the word "nullification" did not appear. Neither did any idea remotely resembling it find place in the discussions. The Madisonian record disclosed that the founders themselves entertained no doubts as to what authority was to pass on the constitutionality of acts of Congress. That this was the function of the judiciary, most of the members who broached the subject took for granted. The doctrine subsequently and most disastrously known as State rights did not show its head on the floor of the convention. Madison's notes contain no mention of a state's right to withdraw after once giving its allegiance to the Constitution. Defenders of secession find little support in the deliberations of 1787.

All these theories were the developments of an aftertime, made to fit particular political contingencies and particular sectional needs. Jefferson evolved State rights as a logical outcome of his faith in government by small units. New England doctrinaires found the same tenet an engine powerful to rid themselves of the embargo. Georgia brought the conception to the front as a means of denying any right in the general government to protect the Indians within its borders. "State rights" in the Cherokee disputation signified the right to steal the red man's lands. Calhoun and Robert Young Hayne found in it a trusty weapon to battle against a tariff policy obnoxious to South Carolina. Similarly in modern times corporations have discovered in State rights a haven to guard them from the "encroachments" of the Federal power. The greatest and most tragic manifestation of the theory developed in the years 1835–1860, which must now be passed under review, when State rights and secession, as formulated by John C. Calhoun, became the instrument by which a social and economic system based on negro slavery was to be made the foundation of the American Union.

II

"Can it be supposed that this vast country, including the western territory, will, one hundred and fifty years hence, remain one nation?" Such was the question propounded to the Constitutional Convention on August 8, 1787, by Nathaniel Gorham, delegate from Massachusetts. The "western territory" which Mr. Gorham had in mind was not the expanse which Americans of to-day understand by that description, but merely the land extending eastward from the Mississippi River to the Appalachians — the region that had been added to the new United States by the treaty of 1783. In far briefer time than Mr. Gorham had suggested events proved him a foolish prophet. At the present writing the century and a half that he proposed as the extreme limit that the Union could survive has expired, and not only has the territory east of the Mississippi been incorporated into what is apparently an indissoluble Union, but additions have been made which, in Mr. Gorham's eyes, would have seemed incredible. Yet soon after 1787 forces had been unleashed that made this development inevitable. In the main, these influences were economic, though "manifest destiny" was an idea that early obtained lodgment in the American mind. The expression itself is a century old; in Jackson's and Van Buren's administrations, spread-eagle orators rhapsodically described the ultimate United States as extending from the Arctic Circle to Cape Horn, and the annexation of Texas and the ravishment of northern Mexico had this earth hunger, as well as the extension of slavery, for justification.

But it was really the evolution of a new economic world that, soon after the adoption of the Constitution, caused Americans to set up new communities in the Southwest and to cross the Mississippi River. European progress in the mechanic arts and wasteful agricultural methods in the Southern states combined to produce this never-ceasing demand for new, rich black earth. The invention of machinery, which resulted in supplanting domestic industry by the factory system, had enormously multiplied the production of cotton goods; European nations, predominantly England, extended their markets to all parts of the world. This set up an insatiable demand for raw material. The old cotton states could not supply this new need. Their crude agriculture quickly exhausted the soil; Virginia, the Carolinas, and Georgia were forced to overflow into new regions, and found them in the territories to the Southwest. Virginia extended into Kentucky, North Carolina into Tennessee, South Carolina and Georgia into Alabama and Mississippi. Thence the overflow burst into the trans-Mississippi country which the Louisiana Purchase had added to the nation, finally comprehending that far-reaching alien country, then part of the new Republic of Mexico, vaguely known as Texas.

The fact which so affected American history was that these new Southwestern settlements were established almost entirely by the Southern states. New England and the Middle states did much to populate the new Ohio country, but few settlers from north of the Potomac joined the invaders of the Southwest. Significantly, in view of subsequent events, the state that furnished the largest percentage of emigrants to the frontier in this period — from 1800 to 1840 — was South Carolina. Virginia and Kentucky contributed to building up communities in the southern tier of the Northwest, Ohio, Indiana, and Illinois — a simple matter, for it meant merely crossing the Ohio River. The migrations of the family of Abraham Lincoln, having its origin in Kentucky and thence finding its way into Indiana and Illinois, are a case in point. The incentive to these transplantations was overwhelmingly economic. The idea that Southerners were leaving their ancient homes to escape slavery is a pleasant tradition once widely accepted, but the real motive is less romantic. The pioneers were seeking virgin land, to replace the exhausted acres of the old cotton and tobacco South. The pressing objective was to supply the demands of the looms of France and Great Britain. The limits to which this impulse extended the frontiers of the United States, and the effect produced upon the Constitution, are to be kept clearly in mind.

The several steps by which the national domain was extended to the Pacific Coast are sufficiently familiar. The purchase of Louisiana in 1803; the establishment of the Republic of Texas in 1836 and its annexation to the United States ten years afterward; the consequent war with Mexico, and the huge stretch of soil exacted from Mexico as indemnity, including California and the regions then known as Utah and New Mexico; the incorporation of Oregon in 1848 as a result of a treaty with England settling disputes of many years' standing — all this is a well-thumbed school-book story.   But the enormous extent of these accessions of national wealth is not always understood.   Nor does everyone comprehend the new constitutional problems directly consequent on this territorial growth.   A glance at the map of the United States, with this idea in mind, will prove illuminating.   Such an inspection discloses that the land comprised in these additions — all that lying west of the Mississippi — is about twice as large as the area which the Constitution originally embraced; twice as large as that "vast country" which, in the eyes of Nathaniel Gorham, could not remain under a single government for a century and a half.   California itself covered as much of the earth's surface as the New England states, with the addition of New York, Pennsylvania, New Jersey, Maryland, Virginia, and Kentucky.   The region then denominated Oregon encompassed the present states of Oregon, Washington, and Idaho, an expanse larger than the old Northwest.   The territory then called New Mexico is the same as that included in the present states of Nevada, Utah, a large part of Colorado, New Mexico, Arizona, and a liberal slice of western Texas.   Louisiana itself was larger than Mr. Gorham's "vast country" of 1787, and from it have been carved the existing commonwealths of Louisiana, Arkansas, Oklahoma, Missouri, Kansas, eastern Colorado, Iowa, Nebraska, Wyoming, Minnesota, North and South Dakota, and Montana.   This, the present domain of the continental United States, was daringly and rapidly accumulated within the sixty years following the inauguration of George Washington.   To put it another way, the new territory added since 1787 was more than twice the size of the land originally incorporated under the Constitution.

This enlargement of the American realm had not been accomplished without pain.   Most nations have consolidated their estates by struggles with external enemies.   Except for the brief and rapidly victorious war with Mexico this was not the case with the United States.   The battles that these riches entailed upon the new country were contested within its own borders — among the states themselves.   From 1830 to 1860 these battles were political, fought on the stump and in the halls of Congress.   Not until 1861 did they reach the conflict of arms.   The fact that brought about the Civil War was this extension of the American demesne from the Mississippi westward to the Pacific Ocean.   This is a truth of which Americans themselves are not always conscious.   There are those who will dispute the statement, but there is a pretty general understanding to-day that the cause of the war was negro slavery.   However, the great point in question was not the slavery in the old South

— in Virginia, the Carolinas, Georgia, and the new states east of the Mississippi and south of the Ohio that really represented the extension of the old South. The Constitution makers, by one of those compromises without which no central government could ever have been made, had settled the great social question in the only part of the country in which they ever expected it to exist. The institution was recognized and tolerated in the land south of the Potomac; most humanitarians, including most Southern statesmen themselves, expected it gradually to disappear; the question, however, was recognized as something for the states to decide. That an infinitely vaster territory would pass under the Constitution, in which the matter of human servitude would open up one of the fiercest arguments that have ever befallen a nation, was something the most imaginative of the statesmen of 1787 did not foresee. Yet the discussion that brought about the sanguinary decision of 1861–1865 concerned slavery west of the Mississippi River, not slavery south of the Potomac. Should this form of labor be restricted to the country in which it had existed since that ominous day in 1619 when a Dutch ship landed twenty "nagurs" at Jamestown, Virginia, or should it be extended in this new pioneer country west of the great river, where it had never been known?

The question at issue was a constitutional one. The Southern planters who migrated to the Southwest went, as already said, for a single purpose: to establish communities in the new land that would duplicate those they had left behind, subsisting, as had the old Southern homes, on cotton raised for the European market. It was their contention that, under the Constitution, they had the "right" to transport such of their "property" as was essential to this end. That they could take property in its universal sense — their horses, oxen, domestic cattle, farming implements, and the like — was undisputed. But they had another "peculiar" kind of property even more indispensable to the kind of agriculture in which they intended to engage. They had their African slaves. The question now arose, had they the right, under the Constitution, to carry these human chattels into this trans-Mississippi country; in other words, could all that enormous expanse reaching from the Mississippi to the Pacific Ocean and from the Rio Grande to Canada be transformed into a slave country? Monstrous as the pretension seems to modern eyes, such was the constitutional dispute of the thirties, forties, and fifties in American history. A strange literary experience to-day is to read the last speeches of John C. Calhoun, and discover him contending for the "rights" of slavery not in his own South Carolina and Virginia, — no one except a handful of fanatics denied its "rights" in that ancient country, — but in California, New Mexico, Oregon, Utah, and the other *terra incognita* of the Rocky Mountain and Pacific region. Can Americans to-day imagine California as a state given up to slavery? Southern statesmen in the fifties fiercely contested for such a privilege. Can we to-day conceive that Calhoun and his followers opposed the organization of the territory of Oregon in 1848 because the pending bill excluded slavery? Can one comprehend the fury with which this school of Southern statesmen opposed the citizens of California in 1850 because those hardy settlers had met in convention, adopted a constitution, and applied for admission into the Union? Incredible as it now seems, this opposition was based on the "impudence" of these "adventurers" because their constitution was one which prohibited the introduction of slavery! No stranger is the fact that the slavery die-hards did establish the right to set up their darling system in the five states that were subsequently made out of New Mexico. And Kansas and Nebraska escaped slavery only by one of the most desperate contests in our annals.

While the extension of slavery, not its abolition in the old states, caused this national convulsion, the two issues, of course, were closely associated. In his abridgement of the *Debates* Benton enters the following note for the Congress beginning January 7, 1836: "At this session the slavery question became installed in Congress and has too unhappily kept its place ever since." Benton had two portents in mind when making this lugubrious notation: first the beginning of the Texas question, and the possible creation of five new slave states on the Rio Grande — for the original Southern plan was to make five states of Texas, thus giving the slavery interests ten new Senators in the Upper Chamber; and secondly the abolition crusade, which was now reaching most formidable proportions. The two movements, the abolition crusade and the opposition to slavery in the trans-Mississippi country, sprang into full fire almost at the same time. The purpose of abolitionism was to destroy slavery in that part of the country — and inevitably in all others — in which its existence was recognized and protected by the Constitution. It signalized a warfare against one of the basal "compromises" of that instrument. Its purpose was to undo the bargain that had been struck in the convention, in which the chief negotiators were the gentlemen from New England and those from the states south of Virginia. It was a humanitarian movement, part of the general antislavery agitation of Wilberforce

and other English leaders, which, in 1833, led to the abolition of
slavery in the West Indies and other British colonies. It was thus
emphatically unconstitutional in its inception. The extreme advocate of the slavery cause, Calhoun, and his supreme opponent,
William Lloyd Garrison, had one point in common. Unless his
slavery ideas could prevail, Calhoun would destroy the Constitution.
Similarly, Garrison ferociously attacked the instrument of 1787,
declaring that, unless the great "crime" to which it had been a
party, the recognition of African slavery, should be undone, that
charter itself should be discarded. "No union with slave holders"
was the line carried for many years conspicuously by his inflamma-
tory paper, the *Liberator*.

Though it is doubtful whether Garrison represented the greatest
influence among the abolition leaders, — in his last twenty years,
indeed, he was pretty well under eclipse, — the man was so startling
a character, he had so many of the qualities of inspiration, even
genius, he was so gifted a journalist, that the word "abolition" has
become synonymous with his name, just as Calhoun is the immortal
defender of the opposite cause. The two men had personal similarities. Both were possessed of that John Knox type of fanaticism
which goes to extremes, accepts the most disastrous consequences of
its logic, recognizes no middle ground, has an irrefutable conviction
of its own personal rectitude, a belief in the absolute sacredness
of its cause, and is utterly unable to comprehend that the question
at issue may have qualifications that make ideal solutions impossible. Such natures see only one truth and are ready to ride over
and annihilate any obstruction to their end. Thus to Garrison
slavery was always the "great sin," and the constant iteration of
the word conveys the Puritanical nature of the Garrisonian onslaught. Slavery was a "sin," irredeemable except by repentance
and immediate and perpetuated abstention; it was personally corrod-
ing, damning to perdition the lost souls that practised it, corrupt-
ing everything and everybody who had the slightest contact with it;
and palliations such as "compromises," localizing the evil, tolerating
its existence for a specified time, were merely compacts with the
devil. In Garrison's mind the thing must be stamped out, wherever
and in whatever form it existed, and stamped out immediately. It
was a matter of soul salvation, of future bliss or punishment, as
much as the election of the Calvinist. Thus Garrison's mission
was not statesmanlike, but evangelical. His purpose was to arouse
"conviction of sin" in the American people. It was a "subject
which involved the temporal and external condition of millions of

our countrymen," he wrote at the beginning of his fight, and though Garrison, in his later period, departed from the orthodox religion of his youth, he never ceased to regard the abolition cause as fundamentally one of righteousness arrayed against the troops of Apollyon.

Garrison was not the only abolition leader; indeed, this cause, like most reforms, was divided into several camps, differing in methods and in aims, above all in the intensity of the advocates. But this spare New Englander was such a vivid personage, and his life, from beginning to end, such an unending and ferocious battle, that history has signalized him as the most veracious embodiment of the antislavery movement. Though the enemy insisted on regarding him as incarnating the most disagreeable qualities of New England, the fact is that he was not a New Englander by inheritance. Both his father and his mother, Abijah Garrison and Frances Maria Lloyd, were Canadians, who emigrated from Granville, Nova Scotia, to Newburyport, Massachusetts, a few months before Garrison's birth in 1805. Still the man's most positive traits — his delight in unpopular causes, his passion for martyrdom, for what he called the "joys and honors of persecution," his utterly sincere desire to make over the world — were in the best tradition of New England Puritanism. And these characteristics were innate. Garrison's initial appearance in print was as a crusader: the black man was not the first cause to arouse his zeal for human improvement; as a boy of eighteen his pen was busy advocating two causes of which much has been heard in recent times — total abstinence from alcohol, and the emancipation of women. Not improbably Garrison's family life as a child had aroused his sensitive nature to the need of both reforms. His father was a drunken shipmaster, who deserted his wife and family when William Lloyd was three years old; his mother was a woman not only of great beauty and dignified carriage, but in character a noble specimen of her sex. Contemplation of the manner in which she, single-handed, solved the problem of rearing her children early implanted that respect for one half of the human race, then little regarded in matters of property and the State, which filled so large a part of Garrison's mature life.

Despite his mother's exertions, Garrison's early existence was a hard one. His educational advantages were limited to a few years in a New England grammar school. At the age of nine he was apprenticed to a shoemaker, afterward to a cabinetmaker, in neither of which crafts was he destined to find congenial employment. It was in 1818, at the age of thirteen, that the boy obtained his first whiff of printer's ink, and this fixed his career. He was as inevitably born to live among types and presses as were Benjamin Franklin and Horace Greeley. And luckily for Garrison his first experience was gained as devil in a newspaper printing office. From sticking type and rolling proofs, the transition to authorship, as in the case of his two noble exemplars listed above, was natural. At twenty-one Garrison was proprietor, printer, and editor of the Newburyport *Herald*. His editorials in praise of the administration of John Quincy Adams, and in general approval of the Whig Party, were never committed to paper. Standing before the compositor's case, the youthful editor arranged the sentences mentally and then himself embodied them in type. Few Americans have been so much the born journalist as this thin, bespectacled journeyman. American newspaperdom lost one of its most accomplished editors when he abandoned the general field and dedicated his energies to special pleading. For Garrison quickly developed into a writer of intensity and power; his sentences resound with a vigor that can be felt to-day, even after time has quieted many of the issues on which he enlightened and infuriated the American public. His is a style which, though hardly graceful, almost never ingratiating, is still clear, emphatic, skillful in phrase and epithet, full of energy and fire, and fairly masterful in vituperation. As a controversialist Garrison belongs to the school of Junius and Cobbett, and his craftsmanship was almost as continuous a riot as was that of his predecessors. "I am aware," Garrison wrote in the first number of the *Liberator*, "that many object to the severity of my language; but is there not cause for severity? I will be as harsh as truth and as uncompromising as justice. On this subject I do not wish to think, or speak, or write with moderation. No! No! Tell a man whose house is on fire to give a moderate alarm; tell him to moderately rescue his wife from the hands of the ravisher; tell the mother to gradually extricate her babe from the fire into which it has fallen; — but urge me not to use moderation in a cause like the present. I am in earnest — I will not equivocate — I will not excuse — I will not retreat a single inch — and I will be heard."

Such were the spirit and literary style of the abolitionist agitation, the cause both of its strength and of its weakness. It was a literary rather than a political phenomenon, enlisting the allegiance of the New England school of writers and orators — Whittier, Longfellow, Lowell, Emerson, Harriet Beecher Stowe, Theodore Parker, William E. Channing, Charles Sumner, Wendell Phillips; its achievements were rather exhortations than effective programmes.

The purpose of the *Liberator* was to liberate slaves, to arouse the nation so practically to its "sin" that the shackles would vanish from the black man. For to Garrison shackles and what the Constitution euphemistically called "involuntary servitude" were inseparable. The genial aspects of the relationship on which the South itself was wont to insist were never visible to him. In Garrison's pages the Southern bondman was always "groaning" at his labor, his "chains" were always "clanking"; always over the dusky droves stood a small army of Simon Legrees, scourging them to unwilling toil. Negro cabins were not, in evening hours, the gathering places of a cheerfully singing and praying serfdom, but of a mournful people, wailing for freedom and gazing pitifully to their Northern sympathizers. The patriarchal amenities of servitude completely escaped Garrison's observation; his more crude description of the peculiar institution was "traffic in human flesh," its beneficiaries were "kidnappers" and "man stealers," "brokers in the trade of blood," while his consistent platform for fifty years was thus succinctly expressed : "We hold slavery to be a blot upon the national escutcheon, a libel upon the Declaration of Independence, a SIN AGAINST GOD [1] which exposes us to His tremendous judgment and which ought to be immediately repented of and forsaken." But Garrison's condemnation extended far beyond the question of slavery itself. He saw, what was similarly apparent to Calhoun and other observers, that the real problem was not the existence of a labor system that reduced two million black men and women to everlasting subjection, but the presence amid a population overwhelmingly white of a people of different race and different color. Thus the fight was not primarily for the slaves, but for the negro; it was concerned not only with Sambo on the plantation, but with the free American of African descent who was found in every section of the North. Garrison opposed bitterly the Colonization Society which had been organized to solve the question by removing American negroes, both free and slave, to land set aside for a black state in Africa. This was merely a scheme, he insisted, to rid America of free persons of color by shipping them to foreign soil. The only real solution was to keep them in the national confines and develop them as American citizens. All discriminations, especially rampant in the North, aroused the Garrisonian wrath. That negroes should have the same privileges as white men; that they should attend the same schools, the same churches, ride on the same cars, sleep in the same cabins in steamboats, live in the same boarding houses and hotels,

[1] Capitals in the original.

eat at the same lunch counters and restaurants — all this was part of his advocacy. Churches that set aside obscure pews for the colored brethren and refused to admit them to Communion in association with whites were held up to scorn. No church should admit slaveholders to membership, he insisted, and those clergymen who defended the institution — and such clergymen were by no means found only in Southern states — came in for unqualified castigation. To what extent Garrison accepted the ultimate conclusion of these equalitarian doctrines is not precisely defined, but that he should be denounced from one end of the nation to another as "an amalgamationist" was inevitable. He ostentatiously fraternized with negroes, spoke constantly in negro churches, — frequently, indeed, no other pulpit could be obtained, — made them traveling companions, and entertained them as guests at his table. The campaign carried on by the *Liberator* for the repeal of a Massachusetts law prohibiting the intermarriage of blacks and whites started rumors that his real desire was himself to take a colored bride — a story so persistent that the editor felt called upon to publish a disclaimer in his own paper.

So far as the most pressing issue was concerned — slavery itself — Garrison saw only one possible recourse. The father of abolition in this country was Benjamin Lundy of Baltimore, and it was Garrison's association, in his twenty-second year, with this pioneer that made him an instantaneous convert to the cause. But the youthful zealot at once took a position far in advance of the experienced Quaker. He favored the immediate unshackling of all slaves, while Lundy, representing a party that grew in strength with the years, thought the matter should be approached by easy stages. These two points of view introduced two new words into the English language, widely used in the first half of the nineteenth century — "immediatism" and "gradualism." The immediatists were those who regarded slavery as such a monstrous wrong that the nation, disregarding all practical considerations, should, at a single stroke, free itself from the degradation. The gradualists, who abhorred the system as intensely as did their more radical brothers, looked upon the institution from the standpoint of history. It had existed for more than two centuries, the whole economic and social structure of the South was bound up in it; to dissolve it suddenly would reduce those eleven states to chaos. It was therefore a change that should be brought about slowly, and adequate preparation should be made for the new adjustment that would ensue. The Garrisonians showed almost as much ferocity against the advocates of "gradualism" as against slaveholders themselves. "Immediate and unconditional emancipation is the right of every slave and could not be withheld by his master an hour without sin." This was the Garrisonian battle cry. The word "unconditional" is significant. England, freeing the slaves in her West Indian islands, had compensated the owners. The proposal that the Federal government should adopt this course was regarded by "immediatists" as supremely wicked. If anyone was to be ransomed, let it be the slave himself! Let no money be given the master. "It would be paying a thief for surrendering stolen property."

All this has an important bearing on the constitutional struggle that now ensued. What was the attitude of the Constitution on slavery? On this point there could be no disagreement. Some sought to argue against that "recognition" of slavery in the Constitution on which proponents of the system relied for its protection, even its extension. But the facts did not support their view. True enough, neither the word "slave" nor the word "slavery" appears in that instrument. The failure to use either word is significant: it betrays the sense of apology, of shame, with which the makers approached a dangerous and even disgraceful subject. It evinces the attitude of most of the leading Americans of the day — indeed of all the states except the three southernmost ones, North Carolina, South Carolina, and Georgia. The incongruity of including in a form of government based on the Declaration of Independence — "all men are created free and equal" — provisions for the perpetuation of slavery impressed most of the statesmen at Philadelphia. It particularly impressed those from Virginia. For this reason, though the delegates reluctantly submitted to clauses that protected the thing, they shrank from giving it the name. The slavery clauses were included for one reason only: without them there would be no Union, the weak Confederation would continue to operate as the only system of government which America could devise. Bad as was a "compromise" with slavery, the alternative would have involved greater infamy; the practical statesmen of 1787 therefore accepted what they looked upon as a temporary evil, but one which the future would rectify. They had not foreseen the invention of spinning machinery, of the cotton gin, of the factory system, of those railroads and steamboats that were to make cotton production so tremendously profitable. Therefore, while they made no provision for "slaves," they did make provisions for "persons."

In those three clauses in which the institution is unquestionably recognized, the black brother always appears disguised as a "person." Under Section 9 of Article I the slave trade is authorized until 1808; until this year "the migration or importation of such persons as any of the States now existing shall think proper to admit shall not be prohibited. . . ." Again, according to Section 2 of Article I, — almost on the very first page of the document, — three fifths of the slaves are given representation in the Lower House of Congress. Only the obnoxious word does not confront one at the very beginning of this new statute of human freedom, for now American serfs become "other persons." In Section 2 of Article IV, the clause that was to have so terrible a history, providing for the surrender of fugitive slaves, the victims are denominated, not by their real name, but as "persons held to service or labor." The same dislike of a hateful word appeared in the daily converse of Southerners, before the war and afterward. With the exception of Calhounites who developed the "positive good" conception, even slave owners preferred to refer to their chattels as "servants." One awkward contradiction was presented by the Fifth Amendment's declaring that "no person shall be deprived of life, liberty, or property, without due process of law," but certain agitators who, previous to 1861, proclaimed this as a constitutional prohibition of slavery received scant consideration. Who could maintain that a document which authorized the slave trade for twenty-one years, provided that slaves should have representation in Congress, and that fugitive slaves should be returned to their owners, did not "recognize" slavery?

These slave clauses have a strange appearance as we glance at them to-day, still embedded in the venerable paper — completely nullified, however, by subsequent amendments; but the interest they stirred in the enemies of slavery before 1861 was not, as it is with us, archaic. Garrison and his extremist associates gazed upon another famous piece of literature — the Bible — and discovered that that also seemed to sanctify slavery. They did not hesitate a moment. They turned against the Bible. Similarly the Constitution proved the bulwark of slavery advocates. So much the worse for the Constitution! That too, like the Hebrew books, did not denounce, but clearly tolerated, the ownership of one human being by another; it was evil and, in this respect at least, should be cast to perdition. "Are you a Christian?" Harriet Beecher Stowe asked Brother Garrison at their first meeting, for the good lady, fundamentalist in religion as in other matters, had been shocked by stories of his "infidelity," his anti-Sabbatarianism and generally cavalier attitude towards orthodoxy. What the editor of the *Liberator* replied on this occasion is not recorded; but he had frequently proclaimed that he was a Christian in a literal sense, a follower who practically applied the teachings of the New Testament, particularly its insistence on human brotherhood, the golden rule, and nonresistance in war — but not a worshiper of ancient Biblical heroes who kept bondmen and bondwomen in perpetual subjection.

Had any similarly pious adherent of the American charter asked Garrison, "Are you a constitutionalist?" the answer would have been a thunderous negative. Extreme abolitionists hated the Constitution as heartily as they hated those slave drivers who depended on its protection. This had been Garrison's state of mind in his earliest days, and it remained so, with increasing intensity, to the end. "The free states are constitutionally involved in the guilt of slavery," he wrote, as early as 1828, "by adhering to a national compact that sanctions it." His fellow citizens were called upon to abandon a Constitution that guarded such a "sin." "If the bodies of millions of rational beings must be sacrificed as the price of the Union, better, far better, that a separation should take place." Wendell Phillips, who denounced Abraham Lincoln as "the slave-hound of the West," because his method of approaching the problem differed from his own, took the same view. The Constitution, shouted Garrison, is "wet with human blood. . . . It makes us, as a people and as a state, the abettors of human degradation and soul murder. . . . It is founded on unrighteousness and cemented with blood." Hundreds of elegant extracts of the same kind could be culled from abolition writers, all demanding the destruction of the handiwork of the fathers of 1787. In 1850 Longfellow published his poem, "The Building of the Ship," containing its noble peroration, "Thou, too, sail on, O Ship of State! Sail on, O Union, strong and great." Longfellow was himself a moderate abolitionist and had helped the cause with a volume of antislavery poems. However, that did not save him from the Garrisonian invective. Longfellow's poem was described as a eulogy "dripping with the blood of imbruted humanity." The Union a "Ship of State" forsooth! It was rather a " 'perfidious bark . . . rigged with curses dark' rotting through all her timbers, leaking from stem to stern, laboring heavily on a storm-tossed sea, surrounded by clouds of disastrous portent, navigated by those whose object is a piratical one [namely, the extension and perpetuity of slavery], and destined to go down, 'full many a fathom deep,'

to the joy and exultation of all who are yearning for the deliverance
of a groaning world."

In this final act of scuttling, the Garrisonians were ready to do
their part. The big scene in Garrison's life came in Framingham,
Massachusetts, on July 4, 1854 — the national holiday, of course,
being selected in a spirit of malignant humor. Three thousand
abolitionists of most virulent type gathered at this sardonic cele-
bration. The Fourth of July orator was Garrison himself, who
in a lengthy and vitriolic address set forth his familiar views. "I
shall now perform an action," he said in conclusion, "which will be
the testimony of my own soul, to all present, of the estimation in
which I hold the pro-slavery laws and deeds of this nation." Then
he held aloft a copy of the Fugitive Slave Law, which he set on fire
and burned to ashes. "And let all the people say 'Amen,'" he
concluded, and a unanimous shout of "Amen!" uprose. Then the
speaker displayed another sheaf of printed leaves, proclaiming that
it was the Constitution of the United States. This instrument,
he exclaimed, was the source and parent of all the other atrocities.
It was "a covenant with death and an agreement with hell." He
then touched a match to this, watching the consuming flames with
an exultation fairly sadistic. "So perish all compromisers with
tyranny," he intoned, "and let all the people say 'Amen!'" And
once more came the echoing "Amen" from the spectators.

III

In the decade before the Civil War, the word "abolitionist" was bandied about as loosely as "Communist" is to-day; under this comprehensive head were grouped practically all citizens who held unfavorable views of negro slavery. The misconception has prevailed up to the present. The average American vaguely believes that abolition, and not slavery extension, caused the Civil War. But the fact is that the abolitionists made no great progress even in the North and West. Unpopular as they were in the South, they were almost as detested in the North. Both Garrisonians and other abolitionist sects, less extreme, were followed, wherever they showed their heads, by mobs, curses, and brickbats. These outbursts, ruffianly and reprehensible as they were, disclose at least one fact of historic importance, the unpopularity of the abolitionists in the North. Emancipation aroused little more favor in the North than in the South. Even historians do not sufficiently draw the distinction between the abolition and the antislavery movement. John Quincy Adams, who, entering Congress after leaving the Presidency, was constantly presenting petitions for ending slavery in the District of Columbia, protested that he was not an abolitionist, as did Abraham Lincoln when he rose to prominence as an antislavery leader in the fifties. Webster's view, as set forth in the reply to Hayne, can be taken as the attitude of the average Northerner, both Whig and Democrat. Slavery was an evil; so far as it existed in the old states, however, it was protected by the Constitution and the assent of the states which had ratified that contract; its abolition would produce greater disasters and problems than the institution itself. It was an anachronism in nineteenth-century civilization and in a republic founded supposedly on principles of universal freedom and liberty; but the process of emancipation could be safely left to time.

That is, it was bound to vanish in the course of events. Only one thing could prevent this inevitable consummation. That was the extension of slavery into the new territories. Here was an issue quite different from that of emancipation in the old-time South. The admission of Louisiana with slavery aroused apprehension in the North, and when Missouri, in 1819, knocked at the door, also with slavery in its constitution, the nation was aroused. The discussion that ensued, in Jefferson's graphic expression, came like "a fire bell in the night." The country now had entered a new danger, different from the prevalence of slavery in the old United States. The question of its extension had become the disturbing element in American life. The old Revolutionary statesmen who still remained on the scene — Jefferson, Madison, Monroe, and others — were as strongly opposed to this extension as were the most rabid Northerners. A new Southern leader, a leader whose one lodestar was love of the Union, finally achieved a settlement that seemed to end the slavery question for all time. Henry Clay proposed to draw a line, at 36°30' latitude, across the territory that had been acquired by the Louisiana Purchase. North of this line slavery should be forever excluded; south of it, it might be permitted. As the expanse lying south comprised only the soil that now approximately includes the states of Arkansas and Oklahoma, — Louisiana for many years had been a state, — and as the land north encompassed the present commonwealths of Iowa, Minnesota, North and South Dakota, Nebraska, Kansas, Montana, Wyoming, and part of western Colorado, it looked as though the antislavery advocates had got the better of the bargain. But as Missouri itself, which lay north of the compromise line, was admitted as a slave state, and as this Northern country at the time seemed little adapted to cultivation by negroes, the extreme men of the South were not entirely without compensation.

The nation gave a sigh, believing that a great danger had passed and that the problem of the growth of slavery had been settled. Practically all the undeveloped country that then formed the United States had been dedicated to freedom. This confidence would have been justified had not a new school of Southern statesmen presently evolved. Their philosophy embraced quite different principles from those of the Southerners who had done so much in framing the Constitution. The career of John C. Calhoun now enters its final phase. In his earlier time, as already described, he had been a Nationalist, a devotee upholding the Union above the states. On the slavery question similarly his views early followed the best Virginia tradition; though not in Congress in 1820, when the Missouri Compromise became a law, he completely approved that arrangement. The change that now took place in Calhoun was a change not only in political opinions but in temperament, even in appearance. The man who had formerly been known as one of the most charming members of Washington society was transformed into one of the most retired and inaccessible. More and more he came to live within himself; not only was he a good deal of a recluse in Washington, but even in his beloved South Carolina he mingled little with the common herd. The man whose reputation extended from one end of the nation to another was, he himself said, personally unknown to the masses in his own neighborhood. The tall handsome figure of his early life became bent and shrunken; the face was emaciated and gaunt, the high cheekbones almost piercing the skin; the hair was gray and thin and the eyes, still eaglelike, melancholic and furtive. Ill-health partly explained this transformation, but probably disappointed ambition had been a more inciting cause. Calhoun's conflicts with Jackson, a statesman he despised and distrusted, had, Calhoun believed, robbed him of the Presidency, while the growing power and riches of the North seemed destined to deprive the South of the political ascendancy that section had wielded since 1789. Thus Calhoun's disappointment was both personal and sectional; with the decline of his own influence was similarly involved the weakening of that political conception in which, he thought, the future of "his country" was involved. Calhoun grew more and more the solitary thinker and statesman, mixing little with his associates, giving up much time to formulating, in letters, resolutions, "addresses," and essays, those strange governmental ideas which, in his own day and since, have given him the name of metaphysician. In this latter period Calhoun stood out as a kind of Jonathan Edwards of the Constitution, spinning strange speculations, evolving interpretations that would have astonished the practical men who drafted it. To those about the man in Washington, the philosopher of new constitutional principles had completely superseded the statesman. The story is told of one of his "mess" companions who fled the common boarding house, as he said, "to get away from thought and Mr. Calhoun."

And all the South Carolinian's powers of disquisition were now centred on two purposes — to secure, if not the dominance, at least the independence of the South, and to preserve slavery. With increasing emphasis he maintained that there was not one nation in the United States, but two. These two sections were so disparate, in social conception, in agricultural and industrial status, in economic organization, in labor systems, that the greatest impending problem was to devise some method of keeping them together under the same Constitution. His final bequest, that *Disquisition on Government* to which the last months of his life were devoted, describes the one possible way in which this miracle could be achieved. Let America frankly recognize that it was composed of two irreconcilable parts. Let its political organism be established on an openly acknowledged sectional basis. Let the Constitution be amended to accomplish this. Strange indeed was the amendment proposed. It should provide for two Presidents, one elected by the Southern states, one by the Northern. No act of Congress should be valid that did not receive the approval of both these executives; each, that is, should have a veto power over the other. This was the extreme expression of that plan of "concurrent majorities" which Calhoun regarded as far more desirable than rule by brutal majority vote; for the man was no Democrat, and objected to "Democratic" as the name of his party. Did not that word imply an endorsement of rule by the mere preponderance of heads? This belated plan of adapting the dual consulship of ancient Rome to the most modern of republics was the inspiration of Calhoun's last days, after fifteen years spent in a bitter struggle to preserve the political power of the South; above all, to preserve and extend that slavery system to which the North was every day showing itself more antagonistic. Probably this scheme of two Presidents was now the only expedient Calhoun could see in which the interests of his section could be protected. He professed great love for the Union and for the Constitution, but only by this recourse, he insisted, could either be saved from destruction.

He returned to the Senate in January 1833, resigning what was left of the Vice Presidency — only two months — in order to take up the slavery battle which he saw impending. It was the disposition of the new land west of the Mississippi River that lifted the slavery issue into the most dramatic episode in American history — an episode famous not only for the exciting problems and incidents that followed, but for the group of powerful statesmen, beginning with Webster, Clay, and Calhoun, and ending with Douglas, Jefferson Davis, and Lincoln, who acted the leading rôle in this stupendous drama. And the object over which these heroes struggled — at times, it almost seemed, the dead body about which the battle raged — was the Federal Constitution. How did that instrument bear upon the growth of the American domain? Three distinct kinds of political organization existed in 1840. There were the states, the District of Columbia, and the territories. What was the "right" of slavery in these communities, so far as the Constitution safeguarded them? About the states there was little difference of opinion. The existence or nonexistence of slavery rested entirely within their control. Congress, under the Constitution, could neither create nor abolish it. Only a constitutional amendment giving power to the central government could make possible that "immediate and unconditional emancipation" which the Garrisonians were so stridently insisting on. But how about slavery in the District of Columbia? According to Southern statesmen, over this ten square miles also the Constitution had no sway. The real estate involved had formerly been parts of Virginia and Maryland, both slave states; the peculiar institution had prevailed in the region from the earliest settlement; Congress therefore had no more right of interference in this area than it had in the old slave states. Abolitionists of all shades, humiliated at the sounds of "clanking chains" and the echoes of the auctioneer's hammer — "traders in human flesh" — under the dome of a capitol devoted to independence and freedom, triumphantly pointed to a clause in the first Article. This gave the Federal legislature power "to exercise exclusive legislation in all cases whatsoever" over the District of Columbia. The phrase seemed comprehensive and plain; did not "all cases" include slavery and the slave trade? Despite the protestations of the South, the North clearly had the better of this constitutional argument; indeed, one of the first acts of Congress, after the outbreak of civil war, was to pass an act ending slavery in the District, no voice being raised, then or since, as to its power to do so under the Constitution.

But the really profound constitutional question arose over the possible existence of slavery in that immense country reaching from the Mississippi to the Pacific Ocean. Had Congress power to permit or abolish it in this domain? Again, what did the Constitution itself say? "The Congress shall have power," reads Section 3 of Article IV, "to dispose of and make all needful rules and regulations respecting the territory or other property belonging to the United States." This sentence would seem to settle two points: first, that the territories belonged to the United States, and secondly that the central power had sovereignty over them, while in the territorial condition. Congress apparently not only possessed this control, but, on several occasions, had exercised it. The Missouri Compromise of 1820 had been based upon this clause. But an entirely new conception of the unsettled country was presently evolved in Southern philosophy and became a cardinal precept of the State-rights doctrine. The territorial land, it was argued, was not the "property" of the United States, despite the constitutional statement to that effect. It belonged to the states themselves. True enough, actual possession rested in the hands of the central government; but that government was merely a trustee. Its business was to administer the property solely with a mind to the interests and "rights" of the real owners, the states. The territories, in this interpretation, were wards of the Union, which could exercise control until they had grown to majority — that is, until they had themselves become "sovereign states," when they would enter into untrammeled possession. During this tutelary period Congress could not deprive the states of their fundamental rights in their own soil. It could not, for example, prevent Southerners from entering their land and carrying with them their "property" — in other words, their slaves. Thus, in that period extending between the time when the land passed into American possession and the time when it became a state, slavery existed in the trans-Mississippi region; it was as much a reality in the section now known as Oregon, Dakota, and California as in South Carolina and Georgia. But when a piece of land was carved from this empire and admitted as a state, could Congress then provide that slavery should not exist in that new commonwealth? No, said the South. California, in 1849, had applied for admission with such a prohibition in its constitution, as Oregon did afterward; but the now rampant Calhounites protested against its admission on such terms. The Federal government, they maintained, had nothing to do with the question. It could insist on only one condition when a new state was admitted, and that was that its form of government should be Republican. The community itself, once attaining statehood, became completely independent and sovereign, and could establish or prohibit slavery. It was the very basis of the Southern creed that the state alone possessed this power. But how about the Missouri Compromise, which forbade slavery north of a certain parallel of latitude? Calhoun's answer was immediate and unqualified. The Missouri Compromise was unconstitutional and therefore null and void. If Southerners wished to cultivate corn in the Nebraska country or wheat in Minnesota, using negro slaves as laborers, Congress possessed no authority to prohibit them from doing so.

It all sounds very strange to-day, and only by turning back a hundred years and looking into the minds of proslavery statesmen can we understand the point of view. What was the motive that impelled them? First of all, a new attitude towards slavery had gained possession of the South. The day when Washington, Jefferson, Madison, and other Virginians proclaimed the institution as evil had gone. The aversion of that Potomac grandee George Mason, who declared, in the Constitutional Convention, that he would rather "cut off his right hand" than sign a document recognizing slavery, had given place to an entirely new point of view. No longer were Southern statesmen ashamed of using the word. After 1840 the outlawed syllables appear almost defiantly in the speeches and writings of the South. No longer is the institution apologized for; no longer is it a "necessary evil"; it is gloried in as a splendid feature of Southern life. Calhoun is now found eulogizing slavery as "a good, a positive good," something that should not be temporarily tolerated, with an eye always to ultimate extinction, but cherished and extended. Not perhaps slavery in general, but slavery as it existed in his beloved Carolina. "I hold that in the present state of civilization, where two races of different origin, and distinguished by color and other physical differences, as well as intellectual, are brought together, the relation now existing between the two is, instead of an evil, a good — a positive good. . . . I hold then, that there has never yet existed a wealthy and civilized society in which one portion of the community did not, in point of fact, live upon the labor of the other. . . . The devices [for accomplishing this] are almost innumerable, from the brute force and gross superstition of ancient times, to the subtle and artful fiscal contrivances of modern." Calhoun and his followers believed this new doctrine with an intensity the present age can never understand. The "patriarchal" society existing in the South represented, in their opinion, justice and the human spirit at their best. Compare the Southern negro, affectionately cared for from birth to death by the kindest of masters, with the "white slaves" of the North, eking out a bare existence in factories and mines, paid the lowest possible wages, worked the longest possible hours, uncared for in sickness, abandoned to an old age of poverty when capitalism had wrung from them the last ounce of strength and profit!

And this idyllic régime had now been viciously assailed by the Northern foe. Southern statesmen made no distinction between the abolitionists demanding the immediate unchaining of black men and the antislavery forces who opposed the creation of new slave territory. Both, in their view, were abolitionists, and in a sense this was true, for the more restrained antislavery spokesmen regarded ultimate extinction as inevitable. One way to make that final destruction certain was to prevent the growth of the system. And that was what aroused the fear of the ever-vigilant Calhoun. The Missouri Compromise, he now perceived, had sounded the knell of slavery. A territorial empire, reaching north from 36°30' to the Canadian line, west from the Mississippi River to the Rocky Mountains, had been set apart for freedom. This included practically all the land then open to settlement, for the country west of the Rockies to the Pacific did not become American until after the war with Mexico. In 1840, when Calhoun's plans began to take definite form, this expanse was all known as Nebraska, just as it had previously been known as Louisiana; it was still occupied exclusively by the red man; no states, not even territories, had been portioned out of it. It has since been parceled into nine commonwealths, each of immense size and, as Calhoun saw, could easily be divided into twenty or thirty. The eye of the pioneer was already looking longingly in this direction; suppose that, within an appreciable time, it should all be settled, all be made into new states, each excluding slavery, each, in addition to its Congressmen, having two members of the Senate? The slave South would then be encircled, north, west, and southwest, by a mighty agglomerate given up to free institutions, looking upon the South and its "civilization" as a blot upon America. Did it require much foresight to see what would happen? This East, Northwest, and West, having a vast preponderance in population, wealth, power of all kinds, would introduce in the Constitution an amendment abolishing slavery in all parts of the United States, even in the old Southland. This was the nightmare that dogged Calhoun's every moment. And of course he was right. It was towards this that the antislavery men were looking when they spoke of "gradual" and "eventual" emancipation. Does anyone suppose that, could slavery conceivably have lasted to the present time, the existing forty-eight states would permit one section of the country to maintain this labor system?

Time was the all-important element, if the "civilization" of the Southern states was not ultimately to be destroyed. As proslavery advocates scanned this continental map, there appeared one way of stopping their encirclement by free territory. Salvation lay in the Southwest. Here, in 1836, a new nation had appeared and won its independence. A horde of hardy, enterprising Americans, mostly from the Southern states, had invaded, with their slaves, the land indefinitely known as Texas, established their own republic, defeated all attempts of Mexico to subdue them, secured recognition as

an independent country from most European states, and applied for
admission to the American Union. Here was the solution of the
Southern problem. In 1844 Calhoun was appointed by Tyler Secretary of State; he cared nothing for the office, but accepted for
one reason, to negotiate the annexation of Texas to the United
States. That war would follow with Mexico was generally believed.
But this Mexican threat merely played into Southern hands, for war
with Mexico was precisely what Calhoun and his companions desired. That the American army would speedily crush the Indian
Republic they confidently believed — an expectation which events
amply justified. As indemnity, the United States could then take
California and New Mexico. This new addition of territory, as
large as that part of Louisiana which had been set aside by the Missouri Compromise for freedom, would thus ultimately be incorporated in the Union and devoted to slavery. Five states were to
be carved out of Texas and as many more out of the proposed
Mexican cession; the freedom obtained by the Compromise would
in this way be more than balanced. The great point to be gained
was of course the increased representation for slavery in the
Senate. This would give the South a permanent veto over all
the abolition enterprises of the future. Thus one is carried back
somewhat ruefully to another "compromise," almost as celebrated
as that of 1820: the one proposed by Connecticut in the Constitutional Convention of 1787, providing for the equal representation
of states in the Senate and representation by population in the House.
This adjustment was certainly having a strange and unforeseen effect
upon the fortunes of the nation. The South, which had almost
unanimously fought this Northern suggestion in 1787, now found
it a contrivance for the salvation of their existence, and the North
discovered that the constitutional arrangement it had so fiercely
contended for was now to be turned against itself. For only the
fact that each state was entitled to two Senators had made possible
this scheme of a Southwestern and Pacific empire based upon
slavery.

The plan succeeded admirably. Texas was annexed; the war
ensued; the American army was soon on the citadel of Chapultepec,
dictating terms of peace to Mexico; and, in addition to Texas,
California and the intervening country were ravished from the descendants of Montezuma. In pity for the defeated country, and
partly perhaps to salve its own conscience and gain an unassailable
title, the United States proposed to pay Mexico $15,000,000 for this
compulsory acquisition. Thus everything had proceeded according

to the Southern plan, but suddenly an unexpected event took place —
one of those happenings that, unheralded, insidious, so frequently
determine the course of history. While the debate appropriating
money for the payment to Mexico was pending, David Wilmot, a
Congressman from Pennsylvania and a Democrat, arose and quietly
proposed the following amendment, using the phraseology afterward
incorporated in the Thirteenth Amendment to the Constitution: that
"neither slavery nor involuntary servitude . . . shall ever exist in
any part of said territory, except for crime, whereof the party shall
first be duly convicted." Instantly the whole nation was in an up-
roar. If a parallel is sought for the rage that swept over the South,
it can be found only in the uprising of the North that took place
when Fort Sumter was fired on. The adoption of this amendment
would have "robbed" the South of all the advantage she had obtained
from the Mexican War. It would have upset the whole scheme
of acquiring a huge slave country and a greatly increased slave
representation in the Senate. The programme that was to make
slavery secure for all time would be transformed into another agency
for destroying it. The Garrisonians hailed the Wilmot Proviso
with a pæan of exultation, but Southern fire-eaters yelled and
threatened secession. The halls of Congress became the scene of
almost incessant riot. Had the Wilmot Proviso become law, — it
did pass the House but failed in the Senate, — civil war would
probably have broken out in 1846, instead of 1861.

So began the terrible contest upon which Americans can hardly
look back to-day without a shudder. The South was determined
to extend its slave system over all the country wrested from Mexico;
the North was just as determined that it should all be free. The
chief participants in the struggle were the three statesmen who were
now to play their final scene — Clay, Webster, and Calhoun. The
one who looms foremost is the Kentucky patriot, older by five years
than either of his companions. Like them, Clay stands in history
as a mournful example of the effect of great ambition in warping
character and distorting a career. Few Americans ever yearned so
for the highest office under the Republic as this great trio, or, on
their merits as statesmen, more deserved the prize. It is little less
than a national humiliation that, in the thirties and forties of the
nineteenth century, the Presidency should have been occupied by
such uninspiring mediocrities as Van Buren, Harrison, Tyler, Polk,
and Zachary Taylor, and that statesmen of the calibre of Calhoun,
Webster, and Clay should have been disregarded. It is said that,
after the election of 1844, the nation fairly gasped when the discovery

was made that it had elected James K. Polk President, and rejected his competitor, Henry Clay. Clay's failure was even more tragic than that of Webster and Calhoun, for neither of these aspirants ever came within measurable distance of the nomination, whereas Clay was an actual candidate four times and, on the last occasion, in 1844, missed the goal only by the barest accident. The reason for the failure reflects Clay's chief weakness as a public man. He had taken a two-faced stand on the annexation of Texas: one day he advocated it, the next he opposed; and herein is pictured the part Clay had played for fifty years of public life. For the Kentuckian was now the idealist, now the practical, self-seeking man; now the statesman, now the politician; now the devoted American patriot, and now the almost unscrupulous pursuer of ambition. History has assigned him a more pleasing title, but one that embodies a similar idea. For Clay was the great "compromiser," the man who watched factions develop into a seething *impasse* and then, at the vital moment, stepped in with an arrangement intended to reduce the disputants to harmony. He had already fulfilled the rôle on two historic occasions. In 1820 he had solved the first great slavery crisis with his Missouri Compromise. In 1833 he had settled the struggle over nullification with his compromise tariff. This function of soother of troubled waters was a complete expression of the man. He loved his country and he loved his fellows; of all American statesmen there has been none more personally popular with the people than Clay. Webster all Americans vastly admired; Calhoun they respected; but Clay they regarded as one of themselves and clasped him to their bosom. No man of his time, at least after the death of Jackson, could command such hurrah-ing, worshiping throngs. Half-crazed, mob-led gatherings assembled whenever it was known that Clay was to speak. His expected appearance in debates caused crowds of both sexes to fill the Senate Chamber to suffocation.

The secret of this magnetism escapes a later generation which seeks it in the printed version of Clay's speeches. Even now, in reading Webster's orations, we can feel the emotion with which his hearers hung upon the words; but Clay's are without lasting literary charm: they seem, after the lapse of nearly a century, inelegant in form, tiresome in repetition, lacking in vivid and distinguished expression; at times they are even dull and vapid. The explanation is simply that, in Clay's oratory, the vital man himself was the important fact. We are not to-day in the presence of that tall, lithe figure; of that ever-mobile countenance, reflecting all varying emotions with the ease and grace of an experienced actor; of the dark eyes, at times flashing and indignant, at others mellow and sympathetic; of that smile and that power, both instantaneously making all men his brothers; above all, of that melodious voice which Clay could use with all the skill that the talented musician applies to his instrument.   One of Clay's bitterest foes was John Randolph of Roanoke; yet when Randolph, dying of tuberculosis, passed through Washington, he insisted on being carried into the Senate Chamber, where, stretched upon a lounge, he listened to another speech from the man with whom he had once fought a duel. "I came," he said, "that I might hear that voice once more."   Thus, all his life, Henry Clay's leadership rested upon his qualities as a human being.   He had received little education; he was not a man of extensive reading; he never attained eminence at the bar; and great as was his devotion to the Constitution, Clay's rank as constitutional lawyer is not an exalted one.   A moralist like John Quincy Adams saw in Clay much to deprecate; he was on occasion a duelist and a gambler; he showed the same carelessness about paying his debts as Webster himself, and, as became a good Kentuckian, had a fondness for hard drink and frequently found the race course more congenial than the Upper House of Congress.   Failings that shocked rigid livers, however, seemed only to draw Clay closer to the American heart.   Above all human frailties the American public saw in Clay a patriot, an honest upright man, devotedly serving his country, a champion almost divinely appointed to lead them out of several of the most dangerous crises in their history.

For concerning the most powerful impulse in Clay's career there was never a moment's question.   He was an idolator of the Constitution and the Union it had framed.   The love he protested for Union was not the kind Calhoun and other statesmen were constantly asserting.   Clay's was unqualified and his love admitted no rival.   Those Virginians who, in 1861, followed the Confederacy not because they believed in its principles, but because they could not fight against their own state, Clay would have scorned.   To him Robert E. Lee would have been no hero.   Virginia, the state in which Clay was born, and Kentucky, the one in which he lived the larger part of his life, did not hold first place in his affection. Before everything else he gave allegiance to the United States of America.   Once in the Senate a Southern member, speaking of Clay, referred to Virginia as "your country."   The man was up in a flash.   "The Honorable Senator," he retorted, "speaks of Virginia being my country. This Union is my country; the thirty states are my country; Kentucky is my country and Virginia no more than any other of the states of this Union. . . . If my own state lawlessly, contrary to her duty, should raise the standard of disunion against the residue of the Union — I would go against her; I would go against Kentucky in that contingency, much as I love her." And this devotion he brought to that Constitution without which, he insisted again and again, there could be no nation. For State rights, when that expression meant encroaching on the strength of the Union, he never concealed his contempt. He foresaw the growth and future power of the United States, and of the Constitution as its bulwark. "Every man," he said, "who looks at the Constitution in the spirit to entitle him to the character of a statesman, must elevate his views to the height which this nation is destined to reach in the ranks of nations. We are not legislating for this moment only, or for the present generation, or for the present populated limits of the United States; but our acts must embrace a wider scope — reaching northwestward to the Pacific and southwardly to the River Del Norte. Imagine this extent of territory covered with sixty, seventy, or a hundred millions of people! The powers which exist in this government now will exist then; and those which will exist then exist now."

The speech in which this imaginative forecast appeared was made in December 1817, in Monroe's administration; but the sentiment proved to be the guiding one of Clay's life for the next forty years. At that time he was a young man, full of energy, lively spirits, and readiness to take the offensive whenever the Union was assailed; in 1849, however, when he returned to the Senate for the last time, Clay was an old man of seventy-one, ill of tuberculosis, feeble and emaciated. He regarded his public life as a failure, for had he not again missed his greatest ambition? "My party always runs me for the Presidency," he once exclaimed, "when there is no chance of being elected, but, when victory is sure, then — " So it had been in 1840, when he was thrust aside for William Henry Harrison, who won; and now, in 1848, when the Whigs again triumphed, they had relegated their founder and leader to the rear and chosen Zachary Taylor, a rough-and-ready general in the Mexican War, a man without the slightest vestige of statesmanship, and, so far as anyone could discover, without political convictions. "What does Zach Taylor represent?" an amazed American public asked, and there was no answer. The fact was, of course, that he represented nothing but the battle of Buena Vista. And it was with an altogether human bitterness that the bent figure, after

Taylor's victorious campaign, retired to his home at Ashland, Kentucky. For his remaining days Clay asked nothing except to be left in quiet and alone. His wishes were ignored. In December, without Clay's wish and almost without his knowledge, he was again elected to the United States Senate. The unanimous vote of the legislature was balm to Clay's injured feelings, but, had another national crisis not arisen, the honor would have been declined. Clay had piloted his country through several great dangers, but the one that loomed in 1850 threatened to become the most serious of all. The abolitionists as usual were raging; Calhoun was every day proclaiming more advanced views on slavery extension, foretelling the break-up of the Union if they were not accepted by the North; in many Southern states secession movements had started. Here was Clay's last opportunity to serve the cause to which his life had been given. If his country had ever needed his rôle of "pacificator" it certainly needed it then. And so in December Clay again made his way to Washington. He took a solitary chamber in the National Hotel, keeping wholly to himself, seeing no visitors, never going into society. Night after night a huddled figure, packed in flannels, drooped in his chair, cold and disconsolate, trying to think of some way out of the abyss into which the country was descending.

IV

One evening in January, 1850, Daniel Webster was sitting in the library of his Washington home. Outside a heavy snowstorm was raging. Webster's spirits were scarcely in more cheery or peaceful mood. The fortunes of his venerated Constitution weighed heavy upon the statesman's mind. He was now sixty-eight and looked older than his years. His body had become corpulent, his face thin and lined, the distinctive cheekbones were assuming a still more definite outline, his hair was grayer and sparser than in the period of his prime, receding from the brow. The man had always been a high liver, and perhaps a too frequent indulgence in alcohol had something to do with rapidly advancing signs of decrepitude. No one, however, had observed any decline in mental and oratorical power. As was the case with Calhoun and Clay, defeated ambition had eaten deeply into his soul. "I want it, I want it!" he once exclaimed to a friend who had deprecated his yearning for the Presidency, arguing that Webster's fame as a statesman and moulder and preserver of the Constitution meant far more than a brief tenancy of the White House, and there is a cry of despair in the words. On the issue that was then rending the nation almost in twain Webster's course had been consistent from the first. In this, as in all things, he took his stand on the Constitution. The guarantees that document gave slavery he had always recognized as a sorry compromise. Especially did the clause requiring the surrender of fugitive slaves seem an offense to human instincts. Yet these concessions to the lower South had made the Constitution possible. Moreover, these sections actually were a part of the Constitution; they represented a contract made between the North and the South; the lawyer who had so brilliantly argued the inviolability of contracts in the Dartmouth College case could not turn his back on this, odious as the "consideration" made by the North had proved to be. Webster insisted, therefore, that the North should honestly fulfill the hateful obligations it had incurred; only in this way could the Southern states be held strictly to their covenants. And one of the things the South must be prevented from doing was to extend its "system" into new countries. In the reply to Hayne, Webster, abhorring slavery though he did, insisted that it be left undisturbed in the old South, for there the Constitution had guaranteed its existence, but he had opposed, with all his matchless eloquence, its invasion of new soil.

While Webster, on this freezing, blizzardous January evening, was sitting by his library fire meditating the problem, a somewhat startled servant entered the room. Mr. Clay, he said, had just appeared at the door and asked to see Mr. Webster. The statesman who tottered in was the mere shadow of "Young Harry of the West." Clay was now seventy-three, so ill and feeble that he could hardly find his way to the chair to which Webster led him. All through the talk that followed his frame was shaken by a persistent cough. No detailed account of the interview has been preserved, though, on personal as well as historic grounds, it was one of the most dramatic in the annals of Washington. The two statesmen had never been upon particularly cordial terms, though they had always maintained an outward show of friendship. Both were full of human failings; for fifteen years they had been the greatest men in the Whig Party, and the rivalries of that period, especially for the Presidency, had left scars. But both Webster and Clay had reached almost the end of their careers; with Clay at least, all Presidential passion had been spent. And now the two statesmen were to close their public lives coöperating in a task from which ambition was absent, the one purpose being an unselfish one to compose a nation's agony. For Clay immediately explained why he had ventured out in this inclement weather. The United States, he said, was on the brink of dissolution and civil war. The word "secession" had become virtually the most familiar one in the speech of the South. That Union which both he and Webster regarded as indispensable to America's future, and which, for forty years, had enlisted the most patriotic efforts of both, was rushing headlong to ruin. Could they not together, and as a final public service, agree upon some plan that would save the situation?

In the solitary hours spent in his room at the National Hotel, Henry Clay had devised such a plan. He wished Webster's advice and hoped for his support. As the old man set forth the details, it bore in every line the familiar marks of his genius. For it was another "compromise." Just as the Constitution itself had been made on the basis of give and take, so it must be saved in the same way. Let the South yield certain things to the North; let the North yield certain things to the South; only thus could the Union, in 1850, be saved. And Clay set forth the items of his proposed settlement. First there was the question of California. Should it be a free or a slave state? Clay insisted that on this point the South must accept the Northern demand. There was really no argument. The convention in California framing the constitution had, by unanimous vote, forbidden slavery; that constitution included sixteen men from the Southern states, who had been even more determined than their Northern brothers! They had seen all they wanted of slavery at home! They did not propose to repeat the mistake their Virginia ancestors had made and introduce the black man to this new, uncontaminated soil. The error of establishing "involuntary servitude" on the Atlantic Coast was not to be repeated on the Pacific.

The question of New Mexico — and always bear in mind that New Mexico meant not only the present state of that name, but Arizona, western Texas, Nevada, Utah, and western Colorado — was a more difficult matter. Southern statesmen were demanding the organization of this domain as a territory, on a basis that would permit slavery. "Why not let them have their way?" asked Clay, in substance, though his precise words are not recorded. Outwardly the North would be yielding to the South and delivering land of enormous extent to a vicious future. But the Southern victory would be only apparent. Slavery advocates would gain the shadow and lose the substance. Nature itself had solved the problem in this region. No one — not even the most excited Southerner — really believed that this country would become a place for African bondmen. The climate and the soil made it utterly unsuited for such development. If ever settled, — and in 1850 its development by Anglo-Saxons was regarded as a matter for the far-distant centuries, — negroes would not be used there. The North, by making this gossamer concession, could win the South to yielding substantial points, and would, in practice, lose nothing; it would merely be playing a stroke in a diplomatic game. The vast country known as California would be gained for freedom. That slaves could be profitably employed there was not improbable. In fact, many Southerners had already taken black bondmen to the region and put them to work in mines. The climate was entirely suited to a sunshine-loving people. Thus, Clay insisted, his plan would give immediate freedom to California and ultimate freedom to

New Mexico. That is to say, the Wilmot Proviso, though abandoned on the surface, would in practice become the fact. Slavery would be excluded from all the territory acquired from Mexico.

The third point was slavery in the District of Columbia. An avalanche of petitions on this subject had been inundating Congress for years. The time had come to take action. Slavery itself could not be abolished there so long as it existed in the states of Virginia and Maryland. But the slave trade could. Clay now demanded that the South agree to end this traffic. In return the North should accept a Fugitive Slave Law more effective than the one that had been enacted in 1793, which had proved unenforceable. Though this provision was the feature of the compromise that caused greatest excitement when announced, Webster had no qualms in agreeing to it. A bargain was a bargain. In 1787 the North had solemnly put its signature to a Constitution that contained the words: "No person held to service or labor in one State, under the laws thereof, escaping into another shall in consequence of any law or regulation therein, be discharged from such service or labor, but shall be delivered up on claim of the party to whom such service or labor may be due." How could any "defender of the Constitution" refuse to carry out its provisions, especially at this time when the very existence of the Union depended on redeeming the promise made by the fathers?

There were other points of minor consequence, but these four were the important ones. On this basis the crisis of 1850 was avoided — as it seemed at the time, permanently. For Clay's wintry visit to Daniel Webster proved successful. The Massachusetts Senator listened sympathetically to the Kentuckian and, after a few days' consideration, agreed to join his old rival in securing a compromise. That his acquiescence would bring the rage of the extreme antislavery partisans on his head, the veteran well knew. That his motives would be assailed, that he would be accused of seeking Southern support for the Presidential nomination of 1852, he understood. Extreme abolitionists were openly advocating the alternative to a compromise — dissolution of the Union, scuttling of the Constitution. Webster's opposition to slavery did not go so far. To him, as to Lincoln afterward, the Union was the thing above all to be saved. As Lincoln declared on a celebrated occasion, the Union without slavery, or the Union with slavery, was the end which he sought. So with Daniel Webster in 1850.

On March 7, 1850, before a crowded Senate that recalled his debate with Hayne on essentially the same subject twenty years before, Webster rose and delivered another speech which, in power, in patriotism, in devotion to the Constitution, deserves to rank with his greatest. In his collected works this oration is called "The Constitution and the Union." More intensely than the speech of 1830 was it a plea for preserving the charter on which the nation rested. It was a mournful occasion, aside from the danger that impended over the country. It marked the last time that the three great statesmen of the slavery issue were to meet in lofty argument. Henry Clay, who a month previously had introduced his proposals with one of his masterly speeches, was an eager and grateful listener. John C. Calhoun had three days before delivered his last oration, opposing the compromise. Only the recognition of the existence of two distinct sections, he had declared, each with its own institutions, protected by a constitutional amendment that would regulate the new association, would settle this and other disintegrating problems.

What that "constitutional amendment" should be was no secret. It was again Calhoun's favorite idea of two Presidents, one for the North and one for the South, each having veto power over acts of Congress. At the time this proposal was advanced Calhoun was a dying man, too weak to deliver his oration, and a brother Senator read his carefully written address. In his crumpled physical condition, sitting silent and inscrutable in a seat just in advance of Senator Mason, who was reading this, Calhoun's final testament, he fittingly symbolized the dying cause which he upheld. The experience had so exhausted the statesman that he had taken to his bed — for the last time, it was generally believed. Webster, therefore, had not expected Calhoun's attendance when, three days afterward, he rose. In fact he referred most sympathetically to Calhoun's enforced absence and the condition of his health that made it inevitable. "The Senator from South Carolina is here!" came in sepulchral tones from the rear of the Chamber. Webster turned and there saw Calhoun stretched upon a lounge. He had insisted on being carried into the Senate to hear Webster's speech. His voice sounded like one from the tomb — as it nearly was, for three weeks afterward Calhoun was dead. "The South, the poor South!" were almost his dying words — words that emblazoned the statesman's conviction that the truce proposed by Webster and Clay was only a temporary matter, that civil war was sure to come, and that his beloved section was doomed to suppression. Far-sighted statesman that he was, Calhoun foresaw that the real problem — that of fitting a huge negro population into the civil and industrial life of the nation — would only rise after this war had been fought. His letters and speeches disclose that he foresaw the chaos of Reconstruction.

Webster and Clay survived their lifelong opponent two years, both dying in 1852. By that time the compromise they had arranged was in working order. That its defects were already becoming apparent is no reflection upon their wisdom. It is not likely that either statesman believed that the measures of 1850 had finally put at rest the slavery question. That was really not their purpose. Clay's Compromise of 1820, in its day looked upon by optimists as forever putting an end to slavery aggression, had delayed the crisis until 1850 — thirty years. It was his and Webster's hope that the new legislation would give the nation another breathing spell. And from this point of view the Compromise of 1850 represented the acme of practical statesmanship. Clay and Webster had made terms with the slavery powers, even consented to one concession which, in the eyes of that generation and this, seems to run counter to human nature itself, the rendition of fugitive slaves, for the same reason that had impelled the framers of the Constitution to play with this particular form of fire — to establish and maintain the Union. The abuse that showered upon their heads, especially on Webster's, for he was a Massachusetts man and a lifetime foe of slavery and its expansion, was such as few public men, in any country, have been called upon to endure. The rage of the abolitionists became fairly maniacal; Boston pulpits and Faneuil Hall resounded with curses on the great "apostate"; Whittier wrote a scurrilous poem, picturing Webster as Ichabod, — "the glory hath gone out of Israel," — and Webster's personal mail became a mountain of reproaches. Yet the orator regarded his "Seventh of March" speech as his finest effort, and the settlement it achieved his greatest public service. Posterity in general agrees with him.

America's most thoughtful historians now believe that the compromise postponed the Civil War ten years. "No man can read carefully the debates in which these two men [Webster and Clay] took part," writes James Ford Rhodes, "at the same time illuminating their public utterances by the light of their private letters, without arriving at the conclusion that the mainspring of their action was unselfish devotion to what they believed the good of their country." "Looking backward," says Edward Channing, "it is astounding to realize the accuracy with which Daniel Webster sensed the situation in the South and recognized that a concession on the part of the North, like that contained in the Fugitive Slave Act of 1850, would cut the ground from under the feet of Barnwell Rhett, Langdon Cheeves, Robert Toombs, Alexander H. Stephens, and William Lowndes Yancey, and put off the inevitable crisis until the North should outstrip the South in man power and resources — so much so, indeed, that possibly secession and war would never come." Had war broken out in 1850, it would have found the two sections fairly evenly matched: the result might well have been a Southern victory and the destruction of the Union. The ten years succeeding were the most prosperous in the history of the North. By the time the decade had run its course, the non-slaveholding states, in population, resources, development of all kind, had left the land of slavery far behind. When the final struggle came, therefore, it could have only one end. It is the glory of Webster and Clay that their statesmanship in 1850 gave the North the opportunity to meet the crisis on more than even terms. The preservation of the Constitution, in 1850, is their greatest title to the gratitude of their countrymen.

V

And so the question of slavery in the territorial sense had apparently been laid to rest. The boundaries of the United States were regarded as fixed for all time. Those boundaries were essentially the ones that exist to-day. North of 36°30′ it had been decided by Congressional enactment that slavery could never exist. The Pacific Coast states — California and the sections that afterward became the states of Oregon and Washington, Idaho and Montana — had, by the will of their own citizens, been set aside for freedom. The Republic of Texas, annexed in 1845, promptly entered the American family as a slave state. The future of the expanse lying between Texas and California, then called New Mexico, had been left to the decision of those who should make it their home. Most Americans regarded the time when even territorial governments would be established in this sandy waste as remote. Would these territories, and afterward these states, be made accessible to slavery? The most optimistic proslavery expansionist did not believe so. Climate and the character of the country seemed to make such a development impossible. So far as the existing limits of the United States were concerned, the Southern states had thus clearly lost the battle. The encirclement that Southern statesmen had so feared, and to escape which they had precipitated war with Mexico and gained a new territorial empire for the United States, was now complete. The platforms of both political parties, in 1852, accepted the Compromise of 1850 as ending the question, and acquiescence in that treaty was looked upon, North and South, as a test of good citizenship.

That Southern hopes for more slave states did not entirely vanish is true. This determination was manifest in directions that astonish the modern reader. There were certain northern provinces of Mexico still unseized — Coahulia, Sonora, Chihuahua; slavery had existed here under the old Spanish régime; peonage — an institution closely resembling it — still prevailed; was it not possible that Mexico could be persuaded to exchange these provinces for some of those millions of gold rapidly accumulating in the American treasury? Parts of Central America were ideally suited, in climate and soil, for growing cotton with negroes. Nicaragua in particular presented a favorite field for Southern filibusterers, all with the vague hope of eventually transferring it into an American state; Jefferson Davis even advocated annexation of Yucatan! But the land that tempted Southern statesmen above all was Cuba. Had the plans of the Pierce administration succeeded, the pearl of the Antilles would have been snatched from Spain — either by purchase or by conquest, for Southerners were quite prepared to wage another war in behalf of slavery — and two or three new states, each having two Senators in Congress, would have been added to the Union. The air was full of such schemes in the years following 1850. Yet the compromise was regarded as sacrosanct, even in the South. Willing as proslavery leaders might be to encroach on foreign nations that bordered the Gulf of Mexico, no voice was raised south of the Mason and Dixon line to suggest the violation of the agreement which had been made respecting the American domain itself. Not until Northern politicians took the first step and showed the way did Southern statesmen evince the slightest disposition to break the compact of 1850 and undo the work of Webster and Clay. The greatest betrayal in American history should, first of all, be ascribed to those Northern schemers who detected in the Southern passion for slavery extension the way of advancing their own political fortunes.

The present fashion for rehabilitating discredited historic characters has not overlooked a man so sorely in need of reappraisement as Stephen A. Douglas. Yet it is not certain that the judgment passed upon this statesman by critics of his own time and by historians since calls for much modification. Jefferson Davis, who became his fellow laborer in the cause of slavery, casting him aside, as did the South in general when Douglas had served its purpose, entitled him a "demagogue"; a much fairer and more judicious commentator of modern time, James Ford Rhodes, does not particularly disagree with this verdict. The "little giant's" policy of 1854, says Mr. Rhodes after a discriminating analysis, "was a bid for democratic support in the next presidential campaign," and he quotes, as "a true statement," the question asked by John Van Buren at the time: "Could anything but the desire to buy the South dictate such an outrage?" These harsh pronouncements have particular force, for they rest upon that trait in the career of Douglas which all biographers, friendly and otherwise, agree was the predominant one. The man, from his earliest view, was almost exclusively the politician, and regarded all public issues, even the profound one with which his period was rife, as matters of expediency. On the question of African slavery he had no moral convictions. At the most exciting moment Douglas exclaimed, "I don't care whether slavery is voted up or voted down," and that phrase may be regarded as sounding the key to his whole public life.

This seems a sad indictment of a man who derived from a long line of New England ancestors, who was nourished in New England schools, who, in fact, spent his early years in one of the cradles of American patriotism, for that part of Vermont that had sheltered his progenitors for three hundred years was the locality of Bennington, of Saratoga, and of Plattsburg. From these beginnings, however, Douglas seemed to have drawn little inspiration. The studious habits, the love of education and reading which are supposed to be part of the New England inheritance, played little part in his early life. That as a young man he was energetic and a hard worker is true; he was always proud that he had learned the cabinetmaker's trade and successfully practised it for a year or two; yet his affiliations were not with the journeyman's bench, or with the agricultural and commercial existence of his ancestral region, but with the new country opening in the West. That Douglas, in his seventeenth year, should have abandoned what had become an uncongenial home and started on Western travels which, by easy stages, landed him at the age of twenty-one in the middle section of Illinois seems a natural evolution. "I found my mind liberalized and my opinions enlarged," he once said, referring to his first impressions of the West, "when I got on those broad prairies, with only the heavens to bound my vision, instead of having them circumscribed by the little ridges that surrounded the valley where I was born."

In every way he fitted immediately into this roughhewn existence. He had precisely the qualities needed for a satisfactory adjustment. His mind was keen and ready; he liked all kinds of human beings and all kinds liked him; he was open, gay, frolicsome, optimistic, fond of taproom conversation, talented in physical encounter, at home in log-cabin courtrooms, a genius in political manipulation, a leader — not so much by powers of persuasion as by personal force. In appearance the man was at first not impressive. His figure was short and squat; his disproportionate head rested, almost without the interposition of a neck, on broad, ponderous shoulders; his movements, while vigorous, were ungraceful, and his speech, while frequently full of animation and eloquence, was rough and overbearing. Yet Douglas exuded confidence and drive. Had he possessed merely the wirepulling abilities that early made him political leader of his section, he would have reached no higher goal than commander of the local machine; from this ruck, however, he was rescued by great inborn talents and boundless personal ambition. In addition to his ability in manipulating men, Douglas displayed qualities that ultimately made him the most skillful parliamentarian of his time; he displayed at an early day that quickness of thought, readiness of retort, improvisation in speech, grasp of public questions, and insight into the ideas and motives of opponents that transformed the "little giant" into the best debater of his day. Had Douglas been merely the pothouse politician, his life would have been spent in those public employments that occupied his earliest days in the West — state's attorney, register of land office, state legislator, Illinois Secretary of State. These offices, however, he quickly outgrew, and at the age of thirty found himself in Congress. Here his immediate rise to importance startled the ever-quotable John Quincy Adams in much the same way that the youthful Andrew Jackson had appalled Thomas Jefferson. "Stephen A. Douglas . . . raved out his hour in abusive invectives upon . . . the Whig party. His face was convulsed, his gesticulation frantic, and he lashed himself into such a heat that if his body had been made of combustible matter it would have burnt out. In the midst of his roaring, to save himself from choking, he stripped off and cast away his cravat, unbuttoned his waistcoat, and had the air and aspect of a half-naked pugilist."

But Douglas's oratory, even at this time, was more than bombastic athleticism; this is proved by the rapidity with which he gained prominence in a chamber then full of able men. The youthful member's opinions, likely enough, had as much to do with Adams's graphic disgust as his manner of speech. For the ex-Vermonter already stood champion for practically everything obnoxious to the New England conscience. The part of Illinois with which Douglas was most familiar had been settled chiefly by Southerners; despite the Northwest Ordinance, slavery had existed in that part of the state in early days, and the views on the institution which possessed the region Douglas had early made his own. Accordingly, from his arrival in Washington, the proslavery leaders in Congress had adopted him as one of their number. They had for years no more zealous compatriot. No gentleman from South Carolina or Mississippi hated an abolitionist quite so fervently. And any man who regarded slavery as undesirable, from the Garrisonian to the philosophic preacher of "eventual emancipation," was included in Douglas's wide-sweeping detestation.   He hailed the Mexican War, rejoiced at the annexation of Texas, entered into all the Southern schemes for the development of conquered territory.   He was a blatant advocate of the extinction of the whole "Empire of the Montezumas" and the incorporation into the Union of everything as far south as the Isthmus of Panama.   The scheme for acquiring Cuba and creating two or three slave states out of that island met his approval.

That Douglas defended the extreme Southern view, easily over-throwing, with wit, sarcasm, readiness at confronting points and deflecting issues, all but the ablest speakers on the other side; that in the more weighty business of framing legislation and steering it through committees he evinced endless resource; that, in addition to these qualities, he showed social adaptability, becoming an orna-ment of the finest Washington drawing rooms as he formerly had been of the drinking parlors of pioneer Illinois — all this made his advancement almost lightning-like at Washington.   He became Chairman of the Committee on Territories, then the most fateful position in Congress.   When, after a brief service in the lower chamber, Illinois sent its favorite to the Senate, he promptly as-cended to the corresponding position.   The fact is that, after four or five years in Washington, Douglas had become almost the most influential Democrat on the scene.   His enemies — a company that included practically all the Whigs and antislavery Democrats — found plenty to criticize in their energetic opponent.   The most vulnerable points concerned his personal relation to slavery.   Doug-las, soon after becoming Senator, had married a beautiful and charm-ing girl of North Carolina: this was supposed to have something to do with his new love for the South.   His wife, by the death of her father, became the owner of a sizable Mississippi cotton planta-tion with a hundred and fifty slaves — a circumstance which, it was charged, explained the conversion of this New Englander to the institution.   To the antislavery mind this meant that Douglas was himself a slave owner, and was fulfilling in his own person the Southern tradition that Yankees, once become the proprietors of black men, developed more fanaticism for the cause than those to the custom born.   Douglas's almost frantic explanation that these slaves belonged absolutely to his wife, and that, under the Missis-sippi law, the husband had no participation in his wife's property, did not entirely remove the brand of "slave owner" with which the enemy insisted on adorning him.

Douglas, in leading the campaign for slavery extension, went to extremes that, up to 1854, had hardly entered the purview of the most ambitious advocate of the South. He had himself favored the settlement of 1850, and approved the Democratic platform of 1852 — a platform that accepted this agreement as ending the slavery dispute. But that same year had witnessed the "little giant's" emergence in a new rôle. That a man so gifted, so able, so popular, so capable of enlisting a large following, should aspire to the same lure that had already led astray greater leaders than himself was in the natural order of things. And the Democratic convention of 1852 demonstrated that the Presidency was, in his case, no will o' the wisp. The death of John C. Calhoun left Douglas the most powerful man in the Democratic Party. Though, in 1852, he was only thirty-nine years old, he stepped forth as one of the four chief candidates for the Presidential nomination; on one of the many ballots taken he obtained ninety-one votes, the largest received by any contestant until the deadlock was broken by the stampede for the previously unknown candidate, Franklin Pierce. The balloting had disclosed one fact bearing upon any future aspirations Douglas might entertain for this distinction. To its realization the support of the Southern states would be indispensable. Douglas's strength in 1852 came entirely from the North; few of his favoring votes had been cast by the region south of Mason and Dixon's line. At almost the same moment came one of those personal events that frequently exercise a powerful influence on a man's public action. His young, slave-owning wife died, and the man was plunged in desperate gloom. Naturally the fierceness with which she and her slaves had been assailed in Douglas's native region penetrated still deeper into his soul. After vainly seeking assuagement of his grief in European travel, a changed man returned to Washington in 1853; his bitterness of spirit, his carelessness in dress, his intensity in assailing one-time compatriots and trampling on their most cherished ideas, made the man an ominous portent. The psychologist must determine the extent to which these several motives explain the rabid course on which the Illinois Senator, now arrived at the peak of his genius, embarked.

From the northern boundary of Missouri to Canada, and from the Mississippi River west to the Rocky Mountains stretched the rich empire then known as the "Indian Country," or Nebraska. This was the land that, by the Missouri Compromise, had forever been set apart for freedom. That the South, failing to establish its system in California and New Mexico, and the possibility of extending it to Central America and Cuba remaining the faintest of hopes, occasionally cast loving glances towards this unknown, mysterious land is true — only momentarily, however, for most Southern leaders regarded the compromise as a sacred bargain and had no desire to break faith with the North. Only two conspicuous voices from this region had been raised in opposition: Calhoun died proclaiming that the Missouri Compromise had been unconstitutional. He had set forth again and again the old familiar argument that Congress had no power, under the national "compact," to prohibit slavery in the territories. The man who aspired to become his successor, Jefferson Davis, was one of the most influential men in the Democratic Party, the representative of the Calhoun constitutional doctrines, the panegyrist of slavery as a "positive good," the advocate of sectionalism. Like Calhoun, Davis proclaimed the theory that two distinct and antipathetic realms existed under the same Federal government and that union could be preserved only by the complete recognition of "southern rights" — above all, the right to carry slaves into all parts of the public domain. Naturally Davis also took over the belief of his great preceptor that this same Missouri Compromise, shutting slavery forever out of the Nebraska country, violated the Constitution. Davis, however, could never have persuaded the South to adopt this conviction, to say nothing of the North. The proposal to destroy this covenant and to betray the Northern states could come only from a leader from the North. The combination that presently was made between the statesman of the deepest of the deep South — from those bottom lands of the Mississippi which the negroes of Virginia and Kentucky held in such horror — and the Senator whose early life had been spent amid the hills of Vermont became, by an unexpected accession, a triumvirate, hastily assembled for the repeal of the Missouri Compromise. This third recruit was important for only one reason — he happened at the moment to be President of the United States.

Franklin Pierce was a man of some personal distinction, but as a statesman he was weak, vacillating, and subject to the influence of stronger wills than his own. One of the strangest of friendships developed between the handsome President and the tall, dignified, intellectual, and forceful Mississippian who was the most powerful member of his cabinet. Both Pierce and Davis were cold, unemotional men, but from the time of their first meeting, when both were obscure, until Pierce's death in 1869 they remained on affectionate and confidential terms — a friendship not dimmed when the South-

erner, in 1861, became head of the Confederacy. And personal
ambition was as active a force with Pierce as with Douglas. Like
all Presidents, he yearned for a second term. The gage in the
Nebraska situation that now rapidly developed was the support of
the South in the Presidential convention of 1856. Weak man that he
was, Pierce was fairly paralyzed with fear that Douglas, by his invention of this issue, would sweep all that power into his own hands.
Certainly to oppose the doughty and reckless innovator would, as
Pierce saw the future, end his own political career.

The Kansas-Nebraska Act, the repeal of the Missouri Compromise, and the violent Kansas-Nebraska disturbances need not be
rehearsed again. What these three men — Douglas, Davis, and
Pierce — accomplished was the repeal of Clay's Missouri measure of
1820 which had closed all the country north of 36°30′ to slavery. So
far as an act of Congress could achieve that end, the domain since cut
up into the states of Kansas, Nebraska, North Dakota, South Dakota,
eastern Montana, most of Wyoming and eastern Colorado, was made
accessible to the Southern system of servitude. Now we know that
the whole thing was an illusion, that a thousand acts of Congress
could not have transformed this land into a kind of country for
which nature had unfitted it. The only excuse apologists have for
Douglas is that he understood this at the time; in other words, the
repeal of the Missouri Compromise was a trick, ostensibly giving
the South a valued boon in exchange for definite favors, of which
the political advancement of Douglas was the most important. The
transaction was concluded on Sunday, January 22, 1854; the seat
of negotiations was the White House; the performers were Douglas,
Davis, and President Pierce. It is significant of the conscience
of the times that almost the only question afflicting the Presidential
compunction was the day selected for the sacrifice; he was not accustomed to receiving guests and transacting public business on
the Sabbath! Davis quieted the misgivings on the ground of emergency; the meeting was held; Douglas explained and justified his
bill, Davis adding emphasis of his own; Pierce agreed to sign such
a measure. A favorite diversion in the Northern and Western
states during the weeks following this Sabbath-day proceeding was
hanging and burning Stephen A. Douglas in effigy. Jefferson
Davis came in for little public odium, for however unpopular his
doctrines were north of the Potomac, they were his own, sincerely
held, and his part in the transaction involved no reversal of his
past; but Douglas was a Northerner, the son of Vermont, the darling statesman of Illinois. The deed therefore was assailed as a

betrayal.   He himself said that he could go from Washington to Chicago by the light of these inflamed representations of his own person.   When he appeared on a Chicago platform to make a speech of justification the hisses and catcalls were so incessant that he was forced to leave with his apology unspoken.   The repeal, it was said, made all the Northern states abolitionist overnight.   The South itself was at first stunned, almost frightened, by this unexpected triumph of its cause.   Presently, however, it became as enthusiastic over its success as the North was appalled.

The principle established by the Kansas-Nebraska Act has passed into history as "squatter sovereignty."   It enunciated the right of the settlers in a territory to determine with no interference from Congress the existence or nonexistence of slavery within their confines.   To antislavery men of all types it seemed the most villainous measure ever placed upon the American statute book.   Could the arrogance of slavery go further?   They were presently to learn that it could.   The doctrine of "squatter sovereignty" proved to be mildness itself; it was the work of Congress and the President, and its passage showed that the South had obtained dominance over two departments of government, the legislative and the executive.   In three years of agitation and growing sectional hatred the Southern states succeeded in adding the third department, the judiciary, to the advancement of their cause.   In 1857 a principle more destructive to freedom than squatter sovereignty was embedded in the Constitution of the United States.

VI

The death of John Marshall, in 1835, fairly appalled the forces of constitutional conservation. Under his guiding hand, exercised for thirty-five years, the bands of Nationalism had been tightly drawn. A loose confederation had changed into a nation. The Supreme Court which, on Marshall's accession, had held no lofty position in popular regard had attained the almost sacrosanct dominance, as the arbiter of the Constitution, which it still retains. That the long reign of Democracy had eliminated the old Federalist control and acquired a majority on the bench is true; these Democratic judges, however, once installed in power, became almost as conservative as the gentlemen they succeeded. But could the tribunal stand the strain of a new Chief Justice, appointed by that enemy of tradition and respectability, Andrew Jackson? Could the man who regarded political office almost exclusively from the spoilsman's point of view, and whose administration had been signalized by an almost incessant warfare on property, be trusted to select a high-minded and able jurist for this position? Despite Jackson's stand on nullification, his general attitude toward the Constitution was suspect. Certain of his remarks on the Supreme Court seem a foreshadowing of comments that have recently come from Washington. When he took oath to support the Constitution, it meant, he had declared, that he should support it as he understood it, not as outsiders — that is, the Courts — understood it. That he depreciated Marshall and many of his opinions was no secret. "John Marshall has made his decision, now let him enforce it," the angry man exclaimed when the Chief Justice ruled that the State of Georgia could not make laws setting aside a treaty the United States had made with the Cherokee Indians. At times Jackson seemed to adhere to the strange Jeffersonian doctrine that each department of government had the right to decide for itself the constitutionality of legislation. The appointment of a Chief Justice reflecting this Jacksonian attitude towards vested interests and these constitutional aberrations would signify, in the eyes of the "more respectable" element, the complete undoing of Marshall's work and the disintegration of the national fabric.

When word came that Jackson had nominated Roger Brooke Taney the worst forebodings seemed to have been realized. In the three preceding years Jackson had appointed this son of Maryland to two lofty posts and in each case the Senate had refused confirmation. It had rejected him as Secretary of the Treasury in 1833, and January 15, 1835, six months before Taney's designation as Marshall's successor, the Senate had refused to approve his name as associate justice of the Supreme Court. That Jackson, having failed to make his favorite an associate justice, should, on the heels of the declination, have proposed him for the head looked at first like sublime audacity. Taney was unpopular in a Senate controlled by the ideas of Webster and Clay because he was regarded as an unscrupulous politician, as a tool of Jackson's in that President's attacks on wealth and capitalism, and the man who, as the President's agent in removing Federal deposits from the United States Bank, had plunged the nation into financial panic and business chaos. Under these prepossessions the enemy was not disposed to examine minutely Taney's career to discover in it evidences of juristic genius. Yet the career of this tall and lean Marylander, with a face which his Protestant critics were accustomed to call "Jesuitical," had been a distinguished one. Though a Marylander and a Catholic, Taney had not sprung from the famous Catholic followers of Lord Baltimore who had settled the colony. His American origin was about the humblest of the humble. It seems a paradox that the jurist most celebrated for his judgments denying civic rights to negroes was himself descended from a slave. Not a negro slave, be it immediately added. But that type of white slave known as indentured servant was as much a bondman, for the period of his servitude, as the African who subsequently supplanted him on the tobacco field. He was bought and sold, just as negroes were, and for "his time" his life and service were at the disposal of his master. One of the refreshing sides of this early Maryland and Virginia society is the extent to which many of these indentured servants, having fulfilled their period of servitude, rose in the social scale. Michael Taney, who sailed from England in 1650, paying his expenses and transportation by selling his freedom for four or five years in the New World, was one of these ambitious exceptions. Before his death Michael was the proprietor of a large plantation in Calvert County, on the Patuxent, and the master of several indentured servants and negroes. His descendants seem to have inherited his energy. The family's Catholicism is an evidence of its rise in the social scale. Just when the ancestral membership in the Church of England was abandoned is not known, but it probably came about through marriage into one of the aristocratic Catholic families of Maryland. The extent to which Chief Justice Taney bore allegiance to his faith has been a matter of controversy. That he was devout in all his religious observances is clear enough; religion was the most important thing in his personal life; yet all his six daughters [1] — his only son died in boyhood — were brought up in the Protestant faith of their mother, a sister of Francis Scott Key.

After a rather desultory education, for the most part at Dickinson College, Pennsylvania, and the usual apprenticeship reading law, Taney opened an office in Frederick, Maryland, and quickly established a successful practice. But law remained only part of his existence. He was born for politics, though his early activities had little in common with the convictions of his afterlife. Most solid families in Maryland, as in South Carolina, in the early days of the Republic, were Federalists; and Taney, settling in western Maryland in the same year that Jefferson entered the Presidency, turned his back on the leveling philosophies and State-rights theories of that statesman. For fifteen years he proved one of the main supports of the Federalist Party, equally useful in backstairs plottings, in writing pamphlets, making speeches, and as a more public-spirited representative in the Maryland legislature. But Federalism with the early Taney was an aristocratic inheritance, and the change which represented real inclination came with the War of 1812. Yet the spirit of his landholding ancestors dominated his new beliefs and, unconsciously, remained ineradicable to the end. Taney approached all questions as an agrarian landlord; usually hailed as the first great American jurist to preach "human rights" in preference to the rights of property, his enmity was launched not against the kind of capital ruling the South, that of land and negroes, but against bankers, merchants, shipping magnates — the type of parvenu millionaire developed by the great centres of population. This devotion to one kind of property and hatred of all other kinds explains Taney's career, both as public man and as jurist. Thus it was natural enough that, after 1812, Taney should break with the Federalist Party, for it was no longer the party of "gentlemen," but the rallying point of rich men, in the more vulgar sense — that is, of shopkeepers, merchants, manufacturers, votaries of trade and commerce. Even an allegiance with so rough a character as Andrew

[1] One of them, in mature life, became a Catholic.

Jackson was not distasteful, since Jackson took his stand as the foe of the new urban capitalism.

Taney became an ardent Jackson supporter in the fierce contest of 1824; in 1828 his energy was unabated, and, with Jackson's triumph, the Marylander advanced close to the throne. "I have appointed Tauney atto. genl.," wrote Jackson to a friend, preserving some semblance to the pronunciation of Taney's name if not its orthography.[1] By this time the new political star had become a State-rights man, a strict constructionist, and a sectionalist. "Moneyed aristocracy of the east" was a cherished detestation, and in this phrase Taney combined his two profound dislikes. He believed — despite Marshall's decision to the contrary — that the Federal government had no right to charter a bank. He was against internal improvements on similar grounds. He had expressed ideas on the Supreme Court that seemed a sad preparation for service on that bench. That justices should be appointed for short terms — four or five years — was one of the less startling. More serious was Taney's hostility to judicial review. He insisted that Marshall had pushed the doctrine of "implied powers" too far. The facility with which Marshall's court set aside unconstitutional laws passed by state legislatures Taney regarded as an invasion of State rights. He even opposed such interference with local sovereignty when the rejected laws contravened treaties made by the Federal government with foreign nations. As main author of Jackson's message vetoing the recharter of the United States Bank, Taney expressed opinions on the Executive's independence of the Supreme Court that made Webster and Clay frantic. "If the sentiments of the message," said Webster, "should receive general approbation, the Constitution will have perished even earlier than the moment which its enemies originally allowed for the termination of its existence. It will not have survived its fiftieth year."

To-day "liberals" would take the Taney of his pre-Supreme Court era to their hearts; the more conservative elements would call him a "rabble rouser." In his mouth the words "money power" were as much a matter of common speech as, sixty years afterward, they became in the fulminations of William Jennings Bryan. And his hostility to concentrated wealth was more effective than the latter-day statesman's, for Taney carried his into practice. Jackson ordered in succession two Secretaries of the Treasury to withdraw deposits from the United States Bank. Both refused and were dismissed. He then promoted Taney to the position for this ex-

[1] It is pronounced as though spelled "Tawney" — as it was in early days.

press job and the deposits were withdrawn.   Historians and economists have not yet ceased wrangling over the results of this
transaction.   The inevitable banking panic followed, for these deposits in large part had been lent for general business purposes, and
the Bank, in order to keep the money liquid to the treasury's demand,
was obliged to call its loans.   Taney declared that the Bank had
itself caused this stringency in order to discredit the administration
and to assure its recharter.   Stump speeches made by Taney defend-
ing his act have the same modern sound.   "Now, for the first time,
the issue is made up, and the question boldly and distinctly presented to us, whether this noble country is to be governed by the
power of money in the hands of the few, or by the free and un-
bought suffrage of the people. . . .   Yield but an inch and you will
be driven to the wall; and instead of the rich inheritance of liberty
which you received from your fathers, you will bequeath to your
descendants slavery and chains — the worst of slavery, that of submission to the will of a cold, heartless, soulless, vindictive, moneyed
corporation."   The speech might have been made at the present time.

Taney's appointment as Secretary of the Treasury had been an
ad interim one; as soon as the Senate came together, the new cabinet
officer was rejected as punishment for his "high handed" act with
the deposits.   When Jackson tried to elevate him to the Supreme
Bench, as noted above, his name was again laid on the table.   In
March 1836, a new Senate entered into power.   When Taney came
up for consideration as Marshall's successor, therefore, the most
heroic efforts of Webster and Clay did not prevent approval.   To use
once more the illustration suggested above, had William Jennings
Bryan, in 1897, been made Chief Justice of the Supreme Court, the
promotion would have appalled the ranks of conservatism no more
than did Taney's nomination to that dignity in 1835.   "The Constitution is gone," wailed Webster, and despair was almost universal.
"The pure ermine of the Supreme Court is sullied by the appointment
of that political hack, Roger Brooke Taney," lamented a New York
newspaper.   "I am last of the old race of judges," wrote Justice
Joseph Story.   "I stand their solitary representative with a pained
heart and a subdued conscience.   To me an attendance here is but
a melancholy renewal of the memory of departed days and pleasures
never to return."

Story had been sitting under the chieftainship of Taney two
years when these pessimistic views were penned.   They therefore
represent his private verdict on the reorganized tribunal and show
that the gloomy expectations held by conservatives on Taney's

appointment had been fulfilled. What Story and his like deplored was that the Supreme Court of John Marshall — "whose name," Justice Story said in a dissenting opinion, "can never be mentioned except with reverence" — had vanished into history. It was not only that the Federalist Court had been superseded and that a Jacksonian Democratic bench had been installed in power, but that new and "revolutionary" ideas had been established as the bedrock of its decisions. Viewing the change in the perspective of a century, the truth now appears that Taney, the first in a series of a "liberal" line of judges that, in latter days, led to Oliver Wendell Holmes and Louis Brandeis, had introduced a spirit of constitutional interpretation made necessary by a new America. Jefferson, in the last twenty years of his life, had fought a bitter battle against the Supreme Court, and had failed; even the judges he and his successor, Madison, had chosen to obtain Democratic decisions — a case of "packing"—discarded his ideas and became as Marshall-like as Marshall himself. With Taney, however, Jeffersonism became triumphant. Taney had derived certain teachings from Monticello: Supreme Court judges should be appointed for short terms; they should not override state legislation; the Executive was not bound by Supreme Court decisions. After his elevation he abandoned these and other Jeffersonian dicta, but another, more profound Jeffersonian idea, the assertion, in the Declaration of Independence, that governments are established, among other purposes, to guarantee "the pursuit of happiness," he made an active principle. He was the first of Supreme Court justices to do so, and his fame as a great jurist rests upon that fact.

In taking this stand Taney adjusted the Court and the Constitution to an America that was rapidly changing. Taney's accession witnessed the rise of reforms then regarded in established circles as grotesque, but now accepted as commonplaces of the body politic. Such were manhood suffrage, even female suffrage, prison reform, abolition of imprisonment for debt, the treatment of bankruptcy "not as a crime but as a misfortune," organized labor, those forms of pre-Marxian socialism represented by Brook Farm and the communities of Robert Owen, the emancipation of married women, feminism; while in the spiritual realm there were such new portents as Unitarianism, Campbellism, spiritualism, and even more unorthodox breakings with the past. Some of this was truly beyond Taney's sympathy, but quotations from one of his early opinions show that his look was forward, not backward. "The object and end of all government," he wrote in his first great decision, "is to

promote the happiness and prosperity of the community by which
it is established and it can never be assumed that government intended to diminish the power of accomplishing the end for which
it was created. . . . While the rights of private property are
sacredly guarded, we must not forget that the community also have
rights and that the happiness and well being of every citizen depends
on their faithful preservation." It was a new note to be sounded
from the Supreme Court Bench — a note that has grown more
distinct from that day to this.

The judgment in which this sentence appears shows concretely
Taney's understanding that a new stage in American progress had
begun. But for his decision in the Charles River Bridge case it is
hard to see how the country could have entered the era of new transportation that started almost on the day of Taney's emergence.
This is the first strong judicial protest against monopoly — an
active issue then as now. And Taney hated monopoly, in transportation or industry, as intensely as does Louis D. Brandeis to-
day. The points which this controversy involved were elementary.
In 1784 the State of Massachusetts had granted a group of investors the privilege of constructing a bridge across the Charles
River from Boston to Cambridge, and of charging tolls to passengers
and vehicles for its use. The growth in population made the undertaking extremely profitable; stock that represented an investment
of about $300 a share had advanced to $2500. The franchise had
thus for fifty years stood for one of those rich monopolies, one of
those "vested interests," which, in conservative eyes, it was the
duty of the state and the courts to protect. Was not the privilege
one of those contracts which, under the Constitution, no state
legislature had the right to "impair"? But the traveling public,
weary of paying the high tolls necessary to yield dividends on the
"market value" of the stock, induced the legislature to grant a
franchise to a competitor, flagrantly paralleling the established
bridge, with the right of levying tolls for six years, after which
period the bridge was to become free. Obviously this new causeway
would completely destroy the investment in the ancient structure.
The Charles River Company and its lawyers immediately sprang
to the defense of their "property rights." A bargain was a bargain.
Boston may have acted foolishly in granting such an exclusive and
eternal privilege; but the charter was a "contract" and, according
to the Dartmouth College case, contracts were sacred and protected
by the Constitution. Naturally the bridge monopolists engaged
the great lawyer who had obtained that decision from Marshall's

Court, and for several years Daniel Webster exercised all his oratory and constitutional wisdom to prove that this rival charter, like the changes attempted in that of Dartmouth College, flew in the face of constitutional guarantee. Most of the great legal authorities of the nation, such as Chancellor Kent of New York and Joseph Story, Associate Justice of the Supreme Court, took the same stand.

The decision of Chief Justice Taney, which came a few months after his elevation to the bench, confirmed the fears of "vested interests" that Jack Cade had usurped the tribunal of Marshall. Most modern legalists, however, look upon it as a masterpiece of interpretation. The charter for the Warren bridge, Taney ruled, did not "impair" the contract made with the older company. That ancient parchment conveyed no exclusive privilege. If it had meant to do so, the fact that it was exclusive should have been nominated in the bond. Webster's argument that monopoly was implied, the Chief Justice dismissed; such vast privileges could never be implied, they must be precisely detailed. Certain transport companies had the right to charge tolls for transportation between two given points. Did that mean that licenses to stagecoaches serving the same territory were unconstitutional? Were franchises to canal boats "paralleling" the operations of stagecoaches an "impairment" of contract? And that new revolutionary method of transportation then looming large, the railroad — was it to be prevented, on the same constitutional grounds, from competing with canals, stagecoaches, and turnpikes? In other words, was modern transportation to be prohibited by a tortured reading of a constitutional clause? Taney's decision did not displace the Dartmouth College case; in that case no implications were read into the contract, for everything had been stipulated; but it struck a lasting blow at monopoly, upheld by the rights of "the community" against the pretensions of the "moneyed few," and made possible the transportation development of the nation. It had the great merit of disclosing that the Constitution, accurately interpreted, was no bar to American progress.

And so the first "liberal" Supreme Court judge, in the modern sense, had gained ascendancy. Other Taney decisions followed in the next thirty years, which an angry conservatism assailed as destructive of "vested" interests. Yet great as Taney's reputation has become for upholding popular rights under the Constitution, his point of view had its narrow side. Fundamentally he was as rock-ribbed a conservative as Marshall himself. He stood as solidly for State rights as Marshall had stood for Nationalism; his "attacks" on banks, on commerce, were largely inspired by a determination to uphold the prerogatives of states against the "encroachments" of Federal power. Moreover, Taney was as stalwart a defender of "property" as Daniel Webster himself, when the kind of property nearest his heart was affected. Taney was hostile to that form of wealth represented by banks, manufacturing, and trade, — the "moneyed aristocracy of the East," — but tender to the kind of property with which he had been familiar all his days — slaves and land. He never realized that the agrarian landlords of his own South were as much "vested interests" as the bankers of New York and the commercial magnates of New England. It would be a simple matter to show that the cotton growers of the Southwest were *nouveaux riches,* as much a part of modern industrialism as the manufacturers of the North. It is a question whether the South was really an agricultural country at all. If we mean by agriculture the product of diversified crops, chiefly for human food, the North was more agricultural than the Southern region. The business of Southern farmers was the raising of the raw materials of industry; the plantations of Mississippi and Alabama represented the first stages in a manufacturing system that ended in Lancashire, England; most of their food — agriculture in the ancient Virgilian sense — they imported from the North.

And the Supreme Court, under Taney, regarded everything pertaining to this property interest with a friendly eye. His opinions, when questions of slavery and State rights were involved, merely reflected the orations of John C. Calhoun. One of his decisions upholding the agrarian point of view has especial pertinence at the present time, for its principles have been completely negatived by the modern Supreme Court. The panic of 1837 brought distress to tenants and landlords — the same difficulty in meeting interest payments with which the existing generation has been made so familiar. And the same measures of relief were adopted a century ago that have figured in contemporary programmes. "Stay laws" were passed prohibiting sales under foreclosure, postponing payment of interest, and the like — alleviations that to-day would be called moratoriums. But did not such legislation violate that section of the Constitution which forbids states from passing laws "impairing contracts" — the constitutional safeguard Webster had found so impregnable a defense in the Dartmouth College case? Taney decided so, and with little ceremony swept the agrarian moratoriums of his time from the statute book. He became as rigid a champion of property rights as had John Marshall, when the kind of property at issue was that land which formed the moneyed background of his own existence; as "class conscious" as Daniel Webster, when the economic basis of his own social environment was threatened. And he showed himself completely separated, as were Marshall and Webster, from the modern point of view — the view which exalts the rights of the great human mass above those of a privileged few. For Chief Justice Hughes and a majority of the Supreme Court have decided as recently as 1934 that "stay laws," when adopted to ease an emergency, — such an emergency as existed after the panic of 1929 and as had prevailed after the panic of 1837, — do not run foul of the Constitution.

VII

Thus Taney's career as judge presents a study in contradiction — he united a devotion to the traditional view of property rights, when the rights in question involved the landlord system, with a hostility to wealth, when by wealth was understood commerce and trade. His attitude, that is, was primarily social and sectional. Though not an extreme friend of slavery, no more vigilant upholder of its rights as "property" ever lived. No constitutional theory would have shocked John Marshall quite so profoundly as Taney's view that the states, by themselves, could regulate interstate commerce. This notion, once popular in the South, would also receive short shrift in the Federal courts to-day. Such a strange perversion of the Constitution was evolved to make legal the exclusion, by South Carolina and other states, of free negroes from their borders and to give control over the interstate traffic in slaves. From a similar motive Taney ruled that states could pass laws that contravened treaties made by the central government with foreign nations. Again it was his desire to protect property rights in slaves that induced this monstrous interpretation. But regard for State rights and slavery attained its most complete expression in the decision with which Taney's name is historically identified — the one promulgated March 6, 1857, which has come to be known as the most preposterous judgment ever issued from that bench.

A picturesque aspect of judicial annals is the way in which extremely modest citizens have caused the most momentous rulings on the Constitution. The ambition of a plodding citizen of the District of Columbia to become a justice of the peace established, in Marshall's hands, the greatest of judicial prerogatives, the right to adjudge the constitutionality of acts of Congress. An even humbler inhabitant of Missouri inspired the dictum which gave victory to the Southern states in the tremendous argument over slavery. For this obscure individual can be described only as an "inhabitant" — the question at issue being the precise one of

whether he could claim citizenship under the Constitution. Dred
Scott was one of those "persons" who make shamefaced appearances three times in the Constitution of 1787.   In afterlife, though
immensely proud of the prominence attached to his name, Dred
used to wonder why all this excitement had been aroused over
"a po' ole nigger" like himself.   The explanation was that, born
a slave, of slave parents, Dred Scott had engaged in certain wanderings that made him an object of interest to the Federal compact.
From the standpoint of interpretation, Dred Scott's voyages into
unfamiliar country were the most portentous ever undertaken by a
black man.   His Odyssey had started in his birthplace in Virginia,
had led to what seemed a permanent domicile in Missouri, thence
carried him into Illinois, thence again into that part of the Louisiana
country now known as Minnesota, and then back again to St. Louis.
These divagations had comprised no heroic adventures, celebrated
as they became in the nation's history.   At a critical moment Dred
had been sold as "property" to an army surgeon, Dr. John Emerson,
and, like other personal "property," had accompanied his master in
the sojournings at army posts that make up the military career.
His handiness as a body servant explains his travels.   All through
these years Dred's status had been that of a slave, a condition to
which he had submitted with a cheerfulness shocking to the
Garrisonians.

Dred's two stopping places of chief importance were those in
Rock Island, Illinois, and at Fort Snelling, Minnesota.   The
Ordinance of 1787 had made slavery forever illegal in Illinois and
the other states carved from the Northwest Territory.   At the time
neither Dred nor his master suspected that the moment the black
man stepped upon this soil of freedom he had ceased to be a slave.
Even more decisive was the arrival in Fort Snelling, Minnesota.
This was part of that *terra incognita* lying north of 36° 30' which,
under the Missouri Compromise, could never become the land of
"persons."   Thus Dred had established not one claim to liberty,
but two.   Had he not made one fatal mistake, the question of his
future status could never have arisen.   If Dred Scott had remained permanently either in Illinois or in Minnesota there is
not the slightest question that he, and the wife and two children acquired in the course of his migrations, would have been "forever
free."   At any moment, in either place, he could have defied his
so-called proprietor, refused to serve further as valet, and set up
as an independent citizen.   He could not even have been a "fugitive
slave," for he had not escaped into free territory, but had been taken

there. But, in 1838, Dred returned with his so-called master to St. Louis, Missouri, a slave state. Did this removal undo all the good work in freeing the man that had been accomplished by his four years' sojourn in a non-slave country? The question did not arise in Scott's mind until the death of his master, Dr. Emerson. He continued in his service several years, never giving a thought to constitutional and legislative guarantees. Apparently his treatment by Mrs. Emerson, who fell heir to this and all her husband's other property, irked the negro. She "hired" him out to other keepers — a practice common at the time, but never pleasing to black men. Sympathizing friends interceded in his behalf. It was a serious question, after all, whether Dred was really Mrs. Emerson's property! Had not his residence in places where slavery was illegal loosed him from his "shackles"? Clearly it was a matter for the courts to decide. The family of his old owners in Virginia had always kept a friendly eye upon their servant, born on their plantation, and now advanced the money needed for testing the case. Dred Scott made his mark on the legal documents, and the suit came up in the Missouri State Court in 1846. Here Dred's petition received summary handling. His return to Missouri, it was ruled, had reconverted the negro into a slave. The Northwest Ordinance and the Missouri Compromise may have given him a brief whiff of freedom, but when the man came home his old status was automatically resumed. The negro's supporters decided to take the case to the Federal courts. To do this, a fictitious sale was made to John A. Sanford, of New York, thus establishing that "diversity of citizenship" necessary to suits under the Federal Constitution. And so began the Federal case that has become immortal in American history as that of *Dred Scott* vs. *Sanford*.

Under ordinary circumstances the case would not have aroused great attention. In fact the point involved had already been decided, by an opinion of Taney's own, in 1851. This lawsuit concerned a company of musicians, negro slaves who had been taken from Kentucky to Ohio for exhibition purposes. Ohio had also been set aside by the Northwest Ordinance as land forbidden to slavery. The claim had been set up by these negro minstrels that their residence in this state had therefore transformed them overnight into free men. There were slight differences in circumstances between the two cases, but the point whether a slave who had theoretically regained his liberty by migrating into free soil lost it by going back into the scene of his original servitude was the same in both. And Justice Taney's decision, so far as the Federal courts were concerned, had seemingly disposed of the constitutional issue forever. He ruled that it was not a matter with which the Federal courts had any concern. The future of such a negro was something to be settled by the courts of the states in which the question arose. The Federal courts lacked jurisdiction. It therefore seemed a reasonable conclusion that the Supreme Court would abide by its own precedent and send Dred Scott back to the mercies of his own state. As the Supreme Court of Missouri had already decided the matter adversely to the negro's claim, such a ruling would have brought him little comfort.

Had it not been for the stirring conditions prevailing in the United States at that time, such would have undoubtedly been the course of procedure. Dred would quietly have relapsed into slavery, and the vast library of legal literature that has accumulated about his name would never have come into existence. What the conditions were which assigned him to a different fate has been set forth in the preceding pages. The years during which the Dred Scott case had been dragging through the Federal courts, from 1852 to 1857, had been the years of the Compromise of 1850, of the Fugitive Slave Act, the Kansas-Nebraska Bill, the repeal of the Missouri Compromise. The question of slavery extension had led to the rise of a new political party, built on sectional lines, called into being to end that extension. These events gave a new significance to the tribulations of this illiterate darky. The people began to realize that his fate involved pressing constitutional questions; already, in the spring of 1856, certain newspapers were speculating on the bearing of the decision on great national events; the excitement over Dred Scott became so tense in the Presidential campaign of 1856 that the Supreme Court thought it the part of wisdom to postpone its decision until after election. What made the Dred Scott case a possible bombshell was its bearing upon the Missouri Compromise. Scott's claim to freedom rested mainly upon the act of 1820 which outlawed human servitude in the district extending west from the Mississippi. That this simple principle was obscured by certain perplexing complications is true. Thus if the court dismissed the case on the ground of no-jurisdiction the constitutional point would not arise. But, in view of the pending argument on slavery, there was no certainty that Taney and his associates would avoid this contention. Again the country-store jurists remarked, What difference did it make anyway? Hadn't the Missouri Compromise been repealed? To which the answer was that such a decision would matter a great deal. The Missouri line had been obliterated by an act of Congress, but an act of Congress could restore it. It would have difficulty in doing so, however, if the Supreme Court declared such legislation unconstitutional. If Congress had no power over slavery in the territories, what would become of the new Republican Party, organized to obtain legislation restricting it? That party would be decreed unconstitutional itself, in the sense that it would be advocating a national policy which, under the Constitution, Congress had no right to adopt. As well might a party be founded advocating the establishment of Anglicanism as a state church! And the Republican Party had nominated its first candidate for the Presidency, John C. Frémont, and in the campaign this very question involved in the Dred Scott case — the extension of slavery in the territories — was being discussed from a thousand angry platforms.

The old Dred Scott case possesses several facets of interest, but to the present generation one phase remains preëminent. It is indicated by the fact recorded above — that the Supreme Court, not wishing to add to the furies then raging in the Presidential campaign, decided to postpone its decision until a calmer season had arrived. In doing this, of course, the Court stepped out of its province as a coldly judicial body concerned, not with influencing public events, but in the impersonal dissection of the law. Public opinion, at that time and since, has not harshly criticized the judges for this particular interference with current affairs. That it was an interference the sequel showed, for, had the Court promulgated, before the Presidential election of 1856, the judgment which followed five months afterward, there is little doubt that James Buchanan would never have reached the Presidential chair. But this postponement was a mild wandering from the judicial field compared with what subsequently took place. The whole course of the Court in these years 1856 and 1857 propounds the question, What part can be properly played by the Supreme Court in the American system of government? That the background and settled convictions of judges inevitably influence their decisions is manifest. It always has been true and it always will be true. Judges are commonly chosen because they are "right" — because their attitude on public questions and the law is regarded as sympathetic with those of the President who appoints them. Washington and Adams appointed only Federalists; Jefferson and Madison ostentatiously chose only Democrats; and Jackson and all his successors have commonly looked to their political followers for candidates.

Naturally a majority of the Supreme Court in 1857 were Southerners, sympathetic to slavery; in addition, two were Northerners of the type irreverently called "doughfaces" — Northern Democrats who advocated the Southern viewpoint and upheld it in their public career. But what places the Dred Scott case in a class by itself is that, for the first time, the Supreme Court stepped outside of its function as a judicial and became a political body — really a third house of legislation. Furthermore, its conclusion represented something which dangerously resembled a joint agreement between the Executive and the judges. That President Buchanan "interfered" with this tribunal and "brought pressure" to bear upon it to obtain a decision favorable to his political programme is now pretty evident. For a long time this belief remained merely a suspicion. Practically all American historians up to 1910 indignantly defended the President from this accusation. Even a writer who held Buchanan in such low esteem as Rhodes comes to his defense on this ground. The President's inaugural, delivered March 4, 1857, contained one passage that startled the public then and has been the subject of much speculation since. The future of slavery in the territories, said Buchanan, was a matter for the Supreme Court to decide, "before whom it is now pending and will, it is understood, be speedily and finally settled. To their decision, in common with all good citizens, I shall cheerfully submit, whatever this may be." How, an astonished public asked in 1857, did the President know that the constitutionality of slavery in the territories was to be discussed in the Dred Scott case? That was the precise question on which public animadversion had been active throughout the past year. The opinion was generally held that the Court would dismiss the suit on the ground of no-jurisdiction. It had already ruled, in the case of the Kentucky musicians, that slaves who had sojourned in a free country and then returned to the place of their early subjection had no standing in Federal courts; that such an issue could properly come before their state courts only. That Taney and his associates might go further and consider the question of constitutionality was regarded as possible; but no one not in the confidence of the Court could know this in advance. Yet here was the President informing the public that such a daring step was to be taken!

One of those little incidents of the inauguration which newspapers so relish added to the general suspicion of "collusion." Just before the oath of office was administered, the Chief Justice and the President were observed engaged in subdued conversation. When this episode appeared in the press, it was related that Taney had "whispered in the President's ear."   This gave ground for the story that the news of the forthcoming decision had been conveyed to Buchanan in this casual manner, and that the President, departing from his manuscript, had hastily incorporated it in his address. William H. Seward afterward added dignity to the incident by charging it, as a fact, in a public speech.   Abraham Lincoln, in his subsequent debates with Douglas, similarly intimated that there had been collusion between Taney and the new President.   Both Buchanan and the Chief Justice denied the scandalous statement in heated words, Taney in his anger declaring that, should Seward ever be elected President, he, as Chief Justice, would refuse to administer the oath of office.   Buchanan, in a note found among his papers, describes the charge as "the infamous and unfounded assertion of Mr. ——— [1] that in a conversation with Chief Justice Taney he had informed him [Mr. Buchanan] in advance of the inaugural what the opinion would be."

For fifty years after the event most historians accepted these fervent disclaimers as completely candid.   "However Buchanan got his intelligence," wrote Mr. Rhodes in 1892, "his character and that of Taney are proof that the Chief Justice did not communicate the import of the decision to the President-elect.   That either would stoop from the etiquette of his high office is an idea that may not be entertained for a moment; and we may be sure that with Taney's lofty notions of what belonged to an independent judiciary, he would have no intercourse with the executive that would not brook the light of day."   Had Mr. Rhodes consulted the Buchanan papers in the Library of the Pennsylvania Historical Society, he would never have written these words.   Their publication in part, in 1910, put a completely new face on this transaction, and made somewhat ridiculous the furious denials of Taney and Buchanan in 1857.   Fierce as was the tempest aroused by the Dred Scott decision, it was a mild affair compared to what it would have been had Horace Greeley and the other declaimers been admitted to the secrets of Buchanan's correspondence.   These letters do indeed disprove the accusation that Taney "whispered" the main points of his forthcoming judgment in the President's "ear" a moment before the inauguration.   They also disclose that such dramatic confidences were not necessary, for the complete story had already been transmitted to the President, in writing, and with Taney's full approval.   They betray an even more astounding fact, for they show that, from the day of his arrival in Washington, in February 1857, Buchanan had

[1] Unquestionably Seward.

been exerting pressure upon the Supreme Court for an early decision, a decision which, he seemed to understand, would be in accordance with his own views. Nor is it an exaggeration to say that the Court had acceded to this demand.

James Buchanan came to the Presidency in 1857 with one persistent ambition. The settlement of the slavery question and the consequent preservation of the Union was to be the great achievement of his public life. Deeply religious as he was, Buchanan looked upon such a consummation as a divinely appointed task. He clearly saw that the bitter argument was separating the nation into two parts, and that disunion and war overshadowed the country. No statesman could have cherished a nobler ambition than the ending of this overhanging menace, but Buchanan's conception of the way in which peace could be attained was fatuous, in view of subsequent events. Complete surrender to the South on all points in dispute was Buchanan's recipe for peace. No one hated abolitionists more profoundly than this Pennsylvanian, and even the mildest of antislavery men found no favor in his eyes. The new Republican Party, to him, was an organization called into being for the purpose of plunging the nation into bloodshed. The opening of the national domain, from the Mississippi River to the Pacific, to the extension of slavery was, in his myopic view, the one way to banish the question from national politics. That any statesman, irrespective of the merits of the case, could suppose that the rapidly mounting tide of hostility to the spread of the Southern system would abandon its course, once this great surrender had been made, must be put down as one of the most mysterious instances in self-deception that American annals present. That Chief Justice Taney should sympathize with this view is not surprising. His attitude was completely Southern. His letters of the period bring out this fact. One of the anomalies of Supreme Court history is that Taney remained Chief Justice during the Civil War, despite that he was an advocate of the Confederacy and hardly concealed his hopes for its success. In this he went further than Buchanan, who, after 1861, was loyal to the Federal cause.

But in 1857 the two men were at one. Burning with this desire to end the slavery controversy and disposed to use any means that would advance this purpose, Buchanan arrived in Washington in the latter part of January, 1857, in preparation for his installation as President. He brought his inaugural address, written at his country home, Wheatland, in Pennsylvania. Almost his first act, after taking rooms at the National Hotel, was to write a letter to

John Catron, Associate Justice of the Supreme Court — a rough-and-ready Democrat of the Andrew Jackson school, a self-made frontiersman, who, born in Virginia, had made his way to Tennessee as a young man and risen, by virtue of a determined character and a powerful intellect, to his present eminence. Like Taney, Catron had championed all Jackson's financial measures, like him hated the United States Bank, and almost the last act of Jackson as President had been the appointment of his defender to the United States Supreme Court. Catron, like Jackson, was a strong Union man — an allegiance he maintained even after the secession of his own state, Tennessee — and devotion to the Union, rather than any strong regard for slavery, explains his behavior in the Dred Scott proceeding. Like Buchanan, he hoped to end the excitement that was rending the nation, and regarded a little divergence from judicial propriety as not unwarranted, so long as it served the good cause. Doubtless a justice of the Supreme Court to-day would resent such a letter as the President now addressed to Catron. The document itself is not available, but its tenor is evident from Catron's reply. Buchanan asked whether the Dred Scott decision would be rendered before the inauguration. The fact was not concealed that the President greatly desired a decision by that time. Far from being offended by this nudging from the White House, Catron wrote several letters to Buchanan, revealing the status of the case, and asked for Buchanan's aid in bringing one member of the Court around to the right side. Justice Catron's first letter to the President, February 6, conveyed unwelcome information. The question on which Buchanan so desired a decision, — the constitutionality of the Missouri Compromise, — he informed the Executive, would not be considered. The Supreme Court would rule that it had no jurisdiction in the Dred Scott case — that the matter was not properly before it. The point whether that negro was a free man or a slave was something for the Missouri courts to settle. Justice Catron wrote Buchanan that the Court would confer on the succeeding Saturday, February 14. The session in fact took place; and on that occasion the judges decided the issue precisely as it had been outlined in Catron's letter to Buchanan. Justice Nelson, of New York, was assigned to write the majority opinion to this effect.

Justice Nelson, as directed, wrote this opinion, but it was not adopted as the majority decision. Certain considerations now supervened which caused the justices to regret their decision to ignore the constitutional points, and persuaded them to enter the dangerous ground that formed the subject of popular controversy. "Conferences" of the Supreme Court — those awesome occasions when the jurists meet in secret, argue the case in a little parliament of their own, vote upon the decision, and appoint one of their members to write the majority opinion — are never made a matter of record, but the confabulations in this case were reduced to writing to a sufficient extent to warrant certain conclusions. Between the fourteenth and the nineteenth of February the Court held several such meetings. Some of the sessions were animated. Reports have since come down giving a far different picture of the august tribunal than the one fixed traditionally in the public record. The dissension and excitement that the slavery issue caused wherever it showed its head were disturbing even to the serenity of the nine black-robed gentlemen. The decision to hand Dred over to the mercy of his Missouri judiciary did not, after mature thought, satisfy any of the judges. What then should be done with him? The ensuing debate on this topic was lively, and at times not free from rancor. One vignette of the proceedings pictures the learned jurisconsults rising in their perturbation, beating the table with their fists, and shouting simultaneously in loud tones.

"Brothers," exclaimed Taney in his most waspish accents, "this is the Supreme Court of the United States. Take your seats." "We sat down," said Judge Curtis, relating the incident, "like rebuked schoolboys."

These sessions caused the Court to reverse its proceedings of a few days before. The plan of rendering no decision on the merits of the case, and withdrawing on the ground of no-jurisdiction, was abandoned. The judges voted to take up the whole matter then racking the nation from end to end — the extension of slavery in the territories. Justice Catron at once wrote the good news to President Buchanan, in a letter probably the most indiscreet and unjudicial communication ever to emanate from a judge of the United States Supreme Court. He even wrote a paragraph which he suggested that Buchanan include in his inaugural message. This was essentially the passage that caused so great a scandal when read from the platform of the Capitol on March 4, though the President somewhat changed the phraseology. It was that passage in which the President informed the American people that the Supreme Court was about to rule on the constitutionality of the Missouri Compromise. The decision would be adverse, Judge Catron's letter clearly indicated but did not explicitly declare. Thus when President Buchanan, on March 4, informed the public that this great point would presently be resolved by the body to which that function "legitimately belongs" and blandly set forth his own willingness "cheerfully" to submit to that verdict, "whatever this may be," he was in possession of letters from members of the Supreme Court containing the welcome information that Dred Scott was a slave and that the Missouri Compromise was unconstitutional.

What had persuaded the Court, between February 14 and February 19, to reverse its position and to take this entirely new attitude? Several explanations have been forthcoming. The one on which most emphasis is usually laid is that a hopeless minority of two, composed of John McLean of Pennsylvania and Benjamin R. Curtis of Massachusetts, signified their intention of writing dissenting opinions, declaring Dred Scott free and their belief that the Missouri Compromise, which made him free, was a constitutional enactment. Catron gave this explanation in a letter to Buchanan. "A majority of my brethren," he wrote, "will be forced up to this point by two dissentients." The proslavery majority on the Court were evidently appalled at the prospect of such an unchallenged opinion proceeding from their tribunal. The decision ultimately prepared, it seems, was intended as an antidote to the document which threatened to come from the antislavery judges. To-day it would be said that the majority judges — proslavery in feeling — feared the "propaganda" effect of a powerful antislavery argument issuing from the Supreme Court, even though it represented the views of only two judges. But in all likelihood other motives were stirring the judicial breast. To what extent Buchanan's eagerness for a good Democratic opinion caused this change in attitude is, of course, conjectural, but it is a consideration that should not be disregarded. At any rate the main incentive actuating the judges' minds was political. It is a startling conclusion, but it rests upon definite evidence. The majority judges clearly abandoned, for the moment, the unbiased interpretation of the Constitution and sought to step into a new arena and solve the great political question of the time.

Four days after Catron's letter was written, another justice, Grier of Pennsylvania, wrote the President, giving a fairly detailed account of the Court's secret deliberations. To him the President had also written — on a point to be considered presently. In view of Taney's subsequent indignation over any suggestion of what the enemy called "collusion" between himself and Buchanan, the first sentences of Grier's letter are interesting. "Your letter came to hand this morning. I have taken the liberty to show it in confidence to our mutual friends Judge Wayne and the Chief Justice. We fully appreciate and concur in your views as to the desirableness at this time of having an expression of the opinion of the court on this troublesome question. With their concurrence I will give you in confidence the history of the case before us, with the probable result." He then outlined the incidents of the preceding week, essentially as set forth above. The man mainly influential in bringing about this reversal of programme was Justice Wayne, of Georgia, another of those Southern unionists who believed that the nation could be held together only by permitting the South to have its own way with slavery extension. Judge Wayne had come to the honest conclusion that the responsibility for ending the contention between North and South rested upon the judicial branch of the government. A decision upholding the Southern point of view would produce that result, and the exercise of this power, extrajudicial as it might be, would therefore be a public-spirited act. "Mr. Justice Wayne," writes the biographer of Justice Curtis, "became convinced that it was practicable for the Supreme Court of the United States to quiet all agitation on the question of slavery in the territories, by affirming that Congress had no power to prohibit its introduction. With the best intentions, with entirely patriotic motives, and believing thoroughly that such was the law on this constitutional question, he regarded it as eminently expedient that it should be so determined by the court." Mr. Clement Hugh Hill, assistant Attorney General of the United States, many years afterward made a memorandum of a conversation with Justice Curtis, in which he frankly discussed Justice Wayne's part in persuading his fellow justices to the new point of view. "It was urged upon the court," said Justice Curtis, "by Judge Wayne, how very important it was to get rid of the question of slavery in the Territories by a decision of the Supreme Court and that this was a good opportunity of doing so."

One difficulty still remained. The five justices who desired to use a Supreme Court decision for this political purpose were all Southerners. This sectional division would surely give rise to heated comment and arouse contempt for the projected pronouncement. Could not at least one Northern judge be induced to join this bare majority? Justices McLean and Curtis were known to be preparing dissenting opinions. Justice Nelson was clinging to his original view that the case should be dismissed for lack of jurisdiction. The only hope of the State-rights party was therefore Justice Grier. He was known to be wavering. But he was a friend and fellow Pennsylvanian of President Buchanan, and a

Jacksonian in principle. Present ideals of judicial ethics would hardly justify a member of the Supreme Court who appealed to the President to persuade a hesitating colleague. That is the course, however, which Justice Catron pursued. The fact would hardly be credible, were not his letter in existence. "Will you drop Grier a line," Catron wrote the President, February .19, 1857, "saying how necessary it is — & how good the opportunity is, to settle the agitation by an affirmative decision of the Supreme Court, one way or the other? He ought not to occupy so doubtful a ground as the outside issue. . . . He has no doubt about the question in the main contest, but has been persuaded to take the smooth handle for the sake of repose."

Buchanan wrote the vacillating justice. When the venerable Court publicly delivered its decision on March 6, Grier was found voting on the Taney side. The appointment of Justice Nelson to write the decision had been withdrawn, and Chief Justice Taney himself produced the historic judgment which, far from "quieting the agitation," as Justice Wayne and others anticipated, proved to be a precipitating cause of the Civil War. For it substantiated practically everything for which Southern statesmen had been contending for twenty years. It dragged forth again all the proslavery arguments which the North had been opposing since 1835, and which, jurists and statesmen should have known, that region would never accept. Its spirit and literary style were. precisely the kind that had come from Southern advocates of slavery in the most turbulent debates that had racked the Senate for thirty years. It was, as Northern journalists insisted, a "stump speech," under the guise of a judicial decision. Its real author was not so much Roger Taney as John C. Calhoun. Certain paragraphs, especially those describing negroes — that is, free negroes — as members of a "degraded" class, who could never become American citizens, and thus have no rights as citizens, reproduced statements Taney had made years before, but the constitutional attitude was merely a reproduction of Calhoun's writings. In Taney's decision, as in Calhoun's theory, a Constitution was described as a compact; the rights of states took precedence over those of the central government; the territories were the joint possession of all the states, and no citizen could be prevented from taking his property into them; slaves were such property, and the Missouri Compromise, reserving country west of the Mississippi to freedom, was therefore unconstitutional. Calhoun, though he never succeeded in his own lifetime in forcing these views on the nation, scored this triumph seven years after his death. The Dred Scott decision, so called, was merely another

Calhoun pamphlet. Should its doctrines prevail, the system which Calhoun described as "a good — a positive good," could constitutionally be extended from the Mississippi River to the Pacific Ocean and from Canada to the Gulf.[1] In future Congress could pass no laws forbidding the encroachment of slavery in this imperial domain. When Dred Scott had migrated into the country now known as Minnesota, he did not become a free man, for the law which had apparently granted this boon was now ruled unconstitutional. So John C. Calhoun had insisted for ten years preceding his death, and so Chief Justice Taney and five of his associates now determined. The real significance of the Dred Scott decision is that Calhounism had been written into the Constitution of the United States. The document of 1787 specifically said that "Congress shall have power to make all needful rules and regulations respecting the territory or other property belonging to the United States," but Justice Taney decreed that this comprehensive granting power did not give the right to regulate slavery. That the decision was bad law events and other judgments of the Supreme Court have shown. The Dred Scott interpretation has now merely an archaic and historic interest. It is one of those Supreme Court decisions which the Supreme Court has itself overruled. As jurisprudence it has been disregarded from that day to the present.

In 1854, when Congress repealed the Missouri Compromise, the proslavery party had gained possession of the legislative department of the government. In 1856, when James Buchanan was elected President, the same interest solidified its already powerful control of the Presidency. With the Dred Scott decision it won the judicial branch. All those three departments on which the fathers of 1787 prided themselves had thus passed into the hands of those who, in Lincoln's phrase, were determined to make the United States "all slave." In solving the greatest difficulty that ever faced the nation, the Constitution had therefore failed. The question which the convention of 1787 had evaded now rose to distract their grandchildren. The complacent expectation of Buchanan, Taney, and his associates that the Supreme Court, by going over to one side of the controversy, would "quiet the agitation" was quickly shown to be a tragic absurdity. The question of slavery was now to be appealed to an even higher court than that which met in the Washington Capitol. Only on the battlefield was the issue to be set at rest — and this time set at rest forever.

[1] Except, of course, in California and Iowa, which had already been admitted as free states.

BOOK V

THE CONSTITUTION IN THE MODERN WORLD

I

THE Dred Scott decision had one result which neither the learned judges nor the excited people had foreseen. It heralded the rise of a new figure in American public life — the figure that from this time forward was to wield a dominating influence on the nation's existence. Until the judicial edict was published that negroes belonged to a "degraded race," little had been heard, outside of Illinois, of the man who was destined to fix their status for all time. In Illinois Abraham Lincoln had for many years been a conspicuous character. He had served in the state legislature, had spent one undistinguished term in Washington as Congressman, had won much local fame as orator-lawyer on circuit, above all as an unusual, but vital and commanding human being. His opinions on the slavery question, his growing prominence as a result of the Kansas-Nebraska and Missouri disturbances, had made him the most successful opponent of that other Illinoisan, Stephen A. Douglas. The Lincoln attitude, earnest in its antagonism to the Douglas programme, had been applauded for its wisdom and sanity. He disapproved of abolitionists, of extremists of all types, but took a rocklike stand against the extension of slavery. When Justice Taney's decision was published, therefore, a few sentences came from Lincoln — words that have ever since echoed, almost like a threnody, in American history. The American public at once accepted these phrases as expressing the tragic significance of that pronouncement. " 'A house divided against itself cannot stand.' I believe this government cannot endure permanently half slave and half free. I do not expect the Union to be dissolved — I do not expect the house to fall — but I do expect it will cease to be divided. It will become all one thing, or all the other. Either the opponents of slavery will arrest the further spread of it, and place it where the public mind shall rest in the belief that it is in the course of ultimate extinction; or its advocates will push it forward till it shall become alike lawful in all the States, old as well as new, North as well as South."

Who was this genius who in these few ruthless words, Biblical both in their vigor and in their simplicity, had thus placed before the American people the real issue with which they had come face to face? The speech from which this paragraph had been culled, it presently appeared, had been made by Lincoln in an address accepting from the Republican Party of Illinois its designation as United States Senator from that state. The term of Stephen A. Douglas was expiring, and Lincoln had been chosen as the Republican candidate to contest his seat. Douglas was then the most prominent Democrat in the nation, the man looked upon as the almost certain candidate of his party for the Presidency in 1860, and that Lincoln, obscure in a national sense as he was, had been selected to face this indomitable debater was in itself enough to arouse national interest. This interest grew when the nature of the Senatorial campaign in Illinois became known. Lincoln was planning to wage battle at close quarters. Apparently standing in no awe of Douglas's reputed invincibility on the platform, the uncouth lawyer had issued a challenge, suggesting that the candidates for the Senatorship conduct their argument in the form of public debates. A programme was arranged, by which the two men, dividing time, should appear on the same platform in seven Illinois towns. Thus began that most decisive campaign in the antislavery story, the Lincoln-Douglas debates, the outcome of which was to give the United States its President and leader in the greatest crisis it has ever faced. For though the forum of these discussions was a series of scrambling frontier towns in an outlying state, the real audience was found in the 30,000,000 people that then made the American populace. Even the radio, had it existed at the time, could hardly have brought the two characters and the life-and-death ideas for which they stood more vividly to every American fireside.

Interesting as these debates are, from all points of view, — as masterpieces of oratory and statesmanship, as containing in themselves the issues and arguments on which the Presidential election of 1860 was to be fought, as well as presenting to the American public the inevitable leaders in that contest, — they have one significance which, in the present connection, overshadows all others. The question which had come to the front already several times since 1787, and which occupies so large a space in contemporary discussion, held almost first importance in the Lincoln-Douglas debates. That was the so-called "sanctity" of the Supreme Court and its adjudications. Were these decisions "sacred" in the sense that they were never to be criticized, never to be ques-

Abraham Lincoln

Stephen A. Douglas

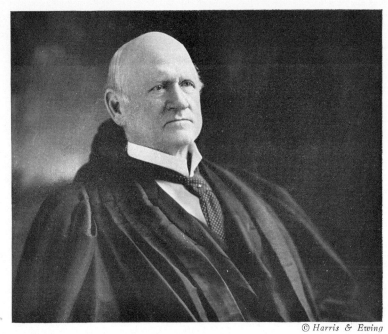

JOHN MARSHALL HARLAN

OLIVER WENDELL HOLMES, JR.

tioned, hardly even discussed? Once that tribunal had spoken, was the argument to be regarded as forever stilled? Had the issue been resolved, and were all private citizens, and all public officials, to accept it as the immutable principle of action?

Lincoln's course in speeches before the debates began had made his position on the inviolability of the Supreme Court a matter of criticism. Few Americans had been more outspoken in denouncing the Dred Scott decision and the judicial and political procedure that marked it. In the whole proslavery campaign, beginning with the repeal of the Missouri Compromise of 1820 and ending with the slavery triumph at the hands of Judge Taney in 1857, he had detected a politico-judicial conspiracy, the purpose of which was to extend slavery all over the United States, in the states as well as the territories. Not yet had the right of slave owners to take their chattels into the states been established by judicial ruling, Lincoln said, but that was coming; it would be inevitably the next step; one more Supreme Court decision was all that was necessary to make the proslavery campaign complete. Once grant the constitutional principle set forth by Judge Taney, and this conclusion could not be avoided. Congress could not prohibit slavery in the territories, Taney had ruled, because slaves were property, and property, under the Fifth Amendment, could not be taken from citizens "without due process of law." The same prohibition would prevent the states from shutting slavery from their borders. A Southern slave master who wished to take his black men to the rocky soil of New England and work them on one of its farms would have the right to do so under the principle of constitutional law just proclaimed. This was what Lincoln meant when he said that the nation would become "all slave" or "all free."

The Chief Justice, as noted above, had angrily asserted that, should Seward be elected President, — and in 1858 Seward was regarded as the predestined Republican candidate in 1860, — he would refuse to administer the oath of office. His reason was that Seward had declared that the Dred Scott decision was the offspring of collusion between the executive and the judicial branch. Strangely enough, Taney did administer the oath to Lincoln, though Lincoln had gone further than Seward in his charges of "conspiracy." For the Illinoisan had asserted that the whole proslavery movement, from 1854 to 1857, justified the conclusion that politicians, Presidents, and Supreme Court judges had worked harmoniously to this end. That such an accusation was not susceptible of legal proof, Lincoln admitted. "We cannot absolutely know that all these exact adaptations are the result of preconcert. But when we see a lot of framed timbers, different portions of which we know have been gotten out at different times and places by different workmen — Stephen, Franklin, Roger, and James, for instance — and we see these timbers joined together, and see they exactly make the frame of a house or a mill, and all the tenons and mortises exactly fitting and all the lengths and proportions of the different pieces exactly adapted to their respective places and not a piece too many or too few, not omitting even scaffolding — or, if a single piece be lacking, we see the place in the frame exactly fitted and prepared yet to bring such piece in — in such case we find it impossible not to believe that Stephen and Franklin and Roger and James all understood one another from the beginning and all worked upon a common plan or draft drawn up before the first blow was struck."

Stephen and Franklin and Roger and James! That is, Stephen A. Douglas, Franklin Pierce, Roger B. Taney, and James Buchanan. Lincoln had not only outlined the conspiracy, but had named the conspirators. The paragraph is a delightful example of that gift for homely illustration of which Lincoln was such a master; never before, however, had the integrity of the Supreme Court been so assailed. And naturally Douglas, in his speeches, pounced upon these sentences as evidencing Lincoln's disrespect for the highest tribunal. Such contempt for judicial integrity, he declared, unfitted Lincoln for the Senatorship. His rival had attacked the most sacred shrine in the American system — the basis on which American justice and freedom rested. Douglas's speeches displayed a reverence for the Supreme Court which Lincoln, with his gift for humor, described as a sudden conversion. "The Constitution," exclaimed Douglas, accepting the Marshall doctrine of judicial review, "has created that court to determine all constitutional questions in the last resort, and when such decisions have been made they become the law of the land." He then denounced Lincoln as a defier of this exalted body — in words that have a familiar sound to-day. "Whoever resists the final decision of the highest judicial tribunal aims a deadly blow at our whole Republican system of government — a blow which, if successful, would place all our rights and liberties at the mercy of passion, anarchy and violence." Lincoln was thus an "enemy" of the Constitution. He was advocating "resistance" to a decision of the Supreme Court. He was seeking to "bring the Supreme Court into disrepute among the people . . . to destroy confidence in the highest judicial tribunal on earth."

"Suppose," Douglas asked in the debate at Galesburg, "he succeeds in destroying public confidence in the Court, so that the people will not respect its decisions, but will feel at liberty to disregard them, and resist the laws of the land, what will he have gained? He will have changed the government from one of laws to that of a mob, in which the strong arm of violence will be substituted for the decisions of the courts of justice. . . . He wants to take an appeal from the Supreme Court to this meeting to determine whether the questions of law were decided properly. He is going to appeal from the Supreme Court of the United States to every town meeting. . . . Mr. Lincoln says he is going to reverse that decision. By what tribunal will he reverse it? Will he appeal to a mob? Does he intend to appeal to violence, to lynch-law? Will he stir up strife and rebellion in the land, and overthrow the Court by violence?"

"I believe that the decision was improperly made," replied Lincoln, "and I go for reversing it." Such was his general attitude, and he saw nothing in this position that was unconstitutional or that in any degree implied "resistance" to the judicial power. Douglas's picture of him, as a subverter of government and an inciter of mob rule, merely appealed to Lincoln's humorous instincts. For the dignity, even the "sanctity" of the Supreme Court no man had a higher sense, but in his eyes there was nothing treasonable in subjecting its decisions to scrutiny, in questioning their wisdom, even in refusing to accept them as good and final law. Was a citizen not entitled to his opinion as to whether a man was a good or a bad judge, whether the interpretation handed down was sound or mistaken? Was he required even to acquiesce in such verdicts as principles of political action? If Lincoln and his political party regarded such outgivings as the Dred Scott decision as evil, as perversions of constitutional law, were they to refrain from efforts to obtain reversals, even to cease working for public policies that contravened them? Lincoln did not think so. He had joined fortunes with the new Republican Party, a body called into being to oppose the extension of slavery. The Supreme Court had decided that such a programme was unconstitutional. Should the Republican Party therefore disband, submitting to this judgment as making forever impossible the object for which it had come into existence? Should no aspirant for public office advocate the apparently outlawed cause? Should voters refuse to cast their ballots for candidates who regarded Judge Taney as a badly mistaken jurist? Should Congressmen or Senators decline to vote for laws that had been declared to run foul of the Constitution? Was a President prohibited from signing measures that ignored the recent pronouncement?

Lincoln frankly said that he did not feel such restraint. His campaign for the Senate was based on a conviction that the Supreme Court had erred, that its judgment, if maintained and acquiesced in, would set back American history for a hundred years, and that the welfare of the nation demanded a reversal. He was prepared to do everything in his power to obtain this reversal. But Lincoln repudiated the Douglas charge that he was "resisting" the Supreme Court. He described his attitude not as "resistance," but "opposition." He drew a distinction between these two words and the policies they implied. As a matter of law, valid until it was reversed, the Dred Scott decision stood. It settled the fate of Dred Scott and all persons in a similar predicament. The Court had decided that he was a slave; Lincoln accepted that decision. He did not suggest that Dred and his champions defy the Court, refuse to submit to further bondage, and summon mobs to assist them in defying the law. That, said Lincoln, would be "resistance." But he held himself, and all good citizens, free to criticize the ruling as mistaken and to do everything they lawfully could to obtain another more in keeping with their conception of the Constitution and sound public policy. That was "opposition" — a right every citizen possessed under a Constitution that guaranteed freedom of speech and of the press.

"We do not propose," said Lincoln, in reply to Douglas's "lynch-law" and "town meeting" charge, "that when Dred Scott has been decided to be a slave by the Court, we, as a mob, will decide him to be free. We do not propose that, when any other one, or one thousand, shall be decided by that Court to be slaves, we will in any violent way disturb the rights of property thus settled; but we nevertheless do oppose that decision as a political rule, which will be binding on the voter to vote for nobody who thinks it wrong, which shall be binding on the members of Congress or the President to favor no measure that does not actually concur with the principles of that decision. We do not propose to be bound by it as a political rule in that way, because we think it lays the foundation not merely for enlarging and spreading out what we consider an evil, but it lays the foundation for spreading that evil into the states themselves. We propose so resisting it as to have it reversed if we can, and a new judicial rule established upon this subject."

Thus those who insist on the immutable sanctity of judicial interpretations will find little comfort in Abraham Lincoln. He believed that the highest court settled the pending cases and fixed the law — until the courts themselves decided otherwise. He believed in the unfettered right of the unjudicial public to criticize the most learned opinion, and, in case it contravened the Constitution, to do all in its power to secure a reversal. Political parties could even advocate policies that "defied" the Supreme Court and not lose standing as decent, law-abiding organizations. Congress could adopt laws, and Presidents could sign them, that embodied constitutional ideas of which the "highest tribunal" had disapproved. Thus when President Roosevelt, in July 1935, recommended that Congress pass the Guffey Coal Bill, "not permitting doubts as to its constitutionality, however reasonable, to block the suggested legislation," his attitude was not especially different from that of Lincoln in the Dred Scott case. "If I were in Congress" — this may be taken as the summation of Lincoln's position — "and a vote should come up on a question, whether slavery should be prohibited in a new territory, in spite of the Dred Scott decision I should vote that it should. Judge Douglas said last night that before the decision he might advance his opinion save it might be contrary to the decision when it was made; but after it was made he would abide by it until it was reversed. Just so! We let this property [that is, the slave Dred Scott] abide by the decision, but we will try to reverse that decision. . . . Somebody has to reverse that decision, since it was made; and we mean to reverse it and we mean to do it peaceably. . . . We mean to do what we can to have the Court decide the other way."

II

Few would deny to-day that Lincoln's attitude represented good law and sound public policy. It involved no disrespect for the Court as an institution; it did involve disrespect, however, for this particular decision — a disrespect that most enlightened citizens, then and since, cordially echoed. How was a reversal of the obnoxious decision to be obtained? On this issue also Lincoln was frank and practical. As a matter of history, events themselves in time obliterated Taney's handiwork; the Thirteenth Amendment, abolishing slavery, the Fourteenth, giving negroes those rights as citizens which, Taney had decided, they were not entitled to and could never attain under the Constitution, made unnecessary any radical proceedings against the Supreme Tribunal itself. That Lincoln was prepared to take measures which many citizens of to-day regard as drastic, even revolutionary, the next few years made clear. Thus an idea so "subversive" as "packing" the Supreme Court did not shock the Emancipator. One of his loftiest ambitions was to appoint enough antislavery judges to secure a reversal of the Dred Scott decision. He made Salmon P. Chase Taney's successor because, as he said to George S. Boutwell, "we wish for a Chief Justice who will sustain what has been done in regard to emancipation and the legal tenders."

Yet no man held the Constitution in higher regard. No President took more care that all his acts should conform to this fundamental law. William H. Seward's dictum that in the matter of prohibiting slavery in the territories there was a "higher law than the Constitution" brought from Lincoln a rebuke. "I agree with Seward's 'irrepressible conflict,' " he said, "but not with his 'higher law' doctrine." Strange to say Lincoln is one of the few American Presidents criticized, in his own time and since, as a "dictator"; a man who, in meeting many crises of the Civil War, brushed aside the Constitution and substituted for it his own will. He has been pictured as a military "despot" who established precedents that, in the hands of less well-intentioned rulers, might wreck American liberties. Others have cited his courage in acting promptly to meet unforeseen difficulties, even in ways not precisely defined in the Constitution, as one of the true signs of his greatness. The actions that have elicited these opposing views were the call for 75,000 volunteers in April 1861, the suspension of the habeas corpus writ in May 1861, the Emancipation Proclamation of January 1, 1863, and the Lincoln programme for Reconstruction. For none of these proceedings, it has been argued, could constitutional warrant be cited.

The last three of the charges are the ones that most conspicuously figure in the discussion. The suspension of habeas corpus has that quality of conflict that animates the historic drama, for this proceeding again brought Lincoln in conflict with the aged Chief Justice. It was against Taney's state, Maryland, that the issue was raised. Though the state itself, as a whole, remained loyal to the Union, the eastern section of Maryland, including the city of Baltimore, was almost as secessionist in feeling as South Carolina. This hostility proved a terrible danger to the Federal cause. Had Maryland joined the Confederacy, the United States would have presented the strange spectacle of a nation with its capital on enemy soil. Washington would have been surrounded by Virginia on the south and Maryland on the north; the city might have become a possession of the seceded states; its officials, its halls of legislation, the departments, even its personnel, — President, Congressmen, Senators, and departmental staffs, — might have passed into the hands of the states in rebellion. Not inconceivably Washington, instead of Richmond, would have been made the capital of the Confederacy! There was more than a possibility, in the first weeks of the war, that such would be its fate. For several days Washington was isolated from the North. The Federal troops, proceeding through Baltimore to its rescue, were met by mobs that impeded progress. Secession sympathizers were destroying bridges, ripping up railroad tracks, and making impassable roads that led to the Capital. A special session of the legislature had been called at Annapolis, and it was no secret that every effort would be made by Southern sympathizers to place Maryland in the Confederacy. Thus almost the first problem that confronted Lincoln, on the outbreak of hostilities, was to stop these riotous excesses in Baltimore, to establish free communication between Washington and the nation, and to preserve Maryland as a part of the Union.

The promptness and thoroughness with which Lincoln acted not only prevented the secession of Maryland, but kept other border states — Kentucky and Missouri — from following her example. Chief Justice Taney, the militant Democratic press of the North, and Lincoln's detractors since, claimed that he accomplished this by violating the Constitution. Had the charge been true, a statesman so practical as Lincoln would not have hesitated; to preserve the Union itself, is it not pardonable to disregard the Constitution? But whether Lincoln actually did so in the habeas corpus cases is a refined problem in constitutional law which cannot be regarded as finally determined yet. For Lincoln's infraction, if infraction it was, concerned this, the most ancient safeguard of Anglo-Saxon liberty. These two Latin words, *habeas corpus,* — "you may have the body," — enshrine one of the greatest privileges of that Magna Charta which the barons wrung from a reluctant king at Runnymede. Until the fall of the Bastille French monarchs enjoyed the pleasant prerogative of seizing any person who had incurred their displeasure and, without making any charges or holding trial, throwing him into prison. There the sufferer would remain until he rotted, for there was no way by which his release could be obtained. Present-day reports from Germany, Italy, and Russia indicate that this is still the common practice in those countries. But such high-handed measures are impossible where the writ of habeas corpus exists. In these countries, friends of the imprisoned man, at any time, may "have the body." The officers of justice can be compelled to produce a prisoner in court, give the reasons for his incarceration, and present the evidence on which the accusation rests. Thus, so long as the writ of habeas corpus prevails, imprisonment on false or unsupported charges is impossible. And this safeguard of liberty is deeply embedded in the Constitution of the United States. Nothing suggestive of French *lettres de cachet* or Hitlerian arrests and executions is possible under the American system.

Precious as is this constitutional safeguard in ordinary times, there are crises when it can become a great public danger. Such times are war and civic upheaval. Conditions may arise in which it becomes necessary to arrest offenders by the hundreds, even thousands, and throw them into confinement. Quick action may be imperative, and there is no time to frame indictments and hold trials. Public safety demands that mere suspicion, or *ex parte* evidence, shall be a sufficient excuse. That injustice in individual cases may result is plain, but the peace and safety of the community as a whole must be preserved, even though a few innocent persons suffer imprisonment. If every disturber, or suspected disturber, could appeal to a court and obtain his freedom from a complaisant judge, the curbing of riot and insurrection would become a difficult process. Thus the power to suspend the writ is granted by the Constitution. "The privilege of the writ of habeas corpus," reads Section 9, Article I, "shall not be suspended, unless when in cases of rebellion or invasion the public safety may require it."

Abraham Lincoln, sitting in the White House, his communication with his country temporarily severed by disloyal Marylanders stoning and murdering Federal troops in the streets of Baltimore and seeking to wreck the trains bearing his army to the scene of war, believed that, in the constitutional sense, a "case of rebellion" existed, and that "public safety" justified his suspension of the writ. The commanding general in Baltimore was therefore ordered to seize all offenders, put them in prison, and hold them without trial. Conspicuous rioters, deprived of liberty under these instructions, at once sued for freedom under habeas corpus. John Merryman, one of the leaders of the disturbances, confined by the army in Fort McHenry for his activities, became the test case. Chief Justice Taney issued the writ, demanding the production of Mr. Merryman's "body" in court, according to the ancient Anglo-Saxon rite. When General Cadwalader refused, informing the Chief Justice that he was acting under orders of the President of the United States, Taney declared him in contempt of court, and wrote a dignified opinion, maintaining that Lincoln, in suspending the writ, had violated the Constitution. Taney's decision was an exceedingly able paper, and most constitutional lawyers believe that, from a legal point of view, it was correct, though this judgment is not unanimous. The section of the Constitution quoted above unquestionably authorizes the suspension of the writ in cases of "rebellion." But the Constitution does not precisely say who shall exercise this power. The paragraph quoted is found in that celebrated Article I which deals exclusively with the powers of Congress. Again, Article II, which enumerates the powers of the President, does not enroll among them the suspension of habeas corpus. Taney therefore contended, with considerable force, that only Congress could suspend the writ. Lincoln never accepted this view, but most lawyers — including John Marshall himself — have done so.

But Lincoln, practical soul that he was, never suffered great mental torture over Taney's decision. And the whole question presently became academic. His measure, including the suspension, crushed rebellion in eastern Maryland, secured the untrammeled transportation of Federal troops, made Washington once more a part of the United States, and enabled the Unionists of Maryland, who were in a great majority, to keep their state in the Union. Lincoln's practical justification for reading his own power into the clause was that the Constitution was indefinite and that, Congress not being in session when the emergency arose, only the President could act. As soon as that body came together, it passed a bill making legal this and several other of Lincoln's acts that had been called in question, so the suspension presently received the constitutional sanction that Taney demanded. And meanwhile the nation had been saved! For Lincoln himself believed that, should the border states of Maryland, Kentucky, and Missouri join what he always called the "insurrection," the Union could not be restored. "These all against us," he wrote in a letter to O. H. Browning, September 22, 1861, "and the job on our hands is too large for us. We would as well consent to a separation at once, including the surrender of this capital."

Lincoln's Proclamation setting free 4,000,000 negro slaves has also been assailed on constitutional grounds. Taney believed it unconstitutional; and that he was never able to write a decision outlawing the document on these grounds is said to have been the great disappointment of his last year. Yet as one reads the story of Lincoln's gradual approach to this subject, his constant respect for the Constitution and the minute care with which he sought to avoid any step conflicting with it are the facts that stand out most conspicuously. If one only grasps the important fact that Lincoln's proclamation did not abolish slavery as an institution, but merely set free the Africans then held as slaves, his constitutional attitude will be better understood. It is a distinction that the Emancipator himself always kept in mind. Neither the President nor Congress had any constitutional right to prohibit the institution. The states themselves alone possessed that power. In the thirty years' agitation that preceded the Civil War, this power had never been called in question. Calhoun and William Lloyd Garrison, little as they agreed upon the general subject, never disagreed on this. The states had created the system; only the states could end it. The Constitution protected the states in this right; that is the reason the extreme abolitionists wished to destroy the Constitution.

Throughout the War Congress had pursued a slavery programme that completely accorded with the views Lincoln had maintained in the discussion that preceded it. An act of 1862 forever prohibited slavery in the District of Columbia. The Congressional right to control the institution at the seat of government Lincoln had always maintained. The compensation to slave owners in the District of $300 per slave similarly coincided with the Lincoln policy for the solution of the general problem. But one step the Lincoln administration did not adopt: it made no attempt to eradicate slavery in the states, even those that were "in rebellion." Here again the Emancipator was consistent. His fixed conviction had always been that Congress had no constitutional right to adopt such legislation. But Congress, in July 1862, did pass certain acts setting free slaves in certain contingencies. Bondmen escaping into the Union lines, negroes belonging to citizens convicted of treason, negroes captured with Confederate armies, or in forts or other positions that had passed into Federal possession, were given their freedom. Nothing more significantly exhibits Lincoln's scrupulous regard for constitutional niceties, even in war time, than that he refused to approve this measure in its original form. Congress, he said, had no right to free a slave; only the states could do that. Congress, however, did possess the power to confiscate the property of persons with whom it was at war. The proper course, therefore, the President counseled Congress, would be to seize slaves, as property, whenever they came into Federal hands, just as horses, mules, artillery, and war material of all kinds were seized. That is, ownership of slaves, as property, would pass from rebellious citizens into the hands of the Washington government. Uncle Sam would thus momentarily find himself a great slaveholder, and would be confronted with the problem of disposing of his new-found wealth. What more natural course than to follow the example of many distinguished citizens, like George Washington, George Mason, Robert E. Lee, and set them free? There was no objection to making it plain, in the act under consideration, that this was the intention. Congress accepted the Presidential modifications and, instead of declaring slaves of these limited classes free, merely "confiscated" them as property of persons engaged in "rebellion."

But as the war went wastingly on, the necessity for action on a larger scale became apparent. More and more it was manifest that slaves were a vast military asset to the Confederacy. They were left at home in charge of plantations and thus released so many white men for army service. They were employed digging trenches, building fortifications, acting as cooks — doing work for which, in the Northern army, the regular forces were pressed

into service.   So far, the Confederacy had not enlisted their black
retainers as soldiers, but the question was being actively discussed
in the South, and in the last phase of the war General Lee advocated the organization of negro regiments.   Could the North
obtain possession of the 4,000,000 slaves of the South, or any part
of them, it would not only weaken the Confederacy, but enormously
strengthen the Northern cause.   Thus emancipation, in Lincoln's
mind, gradually assumed the proportions of a military measure.
It could greatly help the government in winning the war.   From
the beginning, antislavery advocates of all degrees had kept this
issue alive, but in the mind of Sumner, Wendell Phillips, and the
like, the question was moral and humanitarian; here was the opportunity to end an enormous wrong, to perform an act of Christian
justice.   But this was not the point of view that appealed to Lincoln.   Over and over again he declared that he would like to set all
slaves free; but, as a mere stroke of benevolence, neither the President nor Congress had the constitutional right.   Only in the event
that freeing the slaves would promote the end for which the war
had been begun — the preservation of the Union — did he believe
there was any authority to act.   Few of his letters have been so
frequently quoted as that superb rebuke to the rasping Horace
Greeley, who kept constantly at his heels on this issue.   The reason
for quoting it again, in the present connection, is the insight it gives
into Lincoln's constitutional attitude.   "If there be those who
would not save the Union unless they could at the same time destroy
slavery, I do not agree with them.   My paramount object in this
struggle is to save the Union and it is not either to destroy or to
save slavery.   If I could save the Union without freeing any slaves,
I would do it; and if I could save it by freeing all the slaves, I
would do it; and if I could save it by freeing some and leaving
others alone, I would also do that.   What I do about slavery and
the colored race I do because I believe it helps to save the Union;
and what I forbear, I forbear because I do not believe it would
help to save the Union."

The way to save the Union, of course, was to strengthen the
Federal armies and destroy the military power of the Confederacy;
in other words, freeing the slaves was, at this crisis, a military, not
a moral or humanitarian problem.   When once emancipation assumed this shape, the Presidential duty became clear.   The Constitution made the President Commander in Chief of the Army and
Navy; as such Commander in Chief, Lincoln — at least so he
maintained — could adopt any measure that gave force to the mili-

tary arm. He formulated this attitude in his reply, September 13, 1862, to one of the many delegations that visited him urging freedom for the slaves. "I raise no objections to it on legal or constitutional grounds, for, as Commander-in-Chief of the army and navy, in time of war I suppose I have a right to take any measure which may best subdue the enemy. . . . I view this matter as a practical war measure, to be decided on according to the advantages or disadvantages it may offer to the suppression of the rebellion." Even at the time this statement was made, Lincoln had reached the conclusion that the aid of the negroes was essential to the success of the cause. More than one colored regiment had already been organized, with satisfactory results. The use of slaves for the numerous tasks necessary in the organization of an army was a matter of even greater importance. Yet the employment of such recruits involved one paradox almost humorous in its nature. On Lincoln's constitutional grounds only slaves of states and regions in arms against the Federal power could be pressed into service. Obviously, on his theory, the President could not confiscate the "property" of states or sections of states that were loyal. That is, he could not seize the slaves of Delaware, Maryland, Kentucky, Missouri, or the western counties of Virginia, for these communities were all parts of the Union. Even though Lincoln had constitutionally possessed the power, it would not have been politic to exercise it, for all the border states were still wavering between North and South. The President for two years had been exercising his conciliatory gifts in attempts to keep them true to the flag, and an edict depriving them of their wealth would probably have driven them all into the Confederacy. Yet the fact remained that only in these border regions did emancipation seem likely to produce practical results. The President might declare free the slaves of North Carolina and Georgia, but how would a paper edict set them free? Their physical bodies would still remain within the Confederate lines, and the effect of a Presidential ukase would depend on the extent to which the Federal armies prospered in those regions.

Yet there were other considerations involved. Despite discouraging defeats in Virginia, Northern troops were steadily progressing on Confederate soil; nearly all of Tennessee, by the fall of 1862, had been conquered; considerable parts of Arkansas and Louisiana were in the possession of the North; and, as the armies advanced, great numbers of negroes were brought under Union control. The Emancipation Proclamation looked forward to this advance rather than to the existing situation. That the flight of negroes from Confederate territory would be stimulated by the realization that freedom lay across the lines was an expectation that did not prove to be unfounded. Again, while the motive for emancipation was ostensibly military, the accompanying political and diplomatic consequences were expected to exercise a powerful effect — as they did — upon the outcome. That France and Great Britain were on the verge of recognizing the Confederacy as an independent government was well known. The result of such recognition might well be the complete breakdown of the Federal cause. Boldly to proclaim, as Lincoln now proceeded to do, that the extirpation of slavery was a prime issue at stake would make such action, especially from Great Britain, impossible. In the England of Wilberforce, a nation that had taken the lead in the world movement for ending slavery and which for decades had been holding up America to scorn for protecting this anachronism, any cabinet that took sides openly in behalf of an insurrection fighting for the subjection of black men would not have remained in power twenty-four hours. The outcome showed that this was the case, for after that January 1, 1863, when Lincoln issued his Proclamation, all talk in England of recognizing the Confederacy came to an end; the British people would not permit themselves to be put in the position of exerting all their influence for the perpetuation of slavery.

The very phrasing of the document shows how closely Lincoln kept to his conception of constitutional power. His authority for setting free 4,000,000 black men, women, and children is carefully expressed. "I, Abraham Lincoln, President of the United States, by virtue of the power in me vested as Commander-in-Chief of the Army and Navy of the United States in time of actual armed rebellion against the authority and government of the United States, and as a fit and necessary war measure for suppressing said rebellion" — the source of authority and the purpose of the edict are thus succinctly explained. It was a power that Congress could not exercise, either in time of war or in time of peace; only the Executive on whom the Constitution had devolved full military command could proclaim such an edict. Lincoln's little preamble is thus a concise treatise on constitutional government. For the same reason, the Proclamation applies only to those states, or sections of states, engaged in the armed condition that the document describes. More significant still, the Proclamation, contrary to the prevailing belief, did not abolish slavery anywhere, either in the loyal states or in those in "armed rebellion." Lincoln still adhered to the opinion he had so frequently upheld in the debates with Douglas: the Federal government had no right to end the institution; that was the sole prerogative of the states. Congress could abolish slavery in the District of Columbia, and had done so, but no such sweeping jurisdiction over the states themselves resided in the central government. "I declare," said the Proclamation, "that all persons held as slaves within said designated States and parts of States are, and henceforward shall be, free." That is, emancipation affected only those particular individuals who, on January 1, 1863, were held in subjection. Lincoln had not put an end to the acknowledged right of the states to regulate this institution as their wisdom might direct. He had merely confiscated their existing "property" in slaves for the military advantage of the Union. Had the war come to an end, with nothing but the Emancipation Proclamation to determine the future of the evil that had caused the upheaval, the slave states would theoretically have had the right to set up the system again. Their existing slaves had been escheated to the general government as an act of war, but nothing impeded their constitutional right to acquire a new supply. That practically such a revival would have been difficult, perhaps impossible, is true; constitutional prohibitions against the slave trade, for example, would have raised a considerable obstacle. Still, as a matter of constitutional right, slavery could have been reëstablished, despite the Lincoln Proclamation. That is the reason the future of the institution was not entrusted to the status in which that document had left it. Under the leadership of Lincoln a step was taken that completely abolished slavery, and did so in a constitutional way.

The Proclamation measure accomplished the expected result, for it ultimately brought into the Union Army 200,000 negroes, 50,000 of them soldiers in the ranks — an accretion which played an important part in winning the war. But only an amendment to the Constitution could forever end slavery; such an amendment passed Congress February 1, 1865, and was in force December 18, 1865. A simple but majestic sentence, embodied as this Thirteenth Amendment, accomplished the change that no act of Congress or Presidential proclamation could make reality. The words, appropriately enough, were taken from the act of 1787 which had prohibited the extension of the system into the Northwest Territory. "Neither slavery nor involuntary servitude, except as a punishment for crime whereof the party shall have been duly convicted, shall exist within the United States, or any place subject to their jurisdiction." Lincoln lived to see his own state, Illinois, become the first to ratify this amendment, although not until the Presidency of his successor, Andrew Johnson, on December 18, 1865, was it proclaimed a part of the Constitution. This was the first change made in the Constitution since the Twelfth Amendment, changing the method of electing Presidents, was adopted sixty-one years before — on September 25, 1804.

III

Lincoln's constitutional policy did not end with his death. It inspired the administration of his successor in the most important of his problems. The "insurrection" or the "rebellion" had been crushed. The mutinous assaults of eleven Confederate states on the fundamental compact had been put down by military force. But a puzzling constitutional question now arose to try all the resources of statesmanship. What was to be the future of these commonwealths? What was to be the fate of the individuals who had made war against the Federal power? Evidently Section 3 of Article III had some bearing upon the situation. "Treason against the United States shall consist only in levying war against them, or in adhering to their enemies, giving them aid and comfort." These few words sound extremely personal. Evidently they contemplated active, responsible human beings, not abstract entities known as states. "Treason" is something of which only flesh-and-blood citizens can be guilty. Evidently a million and more individuals, according to this provision, had committed this great crime; that is, they had "levied war against the United States." Legal action against that number of persons, even if it could be defended on moral grounds, would involve practical difficulties. But could not action be taken against the states, as states? The Constitution itself did not point the way. Could their governments not be dissolved, their physical areas confiscated to the Federal power, state boundaries obliterated, and such ancient domains as Virginia and North Carolina reduced to a territorial status? Under such humiliating circumstances could they not be forced to spend a period in sackcloth and ashes until new commonwealths, erected on the proscribed soil, could qualify for admission to the Union?

Such arguments were advanced in Lincoln's time, but found little favor at his hands. They appealed neither to his sense of justice nor to his sense of humanity. Neither did such a policy, in Lincoln's eyes, have any standing under the Constitution. To accept the view that the Southern states, by the act of "treason," had ceased to exist would be, he declared, to deny the constitutional theory on which the war had been fought. According to this principle, the states were indestructible parts of an indestructible whole. "Union" was the word constantly on Lincoln's lips, and his Union included the eleven states in "rebellion" as well as the twenty-one that had remained loyal. The North had armed 2,000,000 men and sacrificed 500,000 lives to uphold the constitutional dogma that a state could not secede. Once it was in the Union, no power, not even the unanimous determination of its own citizens, could force it out. The Southern states had been as completely in the Union at the time of Bull Run and Gettysburg as in the time of the Mexican War. They were members of the central government when Fort Sumter was fired upon and when Lee surrendered at Appomattox. The idea of "punishing" states, therefore, contended Lincoln, was a constitutional absurdity — the denial of the principles for which the North stood. Vast numbers of citizens had, at least in the constitutional sense, been guilty of "treason" and, if such a policy seemed wise, could be held responsible for their deeds. But the states themselves were just as stable, just as innocent of wrongdoing, just as insusceptible of reprisals, in April 1865 as they had been in April 1861. You might constitutionally hang Jefferson Davis and Robert E. Lee, for they had "borne arms against the United States" and thus were technically, under the constitutional definition, guilty of "treason"; but you could not wipe Virginia and Mississippi out of existence, for they had never seceded from the Union, despite certain paper declarations to that effect. Once in the Union, always in the Union — such was the constitutional principle on which the war had been fought. This was the foundation of Lincoln's system of Reconstruction, taken over bodily by Andrew Johnson.

As the status of the negro, and especially his right to vote, became the disputed point over which the battle of Reconstruction subsequently raged, it is important to keep in mind Lincoln's attitude. It was by no means the point of view that, from 1865 to 1876, took leadership as the Republican doctrine. The habit of confounding abolitionists with all the other foes of slavery, mild and extreme, has already been emphasized. Perhaps Abraham Lincoln has been the greatest sufferer from this. He suffered from it constantly in his own lifetime. In nothing more did Douglas display his predominance as a demagogue than in his picture of Lincoln as an abolitionist, as a man who insisted not only on freeing all slaves, but in making them the social and political equals of whites. Again and again, in the debates, Douglas held forth his antagonist as an advocate of racial intermarriage — to such an extent that Lincoln was compelled to repudiate the charge in specific terms. "I protest, now and forever, against that counterfeit logic which presumes that because I do not want a negro woman for a slave, I do necessarily want her for a wife. My understanding is that I need not have her for either." Few men held in greater horror abolitionists of the Garrison and Wendell Phillips type. Even in his Civil War messages, when discussing the destruction of slavery, Lincoln avoids the word "abolition" and uses "abolishment"; evidently he wished to escape the connotation usually associated with the obnoxious term. The Civil War resulted in adding three amendments to the Constitution, the Thirteenth, abolishing slavery, the Fourteenth, giving the negro civil rights, and the Fifteenth, endowing him with the ballot. Lincoln proposed and favored the Thirteenth; the Fourteenth and Fifteenth were not introduced in his lifetime, but his principles, frequently set forth in public speeches, would have led him to oppose them both. Previous to 1861, Lincoln had not advocated emancipation in the states where slavery existed, much as he abhorred slavery everywhere; after the appeal to arms, however, and the terrible trials the thing had brought on the Federal government, he determined that it should be brought to an end. But he did not believe, even then, in granting this backward race full civil rights. He was opposed to negro suffrage. He would not have permitted black men to serve on juries, to hold office, to become members of state legislatures or of Congress. No one would have been more shocked than the Emancipator at the processions of negro hordes to polling booths that became common sights of Reconstruction, or the presence of dusky lawmakers in state legislatures and halls of Congress. The complete subjection of the white population of the Southern states by the ignorant and brutal negroes who had formerly been their slaves would have seemed to Lincoln an insult to democracy. He constantly expressed his opposition to making the negro the social or political equal of white men.

Plenty of quotations from Lincoln's speeches could be made setting forth this belief. One or two will suffice. "I will say then," he remarked in a speech at Charleston, Illinois, "that I am not, nor ever have been, in favor of bringing about, in any way, the social and political equality of the white and black races — that I am not nor ever have been in favor of making voters or jurors of negroes, nor of qualifying them to hold office, nor to intermarry with white people; and I will say in addition to this that there is a physical difference between the white and the black races which will ever forbid the two races living together on terms of social and political equality.   And inasmuch as they cannot so live, there must be the position of superior and inferior, and I, as much as any other man, am in favor of having the superior position assigned to the white race. . . . Anything that argues me into the idea of perfect social and political equality with the negro is but a specious and fantastical arrangement of words, by which a man can prove a horse chestnut to be a chestnut horse. . . ."   Despite all this, Lincoln did believe in giving the negro certain rights, and what these were he set forth, as only Lincoln could, in his speech at Ottawa. "Notwithstanding all this, there is no reason in the world why the negro is not entitled to all the natural rights enumerated in the Declaration of Independence — the right to life, liberty and the pursuit of happiness.   I hold that he is as much entitled to these as the white man.   I agree with Judge Douglas that he is not my equal in many respects, certainly not in color — perhaps not in intellectual and moral endowments, but in the right to eat the bread, without the leave of anybody else, which his own hand earns, he is my equal, or the equal of Judge Douglas and the equal of every living man."

It would be difficult to frame a social philosophy or lay a groundwork better adapted to the problem of bringing the Southern states "into constitutional relationship with the Union" than these commonsense ideas.   And the programme Lincoln outlined, even while the rebellion was raging most fiercely, was based upon these convictions. This programme made no attempt to place the black man on a social and political equality with the white.   It contemplated giving the negro his freedom, but made no effort to give him the vote, or to enable him to hold civil office or act as lawmaker.   It still kept the ex-slaves in a position of inferiority to the white.   Above all, Lincoln's Reconstruction gave no scope to hatred or vengeance.   It accepted the fact that Southerners, like their fellow citizens elsewhere, were human beings.   It acknowledged that human beings can go astray; that the Civil War was the culmination of political and sectional passions that had been kept in a state of constant excitement for forty years; that blame rested on the North as well as the South; that its conclusion was no occasion for reprisals, and that the only true statesmanship was that which brought again together the dissevered fragments in perpetual union.   The spirit that actuated Lincoln in this task of reconciliation is that of his second inaugural.   In words of fairly Shakespearean pith he set down the purpose that humanized his whole Reconstruction programme.

"With malice toward none, with charity for all, with firmness in the right as God gives us to see the right, let us strive on to finish the work we are in, to bind up the nation's wounds, to care for him who shall have borne the battle and for his widow and his orphan, to do all which may achieve and cherish a just and lasting peace among ourselves and with all nations."

No proscriptions, no policy of vengeance, no votes to negroes, no domination of the white man by African ex-slaves — none of these vagaries of an aftertime were to serve as Lincoln's preliminaries to "binding up the nation's wounds" and establishing a "just and lasting peace among ourselves." If the South deserved punishment, her devastated fields, her thousands killed in battle, the destruction of her economic system, the obliteration of all her wealth — herein, in Lincoln's view, she had already sufficiently atoned. The task now was to help her reassemble her scattered energies, and bring her once more within the Union from which, according to Lincoln's constitutional theory, the eleven states "recently in rebellion" had never been separated. Lincoln had already begun restoration on this basis. As far back as December 8, 1863, he had published his plan. Relying upon the pardoning power which the Constitution vests exclusively in the President, this document proclaimed amnesty to nearly all participants in rebellion. Certain exceptions were indeed made. Officers of the United States Army and Navy who had thrown up their commands and joined the Confederate forces; Congressmen, Senators, and judges who had taken the oath of allegiance to the Constitution and had then joined the insurgents — these, and a few others, were not yet to be received into perfect fellowship. The Proclamation, however, encompassed the great mass of the Southern people, and almost the only stipulation exacted from them was that they should take solemn oath of allegiance and, above all, swear to observe the Presidential Proclamation freeing the slaves. A scheme for readmitting the seceded states was outlined — inadequate as it must have seemed when most of them were still under the wing of the Confederate government, but significant as setting forth the President's purpose. Whenever 10 per cent of the voters set up a state government, "Republican in form," as the Constitution required, Lincoln was prepared to recognize that as the legal government and, as such, part of the Union. Under this system, even before Lincoln's assassination, Tennessee, Louisiana, and Arkansas had reconstructed themselves, established state legislatures and courts, and had even elected Congressmen and Senators — the latter, however, not having yet been admitted to

Congress. "Ten per cent governments," as they were called by the critics of Lincolnian Reconstruction already rearing their heads in Washington, hardly offered a satisfactory basis for incorporating anew the old South in the Union, but they indicate what a sympathetic friend the South would have found in Lincoln had not the assassin's bullet brought his career to an end.

IV

When Jefferson Davis was accused of having had a hand in Lincoln's murder, he significantly replied: "How ridiculous! Everybody knows that the South prefers Lincoln to Johnson!" Such was the general feeling in the Southern states when this rough Tennessee mountaineer became the heir of Lincoln's problems. That the new President was himself a Southerner, a native of Raleigh, North Carolina, gave his former compatriots no satisfaction. He was precisely the type of Southerner from whom Southerners seemed to have most to fear. For Johnson, in birth, rearing, occupation, and ideas, represented the lowest Southern caste. He himself typified the chief argument that had been urged against slavery and the Southern system. It developed no self-respecting middle class, but evolved a society with a few patricians at the top and a mass of ignorant, half-starved "poor whites" at the bottom. It was to this latter group that Johnson belonged. Whether, as Chief Justice Taney said, the negro was the irreclaimable member of a "degraded race" may be argued, but there seems little question that the order into which Andrew Johnson was born had many stigmata of such a caste. His birthplace was a miserable shack in a back street of Raleigh; his father earned a precarious living as porter of a local bank and bell ringer of the Presbyterian Church. Neither father nor mother could read or write; the son never went to school; though, in some unrecorded way, he did pick up a slight knowledge of reading, he could not write his name until after marriage, being taught this art, as well as the rule of cipher, by his wife. The facts of his subsequent career are well known: how, at the age of fourteen, apprenticed to a tailor, he ran away from his master, finally finding a haven in eastern Tennessee; how he established here what grew into a flourishing tailor's trade; how his native energy, vigorous mind, congenial, if rough-and-ready, companionship, and never-failing interest in political problems made his shop the focus of Democratic activity and launched Johnson on a political career.

To-day the State of Tennessee keeps as a shrine the little building in which Johnson plied his trade, exhibiting the scissors with which he fashioned the garments of his neighbors, the goose with which he smoothed their wrinkles, and even a dress coat made by the President-tailor's own hands. "Mechanic mayor" of Greenville, "mechanic Congressman and Senator in Washington," "mechanic governor," finally "mechanic President" in the White House — such were the titles used to describe Johnson's progress. The story, in its external phases, has much in common with Lincoln's own, but in the spiritual aspects it is quite different. Such hardships, which mellowed and humanized Lincoln, embittered Johnson. The neglect in which his boyhood had been passed, the insults his ambitions had elicited from the educated, never faded from his mind. For complacent respectability Andrew Johnson's hatred was intense. Every snub endured from "patricians," as he called them, remained an unforgettable memory. This feeling explains much that was least desirable in his deportment. No self-made man so gloried in the depths from which he had risen. In his early Tennessee campaign, in his speeches as Congressman, even, indeed, as President, no word was more constantly in Johnson's mouth than "plebeian." This, Johnson would shout, — and his voice, usually uplifted in the open, would carry to the reverberating hills, — was what he was and what he was proud to be; this was what all men were, he insisted, whose lives meant anything to the state. Something of this appears to-day in the Johnson portraits. The high forehead, indicating the brain power that the man indisputably possessed, the neatly brushed black hair, the firm-set mouth, the shaggy brows, the well-poised head, the powerful erect shoulders, have dignity, force, and character, but they bear witness also to the hardships that had made his existence. The face looks out at the world a little doubtfully. With all his furious self-assertion, the general feeling is still that of the poor mountain white unexpectedly thrust into high position, the tailor lifted from the tailor's bench to perform a great rôle in his country's history. In it all there is a suggestion of Christopher Sly.

About one phase of Johnson's career, however, there was nothing questioning. In all stages of his advancement the Constitution had been the rock of his political creed. From childhood he had idolized it and had proclaimed its survival as the one overshadowing question at issue in the war. Even Webster himself had shown for the Constitution no greater devotion. A companion piece to Webster the boy, studying the Constitution on his cotton handkerchief, is that of Johnson working at his tailor's bench with thread and needle as his young wife read the newspapers of the day, filled with accounts of Jackson's controversy over nullification. Calhoun and his followers had no greater enemy than the Greenville oracle whose zest in echoing the Jackson toast on the Union was a local tradition for many years. Johnson had a more comprehensive knowledge of the Constitution than the President he had adopted as model, for, despite his early educational shortcomings, he had studious qualities that Old Hickory lacked. There are no signs that Jackson had ever studied the writings of Madison and Hamilton, but the "mechanic statesman's" first-hand acquaintance with these constitutional authorities constantly illuminated his orations. Johnson was a stump speaker in the days when that expression had its literal meaning; his manner, too, was the loud, sometimes obstreperous oratory associated with the recently leveled forest; but his outgivings frequently possessed substance, a genuine knowledge of American history and institutions. This same familiarity he displayed when his mountaineer admirers, much to the disgust of the more dignified elements, sent the tailor to Congress, and afterwards to the Senate. Here he developed two antagonisms, — and on antagonism the Johnsonian temperament thrived, — both of them based on a worship of the Constitution.

It would be difficult to say whether Johnson, at this stage of his career, held in greater detestation his colleague Charles Sumner, spokesman of Boston abolitionists, or his colleague Jefferson Davis, advocate of secession. Both offended for the same reason, for both regarded the Constitution as something to be defied when it interfered with a favorite policy. The principles of both, if logically persisted in, meant destruction to the Union. Few speeches from the Senate have resounded over the nation as did Johnson's address on the "Constitutionality and Righteousness of Secession" delivered on South Carolina's withdrawal from the Union. He adopted his text from Madison, proving, to his own satisfaction at least, that this doctrine contravened the teachings of that great Virginian. John Marshall was summoned from the grave to assert the indestructibility of the Union. "Though I fought against Lincoln [1] I love my country; I love the Constitution. Let us therefore rally around the altar of our Constitution and swear that it and the Union shall be saved as 'Old Hickory' Jackson did in 1832. Senators! My blood, my existence, I would give to save this Union."

All the time the fiery Tennessean was delivering this onslaught

[1] As a good Democrat Johnson had supported Breckinridge in the campaign of 1860.

on his fellow Southerners, the Senate gallery was filled with Southern sympathizers, men and women, who created such a hubbub of opposition that for moments he could scarcely be heard. Fellow Senators from the South kept interrupting, and even threatened violence. As the orator left the Chamber and proceeded on foot to his quarters in the Kirkwood House, adherents of the Southern states greeted him with yells and hisses. For months afterward he was burned in effigy all over the seceded South. Letters and telegrams threatening death fell in heaps on his desk. On his return to Tennessee Johnson experienced more direct forms of disapprobation. The railroad journey through Virginia degenerated into a continuous riot. Howling mobs assailed the train as it passed through the towns; when it halted, local roughs attempted to board the Johnson car and administer physical chastisement. At Lynchburg they succeeded. Johnson was jerked from his seat, a halter thrown around his neck, and the champion of the Constitution was dragged in the direction of the most convenient tree. "Don't hang him, boys," one old-timer shouted, "his friends in Tennessee are planning to do that, and we should n't deprive them of the pleasure." Whether this argument saved him is not certain; however, Johnson succeeded in escaping from the crowd with no more serious affront than a pulled nose, this feature being of a generous size inviting such familiarities. The next few weeks, however, Johnson kept at his valiant work, stumping many of the most disorderly parts of Tennessee, armed with ever-ready pistol, denouncing secession, crying for loyalty to the fundamental law, seeking to keep his state within the Union lines. So far as his own section, east or mountain Tennessee, was concerned, the plea was successful; the state as a state joined the Confederacy, but the Johnson part remained faithful to the flag throughout the war, and contributed thousands of volunteers to the Union Army. Johnson wished, following the example of West Virginia, to detach eastern Tennessee from the present commonwealth and organize a new state, but this plan miscarried. On the reassembling of Congress in June, however, the intrepid statesman returned to Washington and resumed his position in the Senate.

His presence in that Chamber has a constitutional significance that was not fully realized until Reconstruction began. In 1861, the United States theoretically included in its membership twenty-two Senators from the eleven seceded states, but only one of them, Andrew Johnson of Tennessee, was found at his station. All the rest abandoned their Federal associations and betaken themselves to the land of the Confederacy. Johnson himself represented a state that had gone through the motions of secession. Even loyal Northerners began to question his right to sit in such an assembly. But his action was consistent with the policy on which the rebellion was being fought. It was in complete accordance with the doctrine that Johnson had proclaimed from the Senate floor a few months previously. Had he not summoned Madison, Hamilton, John Marshall, and Andrew Jackson to substantiate his thesis that no state could constitutionally secede? Had not Lincoln proclaimed the same doctrine as justification for calling armies into existence to put down the "Insurrection"? That is, all the eleven states that had withdrawn were still members of the Union. Their departed Senators — Jefferson Davis, Judah P. Benjamin, and the rest — were still United States Senators, temporarily absent from duty. And so Tennessee, despite its act of "so-called secession," was still in the Union, and Johnson, as one of its Senators, was constitutionally entitled to occupy his seat. Lincoln accepted this doctrine and was grateful to Johnson for upholding it, not only in his campaigns at home, but in his personal appearance on the Senate floor. So grateful that, when Grant had cleared most of Tennessee of Confederate armies and the time had come to arrange for its Reconstruction, Johnson was selected to head the movement. He was made military governor of Tennessee, with the rank of brigadier general. His commission, dated March 4, 1862, was Lincoln's first step in Reconstruction. So loyally did Johnson perform his task that, in 1864, he was nominated for Vice President of the United States on the ticket with Abraham Lincoln. On the night of April 14, 1865, the assassination made him head of the nation. From "mechanic alderman" of Greenville, Tennessee, Johnson had advanced by the usual grades of political promotion to become "mechanic President" of the United States.

Despite the man's record of patriotism, the country did not acclaim this unexpected elevation with enthusiasm. There were certain unfavorable episodes in the man's career. His inauguration as Vice President did not hold forth high hopes that the new office would be filled with dignity. The fact is that, on this great occasion, the new Vice President was indubitably drunk, and the wandering harangue delivered on taking the oath, more redolent than usual of references to "plebeians" and the incumbent's rise from poverty, caused Charles Sumner to cover his face with his hands and shed tears. This, one of the most celebrated and certainly one of the most calamitous sprees in history, was actually to have its influence on the development of the Constitution, for it did much to prepare the public mind for the impeachment of Johnson that took place three years subsequently. In a twinkling it transformed the picture, up to that time held by the grateful North, of Andrew Johnson as the one great Southern leader who had seen the issue clear, into that of "the drunken tailor at the other end of the avenue," as Thad Stevens called him. Johnson has had to wait until the present generation for vindication on this, as on so many other matters. All his recent biographers, however, have shown that he was by no means a man of intemperate habits, and that it was part of the misfortunes persistently dogging his Presidential career that the one occasion when he had made this spectacle of himself was precisely the one when he should have appeared to best advantage. They insist that he reached Washington ill and fatigued, that his nerves needed soothing in view of the prospect, and that the strong drink taken just before ascending the rostrum produced these deplorable consequences. Johnson, despite this sad lapse, was really one of the most seemly living men who ever adorned great office. As domestic in his tastes as Andrew Jackson, he far surpassed that statesman in dignified manners and careful accoutrement. (The second Andrew had not been a tailor in vain; he was a fashion plate in dress, was always exquisitely barbered, and was one of the few public men of his era who took a daily bath.) But this "bad step," as Lincoln called it, has overbalanced all other excellencies of deportment.[1] Until the work of rehabilitation began, the average American's conception of Andrew Johnson was that of the man who got drunk when inaugurated Vice President, who used the Presidency as a vehicle for restoring "rebellious" Southerners and Northern copperheads to power, and who escaped removal from office — which he richly deserved — by the margin of one vote. Things are seen in a different light to-day. He has a growing importance in the story of American political stability, and should be regarded as a martyr to the Constitution. He was the sacrifice apparently needed to show that the Presidency was not to be regarded as the prey of excited, fanatical, and dishonest politicians; that in dignity, power, and security it remained aloof from the passions of the moment. Had the impeachment of Johnson succeeded, that office would have been so diminished, would have so become the sport of legislators, that the constitutional fabric would have been shaken almost beyond repair. It has been the strange fate of the "drunken tailor" to enhance enormously the dignity of the Presidential office.

[1] See the biographies, R. W. Winston (1928), Lloyd Paul Stryker (1929), and George Fort Milton (1930).

And this is the main significance of Johnson's career in the present connection. There is no need of telling again the long and ghastly story of Reconstruction. That subject also has been canvassed by many modern historians, and with their verdict there is no occasion, in the main, for disagreement. The merits of the sad transactions of the ten years succeeding the Civil War can now be regarded as definitely fixed. Lincoln was right, and so was Johnson, who followed closely in his track; Stevens, Sumner, Boutwell, Wade, Stanton, and other fanatics who elevated the negro to power were damnably wrong. Whether their motives were as evil as those commonly attributed to them, or their main failings those of an overzealous humanitarianism, an idealism that pays no regard to the commonplaces of existence — on this point there can be some argument. But the result, whatever the inspiration, provides the sorriest chapter in our history. Never has the Constitution suffered greater attacks than in this unscrupulous era. That it finally emerged more powerful than before is only another instance of its vitality. As to the constitutionality of the Reconstruction measures, there is now little dispute. Probably no lawyer of authority to-day would undertake their defense on this ground. Their main purpose was to destroy the governments that had been created in the Southern states by the slow processes of history. The Virginia of Washington, Madison, and Jefferson, as an independent sovereignty, vanished from the map and, joined by North Carolina, became Military District No. 1. State constitutions, state legislatures, state courts, state departments, state authority of all kinds disappeared, and in their stead arose the military power of a brigadier general of the United States Army. The one way in which a one-time state could regain its former status was to adopt a constitutional amendment which gave the franchise to recently emancipated slaves and practically disfranchised the white population — in other words, to convert itself into something resembling a Haitian or Santo Domingan republic, under negro rule.

Modern constitutionalists have not wasted much time on this scheme of disunion. There is no disagreement with the dictum of Professor Burgess: "There was hardly a line in the entire bill which would stand the test of the Constitution." It was "tantamount to the creation of a new sort of Union with another kind of Constitution by an Act of Congress." President Johnson's message, vetoing this Reconstruction Act, is one of the greatest state papers in Presidential literature. In it he abundantly sustains the judgment passed upon him by his Secretary of the Navy, Gideon Welles, as "the defender of the Constitution." This Constitution, said Johnson, "is the only system of free government which we can hope to have as a nation. When it ceases to be the rule of our conduct, we may perhaps take our choice between complete anarchy, a consolidated despotism, and a total dissolution of the Union; but national liberty regulated by law will have passed beyond our reach. It is the best frame of government the world ever saw. No other is or can be so well adapted to the genius, labor or habits of the American people. Combining the strength of a great empire with unspeakable blessings of local self-government, having a central power to defend the general interests, and recognizing the authority of the states as the guardian of industrial rights, it is the 'sheet anchor of our safety abroad and our peace at home.' . . . It was to punish the gross crime of defying the Constitution and to vindicate its supreme authority that we carried on a bloody war of four years' duration. . . . Shall we now acknowledge that we sacrificed a million lives and expended billions of treasure to enforce a Constitution which is not worthy of respect or preservation?"

It was for upholding views of this kind — for maintaining the integrity of the Constitution — that Andrew Johnson suffered the greatest humiliation ever inflicted upon an American President. Of the thirty-two men who have filled that office, the Tennessee tailor is the only one to have undergone impeachment. He was the only one to be haled before the bar of the Senate to answer charges of having committed "high treason and misdemeanors." Few historians to-day take any other view than that Johnson's trial under this constitutional charge was purely political. That he had violated any valid law or any constitutional regulation is now hardly pretended. The purpose of the investigators was to remove from office an executive who was constantly opposing their infractions of the fundamental charter. The chief engineer of the trial, Ben Butler, practically admitted this charge. Impeachment, he insisted, was not a judicial proceeding at all. "High crimes and misdemeanors" need not necessarily be proved. "Common report of misconduct" was adequate reason for removing a President. "If any man stands in the way of the great march of this country to honor, glory, peace, unity, happiness, liberty and law he must be taken out of the way." That is, if two thirds of the Senate regarded the incumbent as an unworthy President, they could depose him, despite the fact that he had been the free choice of the citizenry. If he promoted policies unpopular with a Congressional majority, that was justification for sending him back to private life! Impeachment, in this view, was merely a convenient device for getting rid of a Chief Executive of whom Congress disapproves.

No statesman of that time saw the real issue so clearly as Johnson's able and loyal Secretary of the Navy, Gideon Welles. No man was so outraged by this attempt to substitute the despotism of an unfriendly Congress for the rule provided in the Constitution. Over and over again in his diary does this honest and clear-visioned Connecticut Yankee lay bare the motives inspiring the Congressional onslaught. "It is a party scheme for party purposes, not for any criminal or wrong act of the President. . . . There is nothing judicial or fair in this proceeding. It is sheer partisanship with most of them, a deliberate conspiracy with the few. A committee is sitting in secret — a foul conspiracy — trying to hunt up charges and evidence against as pure, as honest, as patriotic chief magistrate as we have ever had. It is for his integrity they conspire against him. . . . The whole impeachment scheme is a piece of party persecution, which, if successful to party, will be ruinous to the country. . . . It is like slaughtering, shooting down the faithful sentinel because of his fidelity in standing to his post. . . . The President is arraigned for doing his duty and striving to defend the Constitution in conformity with his oath. The Constitution-breakers are trying the Constitution-defender; the law-breakers are passing condemnation on the law-supporter; the conspirators are sitting in judgment on the man who would not enter into their conspiracy, who was, and is, faithful to his oath, his country, the Union, and the Constitution. What a spectacle! And, if successful, what a blow to free government! What a commentary on popular intelligence and public virtue!"

V

And the Presidency was only one department that the fanatics were seeking to subvert. Their campaign was aimed at what was perhaps even higher authority. Side by side with this effort to seize the executive office, the radicals were making warfare on the Supreme Court. "There is a conspiracy maturing," writes Welles, January 11, 1867. "How can they reduce the states to the condition of corporations, territorialize them, deprive them of their original reserved and guaranteed constitutional rights, without the aid of the judiciary? How can they get control of the Court except by enlarging its members? If the number is to be increased, how can they get Radicals except by displacing Johnson and getting Wade [1] or one like him in his place?" That all these Reconstruction acts would come before the Supreme Court was the general expectation; that the Court would set them aside as unconstitutional was the opinion of constitutional lawyers. Inevitably, in an *impasse* of this kind, — before and since, — this tribunal became an object of suspicion and hate. The Court must not be permitted, on constitutional grounds, to step between Congress and its will and set aside its legislation. The resources that were now brought forward to forestall this calamity have a familiar sound. There is really nothing new in American history! Each generation seems to revive all the departed ghosts of its predecessors. The first move, as Gideon Welles foresaw, was not to increase the membership of the Supreme Court, but to decrease it. A good deal has been heard recently of adding to the size of the Court, in order to obtain a friendly majority, but Congress, in the late sixties, hoped to achieve the same result by the reverse process. On Johnson's accession the number of judges was the same sacred nine as are found to-day, but the death of two left a court of seven. Why not keep it at this figure? Why let the President appoint two new judges who,

[1] Benjamin F. Wade, of Ohio. As president of the Senate he would become President in case of a vacancy in that office. Despite his interest in the result, Wade was one of the leaders in this attempt to displace Johnson.

if the unpopular Johnson followed the practice usual with all his predecessors and successors, would certainly be men generally sympathetic with his attitude? Congress therefore passed legislation limiting the membership of the Supreme Bench to seven. The idea was, unblushingly, to forestall any Johnson appointments.

That the Congressional leaders had reason in plenty to fear an independent judiciary, events disclosed. In April 1866, the Court rendered a decision that meant death to the Reconstruction programme. The rule of communities in peace time by military power was the point in question. Thaddeus Stevens's Reconstruction Act had established such military rule in the Southern states, once in rebellion but now at peace. Brigadier generals had been given authority to set up military courts and try civilians for all breaches of law. The Supreme Court, in the Milligan case, had already decided that such procedure was unconstitutional. Military courts could be established only, this judgment propounded, in places that were scenes of war, insurrection, or civic disturbance. Only when the ordinary civil courts were unavailable could the military power step in. The principle of this decision apparently made invalid nearly all the Reconstruction laws. "Martial law can never exist," said Judge David Davis, "when the courts are open, and in the proper and unobstructed exercise of their jurisdiction. It is also confined to the locality of actual war." How, then, could martial law be introduced in the Southern states in 1867? In all of them the war had come to an end; in all, the ordinary courts of peace time were normally functioning; under the Milligan decision, therefore, citizens could not be summarily hustled before military tribunals and tried and sentenced for their crimes. Yet this is precisely what the Reconstruction Act provided — that is, it had established seats of so-called justice which the Supreme Court had pilloried as unconstitutional. A test case was now pending adjudication. A Mississippi editor named McCardle had published statements about the military governor of his district, General Ord, which that potentate regarded as actionable, and, for this offense, had been tried and convicted by a military court. McCardle promptly appealed to the civil law, making the plea that, under the Milligan decision, the proceeding transgressed the Constitution. The verdict of the Supreme Court was expected to be delivered in the latter part of February, 1868. Little doubt was generally entertained as to what this decision would be. The "seven old men," if they followed the rule they had themselves laid down in the Milligan case, would sustain McCardle's plea and pronounce unconstitutional the law

under which he had been tried.   Such a decision would practically
destroy the Reconstruction Act and cast down in ruins the elaborate
fabric which the Congressional leaders had so laboriously constructed.

As always happens in a crisis of this kind, the guns of the enemy
were directly trained against the power that was meditating this
frustration of its will.   For the moment, Southern "rebels" ceased
to be the prime object of aversion; the Supreme Court itself assumed that odious rôle.   Evidently the moment had arrived to
"clip" that body of power and thus forestall intercession on its
part in the interest of the Constitution.   And the particular method
of attack now devised by the reformers was the one which had been
suggested in similar contingencies many times before.   No more
majority decisions!   Require a two-thirds vote in decisions that
set aside an act of Congress!   How reminiscent, almost hackneyed,
the remedy seems!   A bill embodying this popular restriction was
introduced and passed the House, but failed in the Senate.   Bitter
as was the antagonism felt in the Upper Chamber against the Court,
and fearful as were such leaders as Sumner and Wade that the
Reconstruction plan was facing dissolution, that body was still too
conservative, still too respectful of the judiciary, to adopt the plan
which had found favor with the impetuous majority of the Lower
Chamber.

Only for a brief period, however, did the Senate maintain its
forbearance.   It did not change its view on the two-thirds proposal,
but it presently joined the House of Representatives in a scheme to
"clip the wings" of the Court which went much further, which,
indeed, almost obliterated that body as an interpreter of the Constitution.   As the time drew near for the dreaded McCardle decision,
tension and hostility increased in fervor.   Nothing like the hatred
which now burst into flame against "the world's greatest tribunal"
had been known in the fiercest Jeffersonian days.   Newspapers, Congressmen, pulpit orators, and other makers of public opinion participated in the fury.   The present generation is inclined to think of
"attacks" on the Supreme Court as emanating almost exclusively from
the "underprivileged" — labor leaders, discouraged farmers, social-
ists, Communists, and other "subversive elements."   But the campaign of 1868 was not linked to men and classes of this type;
the advocates of "curbing" judicial review in those days belonged,
for the larger part, to those whom John Adams called "respectable" — the "well born" and "propertied" elements.   They were
the millions of patriotic citizens who had loyally supported the nation

in four years of war, had fought its battles and led its armies. These sections of society, in the main, supported Reconstruction legislation, believing that only in this way could the fruits of the war be won and Federal authority be reëstablished in the Southern states. To them the United States Supreme Court loomed as an ominous and sinister portent. Was it not about to intercede in behalf of "rebels," to do its part in restoring control of the government to "traitors" who had done their best to annihilate the Union? What Southerners had failed to accomplish by arms, they now seemed likely to achieve by the help of the judicial power.

"The Reconstruction acts," wrote the Indianapolis *Journal,* "are full of the rights and liberties of millions of men; and to have these stricken down by the decision of some old fossil on the Supreme Bench whose political opinion belongs to a past era would be an outrage on humanity." Similar quotations could be extracted from the most dignified journals of the time. Clergymen like Henry Ward Beecher joined in the pursuit. All this reasoning was topsy-turvy, but it inspired action against the hated tribunal more drastic than anything suggested in recent controversies. Nor was the problem a difficult one; the Constitution itself pointed the way. Under that instrument, no branch of government is so vulnerable as the judiciary. The powers of Congress and the Executive are stipulated with a fair degree of certainty, but those of the courts are left in most indefinite form. The control which Congress possesses over its cognate branch is almost without limit. It is hardly too much to say that the legislative department, by passing a few laws, can reduce the courts practically to inanition. Nearly all the strength the courts possess is derived from the Judiciary Act of 1789, with amending laws since passed; without these Congressional grants the courts could not function, and what Congress has created it can destroy. Old Oliver Ellsworth, the chief agent in establishing the American judicial system, was not the Constitution; he was merely a Senator from Connecticut, and his great Judiciary Act was an act of Congress, which Congress can at any moment repeal, in whole or in part.

The atmosphere of 1868 was full of threats of this kind. Did not the Supreme Court know that Congress could all but end its existence? Were Supreme Court justices ignorant of the fact that a simple vote in the legislative branch could exterminate all the district and circuit courts in the nation? That a Supreme Court of one or two judges, drawing a nominal salary, — a dollar a year for example, — would fulfill all the requirements of the Constitution?

More important still, that Congress, according to Article III, Section 2, could "except" from the jurisdiction of the Supreme Court such matters as its wisdom might suggest? And it was this clause which the foes of "judicial usurpation" now pressed into service. According to a law passed as recently as 1867, Congress had extended to the courts jurisdiction "in all cases where any person may be restrained of his or her liberty, in violation of any treaty or law of the United States." It was under this law that the ex-rebel McCardle was seeking release, and under this that, with the aid of Chief Justice Chase and his associates, the Reconstruction programme was expected to fall. How simple was the problem! Another act of Congress, repealing this provision, would throw the case out of court and prevent the judges from passing upon the issue. Congress could, figuratively speaking, walk up to the highest court just as it was preparing to issue its edict, roughly lay its hand across the judicial mouth, and prevent it from speaking.

That is what Congress now proceeded to do. Only a few lines, passed by both Houses and repassed by a two-thirds vote when Andrew Johnson vetoed the new law, sufficed for the application of the gag. "Judicial review," so far as the constitutionality of Reconstruction acts was concerned, ceased to exist. Had Congress, in May 1935, on the eve of the decision on President Roosevelt's National Recovery system, passed a law removing the whole matter from the jurisdiction of the Supreme Court, the famous unanimous judgment could never have been rendered, and that entire organization would conceivably be in operation to-day. There seems no question that the national legislature would have had constitutional authority for such interposition.

And not only constitutional authority, but precedent. For the enemies of judicial review in 1868 repealed the clause of the amendment to the Judiciary Act which gave McCardle the right to take his case to the highest Court. They did so just as the Court was preparing to issue its decree. Thus the Reconstruction Acts, which few lawyers to-day would pronounce constitutional, were never passed upon by the seven "old fossils" of 1868. But was this proceeding in itself constitutional? Did Congress have the right, by passing a simple law, to snatch these cases from under the very nose of the judges; to silence them at the very moment they were girding themselves for interference? The best authority decided that Congress possessed this power. That was the United States Supreme Court itself. For in due course — in a few months — this newly asserted power of Congress came before that tribunal. In a decision rendered by Chief Justice Chase, the Court said that the act of Congress depriving it of jurisdiction was authorized by the Constitution. Moreover, this decision against itself was no four-to-three affair; it was unanimous. "Judicial duty," wrote the Chief Justice, "is not less fitly performed by declining ungranted jurisdiction than in exercising firmly that which the Constitution and the laws confer." The Constitution confers appellate powers upon the courts "with such exceptions and under such regulations as the Congress shall make."

That other Yankee, Gideon Welles, whose diary performs for this era the same sombre service of Greek chorus that the Adams diary did for a former generation, was aghast at the development. "These are indeed evil times," he wrote. "The action of Congress and particularly the Senate, in taking from the Supreme Court certain powers to prevent a decision in the McCardle case is shameful and forebodes an unhappy future for our country. There is no exercise of reason, judgment, intelligence or patriotism of the Radical majority on any subject whereby their party is affected. Truth, justice, right, laws of Constitution are broken down and trampled under foot by Senators."

"Congress, with the acquiescence of the country," said Benjamin R. Curtis, "has subdued the Supreme Court as well as the President."

This particular battle the Reconstructionists won, but in its great objective the Congressional party failed. By the margin of one vote Andrew Johnson escaped removal from office. In its ultimate bearing upon the Constitution that was as great a gain as the loss suffered by the temporary eclipse of the judiciary department. For had that proceeding succeeded, impeachment would have become a permanent engine of political manipulation. The fundamental question at stake in this proceeding to displace a President was the same as that involved in the impeachment of Justice Chase in Jefferson's administration. Both trials were founded on the same clause of the Constitution, that which gives the Senate power to remove civil officers, by a two-thirds vote, for "treason, bribery or other high crimes and misdemeanors." Johnson certainly had not committed treason; no man had the effrontery to charge this simple, honest soul with bribery; neither could there be laid at his door any high crimes and misdemeanors. His one cause of offending was that his policy as President had proved obnoxious to the ruling majority in Congress; he had been a constant obstruction to their schemes for establishing the rule of negroes in the Southern states. Therefore his displacement was desired. The Johnson trial was the last attempt made to enforce the Jeffersonian dogma that impeachment was not necessarily a judicial proceeding, in which definite evidence of crime should be presented, but a political contrivance for cashiering public officers obnoxious to the Congressional majority. John Quincy Adams had described the Jeffersonian theory as "nothing more than an inquiry, by the two houses of Congress, whether the office of any public man might not be better filled by another." The scheme failed in 1804–1805, in the trial of Justice Chase, and failed again in 1868 in the impeachment of Andrew Johnson.

Thus in 1865 and 1868 two great constitutional principles were established by events, not by the interpretation of the Supreme Court. The Civil War established irrevocably the unconstitutionality of secession. It cemented the indestructible union of indestructible states. The verdict of the Senate in 1868, sitting as a Court of Impeachment, put a quietus on another heresy that had broken out periodically since 1787. It was now determined, for all time, that impeachment was a trial, not to settle a political argument, but to establish crime. Since 1868 Congress has had more than one President "on its hands" whom it would have liked to dismiss by the simple mechanics of a party vote, but the precedent in the Andrew Johnson case has forced it to refrain.

Had Johnson been compelled to leave the White House and retire to his home in eastern Tennessee, there would have been set up in this country something comparable to the Parliamentary system of England. The United States would have instituted a cumbrous and undignified order of Congressional government. All Presidents, judges of the Supreme Court and other courts, would have held power subject to a two-thirds majority in the two Houses. The Constitution, as adopted by the Fathers, providing a decidedly different scheme of things, would have been overthrown. Considered from this point of view, the impeachment is one of the great episodes in the history of that instrument.

VI

For this desirable outcome the nation was indebted to the Chief Justice of the United States, Salmon P. Chase. After considerable hesitation Lincoln had selected his Secretary of the Treasury, in 1864, to succeed Taney, dead at the age of eighty-seven; an appointment that was justified, if by nothing else, by the firmness and regard for constitutional procedure which marked Chase's conduct of the Johnson trial. From the first, the Chief Justice set his face against politicians of the Ben Butler and Ben Wade stripe, who sought to make the whole affair a kind of inquisition, in which accusation should take the place of evidence, political expediency the place of justice, and the methods of the hustings supplant the orderly procedure of a court. In curbing violence of this kind, in insisting that the tribunal was a judicial trial and not a party convention, in affirming that the rules of testimony usually prevailing in a court should rule this attempt to remove a President from office, Chase gave dignity and honesty to a convocation which, in its purposes, decidedly lacked both these qualities. It is not too much, therefore, to attribute the fortunate conclusion largely to the Chief Justice. The man's very presence served as a sobering influence. For Chase was one of the most commanding figures in the American panorama. No man, save Webster, exercised greater weight by the sheer energy of presence. More than six feet tall, with bulky but symmetrical body, a great head, like Webster's, keen blue eyes, solid jaws, tightly pressed lips, a face which, on the whole agreeable, even benevolent, still reflected the reserve and the consciousness of power and inner rectitude that are inseparable from the Puritan character — in this majestic, massive frame, America possesses one of its few Jovelike public characters. No man ever quite looked the Senator like Webster, and no man quite the Chief Justice like Salmon P. Chase.

The comparison could be carried further, even into details. Both were New Hampshire boys, both graduates of Dartmouth, both lawyers who had struggled from the hardships of the farm to high position at the bar. Chase was born at Cornish, about twenty miles from Webster's childhood home, in 1808 — too late to feel that personal association with Revolutionary heroes that did so much to frame Webster's ideas. But Chase's early years had reminders in plenty of a sturdy past. He came of yeoman stock — that stock in which the task of winning a livelihood from unfruitful soil did not prevent the cultivation of the mind. The sight that Chase presented, that of a boy working in the fields and simultaneously studying Greek, was not an unusual one at the time. This was more or less the usual thing and did not signify that Chase was a deep scholar, as he was not; his record at Dartmouth was not high, though he did develop a strong and lifelong taste for miscellaneous reading. Between his childhood at Cornish and his life at Keene — to which latter place the family moved soon after Salmon's birth — there came an interregnum in Ohio, Chase having been sent there at the age of eleven to be trained by his uncle, Philander Chase, first Episcopal bishop in that frontier state. It is owing to this sojourn at Cincinnati, where, overlooking the Ohio River, Chase could see the slaves at work on Kentucky farms, that, when he became an abolitionist, his brand of the noisome creed was of a Western, not a New England, flavor. The quality of slavery was much gentler in Kentucky than in the lower South; Chase, unlike Garrison, thus knew the thing at first hand and, like most Westerners, was careful to disassociate his campaign from that of the Garrison school. Thus he was no advocate of destroying the Constitution to get rid of slavery; rather he would use that instrument as an engine for ending human bondage, even going so far as to develop the theory — palpably unsound — that the Constitution offered no protection to the institution. Runaway negroes were also common sights during Chase's residence at his Uncle Philander's home, and these phenomena laid the groundwork of the boy's future career as "the Attorney General for fugitive slaves."

Although at the age of fourteen Chase returned to the paternal roof in New Hampshire and spent four years at Dartmouth, his Ohio experiences clearly exercised a stronger pull than did those of New England. After a brief time at Washington, where, as schoolteacher, he became an intimate of the family of William West. he scrambled together enough knowledge of the law to leave for Ohio and open an office in Cincinnati. Neither then, nor afterward, was Chase a great lawyer. Indeed, when he came up for examination before Justice Cranch, of the Supreme Court of the District of Columbia, that learned judge was not impressed by the legal attainments of the handsome young man. Only when informed that the candidate intended to practise in Ohio did Cranch consent to sign his certificate; for that wild region, he said, Chase probably had learning enough! A striking physical appearance, a keen intelligence, and attractive manners were more important on that frontier than an intimate knowledge of constitutional law. Perhaps Cranch discerned, what speedily proved to be the fact, that the social and political concerns of Ohio would occupy Chase far more than the dingy routine of its courts. The Western attraction must have been strong, for Chase left Washington at a great moment — with the echoes of the Webster-Hayne debate sounding in his ears, and just as the scene was being set for Jackson's attack on Calhoun and nullification. Such topics, however, were almost as lively on the Ohio as on the Potomac, and proved sufficiently vital to turn the young man's energies into their natural channel — politics and the public platform. A decent practice in commercial law was quickly acquired; in all likelihood Chase could have enlarged this to great personal profit, but those two forces at work in the man — a desire for personal distinction, selfish ambition if you will, and a genuine sense of public duty — quickly made him a leader in the cause that was then agitating the public. Although Chase's vanity and pursuit of station were his great weaknesses and frequently displayed themselves in petty fashion, the fact is that neither as seeker of governorship or Senatorship in Ohio nor as seeker of the Presidency in the nation did he ever sacrifice principle to ambition.

To relate his public career, from his appearance in Cincinnati in 1830 to his accession to Lincoln's cabinet in 1861, would be simply to tell once more the story of the slavery agitation. His work in this was so important that when he resumed his Washington life Chase was a great public figure, and when Lincoln expressed his determination to gather in his official family the ablest members of his party, Chase automatically became one of his counselors. The magnanimity of Lincoln's character appeared to particular advantage in his relations with this New Englander. The two men had little in common — were indeed unsympathetic. Chase was a polished man of the world, grand in manner, showy, if not profound, in intellect, the head of a brilliant social circle the glory of which was his daughter, Kate Chase, beautiful, dazzling in charm and conversation, even, it was whispered in Washington, more gifted mentally than her father, and the real inciter of the unsleeping desire for the White House that urged him on. Beside all this, Lincoln and his household cut a poor figure, but Chase did not have a vestige of the understanding and humor that were Lincoln's main assets. Chase would have been insulted had Lincoln not invited him into the cabinet; once in it his whole behavior was condescending. In 1856 and 1860 he regarded himself as the inevitable Republican candidate, and how a benighted party could prefer this clodhopper from Illinois in preference to himself he could never comprehend. Like William H. Seward, he expected Lincoln to transfer the administration into his hands, and his disapproval of the Presidential policy, especially when it struck out independently, was mighty.

As the three years Chase remained in the cabinet were full of trials for his chief, Lincoln submitted to the man's disrespect and even his disloyalty — Chase's angling for the Presidential nomination in 1864, while still in the cabinet, amounted to that — for the same reason that he endured other bad-tempered subordinates. Despite McClellan's frequently insulting behavior, Lincoln declared that he would hold the General's horse if that would help to win the war; and he ignored the petulance of Chase for the same public reason. As Secretary of the Treasury, for a time at least the man was indispensable to the country. As the war went on, however, Chase's frequent resignations — whenever the President became especially annoying to his Secretary, Chase's resignation would promptly fall on Lincoln's desk, to be ignored and pigeonholed — reached the limit of Lincoln's patience. The crisis came in June 1864, over the appointment of an Assistant Treasurer of the United States. The matter, like all previous difficulties, was susceptible of adjustment, but Chase could not forbear the luxury of having another resignation declined. When Lincoln promptly accepted it the Secretary was the most astonished man in Washington. He never wished or expected to leave the administration. Sumner tried to comfort him. Necker had once been ousted as Finance Minister of France, but, when conditions grew desperate, had been recalled. That would probably be Chase's fortune, he said. To which Chase replied, "Lincoln is not Louis the Sixteenth" — showing that, despite his failure to appreciate all the man's qualities, he had learned something of his seriousness and determination.

So far as anyone could see, Chase's public career was at an end. His daughter Kate was frantic, for her father's advancement was the one thing for which she lived and intrigued. One possibility loomed. The Presidential nomination of 1868 was only three years ahead. Again letters went forth from Chase to his friends: "I think the time has come to organize." Chase's hunger for this office is one of the most pitiful episodes in political history. It is pitiful because there was really only one person in the United States — at least one person of influence — who desired to see this statesman President. That was Chase himself. Yet he was irrefragably convinced that the nation, in all sections and all social grades, was clamoring for him as candidate. The Presidential story is full of men whose lives were blighted by aspiration for this post; yet most of these men commanded a large following who ceaselessly worked in their interest. There was never any such Chase contingent, no faction that zealously wished to promote his ambition. No one, except Chase and Kate, really grieved at his repeated failures to stir the party breast. In 1856, 1860, 1864, 1868, 1872, Chase was writing letters to friends, promoting campaign biographies of himself, making ostentatious tours, displaying his undoubtedly Presidential person, cultivating newspaper editors and reporters, constantly, in public and private, proclaiming himself the destined man — and all this time there was hardly a ripple of response. He was an able and honest man, who would have adorned the office far better than many who have filled it, but his cold intellectual qualities had no attraction for the crowd. Even his elevation as Chief Justice did not still the cankerworm. The Supreme Bench merely became the throne from which he repeatedly put forth this ambition. When in 1868 his party ignored all solicitations and selected Grant, Chase turned to the Democrats, offering, in most humiliating fashion, to become their champion against his ungrateful partisans. In 1872, prematurely old, — he was only sixty-four, — suffering from a recent stroke of paralysis, the poor man again raised his hopes, as a candidate of the Democrats, and it was not until a second attack of his malady, in 1873, ended his life that his feeble grasp on this constantly fleeting aspiration was relaxed. This political ambition must be kept in mind in estimating Chase's work as Chief Justice. It undoubtedly influenced his judgment at the crisis of his judicial career. Indeed, those who deprecate — as did the framers of the Constitution — the coddling of political ambitions by members of the judiciary can find no more lamentable text than the career of Salmon Portland Chase.

Lincoln, when he permitted Chase's departure from the cabinet, was aware of the man's ambitions and well knew that, in 1864, his Secretary had hoped to supplant him. Things of this sort, however, he never let affect his official behavior. For some time before Taney's death there was a general feeling that Chase was the man to succeed him; the political world that regarded Chase as an impossible

Presidential candidate instinctively turned to him as an ideal Chief Justice. Lincoln had given encouragement to this consensus, but after the man's not too dignified exit, and his Presidential wire-pulling, Chase's chances for the leadership of the Court seemed lessened. Lincoln himself hesitated. Not, however, because of Chase's insubordination, or any personal animosity. Neither did the fact that Chase had not opened a law book in twenty years make him impossible as Chief Justice. But Lincoln did think that this desire for the Presidency was an undesirable attribute for the head of the Court. He was afraid that Chase would use the position as a springboard for the White House. That, Lincoln told his intimates, would detract from the even administration of justice and lower the Court still further — it had not yet recovered from the loss of prestige that followed the Dred Scott decision — in popular esteem. Lincoln's instinct in this, as in most things, was sure. In finally overcoming his doubt and sending in Chase's name, he for once acted against his better judgment. Yet to the end he was uneasy. "Will he be satisfied to remain Chief Justice?" he asked those friends who came urging the selection.

As already indicated, Lincoln's qualms were justified. Chase was not satisfied to remain Chief Justice, but continued to drive for what he regarded as a higher prize. And largely because of this he cannot be regarded as a great judge. Under him the Court did not regain the lofty standing it had lost under his predecessor; in fact it sank further. Chase's work as presiding officer in the Johnson trial is a great moment, but his administration, on the whole, was not distinguished. Under him the Court presented one anomaly. From 1789 to 1864, all the Chief Justices — Jay, Ellsworth, Marshall, Taney — were, in popular estimation, the greatest men on the Supreme Bench. That was not the fact under Chase. Several of his associates were abler lawyers and finer intellects. Chase recognized this himself. The man who dominated the Court in his time, according to the Chief Justice, was Samuel Freeman Miller, and other contemporaries who easily outshone Chase as jurist were Stephen J. Field — one of that famous group of brothers, others of whom were Cyrus, layer of the Atlantic cable, and David Dudley, leader of the New York bar — and Joseph P. Bradley.

Miller was one of the most interesting characters in the history of the tribunal. An appointee of Lincoln, he had many of Lincoln's qualities. One day in July 1862, Senator John Crittenden of Kentucky, standing in the lobby of the National Hotel in Washington, was accosted by a lumbering rustic stranger, who introduced himself as Mr. Miller, of Iowa. Crittenden, accustomed to eluding prospective office seekers, attempted to escape. "But," said the stranger, "I want to thank you for a piece of advice that you gave me when I was a young man. You advised me to leave Kentucky and settle in the West. I did so and have prospered." "I am glad to hear that you have done well," said the Senator, edging still further away. "What are you doing now?" "I am to be commissioned to-day Associate Justice of the United States Supreme Court." "Great God! Are you that man?" exclaimed Crittenden. This particular Miller he vividly recalled, though the frame now confronting him bore little resemblance to the young man who, at his suggestion, thirty years before had abandoned Kentucky for a new career on the distant prairie. A seat on the Supreme Court had been a prize Crittenden himself had pursued for years; he had actually been appointed by John Quincy Adams, only to fail of confirmation, and since then had been an almost perpetual candidate. And while he was spending these assiduous years in Washington, as Congressman, Senator, cabinet officer, hoping that each vacancy on the bench would prove his opportunity, this frontiersman, whom he had himself sent West, was building up the reputation and establishing the character that, in 1862, made him fit ideally into Lincoln's plans for "reorganizing" the Court. For this was one of Lincoln's ambitions, and he made no secret of his purpose. That Dred Scott decision which he had so brazenly criticized in his debates with Douglas still hung over the President like a judicial nightmare; he wanted judges who would see that it was reversed! Decrepitude was creeping on more than one of the jurists who had inflicted this blot on the nation — so Lincoln regarded it. By the time the Court reassembled in December 1861, there were three unfilled vacancies — two by death and one by the resignation of John A. Campbell of Alabama, who retired to throw in his lot with the Confederacy. Samuel F. Miller, of Iowa, Noah H. Swayne, of Ohio, and Lincoln's friend, David Davis, of Illinois, seemed to fulfill Lincoln's requirements — undeviating loyalty to the Union and to the Constitution, and complete sympathy with the Lincolnian war policies.

Thus Miller was one of those "country lawyers" who, elevated to the bench, frequently display larger than parochial talents. But law was with Miller an aftermath. The new profession came to him more or less as an accident. Born on a Kentucky farm in 1816, his first lucrative occupation was that of clerk in a country drugstore; this naturally led to an interest in the human body and its ills, with the result that Miller, after spending two years in the medical department of Transylvania University, opened an office as a physician. Visiting ailing human beings in the Cumberland Mountains, plying one's way across hardly perceptible trails on horseback, proved neither a profitable nor a self-respecting profession; medical science was at a low ebb, medical training the merest empiricism, and Miller, not too confident of his qualifications for playing with life and death, early sickened of the trade. As a matter of economy he shared an office with a lawyer, the possessor of a modest law library. In his frequent periods of unemployment the young doctor was accustomed to browse among these volumes. Their contents seemed to him far more interesting than the minute descriptions of the human system which had, up to that time, proved his intellectual pabulum. The more he read, the more fascinated Miller became, until finally, to the astonishment of the neighborhood, the doctor's shingle was removed from Miller's headquarters and another, "Attorney and Counsellor at Law," substituted. Meeting John J. Crittenden on one of the latter's stumping tours, he received the advice referred to above. Miller had another reason for wishing to begin life anew elsewhere. In Kentucky it seemed the general rule for upstanding citizens to possess slaves and hate slavery; this was the case with Miller. He was on the brink of giving his few black men freedom when the new constitution of Kentucky went into effect. This prohibited the residence in the state of negroes whose masters had set them free. Samuel Miller therefore took his "property" under his wing, departed for Keokuk, Iowa, gave them their liberty, and began his juristic career on a soil congenial to emancipation and its promoters.

In one sense the new profession proved to be a continuation of the old. Practising law in pioneer Iowa was as much an out-of-door occupation as practising medicine in Kentucky. Clients were found in a hundred places on the prairie, and circuit riding from county court to county court, frequently amid rain and snow, and camping in the open, not only added to the man's professional prestige but hardened his body, as they softened and made human his spirit. Though Miller did not realize it at the moment, these trips led directly to the United States Supreme Court. For Miller frequently crossed the Mississippi into Illinois, and here, at country taverns and in courtrooms, he met now and then another itinerant legal luminary. That Abraham Lincoln and the Keokuk attorney should find much in common was inevitable. They were both Ken-

tuckians, both frontiersmen, both absorbed in the political problems
of the time, both worshipers of the Union and the Constitution.
"It is my profound belief," Miller said afterward, "that the wisdom of man, unaided by inspiration, has produced no other writing as valuable to humanity," and this conviction, at a time when
its existence was a matter of constant discussion, must have been
conveyed by Miller to his fellow traveler. Lincoln, as he looked
upon his Iowa contemporary, saw a man whose pattern very much
resembled his own. Here was a circuit rider, a giant in frame,
broad-shouldered, large-boned, with a mammoth head, surmounted
by a mass of black hair always in disarray, great swinging arms
and long, lanky Lincolnian legs. There was a carelessness in his
attire and a carelessness in his manner and speech that would also
appeal to a lover of the natural man. And the humor that sparkled
in Miller's keen eyes kept even pace with Lincoln himself. No more
conversable soul ever sat before the fire in a country store, and the
man had a perpetual flow of stories that Lincoln, in all probability,
freely purloined for use in his political campaigns.

These traits give the clue also to Miller's quality as a lawyer.
A scholar's deep knowledge of the law he never had. In after
years his scholarly colleague on the Supreme Bench, Horace Gray,
of Massachusetts, used to lament that such a powerful mind was
not deeply grounded in the books. The trait for which he was
famous was common sense. As a practitioner, and afterward as
a Supreme Court justice, Miller possessed, above all else, what
lawyers call "legal instinct." He could divine the points at issue;
let others quote the authorities! His brain was as massive as his
body; the frankness and honesty that marked his social relations
appeared also in his search for justice, in which instant perception,
not the study of abstractions, invariably set him on the proper
track.

And so when, in 1862, appeals came to Lincoln from Iowa and
the Western regions to make use of this sturdy advocate in his
"reorganization" of the Supreme Court, the suggestion struck a
responsive chord. Miller, like Lincoln himself, had steadily advanced since the circuit-riding days. In the Western country he
stood eminent as one of the staunchest of Union men. Thus he
would well fit in with Lincoln's demand for judges who would
"uphold the war policies." He would be a wholesome antidote
to Taney, eagerly contravening Lincoln's notions of habeas corpus
and determined to set aside emancipation. That the nomination
would arouse unfavorable comment the President understood.

Miller was "unknown" — that is, unknown in the great law circles of more civilized America. But he quickly demonstrated that an unknown lawyer may have in him the makings of a great judge. Miller's first appearance disclosed a fine, if primitive and unornamented intellect. The biggest legal lights of the country began to quail under his searching gaze, always looking for the underlying truth, and his penetrating questions. At times Justice Miller's passion for the substratum and his hatred of unnecessary verbiage showed itself in irascible ways. His voice was frequently gruff, he had no love of fools, and long-winded arguments would start something resembling rage. One warm day Miller, sitting amid a group of somnolent brother justices, his neckband loosened, a fan wearily applied to a perspiring face, leaned over and broke into the endless argument of a particularly tedious advocate. "Damn it, Brown," he shouted, "come to the point!" "What point, Your Honor?" asked the startled lawyer. "I don't know," fairly yelled the jurist; "any point, some point!" Despite these impatient manifestations, when Miller died in 1890, after twenty-eight years' service on the bench, the tributes to him were such as few members have drawn from the profession. He had written more than eight hundred and fifty decisions, many of them landmarks in constitutional interpretation. He had sat under three Chief Justices, — Chase, Waite, and Fuller, — to all of whom he was unquestionably superior both in mental ability and in the endeavor to bring the Constitution into harmony with the new American world.

The era of Chase — from 1864 to 1873 — bridged the tumultuous gap between the end of the Civil War and modern America; the time of Miller, from 1862 to 1890, witnessed the transformation in American politics, finance, and social change that was the outcome of the railroad, the corporation, and the industrialization of the land. Upon many developments of this era Miller looked with an unfavoring eye. He intensely disliked Wall Street and stockjobbers. "They engage in no commerce," he said, "no trade, no manufactures, no agriculture. They produce nothing." Animosities of this kind not infrequently appeared in his opinions. Sometimes there were hard digs at his brother judges. He spoke in one of a decision which was reached by "a stretch of fancy, only to be indulged in railroad bond cases." "The capitalists" — and by these he meant those "who live solely by interest and dividends" — were about as popular with Miller as with the farmers of the West. "It is the most painful matter connected with my judicial life," he wrote in a letter, "that I am compelled to take part in a farce whose result is invariably the same, namely to give more to those who have already and to take away from those who have little, the little that they have." The appointment to the bench of men who had been identified with rich clients also came in for criticism. "It is vain to contend with judges who have been at the bar advocates for forty years of railroad companies and all the forms of associated capital, when they are called up to decide cases where such interests are in contest. All their training, all their feelings, are from the start in favor of those who need such influence." Let no one think that the "liberal judge" on the Supreme Court Bench goes back no further than John M. Harlan and Oliver Wendell Holmes!

The muzzling of the Court on Reconstruction issues gave Chief Justice Chase no opportunity to play a part in the most vital and exciting issues of his time. Thus there are no momentous decisions associated with Chase's name; the one "great case" in which he rendered judgment proved really a humiliation, for, at the succeeding term, his own court turned against its presiding genius and reversed his decree. The legal-tender cases have an important place in the annals of the Supreme Court, for they present the clearest, most unblushing instance of that body's deliberately erasing one of its own judgments and substituting another of opposite tenor. In 1870 the Supreme Court decided that the Legal-Tender Acts of the Civil War period were unconstitutional; in 1871 it decided that they were not. That Chase would regard them as constitutional seemed assured. No man had done more to obtain this legislation from Congress. As Secretary of the Treasury he had rigidly enforced it. That the legal tenders had proved indispensable in winning the war he had frequently asserted. From the day of the enactment, however, doubts had been raised as to their constitutionality. That Congress could emit paper money in war time might be granted, — though there were those who denied it, — but could Congress pass laws making this paper legal tender as good as gold? The point was a doubtful one. Doubtful or not, the whole policy of the Treasury, under Chase, accepted the measures as valid; greenbacks were put forth in increasing number, until, in 1865, there were more than $400,000,000 in circulation. Though nothing but the credit of the government supported these issues, they stood the strain fairly well, the premium on gold, in 1870, not exceeding 20 per cent. After Appomattox, however, the business and financial world became more and more anxious on this subject. Sound policy demanded that the Treasury return as soon as possible to specie payments. The craze for inflation was spreading; the greenback party, which was to torment the country in the seventies, had already blossomed. Holders of securities and contracts calling for payment in gold were growing restive over laws that compelled them to accept paper. That element which, from the first, had denied the power of Congress to print treasury notes and call them money became more clamorous every day. In the latter part of 1869 the Supreme Court found itself facing a decision on this point. "I do not agree with you," Chase had written a friend, May 18, 1864, "that the Constitution prohibits the issue of legal tender notes." Was it not reasonable to anticipate that a Secretary of the Treasury who had taken this stand would, as Chief Justice, uphold constitutionality?

Consternation struck the financial and political community, therefore, on February 7, 1870, when the decision was handed down in the case of *Hepburn* vs. *Griswold* — a decision written by Chief Justice Chase. The Legal-Tender Acts, so far as they affected contracts written before February 22, 1862, were declared to be unconstitutional. Chief Justice Chase had overruled Mr. Secretary Chase! The deadline represented the date the first Legal-Tender Act was passed. Contracts made before such passage, stipulating payment in gold or specie, must be carried out to the letter of the bond. A law making possible the fulfillment of such obligations in paper was an impairment of contracts, and thus amounted to the taking of property without "due process of law" — something unconstitutional under the Fifth Amendment. Defenders of the Legal-Tender Acts had fallen back upon the "necessary and proper" clause. Congress had the right to make war; consequently under the long familiar principle of "implied powers" it had the right to adopt such means as were "necessary and proper" to the effective use of arms. Chase's reply to this was the essence of Jeffersonism. The principle was recognized, but it could be applied only when the need was urgent and indispensable. Legal-tender notes were not absolutely essential to the prosecution of war measures; therefore the "necessary and proper" principle could not be invoked in this instance. It was Jefferson's argument against the constitutionality of a Federal Bank. But the public was interested not so much in fine-drawn disquisition as in the practical outcome of the decision and in the spectacle of Chase crying shame upon the doctrine he had upheld as a member of Lincoln's cabinet. Unsound as greenbacks might be, they had a sentimental hold upon the American public; had they not served a noble purpose in destroying rebellion and preserving the

Union? Was greenback not another name for victory? Chase's ruling came like an insult to a cherished national institution. One man on the Supreme Bench was especially outraged. Justice Miller wrote the dissenting opinion — he was one of a minority of three — roundly scoring the majority view. To outlaw the legal tenders seemed to him a turning of the judiciary back upon the Union cause and a lowering of the Supreme Bench to the low-water mark it had reached in the Dred Scott case. Miller and his two companions — Swayne and Davis — declined to accept this adjudication as finally settling the matter and resolved to use the first favorable opportunity to set aside the Chief Justice himself. His correspondence shows that Miller had no high opinion of Chase as a jurist or as a man. Chase's "stratagem," his "low political trickery," are phrases he does not hesitate to apply to his superior on the bench. He evidently believed that Chase's constitutional view was affected by the man's political aspirations; the supporters of legal tenders were most conspicuous in railroad and corporation circles, and the Democratic populace, almost to a man, hailed the Chase decision. And the Chief Justice was hopeful of the Democratic nomination in 1872!

It soon appeared that the minority judges were to receive reenforcements from a powerful quarter. One of the bad features of the legal-tender decision was that it came at a time when the Court was passing through a crisis of reorganization. Andrew Johnson having retired from the Presidency, and Grant finding greater favor with Congress, the tribunal was again reconstituted with the sacred nine Muses of the Law who had held sway before Johnson's time and have held it since. Eight judges participated in Chase's decision, which nominally stood five to three. But one of these, Grier, — a relic of the Dred Scott days, — was seventy-six years old, physically and mentally enfeebled. He had manifested such weakness in the "conferences" held on the case, at times showing an inability to understand the points at issue, voting one way on one occasion and diametrically opposite the next, that his brethren brought pressure upon him to resign. Grier accepted their advice, with the result that, when the decision was announced, he was no longer a member of the Court. Miller and his two dissentients insisted that the vote was therefore four to three and not five to three, and that, as two vacancies existed, a complete Court might have rendered a verdict the other way. That President Grant and his cabinet were appalled at the result was no secret, and that, on the very day the legal-tender pronouncement was made, two appointments came from the White House to the Supreme Court caused no surprise. The public raised its eyebrows and the opposition press immediately raised the cry of "packing the Court" when the names of the two new judges reached the Senate. They were Joseph P. Bradley of New Jersey and William Strong of Pennsylvania. Both men represented that type of "corporation lawyer" that had sprung into prominence in the new world that followed the Civil War. Both had been largely identified with railroads. Railroads with large outstanding bond issues were especially eager to have the legal tenders sustained. They collected their revenue mostly in greenbacks; to make them pay their interest charges in gold would, they asserted, bankrupt their properties. How did these two new judges, ex-railroad attorneys, stand on the Chase decision? About Strong there was no question. As Chief Justice of the Supreme Court of Pennsylvania he had written an opinion sustaining their constitutionality. That Bradley entertained similar ideas could be taken for granted. Clearly President Grant, as soon as he heard of Chase's decision, — so a large section of public opinion concluded, — had appointed these two men for the express purpose of obtaining a reversal. The United States Supreme Court had been "packed."

The events of the next year gave color to this view. The Supreme Court of February 1870, when the momentous edict went forth, contained four anti-legal-tender men, and three friends of that measure. The next day this same Court contained five legal-tender judges and three opposed. In a twinkling the situation had been completely reversed. Was it in human nature to suppose that Miller, now with a majority on his side, would not struggle to undo what he regarded as a great iniquity perpetrated by Chief Justice Chase? "Struggle" is the word. For the attempts to bring the issue again before the Court caused a long, bitter controversy. Chase and Miller were the leaders of the contending factions. The Attorney General, Ebenezer Rockwood Hoar, had other pending cases involving the same question; every time he attempted to present one, Chief Justice Chase would find some means of shunting it aside, while Miller and his four followers would battle to get it on the calendar. This War in Heaven was fought chiefly in those nonrecorded sessions of the Court known as "conferences"; but occasionally tilts between the two factions would take place in open court. Sometimes occurred a scene that filled newspapermen with delight. When the Attorney General moved one of these cases the Chief Justice coldly informed him that the Court had ordered that all such suits should follow the precedent established in *Hepburn* vs. *Griswold*. "The honorable Chief Justice so ordered," spoke up Justice Miller, "but not the Court." Then an anti-legal-tender judge, Nelson, substantiated Chase's recollection. The Chief Justice repeated his statement with "emphasis and passion," only to meet contradiction from the other camp. "There was a very lively scene at the Supreme Court this morning," wrote a Washington correspondent, "the oldest lawyers practicing there having witnessed nothing like it in their day." But the real battles took place in conference. How tense they were can be gathered from a letter written by Justice Miller. "We have had a desperate Conference in the secret conference of the Court for three weeks over two cases involving the legal tender question. . . . The fight has been bitter in the Conference room. The excitement has nearly used me up. It has been fearful; and my own position as leader in marshalling my forces and keeping up their courage, against a domineering chief and a party in court who have been accustomed to carry everything their own way, has been such a strain on my brain and nervous system as I never wish to encounter again."

But the old circuit rider finally emerged triumphant. The constitutionality of the Legal-Tender Acts came up in *Knox* vs. *Lee,* decided in May 1871. The opinion of the Court was written by one of the two "packed" judges, William Strong. It reversed Chief Justice Chase *in toto*. The language was not over-gentle; a galling reference to the "head of the treasury," who, before ascending the Supreme Court, "had represented to Congress the necessity of making these new issues legal tender, or rather, declared it impossible to avoid the necessity," made Chief Justice Chase wince. The next day Chase, disheartened and humiliated, appeared in the office of George S. Boutwell, Secretary of the Treasury. "Why did you consent to the appointment of judges to overrule me?" he demanded. And then he proceeded to bewail his career on the bench. It had brought him no satisfaction; gladly would he exchange places with Mr. Boutwell and take up his old labors as Secretary of the Treasury! But Chase's period of durance was not to last much longer; in a few months he was attacked by the malady that put a close to his Chief Justiceship.

The conviction that Chase uttered in this wail to Boutwell has furnished a matter for discussion ever since. Did Grant, or did he not, "pack" the Court? That he "packed" it in the sense of making a definite bargain with his appointees to reverse the legal-tender decision no one believed then or has believed since.   But his defenders have insisted that though, in selecting judges, Grant, like all Presidents, picked men of good party faith, loyal in a general sense to the views of the administration, the choice of Bradley and Strong was not made for the express purpose of obtaining the particular verdict he desired.   Their contention has been based chiefly on two facts.   Grant, it is urged, selected his new judges before the Chase decision had been rendered, without any knowledge of what that decision was to be.   Again, he hit upon Bradley and Strong as two leaders of the American bar, — as they were, — with no particular information as to their position on the pending issue.   Reputable historians have accepted these disclaimers at their face value and have acquitted Grant of what they regard as something verging on crime.   Mr. Rhodes, for example, has come to the President's defense, just as he came to the defense of Buchanan, charged with tampering with the Supreme Court in the Dred Scott case. And the outcome of both controversies has points in common.   It was necessary to wait until 1910, when the Buchanan correspondence was published, to obtain the real underground story of Taney and his Court in 1857.   Similar revelations thirty and sixty years after the legal-tender episode have made it necessary to see that matter in true light.

The first important piece of evidence came in 1902, with the publication of the *Reminiscences* of George S. Boutwell.   In this book Mr. Boutwell makes the statement that he knew of the pending Chase decision two weeks before it was delivered.   No less an authority than Chase himself made the disclosure.   The Chief Justice "gave as his reason" for extending this confidence to the Secretary of the Treasury "his apprehension of serious financial difficulties due to a demand for gold by the creditor class."   That is, the necessity of paying obligations and contracts in the precious metal would start a stampede; the Chief Justice apparently thought the Treasury should have time to prepare for such eventualities. It seems incredible that Mr. Boutwell should not have conveyed the important news to the President, with whom he was on the closest terms and in daily association, especially as there was no subject on which the President's anxiety and interest were so keen.   Mr. Boutwell's revelation pretty effectually disposes of the theory that Grant, in appointing Justices Bradley and Strong, known champions of legal tender, had no knowledge when he placed them on the bench that they would be called upon to review what he regarded as an obnoxious decision.

An even more conclusive piece of evidence is disclosed in Mr. Allan Nevins's recently published *Life of Hamilton Fish,* Grant's Secretary of State. No man had been more fiercely assailed on the "packing charge" than E. Rockwood Hoar, Grant's Attorney General; there was the public man, the Democratic enemy declared, who had persuaded the President to place two men on the Supreme Bench for the purpose of reversing the Chief Justice. Mr. Hoar felt the accusation acutely, and spent a considerable part of his remaining days denying it. He regarded it as a reflection upon his honor as a public man. "Neither the President nor I knew what it [the decision] was going to be. The Judges of the Supreme Court kept their own opinions, and, until they were read, nobody knew what they were." If Mr. Boutwell's statement quoted above is accurate, — and it bears the impress of truth, — this statement clearly needs qualification. The President, Mr. Hoar insisted, had nominated Bradley and Strong on the basis of professional standing and high personal character; "their subserviency upon a particular question or a particular interest" had nothing to do with the choice. In 1876 the attacks on Mr. Hoar became so furious that he wrote Secretary Fish, asking him to intercede with Grant and secure a statement that would refute an allegation "as slanderous of the President as it is of me." Mr. Fish, according to his diary, now brought to light by Mr. Nevins, laid the situation before the President, who declined to accede to Mr. Hoar's request. "It would be difficult for him to make such a statement" — such is Mr. Fish's record of his conversation with Grant. "Although he required no declaration from Judges Strong and Bradley on the constitutionality of the Legal-Tender Act he knew Judge Strong had on the bench in Pennsylvania given a decision sustaining its constitutionality and he had reason to believe Judge Bradley's opinion tended in the same direction; that at the same time he felt it important that the constitutionality of the law be sustained, and while he would do nothing to exact anything like a pledge or expression of opinion from the parties he might appoint to the Bench, he had desired that the constitutionality should be sustained by the Supreme Court; that he believed such had been the opinion of all his Cabinet at the time."

It is thus apparent that Grant, in appointing Bradley and Strong, was influenced by his desire to have the disputed act upheld. He exacted no such pledge; not only would that have been improper, but, in view of the known record of the men, superfluous. Incidentally, this quotation implies that Grant had knowledge of the forthcoming decision; otherwise would he have been so concerned as to the likely attitude of his candidates? Does all this mean that the Court was "packed"? If by packing it is meant that the President, before sending in the names, entered into a hard-and-fast bargain with his candidates to decide cases in a certain way, the answer is no; if it is meant that he was affected in his choice by an expectation that his appointees would settle matters in accordance with the administration programme, then the charge is true. That all Presidents "pack" the Court by placing in it men sympathetic with their states of mind, the record shows; but this case is somewhat different, for it concerned a pending litigation. Washington's insistence on appointing only those judges who were favorable to the Constitution, and Theodore Roosevelt's determination to get only men who accepted "my policies," is something different from Grant's act in elevating men who would settle a particular lawsuit in a particular way.

VII

From this point begins a new era in the story of the United States and its Constitution. The nation that had struggled from chaos into unified life from 1787 to 1870 was a different one, in almost every aspect, from the nation that developed, with fairly startling rapidity, into the one we know to-day. From 1820 to 1870 the story of the Constitution revolves largely around the subject of slavery. Other great issues showed their heads in the course of those fifty years, but gained little of their present importance. The historic decisions of the Supreme Court, exclusive of those which turned upon the ownership of human beings, were *Marbury* vs. *Madison* in 1803, the Dartmouth College case in 1819, *McCulloch* vs. *Maryland,* 1819–1824, *Gibbons* vs. *Ogden* in 1824. These cases, vital as were the points they settled, have acquired greater significance in modern times than in the days they were delivered. The first, for example, asserted the right of judicial review — the prerogative asserted by the Supreme Court to set aside unconstitutional laws passed by Congress. For a half century the Court never made use of this power. From 1803 until 1857 not a single act of Congress was declared constitutionally invalid. *Gibbons* vs. *Ogden* established the control of Congress over interstate commerce, but only since the Civil War has this power been used on an extensive scale. *McCulloch* vs. *Maryland* decided, among other things, the lawfulness of a Federal Bank; but the Bank thus sanctified by the Constitution was destroyed by Jackson, and the power so conferred remained unused until comparatively modern times. The great constitutional debates from 1820 to 1860 dealt almost entirely either with slavery itself or with problems that arose in connection with it. In the years from 1876 to 1892 a German scholar, Hermann von Holst, published a monumental work in seven volumes, which appeared in English translation (not quite accurately) as *The Constitutional and Political History of the United States.* This work is really an exhaustive history of slavery in its relation with the Constitution. That the United States, in the fifty years before the Civil War, lagged behind Great Britain in industrial development was owing largely to the absorption of the country and its statesmen in this one department of national existence.

This slavery question, as already made plain, was occupied chiefly with the territorial empire extending from the Mississippi River to the Pacific Ocean. The whole debate revolved around the labor system that was to be established in the twenty-two huge states subsequently carved out of this area. The determination of the North to safeguard this country from negro slavery, the insistence of the South on its "right" to set up there its "positive good," compose, in the main, the constitutional history of that time. The seventy-two years that have passed since Appomattox disclose that this struggle was based on a great illusion; Daniel Webster showed his statesmanship no more prophetically than in the debate on the measures of 1850. No act of Congress was needed, he said, to shut out slavery from this region; climate, soil, and the nature of the country automatically excluded it. "I would not take pains uselessly to reaffirm an ordinance of nature, nor to reënact the will of God." As soon as the verdict of war had decided against such extension of the evil, the new America quickly substantiated Webster's forecast. The covered wagons that now crossed the Mississippi in an endless stream; the armies of European immigrants — largely Germans and Scandinavians — that united with the dispersion from New England and the South to transform the prairie into the greatest agricultural country in the world; the railroads that, with a feverish activity, penetrated by tens of thousands of miles the new domain; the exploitation of mineral wealth that ensued — gold, silver, copper, above all iron; the large cities that magically arose on the plains — such phenomena had little connection with slavery and would never have been possible under such an institution. "Nullification," "compromise," "Southern rights," "fugitive slaves," "squatter sovereignty," and dozens of other catchwords vanish from American history.

The new world — the world of transcontinental railroads, telegraphs, telephones, electric lights, water power, labor unions, corporations, new industries, steel, oil, agricultural machinery, sugar refining, beef packing, street railways, automobiles — gave rise to an entirely new constitutional vocabulary. The courts now began to resound with new phrases, — "due process of law," "immunities of citizens of the United States," "business affected with a public interest," "reasonableness" as applied to constitutional interpretation, "restraint of trade," "trusts," "long and short hauls," "rebates," "unfair competition," "state regulation," "commerce commissions," "holding companies," "interlocking directorates," "international bankers," — words that would have been jargon in the ears of Webster, Calhoun, and the statesmen who wrangled so valiantly over the Constitution in pre-war days. A new America had come into being that had little resemblance to the one they knew. Kansas and Nebraska farmers who had fought so bitterly the slaveholders seeking possession of their fields in the fifties now turned their guns on a different but equally detested foe — the railroad and the monopolist. Humanitarians whose emotions had been stirred in favor of black men found plenty of new causes, now that the negro's shackles had fallen. The humanitarian movement had begun even before this great social change had taken place. Most of the antislavery agitators pursued other reforms as a kind of side line; in the thirties the advocates of temperance, "women's rights," even female suffrage, and the pioneers of improved housing conditions, abolition of child labor, shorter working hours for factory operatives, protective legislation for women, and other similar crusades making for the "more abundant life," were active. Prophets advancing such conceptions were harshly regarded a century ago; in popular estimation they were destroyers of property rights and invaders of venerated convention; when the first woman demanded the right to practise before the Supreme Court of the United States, that body dismissed her plea with an indulgent smile.

None of the social questions intimated above then rose to the dignity of constitutional issues. But this is the form they have assumed in the three quarters of a century that have passed since the Civil War. And such innovations have subjected that instrument to even severer tests than those presented by State rights, slavery, and civil war. Not one of them figured as a critical problem when the Constitution was framed. The history of that charter since 1865 is that of an instrument framed to fit a particular type of social and industrial society suddenly called upon to meet the issues of an entirely different order of life. In 1787, America, north and south, was an agricultural country; transportation differed little from the system that had prevailed in the days of the Roman Empire; farming, in its dependence on the wooden plough and the sickle, was essentially the same art that was practised by the Pharaohs; commerce, with sails and the winds as motive power, showed little progress from the times of the Phœnicians; manufacturing, so far as it existed at all, was an individual matter, largely family work in separate households; the corporation and joint stock company were unknown; associated effort, moderate in scale, took the form of partnership. American foreign trade consisted in the exchange, for certain essential European products, of a few large staples such as cotton, tobacco, rice, and indigo in the South, rum, fish, lumber, ships, and farm provisions in the North. How was the Constitution to serve its announced purposes of "establishing justice, promoting the general welfare, securing the blessings of liberty," in a new world of which hardly a semblance existed when it was framed?

Despite the disappearance of slavery, the negro still hovered over constitutional law and, by one of the strangest perversions of history, exercises a present-day influence on that instrument. In his interest three amendments were added to the national charter. The Thirteenth Amendment made the African slave a free man; the Fourteenth gave him the privileges and immunities of a citizen; the Fifteenth bestowed the right to vote. At least such was the purpose for which these new constitutional guaranties were called into being. But the fact is that only one of these amendments, the Thirteenth, has accomplished the end at which it was aimed. This is the one real tangible gain the black man has derived from his war amendments. Negro slavery no longer exists. The Fifteenth, prohibiting any state from depriving a citizen of suffrage because of his "race, color, or previous condition of servitude," has become a dead letter in all the states in which the negro forms a large part of the population. Literacy tests, "grandfather clauses," and other expedients have kept the sons of Ham from the polls south of the Ohio and the Potomac. The Fourteenth Amendment has similarly disappeared from the Constitution, so far as the reform it was intended to accomplish is concerned — of giving the ex-slave that status of a citizen and the rights of citizenship which the Dred Scott decision said he could never possess. Nearly all this amendment, the longest and most complicated of the twenty-one, has been rendered obsolete by time. The outworn paragraphs still stand gauntly in the Constitution, having no living consequence in the life of to-day, monuments only to the hateful struggles of a long-past era. The second section, for example, provides a method of cutting down the representation in Congress of such states as deny the negro the ballot. As this denial has always been made by indirection, the Southern states have succeeded in nullifying the provision and escaping the penalty. Section 3 disqualifies for public office in state or nation former "members of Congress, or officers of the United States, or members of any state legislature, or executive or judicial officers of any state," who broke their oath to the Constitution and engaged in "insurrection or rebellion" — a punishment that lapsed with Reconstruction. Section 4 forbids the payment by the United States or any state of any debt contracted "in aid of insurrection or rebellion against the United States" and at the same time pronounces the validity of all debts and obligations of the United States contracted to suppress such insurrection and rebellion. That clause ceased to have practical importance a few years after Lee's surrender, and, of course, is not of the slightest consequence to-day.

The first section of this Fourteenth Amendment, however, has shown startling vitality, though in ways not suspected when adopted. "All persons born or naturalized in the United States, and subject to the jurisdiction thereof, are citizens of the United States and of the State wherein they reside. No state shall make or enforce any law which shall abridge the privileges or immunities of citizens of the United States; nor shall any State deprive any person of life, liberty, or property without due process of law, nor deny to any person within its jurisdiction the equal protection of the laws." So many momentous issues were seldom crowded together in so short a space. There is hardly a sentence in that paragraph, hardly a word, that has not produced volumes of juristic literature. The reports of the United States Supreme Court, of circuit and state courts, contain tomes of learning devoted to the interpretation of these clauses. The reputations of justices have risen and fallen according to their reading of these definitions and prohibitions. Every sentence has become a problem, almost every word a challenge. But few of the judicial battles have concerned the colored brother for whose benefit the lines were written. When Reconstruction statesmen put that difficult paragraph in the Constitution they were thinking only of Sambo in the cotton fields. They had before their eyes Chief Justice Taney, old, frail, white-haired, the mere shadow of a man, proclaiming from the Supreme Court Bench that the negro was the member of a "degraded race" who could never be a citizen, or have any rights which the "white man was bound to respect." This clause was an answer to that odious proclamation. The negro never to be a citizen? Here is the reply: "All persons born . . . in the United States, and subject to the jurisdiction thereof, are citizens of the United States and of the State wherein they reside." Practically all the 4,000,000 ex-slaves were "born in the United States and subject to the jurisdiction thereof." And all of them, despite Justice Taney, now assumed the full status of citizens. That, however, did not absolutely ensure all the rights of citizenship. Already the Southern states were passing laws that would have segregated them into a special class — transformed them into an order of helotry, a halfway status between freedom and slavery. The antislavery forces that had been fighting their battle for a generation were determined to thwart this tendency; the endowment of the negro with full civic rights now became their gospel.

But what were the "rights of a citizen"? Suffrage was clearly not one of them, for millions of white men, at several stages of our history, had been denied the ballot; therefore a separate amendment, the Fifteenth, was incorporated. "Privileges or immunities" was the phrase carefully selected to describe all those endowments believed to be inseparable from citizenship. The right to sue, and to be sued; to sit on juries; to hold public office; to serve in the militia, the army and the navy, even to become officers thereof — should not negroes enjoy these "privileges" the same as white men? Sumner and his co-workers carried the doctrine even further. To ride on public carriers in the same cars with white men, to eat at the same restaurants and sleep in the same hotels, to occupy seats in the theatre, — not in "nigger heaven," but in the orchestra, — and sit side by side with the blue-eyed Anglo-Saxon — such was the social plane to which the ex-slave was to be promoted. No state shall "deny to any person" — that is, any negro — "within its jurisdiction the equal protection of the laws." "No state shall make or enforce any law which shall abridge the privileges or immunities of citizens of the United States." So far as negroes and their civil and social rights were concerned these clauses would seem all-sufficient. But the last-quoted sentence, when it emerged as part of the Fourteenth Amendment, had a final clause which has occupied the attention of the Supreme Court from that day to this. "Nor shall any State deprive any person of life, liberty, or property without due process of law."

"Due process of law." There was the rub. What did it mean? The expression is as old as Magna Charta; it was already in the Constitution, in the Fifth Amendment. In the latter section to deprive a person of "life, liberty, or property, without due process of law," was enumerated as one of those things prohibited to the Federal government. In the Fourteenth Amendment it figures as one of the things that no state legislature can do. To the Congressmen and Senators who voted for this amendment, and the states whose legislatures ratified it, there was nothing mysterious about these words. The purpose their proponents had in mind was apparent enough. "No state can deprive *any negro* of life, liberty, and property without due process of law." That was not the precise phraseology, but that was the intended meaning. Certain of the "black codes" passed by Southern legislatures immediately after the peace resembled the laws adopted against Jews in Russia before the Revolution. They prohibited negroes from living in towns, except as domestic servants, required them to remain on the soil and cultivate it, though negroes were forbidden to own land. Certain vagrancy and labor-contract laws, it was urged, practically reëstablished slavery or that peonage which was only a few degrees removed from it. It was to curb these and other anti-negro tendencies that the Fourteenth Amendment was added to the Constitution. Sumner, in his grandiose way, hailed it as "the centralization of liberty" and "the imperialism of equal rights," but less idealistic critics stigmatized it as an attempt "to bleach a negro into a political white man." Justice Miller expressed the intent in more dignified language. All three war amendments, he wrote, were expected to assure "the freedom of the slave race, the security and firm establishment of that freedom, and the protection of the newly made freeman and citizen from the oppression of those who had formerly exercised unlimited domain over him."

"Due process" was to be one of the safeguards against such oppression. The practice of Anglo-Saxon nations for a thousand years clearly showed what "due process" meant. It signified orderly and just court procedure. No man could be put on trial without an indictment; such trial must be by a jury of his peers; certain rules of evidence must be used in proceedings against him; he could not be made to testify against himself or be subjected to torture; he had the right of appeal, of habeas corpus, and other traditional guaranties. If his property was to be taken for public purposes, it must be done by eminent domain and with full compensation. Justice Miller, admitting the difficulty of fixing definitely the scope of the historic phrase, came near to expressing the sense in which it had been used for centuries as "a fair trial in a court of justice, according to the mode of proceeding applicable to such a case." Thus, according to this jurist, "due process" referred entirely to court procedure, and was inserted in the Fourteenth Amendment to obtain such orderly and just court procedure for negroes.

This first clause of the Fourteenth Amendment has not only been transformed into an instrument for entrenching "property interests," but it has failed completely in its original purpose of giving the negro his so-called civic rights. Negroes in many states to-day do not sit on juries, do not vote, do not attend public schools in company with white children, do not eat or sleep in the white man's hotel, do not — at least in the South — ride in the same street-cars or railroad trains. Sumner's "imperialism of equal rights" was promptly shown to be a delusion. His pet measure, the Civil Rights Bill of 1875, passed by a huge majority of Congress, came up for decision by the Supreme Court in 1883. It was based upon the rights believed to have been conferred by the Fourteenth Amendment. The Court voided it as unconstitutional. Congress had no power, the Court ruled, to pass such a measure. Such "rights" as the law conferred, to the extent that they were "rights" at all, did not lie within the purview of Congress; they were exclusively matters for the states. This decision surprised no one, not even Sumner himself, greatly as he bewailed it. It simply repeated decisions already made, which disclosed that, in writing the Fourteenth Amendment, someone had bungled. Its uncertain English had completely failed to frame the ideas of its advocates.

The man who first pointed out this incongruity was Justice Samuel F. Miller. The negro had no warmer friend in America, the Union no more eloquent supporter; and Miller felt far more sympathy for the Reconstruction measures than most enlightened Americans do to-day. Yet in the first "great case" under the Fourteenth Amendment Miller disclosed in masterly English that this supposed change in the Constitution could not be invoked to shield the negro from what the humanitarian spirit of the time regarded as injustice. Curiously enough the litigation which inspired this declaration had nothing to do with the negro.

Giving the black man the right to serve on juries and to live where he pleased was something far removed from the right of white men to slaughter cattle. The right to slaughter cattle was one that sought shelter under the new constitutional guarantee. The carpetbag legislature of Louisiana had passed a law granting a favored group the exclusive right to maintain slaughterhouses in the city of New Orleans. Not far from a thousand butchers in that community were thus suddenly deprived of the right to pursue their trade; at least they were forced to pursue it at the pleasure and will of the entrenched monopolists. Naturally they took their grievance to the courts. In the old days they would have brought the matter quietly before their local tribunals; before the Civil War the clever-est lawyer would never have dreamed that any Federal court had jurisdiction in such a parochial controversy. But now their counsel pointed to the recently enacted Fourteenth Amendment. "No State shall make or enforce any law which shall abridge the privileges or

THE SUPREME COURT, 1937

Left to right, seated: Justices Louis D. Brandeis, Willis Van Devanter, Chief Justice Charles Evans Hughes, Justices James C. McReynolds, George Sutherland; *standing:* Justices Owen J. Roberts, Pierce Butler, Harlan F. Stone, Benjamin N. Cardozo

© *Harris & Ewing*

New Supreme Court Building

immunities of citizens of the United States." Was not the right to slaughter cattle a "privilege" as understood by the Constitution? Was not Louisiana a "State"? And had not this State "made" and was it not at the moment enforcing a law "abridging" this privilege? And was not the slaughterhouse law of Louisiana therefore unconstitutional? To the lay mind the case was as clear as crystal; the legal profession as a whole undoubtedly supported this view; four justices of the United States Supreme Court, including one of the ablest of the lot, Joseph P. Bradley, accepted the interpretation. But Samuel Freeman Miller said "no," and carried four other justices with him, so that his opinion, by the now much deprecated vote of five to four, became the prevailing one.

Miller pointed out one fatal defect that most commentators had overlooked, and which the framers of the amendment in all probability had not considered. The individuals whose "privileges and immunities" could not be ravished by a state legislature were "citizens of the United States." The rôle played by the African in the development of the Constitution has already been suggested; and among his achievements is the creation of an entirely new American phenomenon. That is, a "citizen of the United States." Until the ratification of the amendment, in 1868, no such person had been known to the law. Citizenship was a state matter; the rights in the United States which citizens obtained arose from citizenship in one of the states. But the Fourteenth Amendment, in the first sentence, thrusts a new character upon the national stage. "All persons born or naturalized in the United States, and subject to the jurisdiction thereof, are citizens of the United States and of the State wherein they reside." This clause signifies a sudden jump into Nationalism broad enough to satisfy the most sweeping continental mind. Every American born or naturalized, as this clause describes, acquires a dual citizenship — that in the nation and that in his state. Clearly he becomes the heir to two sets of rights — those conferred by the state and those conferred by the nation.

But observe, said Justice Miller, in effect, what the very next sentence accomplishes — the one upon which the aggrieved butchers had relied in claiming Federal protection. No state "shall abridge the privileges or immunities of *citizens of the United States.*" Was the privilege of slaughtering cattle one that belonged to a citizen of the United States? Of course not. For generations butchers had operated under licenses granted by municipalities. From colonial times this trade was a privilege derived from colonial or state citizenship. It was a right that had existed long before there was any United States; it would endure even though the United States should disappear. Study the Federal Constitution; do you find there that Congress has power to confer the right of slaughtering cattle and hogs? Does that mean then, the opposition asked, that only those privileges found in the Constitution are rights of "citizens of the United States"? Yes, said Miller, that is precisely what it does mean. There are certain rights specifically stipulated in the national charter, and these, and only these, can be regarded as inherent in "citizens of the United States." Thus the privilege of sending one's goods into another state for sale is one that no state can confer; only the United States can do that — and does. The right to navigate the rivers of another state, to drive one's wagons over its roads, to circulate freely in it on equal terms with its own citizens, no state can grant, but the Federal Constitution does. When the motorist of to-day crosses the line separating New York State and Connecticut and proceeds unchallenged on the smooth road of "another state," he is exercising a right which he enjoys as "a citizen of the United States." To enter the harbor of a "foreign" state, to unload one's person and cargoes on its docks, to claim protection on the high seas and in foreign countries, is a right "citizens of the United States" possess, but not citizens of Massachusetts or Virginia or New Jersey. But to imagine that the Fourteenth Amendment gave the Federal government power to act as a universal providence to interfere with states in their most minute concerns, to imagine that in this instance the Federal government had the right to prevent Louisiana from slaughtering its cattle as it chose, was to imagine a vain thing. Justice Miller's adjudication has never been upset, and the slaughterhouse cases, as they have always been known, are a landmark in constitutional law. Had the decision been otherwise the states would have all but vanished as governmental units. Congress and the Supreme Court could have reduced them to the position of "counties" which Madison had envisaged. The Federal government would have become that solidified nation which there is a tendency to make it to-day. It was Justice Miller's privilege to say to the central power: Thus far shalt thou go, and no further!

But as an inevitable consequence it left the poor negro stark and unprotected. What had become of his "privileges and immunities"? For there were very few of them he held as a "citizen of the United States." They were all the fruits of his status as "a citizen of a state." Could Congress pass laws — as it did — permitting him to attend the public schools, instead of being segregated in buildings set aside for his exclusive use? It could not — this was a matter of state control; many states established such negro schools, and the Supreme Court decided that they had the right to do so. The Southern section has universally adopted "Jim Crow" laws for the segregation of negro passengers; the Supreme Court, on the same principle, has declined to set them aside. The South has even succeeded, on a large scale, in depriving negroes of the vote. This has not been done by passing laws mentioning citizens of color in so many words, for that, under the Fifteenth Amendment, would be palpably unconstitutional. But literacy tests, applicable in set terms to whites and blacks alike, do not violate the basal law — though in practical administration they open the polls to all white citizens and close them to Judge Taney's "degraded race."

VIII

Yet Miller's interpretation, as already indicated, did not pass unchallenged. The four dissenters included Justice Joseph P. Bradley, probably the greatest intellect, considered purely as intellect, who ever ornamented the Supreme Bench. Bradley was one of those Grant appointees who joined the previous minority of three in the legal-tender case and reversed the Chase decision. His mental attainments have long since passed into legend. Born in 1813, at Berne, Albany County, New York, descended from an English family that helped to settle New Haven in 1638, Bradley came of a long line of New England yeomen. His parents, however, were very poor; as one of eleven children the future jurist, from childhood, was compelled to make his own way. In the fall of 1833 an exceedingly scrawny youth, diminutive in size and awkward in manners, appeared as a candidate for the freshman class at Rutgers College, New Jersey. Soon his fellow students, who at first were inclined to make fun of Bradley's strange, unworldly behavior, began to respect him for his mental qualities. When not occupied with appointed tasks, Bradley gave himself to such diversions as predicting eclipses of the sun, calculating transits of Venus, and engaging in philological excursions not included in the college programme. In a few years the prodigy had acquired mastery, not only of all modern languages and the accredited classic tongues, but of Hebrew and Arabic, and even cultivated a taste for Egyptian hieroglyphics. Years afterward, when a Supreme Court justice in Washington, Bradley used to keep the Greek Testament in his church pew; whenever the preacher read from the English version of that volume, his parishioner liked to follow the original, finding pleasure in detecting errors of translation. All kinds of learned manuscripts, on such subjects as "The Recurrence of Ice Periods in the Northern Hemisphere," were found among Bradley's papers on his death; they were merely amateur investigations of scientific problems. A calendar constructed by the Supreme Court justice was one of the marvels of the day; at a glance one could determine the day of the week for any given date extending through forty centuries. This mathematical faculty, indeed, went along side by side with Bradley's legal practice. Admitted to the New Jersey bar in 1839, he took up, as a side line, the job of actuary of the Mutual Benefit Life Insurance Company, and left, as his contribution to an abstruse profession, a new set of life tables. "A lawyer should know everything," was his apology for these digressions into fields not directly associated with the bench.

These traits made Bradley a figure somewhat remote; he was not impressive in person — short, slight, keen-eyed and thin-lipped, his sharply chiseled, smooth-shaven features standing out in contrast to the heavily bearded, large-jowled lineaments most conspicuous on the bench during his era. Neither was he especially approachable, at times being definitely given to ill temper. These qualities detracted from his success as a "jury lawyer" and "business getter," and thus more and more turned his powerful abilities towards a kind of practice that, in the seventies, began to assume a new — and in quarters an odious — importance. For Bradley was the first of that procession of "corporation lawyers" whose activities, from this time forward, take on great constitutional importance. The development of railroads, of large joint stock companies, of industry on a continental scale, now brought the need of great legal brains in meeting their complex problems. Bradley, in the retirement of the inner office, became a valued counselor in the biggest cases under discussion. Indeed, few of these pivotal litigations ever got far without the requisition of his services.

Bradley was the lawyers' lawyer, and great, as such, was his professional fame. This for a time forestalled his real ambition. His particular qualities, Bradley believed, and his life study of the law in all nations and civilizations, fitted him for the Supreme Bench of the United States. Few impartial observers disagreed with this judgment. But there were practical difficulties. Bradley was a "railroad lawyer," supposed to be removed in sympathy from the mob, and already the demand for "liberal judges" who would regard "human" rather than "property" rights was in the air — though these particular phrases had not yet been coined. Few lawyers were so well known to the Supreme Court, for few appeared before it so frequently. But Bradley's affiliations with "big business" had so far precluded his appointment to the circuit court and interfered with his desire to become chancellor of the State of New Jersey. President Grant, however, was not squeamish where large wealth was concerned, — his fondness for rich men greatly humiliated his admirers later, — and when, in February 1870, two judges were needed to fill vacancies, for that "packing" which has already been described, he acquiesced in a pretty general demand from the profession and elevated Bradley.

That one of the reasons for his selections was the suit then pending has already been made plain; but it should be emphasized that Bradley's attitude on legal tenders was no sudden conversion and involved no sacrifice of principle. He was one of the most uncompromising Nationalists in the land. The Civil War had only intensified his early convictions that the United States was a nation and that the central government was the one supreme fact. "It seems to be often overlooked," he said, in words that the Virginians of 1787 would have rejoiced at, "that a national Constitution has been adopted in this country, establishing a real government therein, operating upon persons and territories and things." Such, he insisted, was the great significance of the Civil War. And here were people declaring that this government did not have the right of making its circulating medium legal tender! As well might one say that the United States was not an independent nation.

It was for this same reason that Bradley admired the Fourteenth Amendment. Had it not created that new political species, a citizen of the United States? This same enthusiasm led him to disagree with Miller's decision in the slaughterhouse cases. Miller maintained that there were limits, in the exercise of the national power, beyond which Congress could not go; Bradley believed that there were few such limits. For State rights his contempt was profound; this, he asserted, was not a constitutional conception, but a theory that went with little minds. And so Bradley became the proponent of a principle which did not find general acceptance in his day, but which is again acquiring prominence, that the United States, by its mere existence as a sovereign, self-sufficient Union, can exercise all the authority commonly possessed by sovereign powers. A great departure, this, from Calhounism and strict construction! Basing all his reasoning on this idea, Bradley easily reached the conclusion that Congress could have something to say about the slaughter of cattle in New Orleans, as well as give the negroes the right to attend non-Jim Crow public schools and ride in non-Jim Crow tramcars. But his brother Miller and a majority of the Court took a different view. Indeed, Miller stigmatized scornfully the idea that the United States, by the fact of its existence, possessed universal sovereign rights, and showed a tendency to restrict its prerogatives to those specifically conveyed by the Constitution. On this point at least the two finest minds on the Court were at loggerheads.

With men of the calibre of Miller and Bradley on the Supreme Court, the nation was almost appalled in 1873 when Grant, on the death of Chase, appointed Morrison R. Waite Chief Justice. All previous Chief Justices had filled high posts and were men to whom this lofty station had come as an appropriate promotion. Jay had been Secretary of State and Ambassador; Ellsworth one of the framers of the Constitution, Senator, author of the Judiciary Act, and Minister to France; Taney, cabinet officer under Jackson; Chase, Secretary of the Treasury and long a commanding figure in public life. Waite had no national reputation as lawyer or statesman. A response something akin to dismay greeted his appointment — an emotion felt with especial intensity by the Supreme Court itself. Not only Bradley and Miller, but practically all the judges looked upon themselves as candidates for promotion. All were disappointed when their claims were ignored. Soon after Waite came to Washington for induction, a dinner was tendered the new Chief Justice by the Washington élite; naturally his recently acquired brethren of the Supreme Court were obliged to attend. "Did you ever see so many corpses at one funeral?" one of the guests remarked to a neighbor. "Waite is one of those luckiest of all individuals known to the law," said E. Rockwood Hoar, himself one of "those mentioned" for the post, "an innocent third party without notice." The associate justices were shocked that a country lawyer, who had never even appeared before their body as advocate, should have been rescued from obscurity and made their presiding officer. Nor did they conceal their chagrin even from the gentleman concerned. On his appearance they suggested that, for a brief period, he take a lower seat and let one of the associates preside, so that he could learn something about the routine of his job. Waite's response to this suggestion showed that he was not quite such an inconsequential person as his good brothers imagined. He sat himself firmly in the chair formerly occupied by Marshall, Taney, and Chase, called the Court to order, and proceeded to exercise all the duties and prerogatives of the office. "I got on the box, gathered up the lines and drove," — such was Waite's description of this inauguration, — "and I am going to drive and those gentlemen know it."

Though his associates for a time continued to treat the "interloper" coldly, their injured pride presently gave way to personal fondness and professional respect. From the moment of Waite's accession, March 4, 1874, until his death in 1888, there was no question as to who was Chief Justice of the United States. Even those who did not regard him as a modern Coke or Mansfield admitted that he looked the part. A man of mighty frame, with big head and big features, yet with friendly eyes and delightful, smiling courtesy, a bushy crown of white hair and great white beard, Waite's person had a patriarchal bearing eminently appropriate to the dispenser of justice. That his career had not been distinguished up to the day when, at the age of fifty-eight, this great office became his portion is true. Grant appointed him for the same reason that he appointed so many men — the man was his friend and an honored resident of Grant's state, Ohio. Born in Connecticut, educated at Yale, where he had as classmates men who became captains of the American bar, William M. Evarts and Samuel J. Tilden, Waite had made the Western journey, settled in Maumee City, acquired a comfortable practice of a humdrum kind, and risen gradually to the rank of leading citizen. In Waite's case that did not signify public leadership, for he had evaded office, declining appointment even to the Supreme Court of Ohio. The railroads and steel corporations that rose to prominence in the sixties and seventies had not sought his abilities or influence; he remained a faithful journeyman worker in the courts, without fear and without reproach. His one distinction, before attaining the supreme dignity, was his appearance as one of the American counsel at Geneva, in 1873, in the Alabama arbitration; he acquitted himself so well that Grant found in this service justification for making him successor to Chase. Though newspapers praised the appointment faintly, and though prosperous legal luminaries shook their heads in doubt, the chorus of approbation in 1888, when Waite's fifteen years' Chief Justiceship came to an end, was practically unanimous. Agreement was general that he had served his country well during an exceedingly difficult time.

For Chief Justice Waite, in this period, was called upon to meet the challenge with which business now assailed the Constitution under the "due process" clause. When this sentence of the Fourteenth Amendment reared its head, the meaning was something radically different from the one which Sumner and his brother Reconstructionists had fathered. No state can "deprive any person of life, liberty, or property without due process of law." Western legislatures, in the late sixties and early seventies, began to pass "confiscatory" laws against corporations. The "socialistic" and "communistic" assaults — these adjectives were in popular use even then — which have continued without interruption up to the present time then had their beginning. The "railroad" and the "corporation" lawyer, skilled in verbal niceties, quick to seize previously unregarded phrases to serve his clients' ends, suddenly found in "due process" a legalistic godsend. It had accomplished nothing for its expected beneficiaries, Rastus and Dinah, but might hold concealed blessings for transcontinental railroads and Standard Oil companies. One difficulty arose, however. The constitutional entity whose "life, liberty, and property" could not be thus unceremoniously imperiled was "any person." Was a railroad or a steel corporation a "person"? Many years hence, in 1886, the courts decided that such a phenomenon, commonly denounced as "soulless," was a person, in the meaning of the Constitution, but in 1870 this metaphysical height had not been attained. Still the lawyers were not discouraged. They raised a momentous query: Could a state deprive a corporation — that is, a "person" — of its property without "due process"? According to the corporations themselves, the states were doing this almost every day. By this they meant that a stream of laws was issuing from "socialistic" legislatures that accomplished this very thing. The problem was particularly acute with railroads. The amount of railroad construction that took place after the Civil War not only opened great areas to settlement, but gave rise to lively problems. Farmers that had hailed these extensions presently began to attack them in vituperative terms. The roads were expensively and frequently dishonestly built; their stock was grossly watered; their management was careless and extravagant. To earn returns on fictitious capitalization, managements steadily lifted rates. They indulged in other obnoxious practices; abuses arose that were new to society: higher rates for short hauls than for long, discrimination against noncompetitive points, "rebates" and drawbacks to favored shippers. The prairies went wild with indignation and politicians thrived upon their grievances. A new organization, formally named the Patrons of Husbandry, but popularly called the Grange, grew in membership by tens of thousands, and the laws that it succeeded in putting through legislatures, always known as the granger laws, form a momentous chapter in the history of the Constitution.

For these laws introduced a novel and, as conservatives of that time regarded it, a dangerous and revolutionary principle. A new brand of State rights appeared. This was the "right" to "regulate" transportation. Legislatures carried the idea even so far as to pass laws fixing minimum rates for carrying passengers and freight.

Here was anarchy red-handed! On what principle did lawmakers interfere with the private management of property? Did not Commodore Vanderbilt "own" the New York Central system, Jay Gould the Missouri Pacific and the Wabash, and corresponding stockholders all the other lines? "Can't I do what I want with my own?" shouted Vanderbilt. "Hain't I got the power?" This indignant query completely expressed the attitude of the railroad "magnates." A peanut vendor can sell his stock at any price he can charge and customers will pay; that was precisely the position of vendors of transportation. If you don't like what we assess for moving wheat and corn, they informed the protesting farmers, you need not use our services; carry the stuff yourself!

But the granger laws proclaimed a different principle. The purveyor of railroad services was not in the same situation as the proprietor of a corner grocery. One difference was that he operated under a franchise granted by the state, and, for purposes of grade crossings and the like, made use of public property. To encourage railroad building, the government had granted subsidies of millions of acres of land. A community that gives such privileges and bounties can stipulate the conditions under which they are to be used. Among these should be adequate service, equal treatment of all citizens, — no "rebates," — and reasonable tariffs. This is now one of the most unassailable principles of law; it seems so self-evident that one wonders how it could ever have been questioned; but it was fiercely fought by the railroads in the seventies and eighties. And in their support they pointed to the Fourteenth Amendment. When a legislature, or its creation, a railroad commission, fixed railroad rates, it was "depriving a person of property without due process of law." The reasoning is not difficult to follow. When rates fixed by the state reduced the income of a corporation they took from that corporation part of its property — and property of a substantial kind, cold money. It was the same as though the state had lifted so much cash from this "person's" till. That the state had the right to take property for public purposes was granted. But how was this to be done? By "due process of law"! And what was the "due process" used in such cases from immemorial time? Such property must be condemned by orderly procedure and compensation paid. Thus to take property without consideration and money damages was not "due process." It was confiscation. Theoretically then, if the legislature, when it fixed rates that deprived the railroad of "property," had appropriated money to reimburse the company for this spoliation, it would have acted under "due process." As it always neglected this ceremony, the rate laws apparently violated the Fourteenth Amendment. From that day to this, "due process" has been argued in thousands of cases by property interests fighting "confiscatory legislation," and this has been the point involved in them all. The classic words, as Justice Miller said, became the resource of all who wished to bring "to the test of this court the abstract opinions of every unsuccessful litigant in a state court of the justice of the decision against him and of the merits of the legislation on which such a decision may be based."

The country lawyer become Chief Justice, Morrison R. Waite, laid this ghost so far as railroads were concerned. Not only this, but eight of his confreres agreed with him, including the "railroad lawyer," Joseph P. Bradley. Those who love to fall foul of this tribunal should give it the credit of establishing, as far back as the eighteen-seventies, the principle that the state possesses the right of regulating railroads, even to fixing the rate of service. When Chief Justice Waite began work, a large number of such cases were clamoring for attention. Half a dozen states had passed rate-fixing laws, and the railroads traversing all of them were pressing for "justice." One case in particular had attracted wide attention. The transportation of grain from the Mississippi Valley led to the erection in Chicago of great storage warehouses, or "elevators," as they were called. The trains rolled up to these ungainly structures and deposited their freight, where it was held until the needs of the market necessitated a reloading upon lake boats or railroads for conveyance to Eastern seaports. In 1870 there were nine grain elevators on the Chicago lake side, the universal *entrepôt* for distribution. Their ownership constituted a virtual monopoly. According to farmers, prices charged for storing their products were ruinous. Yet they could not live without these facilities. Therefore when the legislature of Illinois passed a law fixing the maximum rates the elevator "baron" could assess on grain, its act was widely acclaimed. But the "barons" themselves set up the cry of "socialism," "communism," and "confiscation." Illinois was "depriving" them of their "property" without "due process of law," and was therefore violating Section 1 of Amendment XIV.

In 1878 Chief Justice Waite, speaking for a majority of seven, delivered his opinion. It is a document that lies at the basis of the vast machinery of regulation that has been set up since, not only in states but throughout the nation, not only of railroads, but of telegraphs, telephones, electric lights, and all other "public utilities."

It is the foundation not only of state commissions, but of the Federal Interstate Commerce Commission. For the Chief Justice did not accept the plea that the elevator law violated the "due process" clause. The first elaborate attempt of "big business" to utilize these words for its own benefit fell to the ground. The lawyers were quite wrong, the Chief Justice said, in thinking that there was anything especially new in the state's fixing the terms upon which an indispensable public service was to be rendered. Illinois and other commonwealths, in legislating rates for elevator and railroad charges, were only exercising a prerogative that had its roots deep in the past. In England and America the principle had been applied, and was then being applied, in countless cases. The community gives a franchise for the operation of a ferry. This is a kind of utility without which existence is hardly endurable. Has the ferryman the right to stand on the bank of the river and refuse to transport wayfarers to the other side unless they empty their pockets of all their money? Not at all. Commonly the rates they can charge are explicitly set forth in the license under which they operate; to charge more is an imprisonable offense. Drivers of hackney cabs had been long accustomed to having their fares specified by the local government; it had never occurred to them that this was a deprivation of property without "due process" of law. What was the principle involved? Waite dove down into a famous ruling of Lord Hale, once Lord Chief Justice of England, and retrieved the phrase that has been echoing in American jurisprudence ever since. This illustrious authority, writing two centuries before, was dealing with the rights and privileges of wharfingers — persons who maintained wharves for common use. "If the King or subject have a public wharf, under which all persons who come to that port must come and unlade or lade their goods as for the purpose, because they are the wharves only licensed by the Queen . . . or because there is no other wharf in that port . . . in that case there cannot be taken arbitrary and excessive duties for cranage, wharfage, pesage, etc.; but the duties must be reasonable and moderate. . . . For now the wharf and the crane and other conveniences are affected with a public interest, and they cease to be *juris privati* only."

"Affected with a public interest"! Here was the touchstone that resolved all the doubts raised by the thousands of pages of lawyers' briefs! Was there much difference between the wharves that Lord Hale described and the elevators that had suddenly arisen on the Chicago lake front? Were not they too "affected with a public interest"? The words fell like balm on the millions of American farmers patiently tilling their fields. It would be hard to-day to find a lawyer — even a corporation lawyer — who would contest the point. When, in subsequent decisions, Waite slightly modified the ruling, he again found the living principle in this same pregnant paragraph. Lord Hale declared, it will be noticed, that the rate must be "reasonable." Here was a desirable check on the states. Just as the rates established by the railroads might be extortionate, so those applied by the legislature might be confiscatory. If the maximum rate were so low that the company could not pay its operating expenses and fixed charges and a fair return to investors, they were "unreasonable" and could therefore be contested. And from this is derived that unique contribution to the science of self-government, the Interstate Commerce Commission, a body which, after minute investigation of all elements involved, has the right of determining, not only rates of service, but service itself, and such matters as capitalization, improvements, competition, and the like.

IX

The annals of the Constitution since the Civil War differ, in one substantial regard, from its tribulations in the quarter of a century preceding that event. In the earlier epoch, "constitutional" crises were mainly civic and political; since 1865 they have, in most instances, reached the judiciary. The first important constitutional problem was the one that culminated in the Whiskey Rebellion of 1794; in this the point involved was whether armed citizens could defy the constitutional provision granting Congress power to levy taxes. That question was not solved by the courts, but by the Executive. Jefferson's Kentucky and Virginia Resolutions presented another issue — whether an individual state could settle constitutionality; this issue proved an active one for thirty years, until the energetic Jackson ended the discussion in 1833. Other "constitutional crises" at once come to mind — those started by the purchase of Louisiana, by the Hartford Convention, by the Missouri Compromise, the Compromise of 1850, and the Mexican War; some of these problems did reach the courts, but for the most part they were determined not by decisions of the Supreme Tribunal but by events. The most momentous constitutional crisis the nation faced — the right of a state to secede, which concerned the very marrow of the constitutional fabric — never reached the courts, but was decided by civil war. That from 1787 to 1866 the Supreme Court set aside only two laws passed by Congress is a point frequently made; this is only another way of saying that constitutional issues in that period were resolved, not by black-robed judges, but by circumstances. That more laws have been invalidated since Reconstruction means that, in the "constitutional" crises of the latter time, the courts, not war or fierce political contention, have played the chief part in settling the disputes.

The judiciary has assumed this new importance chiefly because the questions arising in modern days are more susceptible to judicial interpretation than those of the ante-bellum era. These questions can be divided into two great classifications. They are those developed by the new industrial and economic order — the problems of transportation, communication, "utilities," manufacturing on a great scale, "big business"; and those created by the growth of a new social conscience, the realization that property is unfairly divided, that the masses do not sufficiently participate in the prosperity they do so much to create, that the opportunities, graces, and benefits of civilization do not reach the generality of men and women to the extent that real civilization demands. These problems frequently become acute, but they are obviously more susceptible to adjudication by constitutional umpires than those presented by nullification, State rights, the extension of slavery, and secession. Citizens become excited — and properly so — over the "robberies" of the railroads, the heartless exactions of monopolies, the frequently low wages paid by industry, the long hours and unhealthful working conditions, but they are not likely to resort to war — at least not yet. The story of the Constitution, in this ultimate stage, thus turns mainly on the workings of the judicial department.

The narrative does not possess the simple outlines that mark the era before 1860; the problems are more intricate, the personalities concerned not so "dramatic." Yet here again a few men symbolize and give vividness to a changing world. New characterizations now applied to the courts and their "master minds" are in themselves suggestive of new ideals. Especially significant are such adjectives as "liberal" and "conservative." In a sense such terms are offensive. They apparently negative the very idea of justice. The evenly balanced scale of that deity knows not "liberal" or "conservative." These words imply a predisposition on the part of courts towards the legal problems they are expected to solve. They suggest a prejudice to begin with. Whatever doubts such designations may inspire, however, the fact is that they do describe an existing fact. Nothing is more certain than that particular Supreme Courts, in the last three quarters of a century, have been liberal and others conservative, and that the words may be accurately used to describe particular luminaries of the bench. Neither is it necessary to waste time in making definitions. An English statesman was once asked to define the word "jingo." "I cannot exactly describe him," was the reply, "but I know one when I see him." So we may say about liberal and conservative judges.

The types are not entirely modern. That Taney showed evidence of liberalism has already been set forth. In the seventies and eighties men like Waite, Miller, even Bradley, that "railroad attorney," if not liberal in the contemporary sense, did not regard the

Constitution primarily as a mighty bulwark raised to preserve entrenched property. Similarly Stephen J. Field, Horace Gray, and Stanley Matthews rejoiced in their conservatism. The decade in which justices of this "reactionary" breed most successfully held sway was the eighteen-nineties. Chief Justice Fuller, with his old-fashioned satellites Peckham, Shiras, and Brewer, represents a particularly backward time. In this ten years — 1890–1900 — the Supreme Court smothered the Sherman Antitrust Law — relegating it to the limbo of forgotten things, from which it was subsequently resurrected by Theodore Roosevelt and William H. Taft — and erased the income tax from the statute books. These achievements alone would give that period an evil eminence. Yet the lines cannot be drawn too sharply. "Liberalism" and "conservatism" alternate from decision to decision, so that the composite photograph, even in such an unpopular epoch, is not all light or shadow. Its harshest critics can scarcely maintain that, in the seventy-five years since Appomattox, the Supreme Court has failed to keep abreast of progress. What have been the great legislative measures adopted in that time to curb the greed of property and to protect popular interests? The regulation of railroads stands in the front rank. The Supreme Court has supported practically all, even the most drastic, of the measures passed by states and by Congress to bring these, and other agencies of communication and public service, under governmental control. Rebates, higher charges for short than for long hauls, pools, rate fixing and service by the public, control over capitalization, mergers, even wages of employes — to the multitude of restrictions on these subjects the judiciary has given its blessing. That administration of new powers has not resulted in a railroad Elysium is true, but administration is not the duty of the courts; practical failures in these lines, therefore, cannot be laid at their doors. The other Congressional edict for holding industrial wealth in leash, the Sherman Antitrust Law, despite ten years of inanition, the Supreme Court has restored to vigor. If here again the reforms anticipated have not been accomplished, the fault is not that of the judicial branch. It has raised no impediment — at least no lasting impediment — to the efforts of Congress to destroy monopoly and restore competition. The extent to which the courts have tolerated the extension of the interstate commerce clause must astonish the wraiths of the founders of 1787.

James Bryce described American city government as the one "conspicuous failure" of American democracy; similarly the candid critic to-day must stigmatize the record of the judiciary on "social legislation" as the one great respect in which it has failed to keep abreast of progress. And here again the picture is not entirely unrelieved. If certain judges have displayed a persistent obtuseness in reading their own outworn prejudices into decisions, others have stood forth just as prominently in making the Constitution what it was intended to be from the start — a living and fluid instrument, built not for an age, but for all time, responsive to the needs of a changing world. The most engaging judicial figure of the new dispensation is the character known as the "dissenting" judge. He is the gentleman who differs, not only from the particular majority opinion, but from the spirit that informs it. Three liberals of this type stand particularly in the van — John Marshall Harlan, Oliver Wendell Holmes, and Louis Brandeis. Not that the dissenting judge is exclusively a modern product. One of the greatest "dissents" ever written was that of Justice Curtis against the Dred Scott decision. One of the most pertinacious dissentients was Peter V. Daniel of Virginia, who died in 1860 after nineteen years' service; as most of his many disagreements were uttered in defense of slavery and State rights, they are forgotten and played no part in the building of the constitutional structure. It was perhaps the tenor of Daniel's opinions that made "dissent" for a period unpopular. A judge, it was urged, who voted against the prevailing view should keep silence; courtesy to his brethren called for reticence; he should never write opinions conflicting, and, if he did, these opinions should not be published. Such exaggerated notions of judicial etiquette fortunately have not prevailed. Fortunately, because dissentient judges have exercised immeasurable influence on the development of law. It is now a commonplace that the dissenting opinions of one generation become the prevailing interpretation of the next. Justice Curtis's masterly dissent *in re* Dred Scott, for example, was subsequently written into the Constitution. The dissenting views of Justice Harlan in the Knight case — a case that chloroformed the antitrust law for a decade — ultimately were adopted as the opinion of the Court. Justice Harlan's violent disagreement with Chief Justice Fuller on the constitutionality of the income tax resulted in the Sixteenth Amendment. "If that is the Constitution," the disgusted jurist said, after the Fuller decision was read, "the Constitution cannot be amended too quickly." And the Constitution was so amended — though not quickly enough to satisfy this, the first of the great modern liberal judges.

For Harlan was a dissenting member long before Holmes and Brandeis, and a more persistent one than either. Though he died

in 1911, after a service which equaled, within a brief time, that of
Marshall and Field, he still holds the record for disagreements.
In his thirty-four years on the bench, Harlan wrote 316 dissenting
opinions. In many ways the man was a conservative of conservatives. Nothing, for example, could shake his fundamentalism
in religion. "Harlan retires at night," said his colleague, David J.
Brewer, "with one hand on the Constitution and the other on
the Bible, safe and happy in a perfect faith in justice and
righteousness." There is an old-fashioned American for you;
one might even call him a puritanical mossback. And this religious bias now and then crept, most unjudicially, into the man's
decisions. When Georgia passed a law forbidding railroads to
carry freight on Sunday, Harlan, strict Sabbatarian that he was,
sustained it, though his brothers, in the majority, ruled it invalid.
Harlan was an enemy of strong drink, but this "prejudice," finding
its way into a famous dissent, has had a happier influence. Congress passed legislation prohibiting the shipment of alcoholic liquors
into states forbidding their sale; the Supreme Court overruled this
as an infraction of the commerce clause. Harlan dissented, and
this divergent opinion proved to be the one that afterward became
the prevailing law; for the Supreme Court afterward applied the
Webb-Kenyon measure, constructed on the same principle, and in
1936 it maintained the same constitutional idea in its application
to convict-made goods. Thus, in the view of many authorities, it
has opened the way to the solution of the child labor and other
"social" problems.

Harlan, despite his allegiance to American tradition, was farseeing and modern. This loyalty to conviction led him into many
strange ideas, or so they were regarded at the time. The nation
was astonished, in 1883, by Harlan's opinion that Congress, under
the Fourteenth Amendment, had the right to pass laws giving the
negro general access to restaurants, hotels, theatres, common schools,
and the like. "Jim Crow" laws found in this Kentuckian their
fiercest enemy. Judge Harlan was the only Southerner on the
bench at this time; all his eight colleagues, Northern men, took the
view of negro social equality that was more popular south of the
Potomac. But one of Harlan's principles was that, in interpreting
a law, great consideration should be given to the intent of its framers.
He always looked beneath the verbiage of a particular statute, attempting to find the purpose that animated it. Was it not plain
that the makers of the Fourteenth Amendment intended to convey civic rights to negroes? Was not that the passion that

urged Sumner and the rest in their championship?   Should not the law carrying out that purpose be sustained?   On all constitutional questions Harlan regarded Madison's *Debates* almost as devoutly as he did the Constitution, for that volume pretty clearly indicated, in most cases, what the fathers had in mind.

Naturally Justice Harlan believed that his parents, in naming him John Marshall, were inspired by a happy prescience, for there were few men whom he so venerated and so loyally took for model. Above all did Marshall's devotion to the Union become Harlan's lodestar.   Though born into the Democratic Party, he championed the Northern side in the war, was appointed an officer in the Federal Army, and, at the end of hostilities, went over to the Republicans and even accepted the Reconstruction measures.   Kentucky's loyalty to the Union in 1860–1865, in considerable part, was owing to Harlan's steadfastness.   When President Hayes nominated him Supreme Court justice in 1877, the public was naturally prepared for the vigor and independence immediately shown.   Vigor indeed, even of an eruptive kind, was Harlan's physical and mental quality. One episode in his latter years Washington will never forget.   The nine Supreme Court justices, having an adequate number for a baseball team, challenged the younger members of the Washington bar.   The exciting moment came when Harlan, aged seventy-five, stepped up to the plate; seizing the bat, he made a terrific lunge at the advancing ball, which quickly circled into territory far beyond centre field.   The judicial figure, heroic in size, had progressed as far as third base before the laggard sphere caught up with him.   The Capital had long been familiar with its favorite justice.   Every morning he rode to his duties on the rear platform of a streetcar, ready to discuss pending events with any chance fellow passenger. At lunch time he could usually be found at a low-priced restaurant with his glass of milk and apple pie.   Every morning he bought his newspaper from the same ancient vendor; if this old figure failed to be at his station, the judge, disconsolate, would pass on, patronizing no other.   Every Sunday he was a regular attendant at the Presbyterian Church, conducting his Bible class.   Inevitably the love which Washington always bestows upon its Supreme Court judges was particularly warm for this veteran.   His muscular frame made Harlan an unforgettable sight in the drawing room or on the bench; his "seventy-two inches of commanding body," as someone described it, his gray eagle of a face, his bald, massive dome, his deep organ voice, well accorded with the courtly manners and ever-present sense of humor that made him a lifelong favorite in Washington society. The man's honesty, sympathy, strength, and courage are qualities that vibrate through the several thousand pages Harlan added to judicial literature.

"He was the last of the tobacco-spitting judges," said Oliver Wendell Holmes, but this did not imply any antiquarianism in his colleague's outlook. How modern this was appeared when the Supreme Court, on May 20, 1895, filed in to deliver its opinion on the income tax passed as part of the Tariff Law of 1894. A proper understanding of this measure takes one back to the Continental Congress and the Articles of Confederation. One of the great weaknesses of that instrument was its failure to provide a system of Federal taxation. Congress could raise money only by quotas. It fixed the grand sum needed for governmental expenses; then a "requisition" was made on each state for its share, calculated on the basis of population. That is, it was a direct tax, apportioned among the states. The statesmen of 1787 took over this idea. "No capitation or other direct tax shall be laid, unless in proportion to the census or Enumeration herein directed to be taken." But what was a "direct tax"? This question became acute at the time of the Civil War, when the first income tax was levied. Since this assessment was collected from individuals, the cry went up that this was a "direct tax" and, not having been levied as the Constitution required, was unconstitutional. The Supreme Court, before which the question arose in 1868, dismissed the plea. There were only two taxes, it decided, that were direct in the constitutional sense, a poll tax and a tax on land. So, when Congress in 1894 adopted another income tax, — the war measure had been repealed long since, — it was thought that the Supreme Court had already passed on its constitutionality. But again the cry was raised. It was a "direct tax" and, not being apportioned as the Constitution required, was void. The best legal talent of the day came to the rescue of disgruntled income-tax payers. The arguments had a distinct contemporary sound. This impost was an attack on thrift by disrupters of society! Joseph H. Choate stigmatized it as "a communist march on private property." When the Supreme Court, by a decision of five to four, pronounced it unconstitutional, a great pæan arose in the financial district. Chauncey M. Depew beamed upon reporters, informing them that Cornelius Vanderbilt, more concerned in the decision than any other American, was "pleased by the news."

One prominent citizen did not join in the jubilation. This was John M. Harlan, long become the most dissentient of dissenters. He made no effort to conceal his displeasure while Chief Justice Fuller droned out the lengthy opinion. According to newspaper accounts, Harlan "glared" at his colleagues and, "lifting his eyebrows" and moving restlessly in his seat, with difficulty maintained silence until the end. Evidently the acrid discussions of the conference room were transferred to an open forum, for Justice Field leaned back most contentedly in his chair and the large bland countenance of Horace Gray reflected satisfaction. As soon as the Chief Justice finished his recital, the resonant voice of the Kentucky jurist began to boom. One of Justice Harlan's habits was to deliver his dissents extemporaneously from the bench and afterward to reduce them to writing for the record. This method served him well in the present instance, for his opinion was really an impassioned speech. Nor were gestures lacking: the fist descended, full force, upon the bench; the bulky frame, when an important point was scored, would turn and defiantly face the Chief Justice. When Harlan referred to the "bare majority" by which the law had been killed, there was something in his voice suggestive of a sneer. According to solemn injunction the Supreme Court must not be treated with disrespect, but this restraint, on this occasion, Harlan hardly observed. "This decision may well excite the gravest apprehension. . . . No tax is more just in its essence than an income tax. . . . On my conscience I regard this decision as a disaster." And so on for nearly an hour.

Such was the spirit that ran through all Harlan's opinions, even those given in a more subdued manner. He believed that the Constitution, as it stood, was competent to render justice in the modern world; he saw in it a historic miracle — a charter of government adopted in the eighteenth century that could solve most of the problems presented by the nineteenth and the twentieth. No man did more to interpret it in this sense. Harlan's chief influence was exercised in solving the problems created by modern industry and business — by the corporations and the trusts. The Antitrust Law adopted in 1890 had, as already said, become almost a dead letter in the administrations of Harrison and Cleveland and McKinley, but Harlan, on the bench, successfully seconded the efforts of Theodore Roosevelt to revive it to serve the ends its devisers had planned — to end monopoly, stop price fixing, restore competition as the industrial ideal. If the Sherman Act failed in practice to produce such results, the fault was not Harlan's. His great triumph came in 1904, when he prepared the majority opinion in the Northern Securities case. J. Pierpont Morgan and James J. Hill had parceled out the area extending from the Mississippi to the Pacific — that is, the northern half of it — as a great railroad empire. The Northern Securities Company gathered all the railroads of this area into one company, controlled by these two magnates. The purpose was to end competition, to fix rates. But the Harlan opinion destroyed the plan. The railroads, as a consequence, were segregated and returned to their original owners. The decision dissolving the Standard Oil Company also met his concurrence, though in this case he filed another dissent, not to the judgment itself, but to the principle on which it rested. Despite the fact that the Antitrust Law prohibited "every contract in restraint of trade," Chief Justice White insisted that only "unreasonable" restraint was forbidden; the Standard Oil monopoly was outlawed because its restraint was "unreasonable." The reading of this word into a law of Congress aroused Harlan to a fierceness almost as tense as had the income-tax decision. He was strongly opposed to a practice of which much has been heard recently — that of erecting the Supreme Court into a third house of legislation. When the Supreme Court inserted words into laws that were not there, it became, Harlan said, a superlegislature. This was Harlan's last warning to the American people. He died October 14, 1911, in his seventy-ninth year.

X

But he left able successors. Oliver Wendell Holmes had been appointed by Roosevelt in 1902; Charles Evans Hughes by Taft in 1910; Louis D. Brandeis by Wilson in 1916; and Benjamin N. Cardozo by Hoover in 1932. These men, with Harlan, constitute the great liberal representation of modern times. To them should be added a fifth, bearing the name of the expounder of the preceding generation — Harlan F. Stone. The most original mind in the group was Oliver Wendell Holmes. Indeed he comes close to fulfilling the admonition of the philosopher whom the future jurist knew as a boy: "Beware when the great God lets loose a thinker on this planet." Such a phenomenon has really happened only twice in the history of the Supreme Court — once with Marshall and again with the man who, a century after Marshall's succession, went upon the Supreme Bench. Thus, in accordance with a rule of which there are other instances, Virginia and Massachusetts have joined hands in giving the nation the judicial leaders that have shaped the Constitution.

Of Holmes's preëminence the recognition is abundant, here and abroad. John Morley, returning from his last American visit, declared that in Oliver Wendell Holmes America possessed the foremost English-speaking jurist. Harold J. Laski has characterized him as "law in the grand style." Tributes like these reflect the quality that lifts Holmes above most of his fellow judges; primarily he was not a judge, but a philosopher, a historian, even, as some have called him, a poet. The law on which he concentrated represented only one phase of that comprehensive fact, life itself, to the full realization of which he always made it subservient. "Life is painting a picture, not doing a sum," was one of Holmes's long list of famous aphorisms; and the tendency of so much legalistic lore to treat it as a "sum," a matter that could be reduced to impeccable logic and framed in rigid syllogisms, aroused in him something resembling anger. This broad philosophic standpoint Holmes came by naturally. His surroundings from his earliest days were not legal, but literary and intellectual.   His forbears were not lawyers, but poets, essayists, historians, preachers, reformers; he himself observed the caution of his witty father, who insisted that the wise man selects his ancestors for at least two centuries preceding his birth.   Perhaps the justice's greatest triumph was in giving a new personality to a famous name.   When he was born, and for many years afterward, "Oliver Wendell Holmes" meant one of the most charming of the New England writers, but to-day, when these syllables are uttered, there comes to mind the scholarly gentleman who for so many years gave grace and humanistic philosophy to the highest bench.   Holmes studied Plato long before he turned to the law; as a boy he wrote an essay on that genius, which met the qualified approval of Emerson; at Harvard his chief interests were literature and philosophy, and his most intimate friend was William James.   And when Holmes finally turned to law, as his father, despite gifts as a writer, had turned to medicine, it was not the rough and tumble of the courts that attracted him.

"I am afraid Brandeis is a crusader," he remarked late in life, speaking of the colleague who for years had also been his friend; "he talks like one of those upward and onward fellows."   That is precisely what Holmes never became.   His actual experience in practice was brief; he early began to contribute essays to legal literature, to edit the *American Law Review,* and to write his book on *The Common Law,* which for sixty years, in all countries and all languages, has been accepted as one of the great treatises of all time.   But from the first it was the intellectual aspects of the profession that engaged him.   While Oliver Wendell Holmes, *père,* was lecturing on anatomy in the Harvard Medical School, the son was holding forth to students in the law department.   The year 1882 proved the critical one in his life, when he was forced to decide between two courses, neither of which, however, contemplated practice.   Should he continue the work just begun as professor of law at Harvard, or should he accept the appointment now tendered to the Judicial Supreme Court of Massachusetts?   Holmes decided on the bench, and thus had twenty years' judicial training before Theodore Roosevelt named him for the United States Supreme Court.   Most justices have reached this dignity through politics and legal practice, but there was nothing of the "corporation lawyer" in Holmes's experience.   All his life he had been the meditator on justice and its problems; had been able to view them aloof from his personal interests, and to accumulate, through forty years' study, a reasoned philosophy in the art — for to

Holmes law was as much an art as a science or a department of learning.

By the time he reached this ultimate goal, what were his underlying theories of his profession? His writings, especially the dissents, contain their gist; and they form a contribution, not only to law and the institutions, but to literature. These dissertations from the bench have the quality of little Baconian essays — they are for the most part brief, pithy, epigrammatic, full of humor, satire, occasionally with an impish twist, and the kind of wisdom that endures. The one lesson Holmes had apparently learned from history and the law was the utter fluidity of life. Nature in all its aspects, physical, human, institutional, was in a constant state of motion and change. This was the omnipresent teaching of science and experience. This was the thing above all that Holmes had learned from his beloved Greeks; the old Greek axiom, "Man never steps into the same river twice," constituted a truth applicable to all human development, especially the law. Everything was in a state of flux; a man who had not grasped this fact was not likely to be useful in any field. He who adhered to tradition, simply because it was tradition, who answered the multitudinous questions of the present by a stolid acquiescence in the past, Holmes regarded as an enemy of society.

"The longing for repose and certainty that is in every human mind" aroused his contempt, for "certainty," he said, "generally is illusion, and repose is not the destiny of man." Aphorism after aphorism follows in his pages embodying the same aversion. "To rest upon a formula is a slumber that, prolonged, means death." A great fallacy is that "we have nothing to do but sit still and let time run over us." "The law does all that is needed when it does all that it can." "Legislation may begin where all evil begins." "The Fourteenth Amendment did not enact Herbert Spencer's *Social Status.*" Nothing in the course of the centuries — unless it is theology — has been so encumbered by fixed ideas and accepted rules of action as the law, and for all this lumber Holmes would substitute intelligence, the contemporary use of the reasoning faculty, unencumbered by allegiance to solutions that have long outlived their pertinence, because they have outlived the circumstances that called them into being. "The life of the law has not been logic; it has been experience." "The running waters are full of life and health; only in the stagnant waters is stagnation and death." "It is revolting to have no better reason for a rule of law than that it was laid down in the reign of Henry IV. It is still more revolting if the grounds upon which it was laid down have vanished long since and the rule simply persists through blind interpretation of the past."

One might think that a lawyer-philosopher who holds these ideas would turn his back upon the American Constitution. Here, the critic urges, is a classic specimen of frozen jurisprudence; here are embodied those rusty principles of the past that a modern age has outgrown; here is something rigid, obstructive, not articulate with human progress. Yet Oliver Wendell Holmes did not declaim against the charter of 1787. He admired and respected it. And his admiration was based upon his conviction that it was a flexible instrument. Unless the Constitution could serve the needs and aspirations of the masses of men in a modern world, it had no excuse for existence; but in Holmes's opinion it met this final test. "When men realize," he wrote, "that time has upset many fighting faiths, they may come to believe even more than they believe the very foundations of their own conduct that the ultimate good desired is better reached by free trade in ideas — that the best test of truth is to get itself accepted in the competition of the market, and that truth is the only ground upon which their wishes safely can be carried out. That, at any rate, is the theory of our Constitution. It is an experiment, as all life is an experiment."

Holmes was a thinking patriot; he revered the Constitution, first of all, because it had made the United States a nation. In considering this quality of the man one must keep in mind his service in the war. Holmes fought at Ball's Bluff, Antietam, and Fredericksburg; he was wounded five times, thrice seriously; and these experiences did more than anything else to form his spiritual background. They gave him, above all, a deep love for his country and a belief in it as an agency for advancing freedom and justice. New England Federalism, the creed of his ancestors, which was almost a living faith with the elder Oliver Wendell Holmes, had not become entirely extinct in the son. At any rate, Holmes's belief in the national, central government never left him. "The thing for which Hamilton argued," he wrote, "and Marshall decided, and Grant fought, and Lincoln died, is now our corner stone." At times, in speaking of this Union, Holmes could become emotional in an old-style Websterian manner. "The flag is but a bit of bunting to one who insists on prose. Yet thanks to Marshall and to the men of his generation its red is our lifeblood, its stars our world, its blue our heaven. It owns our land. At will it throws away our lives."

This admiration for Marshall is significant; it explains Holmes's attitude towards the nation and the Constitution. In the law school of Harvard University to-day hang two portraits, facing each other; one is that of Marshall, and the other of Holmes, and in the presence of the Great Expounder, says Learned Hand, his twentieth-century contemporary "need not flinch." It is said that Roosevelt hesitated a month before sending Holmes's name to the Senate, certain of his comments on Marshall not seeming to that intemperate patriot sufficiently fervid. To the more judicious citizen, however, Holmes's appraisement leaves little unsaid. For he designated Marshall as the chief exemplar of American lawyers; could one ask more than that? "When I consider his might, his justice, and his wisdom, I do fully believe that if American law were to be fully represented by a single figure, skeptic and worshipper alike would agree without dispute that the figure could be one alone, and that of John Marshall." And the reasons for so elevating Marshall have contemporary application. Holmes thought it "a fortunate circumstance" that the appointment of a Chief Justice in 1800 fell to John Adams "instead of to Jefferson a month later. . . . It gave to a Federalist and loose Constructionist to start the workings of the Constitution. . . . When we celebrate Marshall we celebrate at the same time and indivisibly the inevitable fact that the one-ness of the nation and the supremacy of the national constitution were declared to govern the dealings of man with man by the judgments and decrees of the most august of courts." There is little comfort for the followers of Jefferson in this. Strict construction, government by minute political visions, the virtual elimination of the courts in constitutional exegesis, State rights, and nullification found no sympathizer in this latter-day champion of Democracy. It was because Marshall employed the basic instrument as a means of wielding a disharmonious people into a nation that, in Holmes's opinion, he deserved the lofty pedestal posterity has put up for him. And there was another reason. Marshall was a "loose constructionist." This is an old-fashioned way of expressing the Holmes epigram that "the Constitution is an experiment, as all life is an experiment," that it is not rigid, but is adaptable to changing conditions and to new problems. When the need arose for Federal banking and Federal improvements Marshall recognized that the Constitution gave them warrant; when expanding American commerce made necessary a curb on local selfishness, Marshall disinterred the almost forgotten interstate commerce clause and endowed it with significance whose full effect has been realized only in modern times. Marshall's spirit no more "longed for repose" than that of Holmes; nor was it hostile to "free trade in ideas"; and to him also the "life of the law" was not "logic." The Great Expounder was no "Black letter man of the law," but a jurist who kept pace with his age.

Nor did Marshall's assertion of the power of judicial review seem to Holmes to violate either the letter or the spirit of the Constitution. The latter-day critics who regard this as a usurpation, as a measure never projected by the fathers, find no supporter in Holmes. Nothing is clearer to students of the convention of 1787 than that the statesmen of that body expected constitutional problems to be decided by the courts. Certainly Holmes had no doubts on this point. "Although research has shown and practice has established," he said, "the futility of the charge that it was an assumption when this court undertook to declare an act of Congress unconstitutional, I suppose we all agree that to do so is the gravest and most delicate duty that this court is called upon to perform." Marshall might have written that sentence, for it accords not only with his belief, but with his performance. Those who oppose this judicial power are forever quoting one of Holmes's dicta that seems to support their view. "I do not think the country would come to an end if we [that is, the Supreme Court] lost our power to declare an act of Congress void." But the rest of this paragraph, equally significant, is not so often pressed into service. "I do think the United States would be imperilled if we could not make that declaration as to the laws of the several states. For one in my place sees how often a local policy prevails with those who are not trained to national views and how often action is taken that embodies what the Commerce Clause was meant to end." It needs no jurist to see that, if states could disregard the Constitution with no check from the courts, the entire Federal fabric would fall in ruins. And this admiration again accorded with the Marshall precedent; although he obliterated only one law of Congress — and that an unimportant one — in his long career, he did set aside much unconstitutional state legislation. This paragraph shows again how far in principle Holmes was removed from Jefferson. Nothing about the Federal judiciary so angered the genius of Monticello as that prerogative of setting aside unconstitutional state laws which Holmes regarded as the very keystone of the national arch.

But here again, as in all questions affecting the Constitution, Holmes believed in moderation. Strongly as he advocated judicial supervision of state legislation, he insisted that it could be carried too far. The same caution the courts should use in voiding national laws should be applied to the enactments of state legislatures. The powers granted to Congress fall naturally into two groups. Some of them are so definitely expressed that no human being, whether a Supreme Court justice or an intelligent schoolboy, could doubt their meaning. If Congress, for example, should lay a tax on exports, would anyone question that such an act was "unconstitutional"? If it should set up the Catholic or the Methodist or the Presbyterian Church as a national religious establishment, would not the unconstitutionality of such legislation be immediately apparent? And there are many other powers about which there could similarly be no dispute. But there are others the meaning of which is not so plain. The opinion of one sensible and honest man is about as good as is another's. In such matters judicial interpretation depends largely upon the particular judge who passes upon them. That the personal predilections of the deciding judge creep into his decisions it would be folly to deny. That is, legislation — frequently introduced, in Holmes's priceless adverb, "interstitially" — sometimes gets into opinions that are supposed to rest exclusively on legal grounds. That the wisdom of the Supreme Court is not infallible is shown by the fact that different courts have decided the same questions in diametrically opposing ways. When the highest tribunal rules in 1870 that legal tenders are unconstitutional, and in 1871 that they are constitutional; when it decides in 1868 that an income tax does not contravene the fundamental law, and in 1895 rules that it does; when, to come down to modern times, it proclaims, in 1904, that no state may fix minimum hours for workers, and in 1908 proclaims that a state may do just that thing, it is a reasonable conclusion that the human element — the personal attitudes of the disagreeing judges — has entered into their conclusions. Theodore Roosevelt, in a cynical moment, said that the validity of a law depended on whether the fifth Supreme Court justice came down "heads or tails."

On such doubtful questions Holmes believed that Congress and state legislatures should be given pretty free sway. When unconstitutionality was not explicit, the Court should not set aside their laws, though it should not hesitate to do so when the Constitution had been palpably disregarded. This problem became especially acute in his own period of service. "Due process of law" became the lawyers' device for thwarting humanitarian legislation which the states desired. The efforts to establish hours of labor, working conditions for women, employers' liability, minimum wages, and other measures for protecting public health and morals and bringing to the underdog a larger share of the satisfactions and conveniences of life than fate had accorded him, were ruthlessly outlawed under the Fourteenth Amendment.   To Holmes, as to most enlightened souls, this remnant of an obsolete controversy thus became an engine of selfishness for thwarting progress.   Why should a phrase, on the meaning of which even the most scholarly justices disagree, be used by unimaginative jurists to impede human progress?   If states wished to indulge in social experiments, and pay for them, and in doing so violated no definitely expressed constitutional prohibition, why should they not be permitted to do so?   And so with constitutional interpretation in general.   "There is nothing I more deprecate than the use of the Fourteenth Amendment beyond the absolute compulsion of its words to prevent the making of social experiments that an important part of the community desires, in the insulated chambers afforded by the several states, even though the experiment may seem fatal or even obnoxious to me and to those whose judgment I most respect."   Wisdom and tolerance cannot go further than that.   And in this attitude again John Marshall would not have disagreed.   For most of the state laws Marshall set aside were brazen defiances of constitutional provisions.   Maryland passed a law that virtually vetoed the national power to establish banks.   Who would deny such a power to-day?   He set aside a Georgia law that arrogated to that state the right to make a treaty, explicitly conferred by the Constitution on the Executive and the Senate.   He quashed a New York statute which pretended to regulate interstate commerce, the unmistakable right of the Federal power.   Holmes would not disagree with such decisions, — and others of the same kind, — for they belonged to that first category of absolute violations which he thought the Federal courts should set aside.

Thus these two great figures — Marshall in the early nineteenth century and Holmes in the early twentieth — may be taken as embodying the spirit and achievements of the Constitution in their day.   And it is a satisfaction that, though separated in time by a century, in thought and aspiration they are so much akin.   And the deep-seated reason was the same.   They were both Americans.   In the estimation of these two great jurists the Constitution, despite demonstrated shortcomings, had accomplished one stupendous result.   To Marshall and Holmes — one a soldier in the Revolution, one a soldier in the Civil War — the Constitution was great, and worthy of protection and respect, because it had created a Nation.

THE CONSTITUTION OF THE UNITED STATES OF AMERICA

THE CONSTITUTION OF THE UNITED STATES OF AMERICA

(The following text is that published by the United States Government, Department of the Interior, Bureau of Education, United States Government Printing Office, Washington, 1935.)

WE THE PEOPLE of the United States, in Order to form a more perfect Union, establish Justice, insure domestic Tranquility, provide for the common defence, promote the general Welfare, and secure the Blessings of Liberty to ourselves and our Posterity, do ordain and establish this CONSTITUTION for the United States of America.

ARTICLE I.

SECTION 1. All legislative Powers herein granted shall be vested in a Congress of the United States, which shall consist of a Senate and House of Representatives.

SECTION 2. The House of Representatives shall be composed of Members chosen every second Year by the People of the several States, and the Electors in each State shall have the Qualifications requisite for Electors of the most numerous Branch of the State Legislature.

No Person shall be a Representative who shall not have attained to the Age of twenty-five Years, and been seven Years a Citizen of the United States, and who shall not, when elected, be an Inhabitant of that State in which he shall be chosen.

[Representatives and direct Taxes shall be apportioned among the several States which may be included within this Union, according to their respective Numbers, which shall be determined by adding to the whole Number of free Persons, including those bound to Service for a Term of Years, and excluding Indians not taxed, three fifths of all other Persons.] The actual Enumeration shall be made within three Years after the first Meeting of the Congress of the United States, and within every subsequent Term of ten Years, in such Manner as they shall by Law direct. The Number of Representatives shall not exceed one for every thirty Thousand, but each State shall have at Least one Representative;

and until such enumeration shall be made, the State of New Hampshire shall be entitled to chuse three, Massachusetts eight, Rhode-Island and Providence Plantations one, Connecticut five, New York six, New Jersey four, Pennsylvania eight, Delaware one, Maryland six, Virginia ten, North Carolina five, South Carolina five, and Georgia three.

When vacancies happen in the Representation from any State, the Executive Authority thereof shall issue Writs of Election to fill such Vacancies.

The House of Representatives shall chuse their Speaker and other Officers; and shall have the sole Power of Impeachment.

SECTION 3. The Senate of the United States shall be composed of two Senators from each State, chosen by the Legislature thereof, for six Years; and each Senator shall have one Vote.

Immediately after they shall be assembled in Consequence of the first Election, they shall be divided as equally as may be into three Classes. The Seats of the Senators of the first Class shall be vacated at the Expiration of the second Year, of the second Class at the Expiration of the fourth Year, and of the third Class at the Expiration of the sixth Year, so that one-third may be chosen every second Year; and if Vacancies happen by Resignation, or otherwise, during the Recess of the Legislature of any State, the Executive thereof may make temporary Appointments until the next Meeting of the Legislature, which shall then fill such Vacancies.

No Person shall be a Senator who shall not have attained to the Age of thirty Years, and been nine Years a Citizen of the United States, and who shall not, when elected, be an Inhabitant of that State for which he shall be chosen.

The Vice President of the United States shall be President of the Senate, but shall have no Vote, unless they be equally divided.

The Senate shall chuse their other Officers, and also a President pro tempore, in the absence of the Vice President, or when he shall exercise the Office of President of the United States.

The Senate shall have the sole Power to try all Impeachments. When sitting for that Purpose, they shall be on Oath or Affirmation. When the President of the United States is tried, the Chief Justice shall preside: And no Person shall be convicted without the Concurrence of two thirds of the Members present.

Judgment in Cases of Impeachment shall not extend further than to removal from Office, and disqualification to hold and enjoy any Office of honor, Trust or Profit under the United States: but the Party convicted shall nevertheless be liable and subject to Indictment, Trial, Judgment and Punishment, according to Law.

SECTION 4. The Times, Places and Manner of holding Elections for Senators and Representatives, shall be prescribed in each State by the Legislature thereof; but the Congress may at any time by Law make or alter such Regulations, except as to the Places of Chusing Senators.

The Congress shall assemble at least once in every Year, and such Meeting shall be on the first Monday in December, unless they shall by Law appoint a different Day.

SECTION 5. Each House shall be the Judge of the Elections, Returns and Qualifications of its own Members, and a Majority of each shall constitute a Quorum to do Business; but a smaller Number may adjourn from day to day, and may be authorized to compel the Attendance of absent Members, in such Manner, and under such Penalties as each House may provide.

Each House may determine the Rules of its Proceedings, punish its Members for disorderly Behavior, and, with the Concurrence of two thirds, expel a Member.

Each House shall keep a Journal of its Proceedings, and from time to time publish the same, excepting such Parts as may in their Judgment require Secrecy; and the Yeas and Nays of the Members of either House on any question shall, at the Desire of one fifth of those Present, be entered on the Journal.

Neither House, during the Session of Congress, shall, without the Consent of the other, adjourn for more than three days, nor to any other Place than that in which the two Houses shall be sitting.

SECTION 6. The Senators and Representatives shall receive a Compensation for their Services, to be ascertained by Law, and paid out of the Treasury of the United States. They shall in all Cases, except Treason, Felony and Breach of the Peace, be privileged from Arrest during their Attendance at the Session of their respective Houses, and in going to and returning from the same; and for any Speech or Debate in either House, they shall not be questioned in any other Place.

No Senator or Representative shall, during the Time for which he was elected, be appointed to any civil Office under the Authority of the United States, which shall have been created, or the Emoluments whereof shall have been encreased during such time; and no Person holding any Office under the United States, shall be a Member of either House during his Continuance in Office.

SECTION 7. All Bills for raising Revenue shall originate in the House of Representatives; but the Senate may propose or concur with Amendments as on other Bills.

Every Bill which shall have passed the House of Representatives and the Senate, shall, before it become a Law, be presented to the President of the United States; If he approve he shall sign it, but if not he shall return it, with his Objections to that House in which it shall have originated, who shall enter the Objections at large on their Journal, and proceed to reconsider it. If after such Reconsideration two thirds of that House shall agree to pass the Bill, it shall be sent, together with the Objections, to the other House, by which it shall likewise be reconsidered, and if approved by two thirds of that House, it shall become a Law. But in all such Cases the Votes of both Houses shall be determined by Yeas and Nays, and the Names of the Persons voting for and against the Bill shall be entered on the Journal of each House respectively. If any Bill shall not be returned by the President within ten Days (Sundays excepted) after it shall have been presented to him, the Same shall be a Law, in like Manner as if he had signed it, unless the Congress by their Adjournment prevent its Return, in which Case it shall not be a Law.

Every Order, Resolution, or Vote to which the Concurrence of the Senate and House of Representatives may be necessary (except on a question of Adjournment) shall be presented to the President of the United States; and before the Same shall take Effect, shall be approved by him, or being disapproved by him, shall be repassed by two thirds of the Senate and House of Representatives, according to the Rules and Limitations prescribed in the Case of a Bill.

Section 8. The Congress shall have Power To lay and collect Taxes, Duties, Imposts and Excises, to pay the Debts and provide for the common Defence and general Welfare of the United States; but all Duties, Imposts and Excises shall be uniform throughout the United States;

To borrow money on the credit of the United States;

To regulate Commerce with foreign Nations, and among the several States, and with the Indian Tribes;

To establish an uniform Rule of Naturalization, and uniform Laws on the subject of Bankruptcies throughout the United States;

To coin Money, regulate the Value thereof, and of foreign Coin, and fix the Standard of Weights and Measures;

To provide for the Punishment of counterfeiting the Securities and current Coin of the United States;

To establish Post Offices and post Roads;

To promote the Progress of Science and useful Arts, by securing for limited Times to Authors and Inventors the exclusive Right to their respective Writings and Discoveries;

To constitute Tribunals inferior to the supreme Court;

To define and punish Piracies and Felonies committed on the high Seas, and Offenses against the Law of Nations;

To declare War, grant Letters of Marque and Reprisal, and make Rules concerning Captures on Land and Water;

To raise and support Armies, but no Appropriation of Money to that Use shall be for a longer Term than two Years;

To provide and maintain a Navy;

To make Rules for the Government and Regulation of the land and naval Forces;

To provide for calling forth the Militia to execute the Laws of the Union, suppress Insurrections and repel Invasions;

To provide for organizing, arming, and disciplining the Militia, and for governing such Part of them as may be employed in the Service of the United States, reserving to the States respectively, the Appointment of the Officers, and the Authority of training the Militia according to the discipline prescribed by Congress;

To exercise exclusive Legislation in all Cases whatsoever, over such District (not exceeding ten Miles square) as may, by Cession of particular States, and the acceptance of Congress, become the Seat of the Government of the United States, and to exercise like Authority over all Places purchased by the Consent of the Legislature of the State in which the Same shall be, for the Erection of Forts, Magazines, Arsenals, dock-Yards, and other needful Buildings; — And

To make all Laws which shall be necessary and proper for carrying into Execution the foregoing Powers, and all other Powers vested by this Constitution in the Government of the United States, or in any Department or Officer thereof.

Section 9. The Migration or Importation of such Persons as any of the States now existing shall think proper to admit, shall not be prohibited by the Congress prior to the Year one thousand eight hundred and eight, but a tax or duty may be imposed on such Importation, not exceeding ten dollars for each Person.

The privilege of the Writ of Habeas Corpus shall not be suspended, unless when in Cases of Rebellion or Invasion the public Safety may require it.

No Bill of Attainder or ex post facto Law shall be passed.

No capitation, or other direct, Tax shall be laid, unless in Proportion to the Census or Enumeration herein before directed to be taken.

No Tax or Duty shall be laid on Articles exported from any State.

No Preference shall be given by any Regulation of Commerce or Revenue to the Ports of one State over those of another: nor shall Vessels bound to, or from, one State, be obliged to enter, clear, or pay Duties in another.

No Money shall be drawn from the Treasury, but in Consequence of Appropriations made by Law; and a regular Statement and Account of the Receipts and Expenditures of all public Money shall be published from time to time.

No Title of Nobility shall be granted by the United States: And no Person holding any Office of Profit or Trust under them, shall, without the Consent of the Congress, accept of any present, Emolument, Office, or Title, of any kind whatever, from any King, Prince, or foreign State.

SECTION 10. No State shall enter into any Treaty, Alliance, or Confederation; grant Letters of Marque and Reprisal; coin Money; emit Bills of Credit; make any Thing but gold and silver Coin a Tender in Payment of Debts; pass any Bill of Attainder, ex post facto Law, or Law impairing the Obligation of Contracts, or grant any Title of Nobility.

No State shall, without the Consent of the Congress, lay any Imposts or Duties on Imports or Exports, except what may be absolutely necessary for executing it's inspection Laws: and the net Produce of all Duties and Imposts, laid by any State on Imports or Exports, shall be for the Use of the Treasury of the United States; and all such Laws shall be subject to the Revision and Controul of the Congress.

No State shall, without the Consent of Congress, lay any duty of Tonnage, keep Troops, or Ships of War in time of Peace, enter into any Agreement or Compact with another State, or with a foreign Power, or engage in War, unless actually invaded, or in such imminent Danger as will not admit of delay.

ARTICLE II.

SECTION 1. The executive Power shall be vested in a President of the United States of America. He shall hold his Office during the Term of four Years, and, together with the Vice-President, chosen for the same Term, be elected, as follows

Each State shall appoint, in such Manner as the Legislature thereof may direct, a Number of Electors, equal to the whole Number of Senators and Representatives to which the State may be entitled in the Congress: but no Senator or Representative, or Person holding an Office of Trust or Profit under the United States, shall be appointed an Elector.

[The Electors shall meet in their respective States, and vote by Ballot for two persons, of whom one at least shall not be an Inhabitant of the same State with themselves. And they shall make a List of all the Persons voted for, and of the Number of Votes for each; which

List they shall sign and certify, and transmit sealed to the Seat of the Government of the United States, directed to the President of the Senate. The President of the Senate shall, in the Presence of the Senate and House of Representatives, open all the Certificates, and the Votes shall then be counted. The Person having the greatest Number of Votes shall be the President, if such Number be a Majority of the whole Number of Electors appointed; and if there be more than one who have such Majority, and have an equal Number of Votes, then the House of Representatives shall immediately chuse by Ballot one of them for President; and if no Person have a Majority, then from the five highest on the List the said House shall in like Manner chuse the President. But in chusing the President, the Votes shall be taken by States, the Representation from each State having one Vote; A quorum for this Purpose shall consist of a Member or Members from two-thirds of the States, and a Majority of all the States shall be necessary to a Choice. In every Case, after the Choice of the President, the Person having the greatest Number of Votes of the Electors shall be the Vice President. But if there should remain two or more who have equal Votes, the Senate shall chuse from them by Ballot the Vice-President.]

The Congress may determine the Time of chusing the Electors, and the Day on which they shall give their Votes; which Day shall be the same throughout the United States.

No person except a natural born Citizen, or a Citizen of the United States, at the time of the Adoption of this Constitution, shall be eligible to the Office of President; neither shall any Person be eligible to that Office who shall not have attained to the Age of thirty-five Years, and been fourteen Years a Resident within the United States.

In Case of the Removal of the President from Office, or of his Death, Resignation, or Inability to discharge the Powers and Duties of the said Office, the same shall devolve on the Vice President, and the Congress may by Law provide for the Case of Removal, Death, Resignation or Inability, both of the President and Vice President, declaring what Officer shall then act as President, and such Officer shall act accordingly, until the Disability be removed, or a President shall be elected.

The President shall, at stated Times, receive for his Services, a Compensation, which shall neither be encreased nor diminished during the Period for which he shall have been elected, and he shall not receive within that Period any other Emolument from the United States, or any of them.

Before he enter on the Execution of his Office, he shall take the following Oath or Affirmation: — "I do solemnly swear (or affirm) that I will faithfully execute the Office of President of the United States, and will to the best of my Ability, preserve, protect and defend the Constitution of the United States."

SECTION 2. The President shall be Commander in Chief of the Army and Navy of the United States, and of the Militia of the several States, when called into the actual Service of the United States; he may require the Opinion in writing, of the principal Officer in each of the executive Departments, upon any subject relating to the Duties of their respective Offices, and he shall have Power to Grant Reprieves and Pardons for Offenses against the United States, except in Cases of Impeachment.

He shall have Power, by and with the Advice and Consent of the Senate, to make Treaties, provided two-thirds of the Senators present concur; and he shall nominate, and by and with the Advice and Consent of the Senate, shall appoint Ambassadors, other public Ministers and Consuls, Judges of the supreme Court, and all other Officers of the United States, whose Appointments are not herein otherwise provided for, and which shall be established by Law: but the Congress may by Law vest the Appointment of such inferior Officers, as they think proper, in the President alone, in the Courts of Law, or in the Heads of Departments.

The President shall have Power to fill up all Vacancies that may happen during the Recess of the Senate, by granting Commissions which shall expire at the End of their next Session.

SECTION 3. He shall from time to time give to the Congress Information of the State of the Union, and recommend to their Consideration such Measures as he shall judge necessary and expedient; he may, on extraordinary Occasions, convene both Houses, or either of them, and in Case of Disagreement between them, with Respect to the Time of Adjournment, he may adjourn them to such Time as he shall think proper; he shall receive Ambassadors and other public Ministers; he shall take Care that the Laws be faithfully executed, and shall Commission all the Officers of the United States.

SECTION 4. The President, Vice President and all civil Officers of the United States, shall be removed from Office on Impeachment for, and Conviction of, Treason, Bribery, or other high Crimes and Misdemeanors.

ARTICLE III.

SECTION 1. The judicial Power of the United States, shall be vested in one supreme Court, and in such inferior Courts as the Congress may from time to time ordain and establish. The Judges, both of the supreme and inferior Courts, shall hold their Offices during good Behaviour, and shall, at stated Times, receive for their Services a Compensation which shall not be diminished during their Continuance in Office.

SECTION 2. The judicial Power shall extend to all Cases, in Law and Equity, arising under this Constitution, the Laws of the United States, and Treaties made, or which shall be made, under their Authority; — to all Cases affecting Ambassadors, other public Ministers and Consuls; — to all Cases of admiralty and maritime Jurisdiction; — to Controversies to which the United States shall be a Party; — to Controversies between two or more States; — between a State and Citizens of another State; — between Citizens of different States; — between Citizens of the same State claiming Lands under Grants of different States, and between a State, or the Citizens thereof, and foreign States, Citizens or Subjects.

In all Cases affecting Ambassadors, other public Ministers and Consuls, and those in which a State shall be Party, the supreme Court shall have original Jurisdiction. In all the other Cases before mentioned, the supreme Court shall have appellate Jurisdiction, both as to Law and Fact, with such Exceptions, and under such Regulations as the Congress shall make.

The trial of all Crimes, except in Cases of Impeachment, shall be by Jury; and such Trial shall be held in the State where the said Crimes shall have been committed; but when not committed within any State, the Trial shall be at such Place or Places as the Congress may by Law have directed.

SECTION 3. Treason against the United States, shall consist only in levying War against them, or in adhering to their Enemies, giving them Aid and Comfort. No Person shall be convicted of Treason unless on the Testimony of two Witnesses to the same overt Act, or on Confession in open Court.

The Congress shall have power to declare the Punishment of Treason, but no Attainder of Treason shall work Corruption of Blood, or Forfeiture except during the Life of the Person attainted.

ARTICLE IV.

SECTION 1. Full Faith and Credit shall be given in each State to the public Acts, Records, and judicial Proceedings of every other State. And the Congress may by general Laws prescribe the Manner in which such Acts, Records and Proceedings shall be proved, and the Effect thereof.

SECTION 2. The Citizens of each State shall be entitled to all Privileges and Immunities of Citizens in the several States.

A Person charged in any State with Treason, Felony, or other Crime, who shall flee from Justice, and be found in another State, shall on demand of the executive Authority of the State from which he fled, be delivered up, to be removed to the State having Jurisdiction of the Crime.

No Person held to Service or Labour in one State, under the Laws thereof, escaping into another, shall, in Consequence of any Law or Regulation therein, be discharged from such Service or Labour, but shall be delivered up on Claim of the Party to whom such Service or Labour may be due.

SECTION 3. New States may be admitted by the Congress into this Union; but no new State shall be formed or erected within the Jurisdiction of any other State; nor any State be formed by the Junction of two or more States, or parts of States, without the Consent of the Legislatures of the States concerned as well as of the Congress.

The Congress shall have Power to dispose of and make all needful Rules and Regulations respecting the Territory or other Property belonging to the United States; and nothing in this Constitution shall be so construed as to Prejudice any Claims of the United States, or of any particular State.

SECTION 4. The United States shall guarantee to every State in this Union a Republican Form of Government, and shall protect each of them against Invasion; and on Application of the Legislature, or of the Executive (when the Legislature cannot be convened) against domestic Violence.

ARTICLE V.

The Congress, whenever two-thirds of both Houses shall deem it necessary, shall propose Amendments to this Constitution, or, on the Application of the Legislatures of two-thirds of the several States, shall call a Convention for proposing Amendments, which, in either Case, shall be valid to all Intents and Purposes, as part of this Constitution, when ratified by the Legislatures of three-fourths of the several States, or by Conventions in three-fourths thereof, as the one or the other Mode of Ratification may be proposed by the Congress; Provided that no Amendment which may be made prior to the Year One thousand eight hundred and eight shall in any Manner affect the first and fourth Clauses in the Ninth Section of the first Article; and that no State, without its Consent, shall be deprived of it's equal Suffrage in the Senate.

ARTICLE VI.

All Debts contracted and Engagements entered into, before the Adoption of this Constitution, shall be as valid against the United States under this Constitution, as under the Confederation.

This Constitution, and the Laws of the United States which shall be made in Pursuance thereof; and all Treaties made, or which shall be made, under the Authority of the United States, shall be the supreme Law of the Land; and the Judges in every State shall be bound thereby, any Thing in the Constitution or Laws of any State to the Contrary notwithstanding.

The Senators and Representatives before mentioned, and the Members of the several State Legislatures, and all executive and judicial Officers, both of the United States and of the several States, shall be bound by Oath or Affirmation, to support this Constitution; but no religious Test shall ever be required as a Qualification to any Office or public Trust under the United States.

ARTICLE VII.

The Ratification of the Conventions of nine States shall be sufficient for the Establishment of this Constitution between the States so ratifying the Same.

DONE in Convention by the Unanimous Consent of the States present the Seventeenth Day of September in the Year of our Lord one thousand seven hundred and Eighty seven and of the Independence of the United States of America the Twelfth. In Witness whereof We have hereunto subscribed our Names.

GO WASHINGTON
Presidt and deputy from Virginia

New Hampshire.

JOHN LANGDON   NICHOLAS GILMAN

Massachusetts.

NATHANIEL GORHAM   RUFUS KING

Connecticut.

WM SAML JOHNSON ROGER SHERMAN

New York.

ALEXANDER HAMILTON

New Jersey.

WIL: LIVINGSTON WM PATTERSON
DAVID BREARLEY. JONA: DAYTON

Pennsylvania.

B. FRANKLIN THOMAS MIFFLIN
ROBT. MORRIS GEO. CLYMER
THOS. FITZSIMONS JARED INGERSOLL
JAMES WILSON GOUV MORRIS

Delaware.

GEO: READ GUNNING BEDFORD jun
JOHN DICKINSON RICHARD BASSETT
JACO: BROOM

Maryland.

JAMES MCHENRY DAN: of ST THOS JENIFER
DANL CARROLL

Virginia.

JOHN BLAIR— JAMES MADISON JR.

North Carolina.

WM. BLOUNT RICHD DOBBS SPAIGHT
HU WILLIAMSON

South Carolina.

J. RUTLEDGE CHARLES COTESWORTH PINCKNEY
CHARLES PINCKNEY PIERCE BUTLER.

Georgia.

WILLIAM FEW ABR BALDWIN

Attest:

WILLIAM JACKSON, *Secretary.*

ARTICLES IN ADDITION TO, AND AMENDMENT OF, THE CONSTITU-
TION OF THE UNITED STATES OF AMERICA, PROPOSED BY CONGRESS,
AND RATIFIED BY THE LEGISLATURES OF THE SEVERAL STATES, PUR-
SUANT TO THE FIFTH ARTICLE OF THE ORIGINAL CONSTITUTION.

*(First ten amendments, the "Bill of Rights," proposed by Congress
September 25, 1789. In force December 15, 1791)*

[ARTICLE I.]

Congress shall make no law respecting an establishment of religion,
or prohibiting the free exercise thereof; or abridging the freedom
of speech, or of the press; or the right of the people peaceably to
assemble, and to petition the Government for a redress of grievances.

[ARTICLE II.]

A well regulated Militia, being necessary to the security of a free
State, the right of the people to keep and bear Arms, shall not be
infringed.

[ARTICLE III.]

No Soldier shall, in time of peace be quartered in any house, without
the consent of the Owner, nor in time of war, but in a manner to be
prescribed by law.

[ARTICLE IV.]

The right of the people to be secure in their persons, houses, papers,
and effects, against unreasonable searches and seizures, shall not be
violated, and no Warrants shall issue, but upon probable cause, supported by Oath or affirmation, and particularly describing the place to
be searched, and the persons or things to be seized.

[ARTICLE V.]

No person shall be held to answer for a capital, or otherwise infamous crime, unless on a presentment or indictment of a Grand Jury,
except in cases arising in the land or naval forces, or in the Militia,
when in actual service in time of War or public danger; nor shall
any person be subject for the same offence to be twice put in jeopardy of
life or limb; nor shall be compelled in any criminal case to be a witness
against himself, nor be deprived of life, liberty, or property, without
due process of law; nor shall private property be taken for public use,
without just compensation.

[ARTICLE VI.]

In all criminal prosecutions, the accused shall enjoy the right to a speedy and public trial, by an impartial jury of the State and district wherein the crime shall have been committed, which district shall have been previously ascertained by law, and to be informed of the nature and cause of the accusation; to be confronted with the witnesses against him; to have compulsory process for obtaining witnesses in his favor, and to have the Assistance of Counsel for his defence.

[ARTICLE VII.]

In suits at common law, where the value in controversy shall exceed twenty dollars, the right of trial by jury shall be preserved, and no fact tried by a jury, shall be otherwise re-examined in any Court of the United States, than according to the rules of the common law.

[ARTICLE VIII.]

Excessive bail shall not be required, nor excessive fines imposed, nor cruel and unusual punishments inflicted.

[ARTICLE IX.]

The enumeration in the Constitution, of certain rights, shall not be construed to deny or disparage others retained by the people.

[ARTICLE X.]

The powers not delegated to the United States by the Constitution, nor prohibited by it to the States, are reserved to the States respectively, or to the people.

ARTICLE XI.

(Proposed March 4, 1794; in force February 7, 1795)

The Judicial power of the United States shall not be construed to extend to any suit in law or equity, commenced or prosecuted against one of the United States by Citizens of another State, or by Citizens or Subjects of any Foreign State.

ARTICLE XII.

(Proposed December 12, 1803; in force September 25, 1804)

The Electors shall meet in their respective states and vote by ballot for President and Vice-President, one of whom, at least, shall not be an inhabitant of the same state with themselves; they shall name in their ballots the person voted for as President, and in distinct ballots the person voted for as Vice-President, and they shall make distinct lists of all persons voted for as President, and of all persons voted for as Vice-President, and of the number of votes for each, which lists they shall sign and certify, and transmit sealed to the seat of the government of the United States, directed to the President of the Senate; — The President of the Senate shall, in presence of the Senate and House of Representatives, open all the certificates and the votes shall then be counted; — The person having the greatest number of votes for President, shall be the President, if such number be a majority of the whole number of Electors appointed; and if no person have such majority, then from the persons having the highest numbers not exceeding three on the list of those voted for as President, the House of Representatives shall choose immediately, by ballot, the President. But in choosing the President, the votes shall be taken by states, the representation from each state having one vote; a quorum for this purpose shall consist of a member or members from two-thirds of the states, and a majority of all the states shall be necessary to a choice. And if the House of Representatives shall not choose a President whenever the right of choice shall devolve upon them, before the fourth day of March next following, then the Vice-President shall act as President, as in the case of the death or other constitutional disability of the President. — The person having the greatest number of votes as Vice-President, shall be the Vice-President, if such number be a majority of the whole number of Electors appointed, and if no person have a majority, then from the two highest numbers on the list, the Senate shall choose the Vice-President; a quorum for the purpose shall consist of two-thirds of the whole number of Senators, and a majority of the whole number shall be necessary to a choice. But no person constitutionally ineligible to the office of President shall be eligible to that of Vice-President of the United States.

ARTICLE XIII.

(Proposed February 1, 1865; in force December 18, 1865)

SECTION 1. Neither slavery nor involuntary servitude, except as a punishment for crime whereof the party shall have been duly convicted, shall exist within the United States, or any place subject to their jurisdiction.

SECTION 2. Congress shall have power to enforce this article by appropriate legislation.

ARTICLE XIV.

(Proposed June 13, 1866; in force July 28, 1868)

SECTION 1. All persons born or naturalized in the United States, and subject to the jurisdiction thereof, are citizens of the United States and of the State wherein they reside. No State shall make or enforce any law which shall abridge the privileges or immunities of citizens of the United States; nor shall any State deprive any person of life, liberty, or property, without due process of law; nor deny to any person within its jurisdiction the equal protection of the laws.

SECTION 2. Representatives shall be apportioned among the several States according to their respective numbers, counting the whole number of persons in each State, excluding Indians not taxed. But when the right to vote at any election for the choice of electors for President and Vice-President of the United States, Representatives in Congress, the Executive and Judicial officers of a State, or the members of the Legislature thereof, is denied to any of the male inhabitants of such State, being twenty-one years of age, and citizens of the United States, or in any way abridged, except for participation in rebellion, or other crime, the basis of representation therein shall be reduced in the proportion which the number of such male citizens shall bear to the whole number of male citizens twenty-one years of age in such State.

SECTION 3. No person shall be a Senator or Representative in Congress, or elector of President and Vice-President, or hold any office, civil or military, under the United States, or under any State, who, having previously taken an oath, as a member of Congress, or as an officer of the United States, or as a member of any State legislature, or as an executive or judicial officer of any State, to support the Constitution of the United States, shall have engaged in insurrection or rebellion against the same, or given aid or comfort to the enemies thereof. But Congress may by a vote of two-thirds of each House, remove such disability.

SECTION 4. The validity of the public debt of the United States, authorized by law, including debts incurred for payment of pensions and bounties for services in suppressing insurrection or rebellion, shall not be questioned. But neither the United States nor any State shall assume or pay any debt or obligation incurred in aid of insurrection or rebellion against the United States, or any claim for the loss or emancipation of any slave; but all such debts, obligations and claims shall be held illegal and void.

SECTION 5. The Congress shall have power to enforce, by appropriate legislation, the provisions of this article.

ARTICLE XV.

(Proposed February 26, 1869; in force March 30, 1870)

SECTION 1. The right of citizens of the United States to vote shall not be denied or abridged by the United States or by any State on account of race, color, or previous condition of servitude —

SECTION 2. The Congress shall have power to enforce this article by appropriate legislation.

ARTICLE XVI.

(Proposed July 12, 1909; in effect February 25, 1913)

The Congress shall have power to lay and collect taxes on incomes, from whatever source derived, without apportionment among the several States, and without regard to any census or enumeration.

ARTICLE XVII.

(Proposed May 16, 1912; in force May 31, 1913)

The Senate of the United States shall be composed of two Senators from each State, elected by the people thereof, for six years; and each Senator shall have one vote. The electors in each State shall have the qualifications requisite for electors of the most numerous branch of the State legislatures.

When vacancies happen in the representation of any State in the Senate, the executive authority of such State shall issue writs of election to fill such vacancies: *Provided,* That the legislature of any State may empower the executive thereof to make temporary appointments until the people fill the vacancies by election as the legislature may direct.

This amendment shall not be so construed as to affect the election or term of any Senator chosen before it becomes valid as part of the Constitution.

ARTICLE XVIII.

(Proposed December 18, 1917; in force January 16, 1920)

SECTION 1. After one year from the ratification of this article the manufacture, sale, or transportation of intoxicating liquors within, the importation thereof into, or the exportation thereof from the United States and all territory subject to the jurisdiction thereof for beverage purposes is hereby prohibited.

SECTION 2. The Congress and the several States shall have concurrent power to enforce this article by appropriate legislation.

SECTION 3. This article shall be inoperative unless it shall have been ratified as an amendment to the Constitution by the legislatures of the several States, as provided in the Constitution, within seven years from the date of the submission hereof to the States by the Congress.

ARTICLE XIX.

(Proposed by the House May 21, 1919; by the Senate June 4, 1919.
In force August 26, 1920)

The right of citizens of the United States to vote shall not be denied or abridged by the United States or by any State on account of sex.

Congress shall have power to enforce this article by appropriate legislation.

ARTICLE XX.

(Proposed in March 1932; in force February 6, 1933)

SECTION 1. The terms of the President and Vice President shall end at noon on the 20th day of January, and the terms of Senators and Representatives at noon on the 3d day of January, of the years in which such terms would have ended if this article had not been ratified; and the terms of their successors shall then begin.

SECTION 2. The Congress shall assemble at least once in every year, and such meeting shall begin at noon on the 3d day of January, unless they shall by law appoint a different day.

SECTION 3. If, at the time fixed for the beginning of the term of the President, the President elect shall have died, the Vice President elect shall become President. If a President shall not have been chosen before the time fixed for the beginning of his term, or if the President elect shall have failed to qualify, then the Vice President elect shall act as President until a President shall have qualified; and the Congress may by law provide for the case wherein neither a President elect nor a Vice President elect shall have qualified, declaring who shall then act as President, or the manner in which one who is to act shall be selected, and such person shall act accordingly until a President or Vice President shall have qualified.

SECTION 4. The Congress may by law provide for the case of the death of any of the persons from whom the House of Representatives may choose a President whenever the right of choice shall have devolved upon them, and for the case of the death of any of the persons from whom the Senate may choose a Vice President whenever the right of choice shall have devolved upon them.

SECTION 5. Sections 1 and 2 shall take effect on the 15th day of October following the ratification of this article.

SECTION 6. This article shall be inoperative unless it shall have been ratified as an amendment to the Constitution by the legislatures of three-fourths of the several States within seven years from the date of its submission.

ARTICLE XXI.

(Proposed February 1933; in force December 5, 1933)

SECTION 1. The eighteenth article of amendment to the Constitution of the United States is hereby repealed.

SECTION 2. The transportation or importation into any State, Territory, or possession of the United States for delivery or use therein of intoxicating liquors, in violation of the laws thereof, is hereby prohibited.

SECTION 3. This article shall be inoperative unless it shall have been ratified as an amendment to the Constitution by conventions in the several States, as provided in the Constitution, within seven years from the date of the submission hereof to the States by the Congress.

INDEX

AAA, xiv–xvii; cashiering of, 186

Abolition, rise of crusade for, 269–271; misconception of, 279. *See also* Garrison, William Lloyd

Adams, Abigail, 131

Adams, Henry, comments on Pickering, 146; on Federalists, 159

Adams, Herbert B., quoted, 27

Adams, John, xxiii, 65, 134, 209, 258, 370; his meeting with Pitt, 36–38; realizes need of union, 38; founder of Federalist Party, 71; describes Sherman, 76, 77; not an accredited Minister, 106; monarchist at heart, 109; Jefferson's letters to, 112, 113; Jefferson's criticisms of, 118; comments on Ames's speech, 126; Taylor's animosity to, 136; political wreck of, 137; his comment on Philadelphia, 145; Pickering makes warfare on, 149; his relations with Hamilton, 153; sends Marshall to France, 172; appoints Marshall to cabinet, 174; robs Jefferson of complete victory, 178, 179, 181–183; in retirement, 203; idolized by New England, 208

Adams, John Quincy, 272, 374; writings of, 13; fails to join secessionists, 152; comments on secession plot, 153; on Giles theory of impeachment, 193, 194; his suspicions of Calhoun, 219, 220; candidate for President, 220; his description of Hayne, 225; chosen President by House, 226; his great intellect, 244; secures purchase of Florida, 251; in Congress, 279; and Clay, 290; his opinion of Douglas, 303; and Crittenden, 381

Adams, Samuel, 60, 92; fails to attend Constitutional Convention, 65; approves Constitution, 104

Adet, French Minister, sent home by Pickering, 148

Adkins vs. *Children's Hospital*, xxvii

Alien and Sedition Laws, 136–139

Alston, Rebecca Motte, second wife of Hayne, 226

Ambler, Polly, 165, 169

Amendments to the Constitution: *Bill of Rights*, xxii, 122

5th, the "due process of law" clause, 276, 337, 398

10th, and Louisiana Purchase, 150; and Madison's *Debates*, 262

11th, ratification of, xxii

12th, changing method of Presidential election, 352

13th, ratified in ten months, xxii; abolishing slavery, 288, 342, 351, 352, 355, 396

14th, ratified, xxii; giving negro citizenship rights, 342, 355, 396; mostly obsolete, 396, 397; and "rights" clause, 397, 398; its "due process" clause, 398, 399, 408–413; Miller's interpretation of, 399–402; Bradley's admiration for, 406; Harlan's interpretation of, 418, 419; Holmes's view of, 429, 430

15th, ratified in thirteen months, xxii; giving negro the ballot, 355, 396, 398, 403

16th, ratified, xxii; caused by Harlan's dissent, 417

17th, ratified in a year, xxii

18th, ratified in thirteen months, xxii

19th, ratified in fourteen months, xxii

20th, ratified in eleven months, xxii

21st, ratified in less than a year, xxii

America. *See* United States

Ames, Fisher, his speech on Jay's Treaty, 126

Annapolis Convention, 11, 52; dominated by Hamilton, 56, 62–64

Antifederalists, 109, 120

Arnold, Benedict, 206

Articles of Confederation, 16, 34, 47, 69, 70, 72, 84, 112; difficulty of amending, 35; Madison's proposal regarding, 48; fail to provide for taxation, 420

Articles of the Constitution:

I, defining extension of legislative right, xiii, xvii, xix; authorizing slave trade to 1808, 276; and Federal legislation over District of Columbia, 283; on habeas corpus, 345

II, on powers of President, 345

III, great weakness of, xxiv–xxvi; defining treason, 353; on jurisdiction of Court, 372

IV, providing for surrender of fugitive